RON BROWN

RON BROWN

AN UNCOMMON LIFE

Steven A. Holmes

John Wiley & Sons, Inc.
New York • Chichester • Weinheim • Brisbane • Singapore • Toronto

This publication is designed to provide accurate and authoritative information in regard
to the subject matter covered. It is sold with the understanding that the publisher is
not engaged in rendering professional services. If professional advice or other expert
assistance is required, the services of a competent professional person should be
sought.

ISBN 0-471-18388-1 (cloth : alk. paper)

Printed in the United States of America

To my father,
Jonathan Chesterfield Holmes

We have tomorrow bright before us like a flame.
Yesterday, a night-gone-thing, a sun-down name.
And dawn today broad arch above the road we came.

—Langston Hughes

CONTENTS

ACKNOWLEDGMENTS

WRITING A BOOK of this nature is never a solitary affair. It cannot be done without the help and support of family, friends, employers, and sources. As such, there are many people whose encouragement and aid I would like to acknowledge. First and foremost, I would like to thank my family, my wife, Marian, and my daughter, Jennifer, for putting up with the long absences—even when I was at home—that my research and writing required. I also want to acknowledge my bosses at the *New York Times* who, when book deadlines loomed, were gracious enough to give me time to complete my work. I am exceedingly grateful to *Times* researchers Barclay Walsh, Monica Borkowski, and Marjorie Goldsborough, who provided invaluable assistance. Also appreciated was the legwork of Elizabeth Gibbens, Sonja Czarneski, Geri Blumenthal, and Matthew Snyder.

I am especially indebted to those who helped me make sense of the research so that I could translate it into coherent thoughts. For that I thank Hilary Hinzmann and my editor at John Wiley & Sons, Carole Hall. In addition, I benefited from the contributions of Wiley production editor Diane Aronson and my agent, Joseph Vallely.

This is not an authorized biography, meaning I produced it without the assistance of Ron Brown's immediate family who, for their own reasons, opted not to cooperate. Still, I am thankful to the more than one hundred sources who did, particularly members of Brown's extended family who graciously aided me in my understanding of his roots, his life, and his promise.

PROLOGUE

THE IMAGES BROADCAST by Black Entertainment Television on April 9, 1996, had both a familiarity and an arresting dissonance to them. The scene on the television clearly was that of a black church, Washington's Metropolitan Baptist, filled to overflowing. The mournful and rich tones of "How Excellent Is Your Name" and "Amazing Grace" rose as the gospel choir rhythmically swayed back and forth. Their beige, brown, and black faces stood out against the red choir robes with white collars.

What was incongruous, however, was the abundance of white faces in the crowd even at the end of the century, when church services remained the most racially segregated events in America. Here, on a Tuesday night, the crowd was decidedly integrated. Their expensive suits and pricey dresses marked them as members of America's establishment. Certain faces so often seen on the network news stood out.

Charles Rangel, the raspy-voiced congressman from Harlem, sat in one row. Tall, erect, and brooding, power lawyer Vernon Jordan sat in another. Senator Edward M. Kennedy, his round, ruddy face framed by steel-rimmed glasses, was also there. Alexis Herman, who would later become secretary of Labor, sat quietly, her light-skinned face seeming even more pale than usual.

Tim Russert, the head of NBC News's Washington bureau, seated himself near the back of the church. One spied Johnnie Cochran, who had gained fame—some said infamy—for his successful defense of O. J. Simpson in the previous year's most sensational murder trial.

They had come to pay a final tribute to a fallen comrade, Commerce Secretary Ron Brown, who had died in a plane crash six days earlier. In front of the pulpit, a photograph stood depicting him in a dark suit and red tie, standing arms akimbo between two white pillars, looking confident and joyous. His mourners did not grieve passively. Groups of them strode to the lectern to tell funny and poignant stories about the man they remembered. Black folks testifying. White folks testifying. Hour after hour into the night. All speaking of their closeness to Ron Brown, of their love, of their loss.

Days before, thousands of mourners had stood for hours to view his casket lying in state at the Commerce Department. Even in Washington, where,

1

like Hollywood, tributes flow like wine, the outpouring of emotion was extraordinary. When Malcolm Baldridge, who was Ronald Reagan's horseback-riding Commerce secretary from Wyoming, was killed in a freak rodeo accident in 1987, the news merited a 650-word Associated Press dispatch in the *New York Times.* President Reagan did attend a memorial service for Baldridge at the National Cathedral, but official Washington barely took note of his passing, and the masses of the American people took no notice at all.

Brown's death, on the other hand, evoked the kind of response normally reserved for heads of state or icons of pop culture: tributes from around the world and live television coverage. Even the catafalque that bore his casket had been used only for coffins of Abraham Lincoln, John F. Kennedy, Douglas MacArthur, and Earl Warren. Never before had it supported the body of a mere cabinet member. It seemed as if an avalanche of newspapers, magazines, and talk shows analyzed the meaning of Brown's life and speculated on what his death signified for President Bill Clinton's reelection chances.

By April 10, a chilly rain soaked the mournful and the curious, dampening the spirit of a capital already impatient for spring. The weather seemed to fit Washington's mood as the funeral cortege wound its way through the city's streets. The line of black limousines flowed slowly from the National Cathedral east on Massachusetts Avenue, passing the stately embassies of the United Kingdom, South Africa, Iran, and other countries. The procession headed east into Shaw, a working-class and poor neighborhood that was once black Washington's cultural and economic hub. South out of Shaw, the cars circled the gray stone Commerce Department building in the heart of downtown, before moving west, past the Washington Monument and the Lincoln Memorial. They then crossed the mud-brown Potomac River to their final stop, Arlington National Cemetery. Along the way, people stood silently as the procession passed by. Some stood bare-headed in the rain. The crowds strained to catch a glimpse of the famous people encased behind the tinted windows of the black limousines. Millions more watched on television.

As I TOOK IN that spectacle of sadness and celebration, several questions flooded into my mind. What was so different about Ron Brown? What was it about this fifty-four-year-old, impeccably dressed African American that could produce such an outpouring? How did he arrive at the table of power? What were the lessons of his life? With these questions, this book began to take shape. I started to look at Brown from different angles and began to see him in a fuller light, which sparked a desire in me to write his story. Without any particular thesis or agenda, I started on the trail and followed where it led.

Right away, it was obvious that as Commerce secretary, Brown had transformed what had long been considered a second-rate department and put it at the forefront of the drive to increase American trade abroad. But trade policy is not the stuff of myth. To the broad mainstream of America, Brown seemed to stand for something much more tangible and easier to grasp.

Who, then, was this larger-than-life public figure? Successful lawyer, quintessential Washington insider, civil rights advocate, political strategist, rogue, pitchman, deal-maker: depending on who you talked to, he was a renaissance man or a chameleon. To the black middle class from which he sprang, he was a favorite son whose entrée into the realms of true power, wealth, and influence was a shining example of the journey of a people from outside to inside the system. They thrilled at his successes and empathized with his ambitions, and quickly railed against those who would bring him down as he moved into spheres of politics, government, and business where few blacks had ventured.

According to what I found in my exploration, however, Ron Brown never wanted to be defined by what he was, only by what he could be. Constantly reinventing himself, he was as much Everyman as a black man. Never satisfied to be merely the beneficiary of progress or to rage against the limits that others sought to impose, he was determined to live as fully as any man could in a world he would help to make.

PART ONE

FOUR GENERATIONS

(1894–1958)

CHAPTER ONE

OUT OF
THE SOUTH

THE YEAR WAS 1894 when Gilbert Dawson Brown Sr., his younger brother, and his seventeen-year-old son, Gilbert junior, rode a rickety buckboard out of Virginia's Fauquier County, in the foothills of the Blue Ridge Mountains. With a team of brown draft horses in the harness, the trio headed north, jouncing along the rutted roads, passing through Frederick, Maryland, and Gettysburg, Pennsylvania, where the tide had turned in the war that had freed the elder Brown from slavery. Being on the move was nothing new to him. His caramel-colored skin, sharp features, thick wavy hair, and penetrating blue eyes bespoke his mixed African, Indian, and white ancestry. A farmhand, experienced in coaxing wheat and corn from the red, loamy clay of northwest Virginia, Gilbert senior, his wife, Mary, and his large family would often journey across the county's rolling hillsides looking to hire on with the farmer who offered him the most money. But this trip was different. He had never traveled this far.

Some family members would later say it was Gilbert senior's brother who had prompted the trio's northward trek. Rumor had it that he had gotten into a scrap with a white man, forcing the Brown men to flee during the 1890s, when Southern racism was at its most violent. The details of the incident have been lost, and some say it never happened. Whether or not the rumor was true, it was time to get out of the South. The Ku Klux Klan was on the march and the number of lynchings soared to more than 100 a year during much of the 1890s. Black elected officials were being tossed out of office and clever and repressive measures from the poll tax to the whites-only primary to literacy tests were robbing African Americans of the ability to vote, leaving them politically powerless to halt their resubjugation.

Gilbert senior's trek North was the first step on a journey that would lift the Brown family up from black Southern serfdom into the race's upwardly mobile middle class. By 1941, when his great-grandson Ronald Harmon Brown was born, the black middle class would still be small, and would still be striving. But the Brown family would be well established in its ranks.

In 1894, however, Gilbert senior desperately needed work. Jobs for farmhands had dried up in many areas of the rural South, a fallout from the tough economic times that followed the Panic of 1893. Gilbert senior had many mouths to feed. He had seven children from his first marriage, of whom Gilbert junior was the oldest. Remarkably, he sired seventeen more with Mary, his second wife, though his descendants cannot remember how many were born by the time he left Virginia.

Word had reached Fauquier County that there was good money to be made in the bustling town of Steelton, Pennsylvania, south of Harrisburg, on the winding Susquehanna River. The town got its name from the sprawling Pennsylvania Steel Company plant that had opened in 1867 and was the first full-scale production mill in the United States using the new Bessemer process, which blasted air through the molten pig iron to burn away carbon and other impurities.[1] The mill acted as a powerful employment magnet, creating an ethnic stew as Irish, Slavs, Croats, Germans, Italians, and blacks poured in to work its open-hearth furnaces and tend its coke ovens.[2]

By 1890 more than 1,200 black people, mainly from Maryland, Virginia, and West Virginia, lived in Steelton, clustered in ramshackle housing on the flat river plain and in an area of the center of town known as Coon Hollow. In 1886, eight years before the Browns arrived, the *Harrisburg Call* derisively described the neighborhood as a "half-civilized community where few white men cared to pass," and said that while "some honest and wealthy colored citizens" lived there, "the other element is by far the majority."[3] In fact, both black and white sections of the bottomland near the river were notorious. Gambling and prostitution thrived in the fast-growing town that drew hundreds of poorly educated single men to do well-paying but often dangerous work. Drunkenness, rowdiness, and fights were common enough to prompt editorials in newspapers and sermons from pulpits urging citizens to avoid "Sabbath breaking," drinking, and other sins.

Work was steady enough, however, to allow a small group of blacks to tenuously inch their way up the economic ladder. By 1912 at least twenty-five black people owned their own businesses in Steelton.[4] More than 700 of the town's African Americans belonged to one of the three black churches. Black social and charitable organizations like the Home Club of Steelton and the Negro Widows and Orphans Committee tried to advance the education of members of their race or raise funds for the needy. Groups like the Young Men's Reform Club tried to steer errant blacks onto a more righteous path. Clearly, Steelton's African American population had cleaved itself into two communities.

From the start it was clear in which of the two communities the Browns wanted to belong. Anxious to build a nest egg and reunite his family, Gilbert senior began his own business, using his team of draft horses to dredge the river shallows for coal that had washed down from the mines upstream. He also hauled stones from the local stone quarry and later went to work there as well. Gilbert junior took a job in a part of the steel plant called the merchant mill, where finished steel products were forged and stacked on shelves for merchants to purchase. Gilbert junior resembled his father in many ways. He had the same short stature, the same smooth café au lait complexion, and the same mass of dark hair. He had a sharp angular nose, thin lips, and a wiry, muscled frame well suited for the arduous work in the steel mill. He also inherited his father's drive and ambition.

By 1903, several years after their arrival, father and son had saved enough money to plunk down $200 for a piece of property. Unlike most of Steelton's African Americans, they did not locate amid the squalor of the river flats. The Browns moved up a rung, literally climbing the hills that rise sharply east of the Susquehanna to build their home in the predominantly German community of Bressler. On a 125-foot-long lot on Chambers Street, a winding east-west thoroughfare, the Browns built a tidy, wood-framed house with seven rooms, three porches, and a large hall. In the backyard, they constructed a large barn where Gilbert senior stabled his draft horses.

When the house was ready, Gilbert senior returned to Virginia to fetch his wife, Mary, and the rest of his children. The overflowing house soon became even more packed in 1905, when Gilbert junior married Nancy Nickens, a Fauquier native who had moved to Steelton some years earlier. She was a light-skinned woman with long, straight hair and hazel eyes. Thin and tall—in fact, she topped her husband by at least an inch—she was sickly throughout her life, suffering from asthma and later arthritis and a heart condition. Still, she bore twelve children, the first two daughters and a son coming into the world in a bedroom at the Chambers Street house.

The Browns were frugal people. In their large backyard they grew potatoes, carrots, onions, and other vegetables for the table. They raised cows, turkeys, and chickens. They butchered a hog every year, providing plenty of pork. Few blacks lived in the area, but that didn't seem to bother the Browns—nor, apparently, their neighbors. "They were progressive people and they just wanted a nice place to live," Charlotte Stewart, Gilbert senior's granddaughter, recalled.[5]

In 1910, with the Browns now bursting through the walls of the house and Nancy once again pregnant, Gilbert junior struck out on his own, first buying his own house down the road, where another daughter was born, and then, in 1914, paying the princely sum of $1,300 for a two-story, boxy white house one block north on Main Street. Tall hedges surrounded the backyard, where the couple cultivated vegetables and raised livestock for the family's consumption. Gilbert and Nancy produced five more daughters and two more sons at their new home. Like all their children, they were brought into the world at home with only a midwife in attendance.

Frail as she was, Nancy Nickens Brown shared her husband's penchant for hard work. She rose every morning at 4:30 A.M. to prepare breakfast for her husband, whose shift at the mill began an hour later. A gifted seamstress, she sewed from dawn to dusk, making everything for her family from underwear to topcoats. She supplemented the family income by making clothes for the wealthy in the area. Nancy never used a pattern. Instead, she asked her customers to describe the suit or gown they wanted, measured them, and transformed their meager descriptions into well-tailored finished products. She also was the neighborhood medicine woman, curing colds and aches with a mixture of herbal concoctions and poultices.

Gilbert and Nancy were models of self-reliance. The family wore the best clothes in the neighborhood, arrayed in garments Nancy fashioned from the remnants of the fine wools and silks her well-to-do customers had provided. The Browns had the neighborhood's first telephone and its first radio. People quipped enviously that the Browns were rich. Some whispered jokingly that they were not really black. It was as though Gilbert and Nancy believed that hard work and frugality would blot out any trace of the degradation, poverty, and servitude of slavery and the Southern caste system from which the family was only one generation removed. "Our parents didn't talk about [slavery]," recalled Charlotte Stewart. "They didn't want to be Southerners and they didn't want to be from a slave background."[6] Nancy even refused to cook collard greens, and seldom prepared rice. "Too Southern," she used to say.

The Browns did not neglect matters of the soul. Gilbert junior was a deacon in the Mount Zion Baptist Church, one of Steelton's three black churches, and the family maintained strict rules about the Sabbath. They rose early on Sunday for prayers and Bible reading before heading down the hill to Sunday school and the eleven o'clock sermon. The children had to return to church at seven o'clock for meetings of the Baptist Young Peoples' Union. If a child missed Sunday school because of illness or for any other reason, he or she could not play outside all day. Gilbert junior also frowned on card-playing in the house and allowed no swear words. Strict though he was, Gilbert junior's demeanor was too gentle to maintain discipline by force. Generally an arched eyebrow or a gruff "That'll be enough of that" halted any mischief. If it did not, Nancy intervened, administering spankings using switches she made the offender break off from the hedges outside.

One of the few children to receive such a punishment from his father was William Harmon Brown, the sixth child and second son. Bill, as he was known, was born on January 31, 1916, the first child to be born in the new house on Main Street. He was handsome, with his mother's height, his father's smooth almond-colored skin, and a perpetual smile. He loved to play, and spent hours shooting a basketball or playing Barbary Lost Track, a kind of hide-and-seek in which the seekers tried to locate their quarry by following their voices. Bill, as is often the case with boys with a bevy of older sisters, was indulged and spoiled. He often skipped his chores, knowing his sisters would cover for him. He took it for granted that others would draw his bath, lay out his clothes, or prepare his meals. He flaunted some of the house rules. One involved a recalcitrant cow he was tending. Frustrated with the stubborn beast, Bill called the animal a "son of a bitch," not knowing that Gilbert junior was nearby and overheard the profanity. The offense earned Bill the only spanking he ever got from his father.

A stylish dresser, and a star on his high school basketball team, Bill was immensely popular. He caught the eyes of the girls, including Elizabeth, a young white girl who lived next door and who liked to sidle up to him as he sat on the family's porch on hot summer evenings. This mild flirting across racial lines seemed to have drawn little notice in Bressler. The Browns were one of only two African American families to live on their block. For the most part, the Brown children did not grow up with daily confrontations with racism and discrimination. They were among a handful of black students attending the high school, where skin color proved to be no barrier. "Regardless of what color you were, if you were good at something you were in it," Stewart recalled. But reminders of racism were never far away. Generally, it just took a trip to nearby Harrisburg or Hershey to remind the Brown children of the prejudice that was the norm outside their town. "We never knew we were really black until we would go to the ice skating rink or the roller rink in Harrisburg and Hershey," Stewart said. "They wouldn't let us in."[7]

Gilbert and Nancy Brown's desire to shed the image and fact of Southern poverty meant their children needed to get an education beyond high school. Half of them did. But in choosing where to go, the Brown children decided that they had had enough of being in the minority and opted to attend black colleges. All but one—including Bill—chose Howard University, a hundred miles to the south in Washington, D.C. "We always felt that that was the place to go and that you would not encounter prejudice there," said Stewart.[8]

NAMED FOR Oliver O. Howard, a Union general during the Civil War who lost an arm during the Peninsula Campaign and was the institution's first president, Howard University had educated successive generations of black leaders in the shadow of the prevailing racism of the nation's capital. Even the school's beginnings were marked by the theme of black advancement in the face of white resistance. President Andrew Johnson, a virulent racist who succeeded Abraham Lincoln, signed the charter establishing Howard on March 2, 1867, the same day that Congress overrode his veto of the bill establishing Reconstruction. Yet Howard—along with such schools as Morehouse and Spelman in Atlanta, Fisk in Nashville, and Lincoln, outside Philadelphia—became the training ground of the black intellectual and social elite. Dr. Charles Drew, blood plasma pioneer, conducted research at Howard's teaching hospital, then known as Freedman's Hospital. Thurgood Marshall, the first black appointed to the Supreme Court, graduated from Howard's law school in 1933, not long before Bill Brown arrived.

With his good looks, serious manner, and country charm, Bill Brown became exceedingly popular on campus. He earned more than just passable grades, maintaining a National Youth Administration scholarship, a New Deal innovation that required its recipients to earn at least a B average. He starred on the basketball team, starting at forward in 1935, 1936, and 1937. A February 1937 front-page photograph in the *Hilltop* depicts a stern-looking Brown, hair cropped close, muscular arms and legs protruding from his basketball uniform, a ball clasped in his hands in a stiff, staged pose. Pictured with him are Edgar Lee and Herbie Jones, the team captain. HOWARD'S BASKETBALL STARS, the headline proclaimed. And they were, leading the team to the championship of the Colored Intercollegiate Athletic Association in 1937.

Bill joined the best clubs, pledging Omega Psi Phi, one of the big three black fraternities, and becoming a member of the "H" Club, an organization of Howard athletes formed to "regulate the wearing of the H, to entertain visiting teams and prominent athletes and to stop the wearing of all foreign letters on the campus." He no doubt fretted over the sad fortunes of Howard's football team, which one year was crushed on successive weekends 35 to 0 by Hampton Institute and 40 to 0 by Morgan State, prompting the *Hilltop* to sob in a front-page editorial, "Why is the Capstone of Negro Education the laughing stock of the Football World?"[9] But Bill also enjoyed the social life, partying and strutting on the "Q" line with his frat brothers and making the rounds of the nightclubs, like the New Green Parrot's Pirates Den, down the hill on U Street.

U Street, at the bottom of the hill from Howard's campus, was the unofficial barrier between the white and black worlds. There, students and people from the neighborhood caught the latest movies at theaters bearing names like the Lincoln, the Republic, or the Booker T that befitted the capital's black neighborhood. They also danced the night away listening to Billy Eckstine or the big bands of Cab Calloway and Duke Ellington at the Howard Theater.

In the Depression years, Howard students played and studied in an atmosphere of rigid segregation. Blacks were barred from hotels, movie theaters, and restaurants in the white parts of town. Taxicabs routinely passed them by, and black patrons in most clothing stores and dress shops could not try on items they were considering buying. One could travel downtown occasionally to buy clothes in a place like Louie's, one of the few white-owned stores that would cater to blacks. But day or night, venturing past the well-understood boundary could be dangerous. "It was a sleepy Southern town," recalled Bill's friend Walter Washington decades after he had become the town's first black mayor.[10] "It was a very segregated city and we sort of lived in a cocoon," remembered Edward Brooke, another of Bill's buddies who went on to fame as the first black person elected to the Senate since Reconstruction.[11]

Washington recalled how the sight of a few blacks walking together at dusk only a few blocks beyond U Street would prompt the attention of the local police, who would remind them that it was nearly sundown. "They wanted to make sure that you headed back up toward campus," Washington said. "We never had any trouble or brutality. They'd just look you in the eye as if to say, 'The time has come.' "[12]

By 1940 the city was nearly one-third black. Divided by income, breeding, profession, and skin color, the bulk of the black population was crowded into substandard shacks, many lacking indoor plumbing, set hard up against each other in the alleys behind residential houses. A tiny black middle class made up mainly of teachers, doctors, lawyers, morticians, and a small but growing number of federal workers lived on "the Hill." But they, like all African Americans, suffered collectively under segregation.

Neither black nor white Washingtonians had the power to change things. Since the 1870s, the citizens of the capital of the world's most powerful democracy could not vote for president. They had no elected representatives in the Senate, nor in the House of Representatives. They had no locally elected mayor or city council. The city was governed by a board of commissioners appointed by the president, but the real power lay with Senate and House oversight committees, bodies dominated by Southern racists like Theodore Bilbo of Mississippi who was elected to the Senate in 1934—the same year Bill Brown entered Howard—and was a former member of the Ku Klux Klan and the author of a book entitled *Take Your Choice—Segregation or Mongrelization.*

Bill did not acquiesce quietly to segregation's slights, however. During two summers while he was at school, a group of students and community residents organized a protest against a local drugstore that refused to allow blacks to eat at its lunch counter. The store, owned by Peoples Drugs, a local chain, was located at Fourteenth and U Streets, in the heart of Washington's black Shaw neighborhood. It was bad enough to be refused service in white stores outside of the ghetto. To be denied service in the black community was more than they could bear. When Walter Washington organized picketing outside the store, Bill regularly showed up to walk the line.

But political activity was more the exception than the rule for Bill Brown. "He was quiet and reserved, but well liked," recalled Washington, who roomed with him during their junior year. "You know, some of us were more politically inclined. We talked more and were more gregarious. But he was laid back."[13] He usually had other things on his mind. For one, as Edward Brooke recalled, "The ladies were very much attracted to Bill. He was a very, very handsome man."[14] Among those women was a pretty, light-skinned student named Gloria Osborne who lived with her father on Fairmont Street, a short distance from the campus.

SHE WAS descended from a Mississippi slaveholder who sired several children by the black women he owned. He favored those born by Gloria Osborne's great-grandmother for "resembling him and being fair-skinned."[15] Light pigmentation literally was the ticket to freedom for Gloria's grandfather, Walter Welborn, and his brother Eugene, who escaped from slavery by disguising themselves as Confederate soldiers purchasing train tickets to the northern reaches of the Confederacy and then making their way to Washington. Good fortune followed Walter Welborn into freedom as well. In Washington, he met and married the daughter of a socially prominent African American Brahmin who bore him four daughters, including Ruth Alma Welborn.

For decades light skin was the sine qua non for entry into African American high society, with black folklore replete with tales of "brown paper bag" soirees, where only those lighter than a brown grocery store sack could get past the front door. Ruth Welborn had no such difficulties. With blond hair and hazel eyes, she could easily have been mistaken for a white woman. She graduated from Dunbar High School in Washington, the top city school for blacks and the one considered the alma mater of Washington's black upper crust.

Ruth Welborn's physical characteristics and good schooling did not, however, ensure her marital bliss. Her marriage to Jerome Bonaparte Osborne, a worker at the Veterans Administration, lasted but a few years. It did, however, produce one child, Gloria, whose looks rivaled those of her mother. Acquaintances of Gloria remember her as a shy child with a pleasing nature. "Gloria was always a lovable person, a sweet person," said Edward Brooke, who attended Dunbar High School with her. "She was very popular, but very quiet. Not an aggressive person by any means."[16] She also was well versed about the nuances of Washington's color caste system and figured out as a young woman that the way around the limited world reserved for blacks was to take advantage of her light skin and smooth straight hair and pass for white.

The benefits passing brought Gloria Osborne were the same for others of her race who "crossed the line"—jobs, access, opportunity. As a young girl, Gloria used her ability to fool whites—and blacks—about her race to gain entrance into restaurants and stores that were closed to African Americans. The advantages of passing were clear; the dangers, at least in most northern cities, were not too great. Though there were instances when people who were discovered were roughed up, most often those who were exposed faced no more than their own shame and embarrassment. Perhaps not as passive as others assumed she was, Gloria took the risk.

On July 17, 1940, over the objections of her father who thought her too young, eighteen-year-old Gloria quit Howard to marry Bill Brown.[17] He was twenty-four years old, and would graduate from Howard the following year. The Brown family back in Bressler celebrated Bill's graduation with a touch of regret, as well as pride. While some of the Brown children had left the Pennsylvania town to attend school, all had returned to live in the area. The lone exception up until that point was Bill's older sister Helen. At college—Howard, of course—she had met a boy from North Carolina and had gotten married. After graduation she moved south with him. Everyone else came back, everyone but Bill.

Following graduation, he took a job in Washington with the Federal Housing and Home Financing Administration, the precursor to the Federal Department of Housing and Urban Development, assisting low-income families to qualify for public housing. It was considered a white-collar job and, as a result, made him the first of two blacks working in a professional position in that agency.[18]

WAR WAS ON THE MINDS of nearly all Washingtonians during that summer of 1941. Hitler's armies had stormed deep into the Soviet Union, having already conquered Poland, the Netherlands, Norway, Belgium, and France. In Asia, the United States and Japan moved inexorably toward battle. Meanwhile in Washington, hundred-degree temperatures and high humidity sucked the air out of the city. Unshaded spots on the Ellipse, a green half oval near the White House usually alive with Saturday afternoon baseball games, were deserted. Public swimming pools overflowed with parched Washingtonians seeking escape from the mind-numbing heat. Six people died from heat prostration; or had drowned while swimming in pools, lakes, and ponds; or had been struck by lightning in violent thunderstorms. Headlines screaming HEAT AND HUMIDITY WILT WASHINGTON and 2 ADDED TO DEATH TOLL competed for attention with news of the war raging in Europe and Asia. Tempers soared with the temperature. A pushing and shoving melee broke out among the crowd, grown ill-tempered and impatient, as it waited in line for the premiere of the new Gary Cooper movie, *Sgt. York,* at a downtown theater. Blacks did not take part in the disturbance. They were not allowed to enter the downtown movie houses.

A more immediate concern to Bill was the fact that Gloria was pregnant and just days from giving birth. The baby—the only child they would have— was born on August 1, 1941. He weighed six pounds, six ounces and was, everyone said, a beautiful child. Photographs of Ron Brown as a baby show him full of the promise of what he would become—handsome, charming, full of life. His face was dominated by sparkling eyes and a warm yet mischievous smile that would melt hearts and disarm skeptics.

When he was barely a few weeks old, Bill and Gloria took him to Bressler. The purpose of the trip was more than to show off the new baby. Bill Brown's mother, Nancy, was dying. Never in robust health, Nancy's heart condition had worsened in 1941, and she was failing.

Standing next to her thin form lying on the bed in the house on Main Street, Bill placed the newest Brown beside Nancy—she was too weak to actually hold him—drawing a wan smile from her. "That's a noble-looking boy," Gilbert junior announced. "He's going to make something of himself."[19] Four months later, on December 14, Nancy Nickens Brown passed away at the age of fifty-six. She and her husband had worked hard, led a pious life, and instilled a commitment to education in their offspring. They had pulled the family out of the poverty that was the legacy of the slaveholding and segregated South and into the middle class. With this foundation, the new baby was launched into the world. But Nancy Brown would never see whether her husband's prophecy would come true, if the newest member of the Brown family would fulfill the hopes of his ancestry.

In the coming years, Ron would be the sole object of all his parents' love, ambitions, and frustrations. He was doted upon, pampered, and spoiled—a little prince who could do no wrong. But he was also being prepared in the best way—perhaps the only way—his parents knew how for coping with the larger world as Bill and Gloria knew it, or at least as they thought they did. Appearance mattered. Frances Perkins, who taught Ron Brown in nursery school, recalled the youngster as "the most meticulously dressed child in nursery school." She remembered that he was "intelligent and had a retentive memory." She also recalled him as "gregarious."[20] His emotional makeup was strikingly like his father's.

Not long after Ron's birth, Bill moved his family to Boston, settling into a two-bedroom apartment in a two-family house on Harrishof Street in Roxbury,[21] at the time a racially mixed area. He continued to work for the Federal Housing Administration. On weekends and after work he spent much of his time playing pickup basketball games at various Roxbury playgrounds and recreational centers and socializing, along with Gloria, with the small group of black professionals he got to know through black organizations like Omega Psi Phi and Alpha Phi Alpha. At some point after his graduation, he had lost the shyness his friend Walter Washington remembered. "Bill was essentially a jocular guy," said Frank Morris, who lived in Roxbury at the time and later became a lawyer. "Boston was a little staid for him."[22] He was ready for some adventure after six years.

In 1947 the housing agency transferred Bill to New York City. After six months there he left the agency and took a new job as manager of the Hotel Theresa. In 1948, the thirteen-story gray-white brick building at the corner of 125th Street and Seventh Avenue was already a longtime fixture on the Harlem landscape. Built in 1913 by Gustav Seidenberg, a cigar manufacturer who named it after his wife, the Theresa initially catered only to whites. The policy reflected both the times and the neighborhood. Despite the storied Harlem

Renaissance of the 1920s, the area around 125th Street remained mostly white until late into the 1930s. The hotel's owners realized that trying to retain a white clientele in the face of Harlem's changing demographics was a losing business proposition. In 1940 the Theresa's owners gave up their futile effort, began renting to blacks, and installed a black manager.[23] Having blacks in charge of a fancy hotel with a staff of seventy-five and a payroll of more than $100,000 was seen by some African American commentators as proof of what could be accomplished if the race was given the chance. Patronizing the hotel was more than a matter of convenience. It was a matter of pride.

The Theresa had become the epicenter of Harlem's high society by the time Bill Brown arrived. With his beautiful wife and their son beside him, Bill was undoubtedly looking forward to having the time of his life.

Perhaps young Ron Brown sensed his father's mood. Without realizing it, the boy was stepping into an extraordinary life-shaping adventure. At the Theresa, Bill Brown's son would grow up relating to all manner of people and situations. One day, he would be seated at a table in the coffee shop talking with Anna Hedgeman, a black intellectual who served in the cabinet of New York mayor Robert Wagner and became the only woman on the organizing committee for the famous 1963 march on Washington. The next day, he would be joshing with porters and bellhops.

If he went into the coffee shop late at night, he often ran into Ellsworth "Bumpy" Johnson, who liked to come in for a snack. The burly gangster who favored conservatively cut suits was a legend in Harlem. Back in the 1930s, he had battled Dutch Schultz and Lucky Luciano for control of Harlem's numbers rackets and had later spent time in Sing Sing prison. An opinionated man, Johnson liked to voice his views to anyone within earshot. Few dared to argue with him. He was, however, friendly toward the young son of the hotel's manager and would engage him in conversation. "How ya doin' Brownie?" he would ask, using his pet name.[24]

CHAPTER TWO

THERESA'S CHILD

A BRIGHT-EYED, impressionable eleven-year-old yanked open Theresa's glass door and bounded inside, as full of energy and life as the hotel itself. On a typical day in 1952, Ronnie Brown, as everyone called him, had just come home from the Walden prep school downtown. As he left the cacophony of sounds on Seventh Avenue behind him, he probably looked around to see who might come strolling across the carpeted lobby, pop out of one of the offices, or turn up at Etienne's, the dress shop on the open mezzanine one flight up. It was fun to spot the celebrities who showed up, and besides, his classmates would pay him five bucks for every autograph he got from one of the luminaries who hung around the hotel.

In 1947, at age five, his parents had enrolled him in Hunter College Elementary School, an overwhelmingly white public school on Manhattan's East Side that only admitted children who passed a challenging entrance exam. He scored well and, as a result, began living in two worlds at a very early age.[1] Now, in middle school, he left Harlem every weekday morning and ventured into the virtually all-white world of his exclusive West Side prep school, where he knew he was expected to interact with his classmates and with everyone he met in a manner that would not reflect negatively on his family or his race. Then he came home to the fabled capital of Negro America. Bill and Gloria's decisions about the best school for their son required him to lead a racially schizophrenic existence. It was a heavy burden to place on such young shoulders. But he appeared to handle it. He learned to look and listen, to sharpen his instincts for survival, to cultivate people, and, no doubt, to be what he would become later in life, a true crossover man.

Resilience was one thing, happiness another. The hotel that Ronnie Brown called home on and off for ten years must have been as welcome a refuge for the youngster as it was for its guests. In New York in the 1950s there were plenty of reminders that blacks were not welcome everywhere they went. In 1951, a survey by a private citizens' group of medium-priced restau-

18

rants on Manhattan's East Side found that half treated blacks "discourteously" or gave them "poor service or inferior treatment."[2] Famous spots and famous people were not immune. In October, Josephine Baker, the renowned singer and actress who was cherished in France because of her work with the Resistance during World War II, charged that she had been given poor service at the celebrated Stork Club because she was black.[3]

But at the Theresa a welcome was a sure thing. "Nothing can compensate you for being turned away at a downtown hotel. So you didn't even go there,"[4] said Evelyn Cunningham decades later. At the time, she was a reporter for the *Pittsburgh Courier,* a leading black newspaper, which had an office across Seventh Avenue from the hotel. If segregation meant limited opportunities for blacks, it also meant that black talent and riches had to congregate in a few places, rather than being diffused throughout the city. In New York, the Theresa became the place for black notables to stay and for black aspirants to go to be near them.

It was a gold mine for a precocious child looking for autographs who also possessed a curiosity about the lives of the people who flowed through the hotel's doors. "He had a real interest in people. He liked to know who they were and what they did," said Cunningham. He often aided her in her work, providing tips on the latest celebrity to check in, allowing her to get a jump on her interview requests. "He would tell me, 'Joe Lewis is coming in; so-and-so is coming in,'" Cunningham recalled. "He knew what my job was."[5]

Sometimes Sugar Ray Robinson stopped in. His own bar and restaurant, Sugar Ray's, was just down the street. Joe Louis was also a familiar figure. In 1950, when he came out of retirement to try to regain the heavyweight crown, Louis made the Hotel Theresa his headquarters for himself and his entourage, and police had to rope off the street to keep crowds back during his comings and goings. But while the proletariat could only view the black celebrities from a distance, Ronnie experienced the Theresa's famous patrons at close quarters. Joe Louis gave him the nickname of "Little Brown." Singer Dinah Washington lived next door and baked cookies for him. Bill Brown allowed his son to have plenty of exposure to the guests. Ronnie brought bottles to their rooms and ran errands for them. He displayed deep curiosity about the hotel's operation and its clientele and was a constant help—some say annoyance—to the staff.

After school, Ronnie generally headed up the elevators to his family's apartment on the twelfth floor to drop off his books. Then, when other boys uptown and downtown were heading to the parks or the side streets for a game of stickball or basketball before dinner, Ronnie would often come back down to the lobby and help the desk clerks assign rooms or sort letters and put them in the proper boxes behind the wooden semicircular front desk. Sometimes he would help the doormen hail taxis on Seventh Avenue or dash around to the Chock Full O' Nuts restaurant on the corner to see if any were cruising up 125th Street. When cabs stopped in front of the hotel's green canopy to drop off a guest, the bellhops would at times let him help carry the bags.

Along the hotel's fifty-one-foot, J-shaped bar in the evenings and on Sunday afternoons, crowds of people lined up drinking, chatting, networking, and seeking companionship overflowed from the lounge and spilled out into the hotel lobby and onto Seventh Avenue outside. Ronnie could peek into the bar and watch the hip men in double-breasted suits and the cool ladies wearing hats with nets that came down over their eyes. Earl, the regular bartender, was usually there, mixing drinks, cracking jokes, and making sure no one hassled the ladies who came in unescorted.[6] The place always was crowded. People were often jammed into the garnet-colored booths. You could look through the big picture window and see crowds milling on the street. Everybody was talking and laughing. Even with the noise you could still hear the piano and Una Mae Carlisle's throaty version of *Stardust.* Sometimes you could spot musicians like Ben Webster or members of Duke Ellington's band, or actors like Rex Ingram.

Crowds seemed to be everywhere: in the lobby, in the bar, on the street. "There were so many people night and day, mostly from out of town," remembered Cunningham. "These were sporting types who went across the country to follow big events. I was so amused to watch men from out of town, swinging their golf clubs or wearing a riding habit because they thought this was the thing to do in New York. They thought you've got to pretend to be a golfer so you arrive in a car, the doorman takes out your golf bag. You are at the world-famous Hotel Theresa so you stand outside to let everybody see you. It used to tickle me to death."[7]

True Harlemites were amused and paid the wannabes no mind. They were just part of the action, and action was what the Theresa was all about. This was where deals were made, contacts established or renewed, and love found—and lost. " 'Meet me at the Theresa' is to Harlem what 'Meet me at the clock at the Biltmore' is to New York whites," *Ebony* magazine proclaimed.[8] Opulence or first-rate accommodations were beside the point. Even before Bill Brown took over as manager the Theresa was a fading beauty. Its carpets were worn, paint peeled from many walls, and its kitchen offerings were hardly imaginative. Patrons complained about being asked to pay cash in advance for their rooms, and that there were no booths in the hotel's beauty parlor. Curtains hung from iron pipes separated the patrons' chairs. "With its dimly-lit hallways, drab, colorless bedrooms, dingy, ancient furnishings and limited room service, the Theresa is anything but a first-rate hotel," *Ebony* magazine sniffed. "But it is the best Harlem has to offer."[9]

What it lacked in amenities, however, the Theresa more than made up for in location. Situated at the most famous corner in black America, it was a stone's throw from the Cotton Club. The bright neon marquee of the Apollo

Theater boasting of names like Jackie "Moms" Mabley and Arthur Prysock was just around the corner. The Red Rooster, Small's Paradise, Basie's Lounge (owned by Count Basie), and other famous Harlem night spots were close by. About a half a block west on 125th Street was L. M. Blumstein, Inc., Harlem's biggest department store. Outside the Theresa's doors, the corner of Seventh Avenue and 125th Street teemed with people and political rhetoric. The intersection at times resembled Hyde Park's famous Speakers' Corner. Street orators stood outside the Chock Full O' Nuts coffee shop and exhorted passersby for hours on subjects from the rights of tenants in Harlem to the need for blacks to return to Africa. The hotel itself was a lodestone for the political activity in Harlem.

Richard Nixon made a campaign stop there in 1952. The appearance was part of the Republicans' strategy to break the Democrats' twenty-year hammerlock on the black vote. At the time, the Republicans' rhetoric and record on civil rights were at least as good, and perhaps better, than those of the Democrats, who were loath to alienate their strong base among white Southerners. Indeed, the visit and the Republicans' appeal to black voters were relatively successful. In November, Dwight Eisenhower and Nixon got 33 percent of the black vote nationwide.[10]

Young Ronnie Brown, however, was unfazed by Nixon's appearance. Avid about politics, Bill Brown had made sure his son was a part of the event, bringing him to the front of the crowd so that Nixon could shake the young boy's hand. In later years, while never explaining what, if anything, Nixon did to offend him, Ron Brown liked to say that the encounter at the hotel convinced him to be a Democrat. Maybe it was simply that the other politicians who gathered at the Theresa were more exciting. Every year the Communist Party, USA, held its national convention there, bringing with it delegates and a number of white men in suits sitting in cars outside the hotel, taking pictures of everyone coming and going. Federal agents—this time U.S. State Department security officers and Secret Service agents—also turned out in force during Fidel Castro's stay in 1960.

Being the only child of hoteliers fostered a kind of independence most children did not experience. Brown roamed the halls by himself, obviating the need for child care. He was the Theresa's version of Eloise, the young protagonist in Kay Thompson's book, who had the run of the Plaza Hotel. The mind pictures him as an energetic little big man, striding down the corridors, the dauphin of the largest hotel in the country catering to African Americans. If he was hungry he wandered into the coffee shop, set just to the left as one entered the lobby through the hotel's front doors. There, he could order a sandwich or a piece of pie. It didn't matter if he had no money. He was, after all, the boss's son. He would chat with the staff or watch the customers, men in business suits, smoking cigarettes, sipping coffee—"java" they liked to call it—and reading the *New York Times* or the *New Age* or the *Amsterdam News*.

As always, a few of the men seated at the Formica counter scanned the racing form and hustled over phones in the lobby. He could probably hear them talking about some place called Pimlico or Saratoga.

Atop the hotel was the Skyline Room, the elegant ballroom that offered Ronnie an even more fascinating window on the world. If there were no affairs going on inside, he could have the place to himself. The room had tall peaked windows on three sides with awe-inspiring views of New York. If he looked east during the day, he could spot planes taking off from LaGuardia Airport. At night, the lights from the Triborough Bridge, to the east, and the George Washington Bridge, to the north, shimmered in the distance. If he looked south he could see all the way across Central Park and pick out the slender frame of the Empire State Building.

It's easy to picture Ron Brown in 1952 in the family apartment, listening to a Brooklyn Dodgers game on the radio. In 1951, when there were only nine African American major leaguers, four of them, Jackie Robinson, Roy Campanella, Dan Bankhead, and Don Newcombe, played for Brooklyn. It was no wonder that Ronnie was a rabid Dodger fan.[11] He kept his favorite players' statistics—home runs, batting averages, stolen bases, earned run averages—inside his head. Jackie Robinson, the first black man to play in the major leagues, was his hero, just like his dad.

As manager of the Theresa, Bill Brown took to this world like a magnet attracting iron filings. On Sunday afternoons he, along with Gloria, hosted cocktail parties in their suite. Musicians like Lionel Hampton and Duke Ellington, writers like Langston Hughes and Gordon Parks, plus journalists, businessmen, doctors, lawyers, and others might drop by to relax, make connections, or just to talk. Adam Clayton Powell Jr., the brash young black congressman who was elected to the House in 1944, sometimes dropped by. Though he was not a regular habitué of the Theresa, Powell's occasional appearance affirmed the hotel's place as a center of Harlem's political and social life.

Bill Brown, who liked to call himself "the innkeeper," held court like Louis XIV, dominating the conversation and the room. According to Martha Lewis, a family friend, "Bill had a lot of charisma. He could engage anyone in conversation, whether they were sports figures, newspaper people, musicians, writers, or political figures. He was comfortable with everybody. I think being exposed to that had a great deal of influence on Ron 'cause Ron certainly had his father's charisma."[12]

Year after year, even among the sporting crowd, the Browns' lively parties sometimes took on a serious undertone when conversation turned to the political events of the day. On May 17, 1954, two months before Ron Brown's thirteenth birthday, the Supreme Court ruled in *Brown v. Board of Education* that racial segregation violated the Constitution. The unanimous (9–0) opinion overturned the doctrine of "separate but equal" that had legally confined blacks into a subservient caste for nearly sixty years. In December of the following year, the first mass protest since the *Brown* decision erupted in Montgomery, Alabama. Led by a compelling preacher few people had ever heard of named Martin Luther King Jr., blacks and whites boycotted segregated city buses in Montgomery. As the Browns held court in New York, the Supreme Court, Rosa Parks (a young seamstress who refused to rise from her seat on a Montgomery city bus), and King had launched the most transforming era in American racial history since Reconstruction.

The changes being wrought would have the most impact on the type of people who occupied Ron Brown's world at the Theresa. The black elite was always a tiny slice of American society. In 1940, the year before Ron Brown was born, only 12 percent of African Americans aged 25 to 29 had finished high school. A scant 2 percent of all blacks had college degrees. Only 1.8 percent of all male professionals were black, with only 2.8 percent of all doctors and less than one percent of the lawyers and engineers. The small cadre of middle-class blacks formed a world unto themselves. Outside of their segregated colleges and universities, their own fraternities and social clubs, their own summer camps for their children and summer colonies like Oak Bluff on Martha's Vineyard and Sag Harbor on Long Island, their aspirations were limited by custom and law. Now, doors of opportunities were starting to open, and it was this group and their offspring who were prepared to stride through. The masses would come later. Members of the black elite would always be the prime beneficiaries of every measure of access to the American dream that the civil rights movement would win. While each generation made the way easier for the next, it was still a journey that produced anxiety. There were dangers as well as barriers, principles compromised as well as mountains climbed. There were tricky relationships with whites—and with other blacks—to be negotiated, traditions to uphold, images to maintain, hard work to be done. The struggle was a common topic for Brown's guests.

Even as momentous change gathered steam, black high society, always a world unto itself, seemed to remain intact. Bill Brown and the staff of the hotel hosted the Guardsmen, Comas, Les Douze, the Smart Set, Tom Thumb (a children's club), Girl Friends, Links, Deltas, AKAs, and a myriad of other fraternities, sororities, clubs, and societies that appealed to the Negro upper crust. Large cotillions and formal affairs tended to take place at the nearby Savoy Ballroom. Smaller, more intimate parties were held at the hotel's Skyline Room. Barred from whites-only entertainment, even those African Americans whose middle-class status stemmed from working as a teacher or postal clerk could for one night dress, dance, and dream of being like the Astors or the Vanderbilts.

"At that time there were so many social clubs, I mean, so many of them," said Juanita Howard, who as a young woman sang at the Skyline Room with a band called Jimmy Jones and the Jones Boys. "There were those you might consider the elites and those at other levels like the Elks, the Masons, the Order of the Eastern Star, the 149th Street Association of North Carolina. So many people had these clubs and they would give these dances all over the place. The Skyline Room was always very busy."[13]

But the clubs were more than just a means for fun and fantasizing. The more elite ones helped hold together the matrix of friends who had met in college. They confirmed your status as one of the "best people." You heard about the latest job opening and kept track of who was moving up and who was moving down. Some taught social graces and networking skills and reinforced shared values like the importance of maintaining the proper appearance. Some, including the Boulé fraternity, engaged in political organizing. Others reveled in sheer camaraderie free of racial self-consciousness.

Like everything else in America involving race, the black clubs were quietly changing in the 1950s. In the past, the elite clubs were highly restrictive, based almost exclusively on lineage and light skin. But in New York, Boston, Philadelphia, Washington, and other urban centers, steady economic gains were slowly softening the rules. By 1950 the average black worker earned $1,300, or 52 percent of the average white worker's income. That compared to $400, or less than 40 percent of the white average, in 1939. The income of middle-class black New Yorkers tripled between 1940 and 1952 to an average of $3,200 a year, according to a survey conducted by WLIB, a local radio station. With increased prosperity, more blacks began clamoring for admittance into high-end black social clubs. The old guard frequently ignored most of the newcomers, though they would often embrace handsome young people with the proper college and family ties—like Bill and Gloria Brown. Gloria was drawn to the Smart Set. In 1952 Bill helped found the Manhattan chapter of the Guardsmen.

"The Guardsmen sprang out of a group of guys who were in college at just about the same time, traditional black colleges and universities," said L. Douglas Wilder, a member of the Richmond chapter who later went on to become the first black man ever elected governor of a state. "They made it as clear as possible that it was not founded to try to be a social action organization. It was never intended to be anything other than entertainment."[14] As in other chapters of the Guardsmen, the Manhattan members were primarily old friends who had graduated from the first tier of historically black colleges. Graduates of Tuskegee or Florida A&M were less likely to be in evidence. Yet for all their fun-loving talk, the club men's paths intertwined in complex ways. Years later, Ron Brown's path would intersect significantly with Doug Wilder's.

In the multilayered world of black America, the old-line clubs like the Guardsmen stood at the apex of social organizations. Below them existed other clubs, often begun by those shut out by the guardians of the established clubs. There was also a host of smaller clubs organized by friends who just wanted a smaller, more intimate, but still formally recognized group. Bill Brown formed one of these, an independent club of young men called the Gaylords.

Recalled James Hubert, a member, "We met at each other's homes, and we would sit up all night long and play poker and tell lies."[15]

Bill and Gloria often included Ron in their clubs' parties, as well as in the drama of the hotel's events. "My earliest years were spent walking the lobbies and the hallways and the dining rooms," Brown said later. "And I was able to absorb the sights and sounds and the mysteries. I was able to watch and learn from the great African American cultural and political leaders and the great athletes who made their way to Harlem."[16] But he learned just as much from the doctors, lawyers, educators, and civil servants who were part of his parents' set. These too were people who made things happen and who had great prestige, prosperity, and flair in an energized, albeit largely black, world. Hanging around them, he could hardly think of himself as anything but special as well.

The world of the Theresa, while inspiring, was also a markedly adult one. To be sure, Bill Brown loved and protected his son. But Bill Brown had a father who was the deacon in the local Baptist church, who abhorred profanity and thought card playing was the devil's work. Gilbert Brown insisted his children attend church every Sunday; Bill Brown sneaked his young son into prizefights and let him hang out with grown-ups at his Sunday afternoon brunches. It is easy to imagine what Gilbert and Nancy Brown would have had to say about their grandson's moral moorings.

Still, the adult world was instructive. Always a keen observer, Ronnie liked checking out the action that went on in a room, making a note of who was saying what, seeing who tried wordlessly to send a message. Observation was a skill he learned early and one that he would use the rest of his life.

One time Martha Lewis was flirting heavily with an eligible young man during one of the Sunday afternoon parties in the Browns' apartment. Following the unspoken rules of the 1950s, Lewis attempted to make her catch with subtle winks, furtive come-hither looks, and timely "sashaying" in front of her quarry. She was convinced her little mating dance was unnoticed by anyone in the room except her target. She was wrong.

"Martha, you should buy yourself some overalls," Ron said to a startled Lewis out of earshot of the others. Lewis recalled him as being no older than eight or nine at the time.

"What do you mean?" she replied, puzzled.

"Because you're working, *so* hard," he said.[17]

Bill Brown would have laughed out loud at this story. He loved the high life and the flamboyant denizens of the Theresa. But his wife, Gloria, did not share in that feeling. Tension in the Brown household was thick. Gloria hated Bill's gambling, his frequent carousing, and, ultimately, his philandering. Bill Brown seemed to shrug off the tension. He liked life on the grand stage the Theresa provided. He worked hard. He liked the constant action as well and grew to need it.

"There's no excuse for being an ordinary Negro," Bill liked to say.[18] He was, however, flirting with danger. According to George Lopez, who knew the Browns in both Boston and New York, Bill tended to spend lavishly and often beyond his means. He always had to wear the nicest suits, go to the best restaurants, and enjoy the best clubs. "He had a great personality," said Lopez. "He had a big ego. . . . He liked to put on a big show—whether he could afford it or not."[19]

THINGS TURNED financially sour for Bill and Gloria in 1956, when Bill was fired in a dispute with the Theresa's owners. The family moved to White Plains, a community in Westchester County, north of New York City. There, Bill struggled to make ends meet, starting a number of different businesses such as peddling beauty supplies and selling insurance.[20] In what became a pattern in his life, each of these ventures failed. He was always on the lookout for a new scheme, some new hustle, and it did not seem to matter whether he had the skills or experience. In later life he decided to become a bail bondsman, even though he had no experience in that field. Like the others, this business also failed, according to friends. "He was the type of person who would get these grandiose ideas about what he wanted to do, whether or not he had the background for it," said Lopez. "We'd hear of some deal Bill was doing and say, 'There goes Bill again.' "[21]

But Gloria and Ron seemed to enjoy the time in White Plains. The Browns rented a yellow split-level house on a quiet street[22] in a middle-class black community called Parkway Gardens.[23] Ron enrolled in White Plains High School, where he ran track, and he spent a lot of time hanging out at the nearby home of photographer Gordon Parks, attracted by both Parks's swimming pool and his oldest daughter, Toni, whom Brown started dating.[24] For Gloria the time in White Plains was an opportunity for the Browns to operate as a normal family, away from the Theresa.

After a year in White Plains, Bill Brown and the hotel's management reconciled and he returned to his post at the Theresa. But although he might have exulted in going back to the hotel, it meant a return to many of the things Gloria disapproved of: the fast life, the late-night poker parties, and the other women. Bill made little attempt to hide his attraction to pretty ladies. Friends from that time often recall his being in the company of attractive women, either sitting alone with them in the hotel bar or in its dining room. Sometimes it was assumed that as the manager of the hotel he was merely being a gracious host. But often his interest was more than just business.

"He was a party guy," said Evelyn Cunningham. "He was very attracted to women, and women very attracted to him."[25] His behavior left some people puzzled. "Gloria was such a beautiful woman," said Dessie Harper, who knew the family since the Browns moved to New York from Boston. "We wondered why he had to be such a womanizer."[26]

The tensions in the Brown home began to take their toll on Ron. In his junior year at the Rhodes School, where he had enrolled after the family returned to the city from White Plains, his grades plummeted, causing near panic among his parents, who envisioned that their son would attend the best college. In desperation, Bill and Gloria put aside their differences and sought psychological counseling for their son from Kenneth Clarke, the noted black psychologist. Even for a black couple as enlightened as the Browns, their turning to psychotherapy in the 1950s is indicative of the extent of their worry. Clarke, who knew Bill from student days together at Howard, confirmed in later years that he worked with Ron for an unspecified period of time. He said he had a vague recollection of Ronnie as "a young man who was not prepared to fulfill his capabilities. . . . I don't remember the specific things we talked about, except friends," he said.[27]

The family crisis came to a head a few months later, in January 1958. The Browns separated. Gloria moved out, living first in the YWCA. She landed a job as a salesclerk at Steuben Glass, an exclusive retail store on New York's Fifth Avenue. Falling back on old habits and assumptions, she hid her blackness from her prospective employers, believing that they would not hire black people to serve their almost exclusively white clientele. Gloria carried out her deception for years, at times embarrassing her son, who could never meet his mother at or near her place of work.[28] Gloria was deathly afraid of being fired if her bosses learned her secret. What she didn't suspect was that management already had seen through her ruse. "I think we all knew that she wasn't pure white," said Sally Walker, who was executive vice president of Steuben Glass at the time.[29]

Perhaps to get away from the tension in the household, perhaps to find places with more people his own age, Ron began to look for ways to escape the Theresa. In his senior year in high school, he virtually moved in with his friend John Nailor, who lived in Saint Albans, a middle-class black enclave in Queens. "It was kind of boring for a young man in high school at the Theresa Hotel," said Nailor. "Some of the things he was more interested in were more abundant in my neighborhood . . . mainly more people of the opposite sex."[30]

OUTSIDE THE High School of the Performing Arts, a Manhattan public school that would later become widely known through the movie *Fame,* John Nailor introduced Ron to Lois Hinton, a striking young girl who lived around the corner from Nailor. Hinton, known to everyone as Lolly, was a stunner. Barely five feet tall, with golden skin, sandy brown hair that she wore long down her back, turquoise eyes, and the lithe figure of a dancer, which she was, she was both beautiful and exotic. She was the type who turned heads, including Ronnie's. She came from a musical family. Her father, a jazz drummer, had played with the big bands of Fats Waller and Earl "Fatha" Hines. Her mother was also a dancer. Lolly attended the High School of the Performing Arts.

Ronnie was immediately attracted by Lolly's perky personality and smoldering beauty. She was taken by his charm, wit, and preppy good looks. "I guess it was his humor, that was the first thing," Hinton remembered. "And handsome, let's not forget that. It was kind of boyish handsome. I just thought he had the cutest mouth and eyes."[31] He also carried the right credentials—smart, from a good family, not a street hustler type, very classy. Definitely someone you could bring home and your parents would approve.

Dating for young African Americans of Brown's and Hinton's social class in New York meant movies in Manhattan and dances thrown by the Guys and Dolls club, an older version of Jack and Jill. They went to house parties in Saint Albans, in Queens, or in the nicer brownstones of Fort Greene or Bedford Stuyvesant in Brooklyn. In the summertime, there were Sunday afternoons at Rye Beach in Westchester or Jones Beach on Long Island; and, most significantly, the ritual of meeting up when the families took their two-week vacations in Sag Harbor, where the black middle class had long ago carved out their own place.

Located on the north shore of Long Island's South Fork, near the Hamptons, Sag Harbor has a rich black history stretching back into the early nineteenth century, when free blacks hired out on whaling ships sailing out of the port.

In the 1940s, middle-class blacks began flocking to Sag Harbor during the summer. They were attracted by the village's long, sandy beach, whose topography made it safe for children to swim alone. As blacks' economic status rose during World War II, Maude Terry, a black Brooklyn schoolteacher who had vacationed in Sag Harbor's Eastville neighborhood, convinced a local resident to subdivide a twenty-acre plot of land into 271 lots and allow her to sell them—at $1,000 for shorefront sites and $750 for those farther inland—to her friends and colleagues. First to come were upper-income blacks. They bought land and put up two- and three-bedroom cinder-block houses in communities called Azurest and Sag Harbor Hills. Later they were followed in the 1950s by blacks somewhat further down the socioeconomic scale: teachers, police officers, and firemen who constructed vacation homes in a community called Ninevah.

The black summer colonists sought more than just a lovely and safe beach. Here was a place where they could raise their families without worrying about hostility. More than a haven from racism, it was a place where upwardly striving black professionals could gather amid people like them, people they knew, people who would be appropriate role models for their children and whose offspring would be suitable playmates.

Neither the Hintons nor the Browns owned homes in the Long Island resort. But they would always be invited to stay with friends, and both Lolly and Ron were eager to see each other there and participate in the social scene, generally parties in the rec rooms with the rug rolled up and the Miracles or

Johnny Mathis crooning a soft ballad. "It was just spinning forty-fives," recalled Hinton. "It was pretty tame stuff. Maybe you might have a little grind up against a wall. That was the big thing. But it was nothing terribly exciting."[32]

Ron avidly followed Lolly's budding career. At one point, she landed a role in the touring company of *West Side Story,* dancing as one of the Sharks girls. He caught her first performance in New York before the company went on the road, bringing her a huge bouquet of roses to congratulate her. "At that age it was like eternal love," she said.[33]

But they were headed in different directions. Years later, reminiscing about her relationship with Ron, Hinton recalled how after he had gone away to college he had asked her to "go steady." She had turned him down, much to the chagrin of a friend in the *West Side Story* cast. "My roommate on the road said, 'Are you crazy? This handsome, nice guy? What are you doing, fool?' "[34] Years later, after he had been elected chairman of the Democratic National Committee and newspapers and magazines were full of stories of this dashing and highly successful African American, Hinton's former roommate called her. "She said, 'Do you remember? Didn't I tell you he was a terrific guy?' "[35]

PART TWO

ON HIS OWN

(1958–1979)

CHAPTER THREE

TWILIGHT'S SCHOOL

ALEXANDER TWILIGHT, overcoming his sense of being different, entered Middlebury College in 1821 when he was twenty-six years old, five years older than the school itself. But it wasn't his age that made Twilight an unusual student. It was his race.

He was born in 1795 in Corinth, Vermont, the third of six children of Icabod and Mary Twilight. The census of 1800 listed his father as being neither white nor Indian, thus strongly suggesting that he was black. Corinth town records were more specific. They say Icabod and Mary were "both colored." As an African American, Twilight was one of only 557 black people living in Vermont in 1800. He became the first to attend Middlebury College, and in 1823 he became the first African American in the country's history to earn a college degree.

Diaries or letters describing Twilight's feelings and experiences at Middlebury have been lost or never existed in the first place. It is not known whether his white classmates accepted Twilight or even if they knew the race of the very light-skinned mulatto who sat next to them in class. Twilight had ample reason to keep his racial identity hidden. Middlebury, like most colleges at the time, was not very supportive of the interests of black people. In 1833 Middlebury students repeatedly heckled an abolitionist speaker whose anti-slavery speech was interrupted by "the scraping of feet, frequent showering of corn over the room and other disturbances designed to break up the meeting."[1] Two years later the school rejected an African American applicant, declaring it "had a policy" of not admitting blacks.[2]

The racial climate had only changed by a few degrees by the last week in August 1958, when another unsuspecting pioneer, Ron Brown, drove up from New York with his father to begin his studies at Twilight's alma mater. Blacks were still a rare sight in the town of Middlebury and the college that bore its name. Only 5 blacks out of a population of 5,305 lived in Middlebury and the student body of 1,200 could boast of only 3. Middlebury lies less than 300 miles from New York City, but in appearance and culture it was light-years away from the crowded streets of Harlem or even the leafy avenues of Saint Albans where Ron had spent his childhood.

At Middlebury, Ron found himself in an environment more alien and sterile than anything he had experienced before. Sure, he had spent his formative years in mostly white elementary and secondary schools, an experience that softened whatever cultural shock he might have experienced. But during that time he returned every afternoon to the familiar black world of Harlem and Saint Albans. This was total immersion. Whatever coping mechanisms he had learned as a youth would now be put to a test. Unlike his father, who had also gone to white primary and secondary schools, Ron had opted to move out of that part of his life that was decidedly African American. Bill Brown had gone to Howard and made a career in Harlem. But with Bill's support, and perhaps encouragement, Ron Brown chose to continue his education in the white world.

Prior to his senior year in high school, the two had taken a car trip with a friend to scout out various schools in New England. The trip was part of Bill Brown's efforts to stimulate his son's interest in academics during a time when Ron's grades were slipping. Bill had also arranged for Ron to visit Hampton Institute, a historically black school founded in 1868 on the Chesapeake Bay in Virginia's Tidewater area. But it was the bucolic beauty of Middlebury that caught the young student's eye. The town sits peacefully in the southern end of the Champlain Valley, bounded on the east by the Green Mountains, home during the Revolutionary War of Ethan Allen and his famous raiders. Walking across campus, Ron would have caught sight of New York's Adirondack range, looming in the hazy distance. All around him craggy peaks, studded green by tall stands of pine, spruce, and fir, cut irregular patterns into the clear blue horizon.

"I had it in my mind that I wanted to go to a small coed school," he would recall. "I came up to the campus and really liked it . . . and I just pretty much decided on the spot that this is where I wanted to come."[3]

But John Nailor, his high school buddy, remembered that the decision to attend Middlebury was not so cut and dried. Ron vacillated for some time, trying to make up his mind whether to place himself in an environment so overwhelmingly white and isolated. "He was hesitant about it," Nailor said. "But as it got closer and closer he became more directed."[4] Nailor and Lolly Hinton recalled that Ron was intrigued by the "challenge" of attending Middlebury as much as he was by its pastoral setting and its reputation as an academically solid school. Attending Middlebury was also in step with his close friends. Nailor, Dalton Jones, and Gaylord Nelson, all of whom were black, attended white colleges. Jones went to Rutgers and Nelson to New York University. The fact that they were guaranteed to be, at most, among the few blacks on their campuses was a badge of honor for a generation that had grown up cheering Jackie Robinson.

Some folks at Middlebury were eager to enroll Ron as well. Though the numbers did not show it, Middlebury officials were on the lookout for black students at the time. Officials at a number of New England colleges, seeing images on television and in the newspapers of blacks in the South fighting for integration, began to question why their campuses were so lily-white. "Civil rights was in the air," said Thomas H. Reynolds, the former dean of men at Middlebury. "I think the nature of the times was such that those of us who were thinking about this understood that you had to do more than just accept blacks. We had to recruit them."[5]

That sentiment, however, was not unanimous among Middlebury alumni. John Handy, the director of admissions who had met Ron during his scouting trip to New England and had encouraged him to apply, recalled some Middlebury alumni upbraiding him for admitting Brown, one more black student. The tiny number already attending the school was quite enough for them. Given that there was some protest, albeit small, over his admittance, it was clear that in Ron Brown the school found all that it hoped for: a soft-spoken African American who was used to being around whites. His presence would allow them to claim that Middlebury was moving toward a more integrated student body, and he did not appear to be the type of person who would rock the boat.

Indeed, not rocking the boat was the accepted Middlebury style. Campus life centered around events like the Winter Carnival, where students molded huge ice sculptures; sports; fraternity parties; and figuring out who was driving over the state line to New York, where the drinking age was only eighteen. The activism kindled by the free speech movement and the anti-Vietnam protests were a generation away.

Middlebury students seemed clueless, even though the civil rights movement, the most significant large-scale domestic event since the Great Depression, had already begun to make headlines. In September 1958, Governor Orval Faubus of Arkansas continued his defiance of court orders to integrate schools in Little Rock and other cities. Local newspapers, the *Herald* in Rutland, and the *Free Press,* out of Burlington, splashed stories on their front pages daily on the breakdown of Southern apartheid. Ron and the other students could hardly have missed them. They did not live on the other side of the moon. As was the case at other campuses, the apathy of Middlebury's students did not arise from ignorance.

Brown felt he knew how much energy to expend and where to direct it in order to survive in his new surroundings. He threw himself into campus activities. He took a full load of courses, including math, chemistry, Spanish, English, and sociology. He joined the track team, continuing with a sport he had done at White Plains High School. He played intramural basketball, enrolled in the Reserve Officer Training Corps, and waited tables in the dining room of one of the student dormitories, making extra money and indulging his prodigious appetite.

"He was rail-thin, an athlete with an enormous appetite for so many things—for life, for sports, for music, for clothes, and for food," said Thomas Meehan, his college roommate. "We were waiters, which meant we got to eat early and as much as we wanted. Ronnie became a legend because of his ability to consume such enormous amounts of food so quickly, and he never gained an ounce."[6] Exhibiting the charm that had been and would remain his trademark, Ron soon acquired a stable of friends, mainly among those whose interest in sports matched his. He was experienced in the ways of white students. Many of the whites he met had never had any contact with black people, so his ability to put people at ease made him extremely well liked.

There were signs, however, that even for Ron the isolation of northwestern Vermont was stressful. With nowhere to retreat, he could not help at times feeling at sea. "It was a different time in history; there was not a whole lot of racial awareness—well, it was difficult for me," Brown once said. "I grew up in Harlem and came from a predominantly black experience, but human beings are very adaptable people and so I managed."[7]

ONE AFTERNOON during Ron's freshman year, Ralph Cobb, a senior, was walking out of the Middlebury Book Shop in the town with a Miles Davis album tucked under his arm. As he did, he noticed a skinny black kid leaving the store carrying an album by Charles Mingus. A discussion ensued. Cobb was a bit of an anomaly on the Middlebury campus: a white student with an abiding interest in jazz. He often pored through the meager jazz selection in the town's bookstore to find records by jazz artists, especially bebop legends like Davis, Thelonious Monk, and Dizzy Gillespie. He would spin the jazz tunes on an old hi-fi in his room on the third floor of his fraternity house, accompanying the riffs on his own drum set. In Brown, Cobb found a kindred spirit in the bebop wasteland of Middlebury. The two spent hours in Cobb's room listening to the work of artists like Davis, John Coltrane, and the Modern Jazz Quartet, and talking about the music. After some prodding, Ron would regale Cobb with tales of some of the jazz greats who stayed at the Hotel Theresa, about playing catch in the main ballroom with Cab Calloway or having cookies baked for him by Dinah Washington. But Cobb sensed that Brown's interest in talking about jazz artists might have been more a symptom of homesickness than anything else. "He had a personal relationship with these people and an interest in the music," Cobb recalled. "But I think he was just more anxious to talk about New York black stuff than it was any real specific interest in bebop."[8]

Curiously, Ron and the few other black Middlebury students never developed a closeness. During Ron's time there, the number of African Americans at Middlebury never exceeded four, and they were all from the New York area. But, for the most part, they eyed each other warily and seldom hung out together.

"There was no banding together in an us-versus-them situation," said Joseph Fielding Ferguson Jr., who was in the class ahead of Brown's. "We kind of went our separate ways. It wasn't a question of having to do things together or else we couldn't do anything at all. We kind of spoke to each other and kind of acknowledged each other. But, essentially, we had our own activities in a sort of separate sense."[9] The estrangement that Middlebury's blacks felt toward each other is not surprising, given the times. The black consciousness movement, with all the trappings of racial solidarity such as "black tables" in the cafeteria, did not begin to touch African American students on predominantly white college campuses until nearly a decade later. It was not unusual for black pioneers who integrated white settings in the late 1950s to feel a sense of uniqueness in what Wallace Lucas, another African American Middlebury student, termed their "F&O"—first and only—status. The presence of other blacks was sometimes viewed as a threat to that specialness, and the resulting competition among token blacks often threw up barriers to friendship.

"I mean, Ron was who he was," said Lucas, who was a year behind Brown. "He seemed to get over in that environment of being the only black on that campus, while I just found it kind of difficult. They weren't New York . . . I needed some homies. And Ron wasn't a homie in my sense."[10]

Lucas grew up in a housing project in the Bronx—though he did attend Horace Mann, an exclusive prep school—and his family operated newsstands in Harlem. His was a world far removed from the Browns' soirees with black celebrities and intellectuals and summers in Sag Harbor. The distance between their two social orbits appeared to be too great for friendship to thrive. Many of their white peers assumed the two were alike. "In fact, we were very different," said Lucas. "Given the competitive nature of that situation in those days, I'm not sure I fully understood all the forces that were at work. But as I look back, I realize there was not only a race issue on those early integrated campuses, there were also class issues."[11]

ON AN AUTUMN DAY in Middlebury's Mountain Club, Ron met a pretty, auburn-haired, hazel-eyed freshman from Midland, Michigan. Known to her friends as Bonnie, Jean Chisholm immediately felt comfortable with Ron. "He was a great deal of fun to be with," she recalled. "He was bright. He was funny and very sweet-natured with a terrific sense of humor at himself as well as other things. I just found him a total delight." The two went to movies in the town, held hands during long walks on crisp days as the Vermont hillsides burst into autumn colors, attended football games, and talked for hours about themselves, their high school days, and the differences in how they grew up—most of the differences, anyway. "If you can imagine how this was possible, we did not talk about race," she recalled. "We never acknowledged the fact that he was black and I was white."[12]

But if Jean and Ron decided to look past their racial differences, others at Middlebury did not. The two dated until Christmas break. Then suddenly he stopped calling. She was puzzled, hurt, even a little angry. But this was 1958, and it was considered too gauche and too forward for a woman to ask a man why he had broken things off. So she bit back her hurt, started dating someone else, and for more than twenty-five years wondered what happened.

The answer came when the two ran into each other at their twenty-fifth reunion. During a moment when they found themselves alone, Brown asked, "Did you ever wonder why I stopped calling you freshman year?" He said that one day as Christmas break approached he was called into the office of Elizabeth Kelly, the dean of women, who told him bluntly that he should not be dating white women. "He said, 'I never dated at Middlebury after that. There were no black women there,'" Jean recalled. "He said, 'That was it. My dating career at Middlebury was at an end.'"[13]

Other black students at Middlebury like Wallace Lucas and Joe Fielding Ferguson recalled dating white women without incident and were skeptical that such an admonition was given to Ron. No one knows. All that is certain is Ron's desire to avoid confrontation. The relationship was not strong enough to get in trouble over. Ending it relieved some of the pressure of finding his place in Middlebury's overwhelmingly white environment.

LOLLY HINTON visited Ron several times at Middlebury during his freshman year, including a trip during Winter Carnival. "The place was just covered with snow and with ice sculptures; just these magnificent ice sculptures that each frat house would make," she recalled. "It was like a winter wonderland."[14] But Ron welcomed respites from western Vermont.

During Christmas break, Bill Brown, in an attempt to teach Ronnie a lesson about the value of work and money, decided to have his son sell Christmas trees on a corner in the South Bronx. Ron took along John Nailor and his girlfriend and turned the lesson into a lark. "We sat out and drank cups of hot chocolate and sold Christmas trees," Hinton remembered. "He was an easy salesman. 'Oh, you don't want to spend five dollars? Okay, give me three.' I'm telling Ronnie, 'No, that's not how you do it.' It was just fun. It wasn't like oh my God, I've got to do this or the rent won't get paid. It was nothing like that kind of pressure."[15]

Fun-loving as he was, Ron wanted the relationship to be more serious. In his sophomore year, he told Hinton that he wanted to "pin" her, give her his fraternity pin as a symbol of the fact that she was his steady girl. She refused. Traveling as part of a national touring company of *West Side Story*, seeing the possibilities of a career in show business, Hinton could not envision going steady with one guy. "I was at that point feeling like, oh, I had this major career ahead of me and I thought I can't be tied down like that," she said. "It became a bone of contention."[16]

Brown's heartache over Hinton's decision did not last long, since he was already seeing someone else.

DURING the 1959 Labor Day weekend Ron met a young black woman from Brooklyn named Alma Arrington who asked a friend to introduce them. "I thought he was cute and nice," Alma recalled later.[17] The two came out of the same black bourgeois world. Their fathers were both members of the Guardsmen. Both belonged to Jack and Jill. Alma belonged to the Laureliers, a social club of middle-class black girls. Like Lolly, Alma was also drop-dead beautiful: medium brown skin, long dark hair that she wore straight and down to her shoulders. And always dressed to the nines. During the summers her parents sent her to Camp Atwater, in North Brockton, Massachusetts, the penultimate upper-middle-class black camp at the time, whose alumni include Vernon Jordan, Hazel O'Leary (who would later become Energy secretary), and Kenneth Chenault (who later became the chief executive officer of American Express).

But while they came out of similar environments, Ron seemed a little square for a girl like Alma, who went to Fisk, the elite and historically black women's college in Nashville. By contrast to Ron, Alma was in a crucible of the revolution that was transforming the country. Students from Fisk, Tennessee A&I (later Tennessee State), and American Baptist College were in the vanguard of the student movement that desegregated lunch counters in Nashville's downtown establishments. Student leaders like John Lewis, Diane Nash, and James Bevel also played leading roles in the Freedom Rides in 1961, later founded the Student Non-Violent Coordinating Committee, and became trusted advisers to Martin Luther King. During her student days, Alma participated in sit-ins at Nashville's restaurants, distinguishing herself from Ron, who, during this phase of the civil rights struggle, found himself on the sidelines.

Their first date didn't end very well. Brown fell asleep during the cab ride from Greenwich Village to Alma's home in Brooklyn. But, she later told a reporter, as soon as Ron awoke, the two of them started planning the next date. With Lolly Hinton having spurned Brown to pursue her stage career, he and Alma began seeing each other regularly—or at least as regularly as was possible for two people who attended schools in different parts of the country. "There was always something different about him," Alma recalled years later. "He was much more mature than the other boys, and sure of himself."[18] Friends of Alma were surprised when she started seeing Ron seriously. She already had serious beaux at Meharry Medical College, the black medical school in Nashville, and they considered Ron a step down. "She was much more sophisticated," said Betty Jean Murphy, who went to Fisk with Alma, "not worldly in a tawdry way. She just had a bigger view at the time, more knowledge of the world. He was kind of geeky."[19] But the two found a common ability to make each other laugh, to see the humor in each other and in the world. Their parents also approved of their dating. They were, after all, from good families.

ISOLATED IN western Vermont without a car in 1959, Ron looked around for a center for his social life. The fraternities were a focal point, and Sigma Phi Epsilon had the reputation of being the hot house. The red-and-white Sig Ep house, on the western edge of the campus, enjoyed a reputation for raucous parties and for having many of the school's top athletes as members. It was a natural fit for someone like Ron, who liked sports and having a good time. He already had some familiarity with the fraternity. Ralph Cobb, the jazz enthusiast, belonged, and Brown had spent hours in his room listening to music. So in February 1959, Ron pledged Sigma Phi Epsilon at Middlebury.

Every evening as they waited for dinner to be served, fraternity brothers and pledges gathered in the knotty pine living room of the Sig Ep house and engaged in what they termed "mocking," gentle repartee laced with playful insults. They jokingly called him *Mister* Brown, pronounced with a jivey inflection the white Sig Ep brothers assumed was common in black street patois. When Brown heard the name applied to him he often would strut around the room, giving his best imitation of a street tough, until a put-down from a frat brother deflated him. Brown was hardly a passive target of verbal thrusts. Having played "the dozens" with friends and relatives back in New York, he gave as good as he got. "It was a sort of a sport," said Gil Owren, one of the Sig Ep brothers. "Everybody enjoyed it, for the most part. And Ronnie was one of the best at it."[20]

But the Middlebury chapter of Sigma Phi Epsilon was part of a national fraternity with most of its chapters in the South. In early 1959, the fraternity's national bylaws still contained a clause restricting membership to "whites of Christian birth." Sig Ep had recently allowed chapters to accept blacks and Jews as so-called social members, meaning they could enjoy all the privileges of the house but could not be initiated officially into the fraternal brotherhood. That was not good enough for the Middlebury chapter, known as Vermont Beta. Its members decided they would make Brown and Barry Gershweir, a Jewish pledge, full-fledged members. "The Sig Ep house was very, very troubled by that clause," John Halpin, former president of the local chapter, said. "We had Jewish guys who wanted to become members and blacks too who could only become social members. The sentiment was, enough was enough. We weren't going to go through this bullshit anymore."[21]

Vermont Beta was not alone in being disturbed by the fraternity's discriminatory policies. With the civil rights revolution heating up in the South, fraternities across the country were coming under increasing pressure from universities and activists to abandon such racist restrictions. At Dartmouth College, a short distance away from Middlebury, officials set a deadline of April 1,

1960, for all its fraternities to do away with restrictive clauses or face expulsion. As a result the Sig Ep house at Dartmouth, along with chapters from a number of other schools, strenuously lobbied the national organization to drop the white Christian clause.

In response, the fraternity's national officers put the issue of repealing the restrictive clause to a vote of Sig Ep's biannual conclave meeting in Washington in the summer of 1959. The conclave adopted the resolution, dropping the white, Christian restriction by a vote of 134 in favor, 37 opposed.[22] In September, following the vote to repeal the clause, the Middlebury chapter initiated Brown as a full-fledged member. "We were not outside the law anymore, and we didn't think it would hurt anybody if we did this," said Breck Lardner, the vice president of the Middlebury chapter. "So we made the decision and went ahead with it. And then we were notified by the national that they were coming up to remove our charter."[23]

The tale of the Middlebury chapter's defiance and martyrdom sounds dramatic and heroic and has been a central part of the Brown story. But it is more the stuff of folklore than reality. Given the lopsided vote, it stretches credibility to imagine officials of the national organization shocked and angry that one of the chapters would carry out the more tolerant policy. In truth, the chapter had a reputation for high jinks and thumbing its nose at the fraternity's rules and traditions. In the period just before they pledged Ron, members of Vermont Beta had held the fraternity's secret initiation rite in public view on the frat house's front lawn. They had ransacked a Sig Ep house at neighboring Dartmouth College. They had failed to forward initiation fees to the national office as required by the fraternity's rule. Former members of the fraternity's national office point to those reasons for disciplining Vermont Beta, not its decision to admit an African American.

At the time, officials at the Middlebury house admitted guilt to some of the infractions, declaring in a statement that "the actions and behavior of the persons involved were wrong and as such were grounds for serious disciplinary action."[24] The chapter felt, however, that expulsion was too severe a penalty. And the harshness of the penalty, no doubt, contributed to the perception among many of the members of Vermont Beta that the transgression for which they were being punished was admitting a black man into the brotherhood.

Brown's initiation into Sig Ep did play a role in the sequence of events that led up to the Middlebury chapter's expulsion. Vermont Beta officials admitted they had failed to submit initiation dues to the national headquarters. They said that, despite the vote by the conclave in the summer of 1959, all of its new pledges still feared the national would somehow keep Brown out. If that happened, the incoming pledges said they would quit in protest. Officials of the Middlebury chapter decided to withhold the initiation fees until the fraternity accepted Brown. When it did, they simply never got around to sending the money in. But over the years the planned protest by the incoming pledges

at the Middlebury chapter has been transformed into a heroic act of principled martyrdom, and the fact that the protest became unnecessary somehow
became lost.

BEYOND THE CONTROVERSY surrounding his pledging a fraternity, Ron had
another problem: academics. He found his course work difficult to handle and
was doing poorly. His college transcript showed him getting D's in math and
chemistry during his freshman year.[25] In March 1959, the school placed him
"on warning" that he was dangerously close to failing chemistry. And in
November, during the first semester of his sophomore year, officials again
warned of the possibility of failure, this time in French. "Ronnie was popular,
well known, and charismatic," said his friend Tom Meehan. "He wasn't a great
student."[26] In many ways, Brown was following a pattern he had exhibited in
high school. Clearly smart, he lacked the discipline to reach his full potential,
often preferring his social life to studying.

"He was lazy as far as academics was concerned," his father once told an
interviewer. "He had the IQ and the intellect where he could read something
once and he had it. He didn't spend all night long with the lights burning reading. He wasn't that type of student. As a result, he came out with grades that
were satisfactory, but he should have come out with all honors with his intellectual capacity."[27] It seems that the sense of specialness bred into Ron by dot-
ing parents and celebrities at the Hotel Theresa, and the sense he had of his
ability to get by through charm and glibness, were now about to be his undoing. Years later he confessed to friends and work colleagues that in the soft,
easy life of his early childhood, he had not learned the lessons of hard work.

"I had a fascinating conversation with him once about his elementary
school years, and about how he'd get in all these gifted programs and how he
learned he could get by doing almost nothing," said Mark Steitz, who later
worked with Brown on Jesse Jackson's presidential campaign and at the
Democratic National Committee. "[He said] it had almost destroyed him 'cause
once he got to serious high school and college work, he still did very little. He
just coasted by. He didn't do any real work."[28]

The lack of discipline finally caught up with him. After getting F's in both
chemistry and French in the first semester of his sophomore year, Brown was
declared an "academic failure" on February 8, 1960.[29] He had flunked out.

School records indicate that he served only a brief time in academic pur-
gatory. Three days after being officially booted out, he was allowed to reenter
the school. College officials, including Thomas Reynolds, the dean of men at
the time, could not recall how Brown came to be readmitted, though they say
it was unusual for someone to be given a second chance so quickly. Generally,
students flunking out of Middlebury were required to prove their academic
mettle once again at some other college before being let back in. But Ron

probably employed his considerable skills of persuasiveness on the faculty committee that ruled on such matters. He talked his way back in. For his part, Reynolds is adamant that one factor played no part in Ron's redemption. "It certainly would not have been simply because he was black," he said.[30]

The close brush with expulsion had had only a marginal effect on Ron's grades, but it changed his life. He switched his major from pre-med to political science. With humanities courses now dominating his class schedule, his grades improved somewhat in the second semester of his sophomore year. "I started off as a joint major in bio and chem until I took organic chemistry," Brown recalled. "Organic chemistry turned me into a political science major."[31] It was a major life change that Brown probably did not appreciate at the time. Had he continued on with medicine, he might have had a rewarding career as a doctor, but it is doubtful that he would have reached the heights of influence and acclaim that he later attained. The switch, however, now pushed him in the direction of law—and of politics, where he would make a name for himself.

First, however, he had to graduate. Foreign languages still gave him trouble. Problems in this area were especially critical for a Middlebury student since the college prided itself on its foreign language curricula and passing at least one foreign language course was a requirement for graduation. But after dropping French, Ron failed Spanish in the first semester of his junior year, and just squeaked by with the equivalent of a D-minus his senior year. He ended his four years at Middlebury with an overall C-minus average, and graduated in the lowest third of his class, ranked 118th out of 145 male students.[32] Years later, after becoming a successful Washington lawyer, Brown made light of his academic shortcomings in a magazine for Middlebury alumni, declaring that his graduation "was in serious doubt until the very last minute."[33]

He made it through, if just barely. All in all, it had been worthwhile. As the dutiful son, he had fulfilled his parents' dream of graduating from college. He had broadened his horizons and discovered a strong field of interest. But if Brown gained from Middlebury, the college also benefited from him. And despite Reynolds's protestations that college officials did not look at his race when they decided to give him a second chance, his color was clearly on the minds of some school officials in later years. In the late 1970s, when Middlebury officials were contemplating putting Brown on the school's board of trustees—something they would finally do in 1988—an unidentified school official scribbled some thoughts on a copy of Brown's résumé. "Remember Ron as a very fine man," the official wrote. "His background certainly shows he has done well since leaving [Middlebury]. A good choice if there is a need for more minorities on the board."

CHAPTER FOUR

THE ARMY

A T SIX A.M. the sounds of reveille echoed across the fields of Fort Devens, just as the morning sun peeked over the green wooded hills of central Massachusetts. The bugle call rousted Ron Brown in the wooden two-story barracks, as it did all ROTC candidates at the military base. Like the others, Brown hustled down to the shower for a fast wash. He returned quickly to his sleeping area, cleaned up the space around his bunk, tidied up the shirts, underwear, socks, and other gear in his footlocker, lined up his shoes in a razor-sharp straight line under his bed, and tucked in his sheets and blankets tightly in case the platoon sergeant tried to bounce a quarter off the bed during morning walk-through. After inspection, he and his platoon hurried to eat, stopping at the metal bar outside the mess hall to do as many chin-ups as the sergeant required that day to gain admission for breakfast. The routine was immutable, unerringly followed by generations of ROTC cadets who slogged their way through basic training at Fort Devens in the 1950s, 1960s, and 1970s.

Brown spent six weeks at summer camp at Fort Devens following his graduation from college. He was supposed to have completed summer camp after his junior year at Middlebury, but he had not been allowed to attend because he had failed Spanish. So in the summer of 1962 Brown underwent what was, in essence, army basic training.

Pampered as a child, undisciplined as a college student, Brown found military life a completely new experience. Middlebury required all freshmen and sophomores to take ROTC. It was optional in junior and senior years, though taking it meant earning extra money. The only catch was that signing up for ROTC in the last years of college obligated the student to at least two years of active duty in the army following graduation. But that probably had seemed a long way off to Brown while he was in school. At Middlebury, ROTC entailed taking a few classes on military science and marching around the grounds near the field house every Thursday afternoon doing close-order drill. Even though ROTC required little effort, he was an indifferent, quietly rebellious cadet at college. He disdained discipline. His uniform was often unkempt, his shoes scuffed. He clowned around during the weekly drills. His lackadaisical attitude drove his ROTC superiors to distraction. "We got paid twenty-seven dollars a month, and that was good beer money or good dating money for some people and that's why they were in ROTC," said John LeTowt, commander of the ROTC guard at Middlebury. "But there were others who were in there because they loved the military. Ron was in the former group."[1]

Suddenly at Fort Devens, Brown confronted the full rigors of military life. He sweated through calisthenics, push-ups, sit-ups, and jumping jacks on the parade ground outside of his barracks. He sprinted through obstacle courses. He labored through twenty-mile hikes with full packs, and shorter jaunts, trotting in T-shirt and khaki pants in step with other cadets to the cadence called out by the sergeant. He pulled KP duty, peeling mounds of potatoes and scrubbing huge cooking vats until they gleamed. Huddled with other cadets in the back of a canvas-roofed two-ton truck, he bounced along loose gravel roads on the hilly 9,300-acre base on the way to firing ranges. There he learned the intricacies of disassembling, cleaning, and reassembling an M-1 carbine, a .45-caliber pistol, and light and heavy mortars. He learned to keep his shoes shined, his uniform creased, and his mouth shut except to give the only acceptable answer to the drill instructor: "Yes, Drill Sergeant!"

Brown emerged from basic training on August 3 and received his commission as a second lieutenant in the U.S. Army Reserve, Transportation Corps. Eight days later, on August 11, he and Alma were married at her family's church. It was a traditional wedding at St. Philip's Episcopal Church in Brooklyn, with bridesmaids, ushers, a ring bearer, and flower girls. His white college buddies, Tom Meehan and Charles Tobey, brothers from the Sigma Phi Epsilon fraternity, attended as well as friends of the Brown and Arrington clans.

Ron wasn't the only person in the Brown family thinking about wedding vows. During the next year, Bill Brown remarried. His new bride, Peggy, was a comely Harlemite, the daughter of a railroad worker, and considerably younger. The two had started dating not long after Bill's divorce from Gloria. Both Peggy and her daughter, Leslie, had been dazzled by Bill's zesty charm. He loved to show off his new catch at Guardsmen functions. They ate at fancy restaurants and showed up in society columns in the *Amsterdam News*. He lavished spending on her, always making sure she was outfitted at tony downtown retail stores like Bonwit Teller. The couple would later have another child, William Harmon Brown Jr., known as Chip, and Peggy would go on to earn a doctorate in education. But the union would also undergo strains, mainly as a result of Bill's continued financial problems.

LIEUTENANT BROWN was not called to active duty for another seven months. While waiting, he enrolled in St. John's University Law School and tried to support himself by becoming a caseworker for the New York Department of Social Services. He worked in a welfare office in lower Manhattan, helping people apply for Aid for Families with Dependent Children, checking that they obeyed the rules, and guiding them through New York's often confusing education, legal, and social service bureaucracy. He did not relish the job. "My first job, a truly humbling but character-building experience, was that of a caseworker for the New York City Department of Welfare at $4,800 per year," he later wrote.[2] To others he was more blunt, telling them later that he hated the work and recoiled in horror when confronted with the reality of urban poverty and underclass pathology.[3] Whatever the truth, his career as a social worker did not last long. In March 1963 he was ordered to report for active duty.

Scheduled to report to the army's transportation school at Fort Eustis, Virginia, Ron and Alma piled their belongings into their brand-new Mercury Comet convertible and headed south. Except for one trip to Hampton Institute in Virginia as a high school student, Brown had spent his entire life in the North. This journey south with Alma offered a rare confrontation with Jim Crow. As the couple pulled into Hampton, Virginia, they stopped at a drive-in restaurant to grab a quick bite to eat.

"Sorry," a white waitress told them when she approached their car. "I can't serve you here."

"Why not?" Ron asked, perplexed.

"I can bring you food in a box and you can eat it over there," the waitress said, pointing to a spot off the premises. The Browns left in a huff, without ordering any food, but with Brown wiser over the legal ways in a part of a country he could be called on to defend with his life.[4]

In some ways, Ron and Alma were lucky. The waitress hailed from Ohio and apparently was apologetic at having to follow local customs and not angry over what many a white Southerner might have felt was Brown's cheeky question. At the time of the incident, blacks in several Southern states, backed by court orders, had begun challenging the refusal of private establishments to serve them. A few weeks before, authorities in Albany, Georgia, had thrown four African Americans in jail for seeking service at the drugstore counter. Scores of black people had been arrested in Rome, Georgia, for daring to do the same thing. On March 19, ten days before Brown had to report for duty at Fort Eustis, the Supreme Court had ordered South Carolina to reconsider breach of the peace convictions of 373 black demonstrators arrested in Orangeburg.

Antisegregation efforts dominated the news. In many areas of the South, whites were on the lookout for what they thought were "outside agitators," people coming down from the North to "make trouble." In this climate, Ron and Alma Brown, a young black couple driving a car bearing Northern license plates into a drive-in restaurant in Hampton, Virginia, and then questioning why they were not served ran the risk of landing themselves in serious physical danger. The fates were shining on them when the waitress they drew was another Northerner.

Reporting to Fort Eustis, Brown continued to undergo the change that had begun at Fort Devens. In the army he could no longer get away with the kind of careless attitude toward military affairs that he exhibited in college. Every screw-up, instance of sloppy dress, or lax discipline could cost him status, rank, respect, and comfort. A junior-grade lieutenant in the army who doesn't perform well can have his life made miserable by his superior officers, by a savvy master sergeant, or by the men in his unit who disrespect his authority. For the first time in his life, Ron Brown had to face the immediate consequences of his actions, and he could not talk his way out of trouble. Not surprisingly, in the military he shaped up. Instead of being depicted as merrily slothful, his efficiency reports portray him as a diligent, resourceful officer, able to assume responsibility and to lead his men.

RON'S FIRST overseas posting was in Kassel, West Germany, only about twenty-five miles from the border with East Germany. A major listening post, Kassel's purpose was to detect military activity among Warsaw Pact troops in Communist East Germany. Assigned to the motor pool as a transportation officer, Second Lieutenant Brown quickly impressed his superiors with his intelligence and warm personality. "His high spirits and usual cheerful demeanour [*sic*] make him well liked by both supervisors and subordinates," his immediate supervisor wrote four months after Brown arrived. The officer, Captain John H. McGinnis Jr., noted that Ron ran his section of the motor pool efficiently with little or no supervision, "a remarkable accomplishment, in view of the fact that he was assigned here directly from the transportation officers basic course, having no experience in the field."[5] For Brown to have received such high praise was noteworthy for another reason: the post, including the unit he commanded, was all white.

In the ensuing months, he continued to draw solid performance ratings. "Lt. Brown readily accepts additional responsibility and can be depended on," Captain McGinnis wrote in an evaluation in April 9, 1964. "Lt. Brown should be capable of superior performance with further training and experience."[6] Five months later he was promoted to first lieutenant,[7] and in December 1964 he was given another glowing evaluation, one that would have been a surprise to his former colleagues at ROTC and his classmates at Middlebury. "Based on my observations of other officers of a similar grade and experience, I would rate Lt. Brown in the upper ten percent," wrote Captain James P. Brady, at battalion headquarters in Giessen, West Germany. "In addition to being an outstanding transportation officer he is also an exceptional soldier who sets a good example and insists on the same high standard of appearance, conduct and discipline from his men."[8]

Despite the proximity of his post to the East German border, Brown's German posting consisted of the routine day-to-day activities of an officer in

a support battalion during peacetime. The Cold War tensions of 1961, when
the Soviet leaders constructed the Berlin Wall and sealed off the Communist
East, had faded by the time he and Alma arrived at Kassel, a former training
center for Luftwaffe pilots located on the Eder River. Consequently, his efficiency reports, while overflowing with praise, describe him performing mundane administrative duties. He supervised the movement of household goods
for officers and men who were being transferred. He set up a snack bar for his
men. He organized a recreation program for officers and men, as well as their
wives and children. He drew particular praise for overseeing an effort to rid
the base of more than 150 abandoned private vehicles. It was hardly John
Wayne heroics.

Still, a task well done is a task well done, and Brown performed all his
assignments with speed and efficiency. He thrived in the military life, and at
one point seriously considered making the army his career. His military experience, with its premiums on delegating responsibility, learning how to give
orders, getting the most out of his troops, and a single-minded pursuit of a
goal, later proved invaluable. Years later, when times got tough at the Democratic National Committee, he would always know how to boost morale,
whether it was giving someone a pep talk, telling them to drop their work for
an afternoon and taking them out for a meal, or setting specific goals.

Military training gave Ron Brown a management-by-objective outlook that
he used well. "That was the thing that I loved about him then, and I still love
about him," said Dan Carol, who later worked for him at the DNC. "He was a
really great leader. He had that army-captain-focus-on-the-mission-take-the-hill
mentality. He just gave out this sense that we can do it."[9]

The means by which Brown developed these leadership skills would
make him a rarity among black civil rights and political leaders. While the military has long been an avenue for the poor and working class—both black and
white—to ascend into the middle class, it has not been particularly popular
among those who would become black leaders. One recent study of blacks
from the World War II generation found that while 68 percent of those listed
in *Who's Who Among Black Americans* had served in the military, only 21
percent of civil rights leaders did, probably because so many of these leaders
were clergy and thus exempt from military service.[10] Even those leaders who
were too young to have served in World War II tended to have eschewed military service. Martin Luther King Jr. never served, nor did Adam Clayton Powell, Thurgood Marshall, Malcolm X, Clarence Mitchell, Roy Wilkins, Vernon
Jordan, Andrew Young, Julian Bond, or Jesse Jackson. Brown's military service
gave him an experience that was rare among African American civil rights
and political leaders. He was one of the few to have worked in close quarters
and in direct competition with whites. Most black leaders in the civil rights and
political fields came out of black institutions, generally the church or histori-

cally black colleges. Their contact with whites during their formative years of college and right after graduation was episodic at best. Brown's was constant. And it was constant in an institution that tried—though not always successfully—to play down racial differences (indeed, *all* personality differences) in order to meld men into a cohesive unit. Studies have shown what effect the military has had on black veterans. "Blacks are about half again more likely than whites to rate their military experience high on specific dimensions such as self-pride, self-discipline, ability to make friends, develop job skills and ability to work with others," two sociologists have written.[11] Brown's ability to work comfortably with and be accepted by whites was clearly honed by his military experience. It is not surprising that in the 1990s only one other African American leader would be seen as having as much "crossover" appeal: General Colin Powell, another product of the military.

Brown did more than just work with whites in the military, however. He commanded them, something that was a rarity for any African American. He was the only black officer at his first posting in Germany, and during his entire time in the army blacks never made up more than 3.5 percent of the officer corps.[12] Being an officer not only meant giving orders, it also meant taking care of your men, listening to their difficulties both great and small, and figuring out how to help them. "Leadership is solving problems," Powell wrote in his autobiography. "The day soldiers stop bringing you their problems is the day you've stopped leading them. They have either lost confidence that you can help them or concluded you do not care. Either case is a failure of leadership."[13]

There is no indication from his efficiency reports that Brown had lost the confidence of his men. Indeed, he would later say of his time in the army that he learned to be comfortable taking command. Ordering white men around and taking care of their personal difficulties, Brown could hardly have seen all whites as unreconstructed racists or ten-foot-tall supermen. If his childhood at the Hotel Theresa exposed Brown to successful black role models, his time in the military gave him a view of whites in all their ordinariness that was equally as valuable.

Surprisingly, however, Brown seldom spoke publicly about his military career—indeed, when he ran for chairman of the Democratic National Committee years later, his aides only found out halfway through the campaign that he had been in the army. Brown's shyness about his military career might have stemmed from its banality. For a man who later came to believe in the power of projecting a certain image, Brown had the misfortune of having missed out on the two defining events of the 1960s—the civil rights movement, both the nonviolent protests in the South and the urban rebellions in the North, and the Vietnam War. Instead of being where the action was, either in the rice paddies of Southeast Asia or in the civil rights or antiwar protests back home, Brown was in Germany and Korea carrying out what seemed to be run-of-the-mill duties. Years later he confided to Alma how much he regretted not participating in either of these two seminal events.[14]

BROWN ENTERED the army five months before the March on Washington, perhaps the zenith of the drive for racial integration. As he learned the duties of maintaining buses, jeeps, and other vehicles in the motor pool at Kassel during the last seven months of 1963, the pace of the civil rights movement quickened back home. In April, Eugene "Bull" Connor, the police commissioner of Birmingham, Alabama, turned high-pressure fire hoses and police dogs on black and white civil rights demonstrators. In May, police in Greensboro, North Carolina, arrested hundreds of black students who tried to eat at whites-only lunch counters. A month later, Medgar Evers, field secretary of the Mississippi NAACP, was shot in the back and killed in front of his home in Jackson. A week later, President John F. Kennedy proposed a sweeping civil rights bill that would ban discrimination in employment, education, and even privately owned establishments like restaurants, movie theaters, and retail shops. In August, Martin Luther King Jr. gave his famous "I Have a Dream" speech—perhaps the most famous plea ever made for racial conciliation—at the Lincoln Memorial during the March on Washington. Throughout the summer and fall, demonstrations broke out all across the South by blacks and whites demanding segregation's end. In many places whites furiously resisted, sometimes violently. In September, a bomb exploded beneath a black Baptist church in Birmingham, killing four young girls. National Guard troops and state highway patrol troopers were mustered into action to halt the subsequent rioting.

Things did not quiet down any the following year. Malcolm X, the charismatic black leader, broke with Elijah Muhammed and the Nation of Islam, saying the black Muslim group was too narrowly focused. In June, the Senate voted 71 to 29 to end debate on a civil rights bill, ending a seventy-five-day filibuster by Southern lawmakers. Northern students, shaking off the apathy that had enveloped them during Brown's time in college, rushed down to Mississippi during Freedom Summer to help blacks register to vote. Two white civil rights organizers from the North, Andrew Goodman and Michael Schwerner, along with a black organizer, James Chaney, were stopped on a lonely road outside of Philadelphia, Mississippi, and killed. Their bodies were found buried in an earthen dam some months later. The murders spurred Congress to pass the Civil Rights Act of 1964, the most sweeping antidiscrimination measure ever enacted. In July, thousands of blacks, angered by the shooting of a fifteen-year-old African American youth by New York City police officers, rioted in Harlem. The movement had come north. In March 1965, club-swinging Alabama state troopers mounted on horseback charged into peaceful civil rights protestors on the Edmund Pettus Bridge in Selma, Alabama. The brutal attack and the Selma-to-Montgomery march that followed it prompted Congress to pass the Voting Rights Act of 1965. Malcolm X was shot dead as he started to address a crowd in New York City's Audubon Ballroom. In August, blacks in the Watts area of Los Angeles rioted, and the slogan "Burn, baby, burn!" became a rallying cry for some African Americans and a frightening call to some whites.

All the while, Brown earned solid evaluations for carrying out duties that entailed making sure there was enough motor oil for the buses on the Kassel base and supervising the towing of abandoned cars. As history rushed forward, he was little more than a Cold War soldier, passively sitting on the sidelines thousands of miles away, reading about the dramatic events in American news magazines purchased in army PX stores. He was learning how to command men. But in the biggest battle to date for his people, Brown was AWOL. He felt the loss acutely. "I probably felt a lot of guilt and detachment about being out of the country," Brown later recalled. "I read about what was going on in *Time* and *Newsweek*. I wasn't there during the riots when the heavy action was taking place."[15]

Brown should not have felt so bad, if indeed he did. He was doing nothing different from what thousands of African American men and women were doing at the time—serving his country, doing his time in the military, and becoming a family man. On March 4, 1965, his son Michael was born. The presence of the baby caused a little bit of a stir at Kassel since so few of the Germans and Americans had ever seen a black infant. "Everybody—every doctor, every nurse—had to come see Michael," Alma said. "They had never seen a little baby like this before."[16]

There is perhaps another reason for Brown's reticence to speak of his military career. By the time he mustered out in 1967, the rhetoric among black intellectuals and leaders had shifted. King's conciliatory message had been supplanted by the angry "black power" slogans of Stokely Carmichael, H. Rap Brown, and Floyd McKissick. In this new climate the view of black intellectual, political, and cultural leaders toward the military shifted from indifference to outright hostility. The military was seen as an institution that drained needed resources away from domestic programs that would help blacks. During the Vietnam era it was accused by those on the left, including black radicals like Carmichael and the Black Panthers, of conducting a "genocidal" war in Vietnam. The view that no self-respecting black should serve in the "white man's army" took hold among the black elite. Those who did so voluntarily, as Brown had, were often looked upon with suspicion. Given the times, it is hardly surprising that Brown played down his military career, even if it had benefited him immeasurably.

IN APRIL 1966, Brown was promoted to captain, and was scheduled to be transferred to Korea.[17] Because the new assignment was near the Demilitarized Zone between North and South Korea, wives were forbidden. During a two-month leave he set up Alma and Michael, now one, in a two-bedroom apartment in the St. James Towers,[18] a middle-income high rise in the Fort Greene section of Brooklyn, across the street from the Pratt Institute of Technology.

Captain Brown's new posting was with the Eighth Army's 38th Replacement Battalion, commanding the Korean Augmentee to the U.S. Army, or KATUSA, Training School. The KATUSA program had been started by Gen. Douglas MacArthur, who, in the opening weeks of the Korean War, found himself critically short of troops. The program essentially took Korean nationals, provided them with uniforms and weapons, and with barely any training assigned them to American military units in a desperate attempt to stem the advancing North Korean troops. Often the Koreans spoke no English and were placed under American officers who spoke no Korean. The results, as might be expected, were at times disastrous. The Koreans often fell asleep on guard duty, and the Americans initially had a hard time breaking them of the habit of greeting the day with a song, which often gave away their positions to the enemy.[19]

But as the war progressed, the KATUSA troops began to prove their value. They served as valuable liaisons between the American troops and the Korean population, dealt with refugees, and questioned prisoners. The KATUSAs provided another valuable service to the Americans. Their presence kept many U.S. soldiers off the front line, and therefore reduced American casualties. At the zenith of the experiment with Korean troops in 1953, there were nearly 24,000 KATUSAs in American units. After the shooting war ended, the United States began shifting many of its troops back home. But since no peace treaty was signed and many American units faced fully armed North Korean troops just north of the 38th Parallel, American commanders, especially within the Eighth Army, continued to use KATUSAs to fill out two full divisions. By the time Brown arrived in Korea there were still 11,000 KATUSAs in American units.[20]

By 1966 the system of providing KATUSA replacements had become much more organized than it was in the chaos of the first few days of the Korean War. The recruits were sent to a school maintained by the 38th Replacement Battalion at Ascom City, near Seoul, for medical examination, English language orientation, and two weeks of aptitude testing before being sent to their American units. It was this school that was placed under Brown. In the year that he commanded it, he rewrote the school curriculum and upgraded its recreational facilities, despite being hampered by a shortage of personnel and funds.

"He built the school into one of the most unique and outstanding schools of the United States Army," Brown's immediate supervisor, Lieutenant Colonel Milford R. Downey, wrote in an April 30, 1967, evaluation of Brown. Downey gushed, "Beyond doubt, he is one of the most competent officers I have ever known in the service."[21]

Brown's time in Korea also provided another valuable experience. It was the first time he had to deal with a culture and a people markedly different from Americans. In Germany his main interaction was with Americans, and while German culture is quite different from that of America, it provided nowhere near the culture shock of Korea. In Korea, the culture was unlike anything Brown, or most Americans—black or white—had ever seen. And he had to deal directly with the Koreans, seeing to their needs and making sure they were integrated into American operations. Lieutenant Colonel Downey's evaluation provides evidence that Brown handled his duties in a way that was at the very least inoffensive to Korean sensibilities and foreshadowed his ability to deal easily with other cultures. "Captain Brown has distinguished himself in the field of Korean-American relations," Downey wrote. "His natural tact, diplomacy and understanding of human relations established a rapport with his Korean counterparts and students."[22]

There is little question that Brown was considered an outstanding officer. If any further evidence was needed it came in October 1966, when he was selected to command the presidential motorcade when Lyndon B. Johnson visited Korea. Johnson's three-day visit was part of a seven-nation Asian tour that included a surprise stop in Vietnam to meet with American troops there. The operation would be dicey at times. Huge crowds greeted the president's motorcade wherever it went. At one point on October 31, a crowd estimated at between 1 million and 2 million people jammed into City Hall Square in Seoul, many of them pushing up against the soldiers lining the streets in an attempt to get closer to Johnson.[23] Tensions were heightened during the visit when North Koreans attacked American and South Korean units just south of the Demilitarized Zone, killing six American soldiers and one from the Republic of Korea.[24] The presidential visit tested the nerves of both civilian and military security officers. According to his efficiency report, Brown's handling of his motorcade duties was "flawless."[25]

"Captain Brown's potential as an officer is practically unlimited," Downey wrote. "If he remained in the service I would unhesitatingly recommend him for promotion ahead of his contemporaries."[26] But Brown was anxious to get back to civilian life and law school. Having been so far from where history was being made—either physically distant in the army or psychologically isolated at Middlebury—he was anxious to make up for lost time.

CHAPTER FIVE

THE LEAGUE

R ETURNING TO AMERICA in May 1967, Brown was eager to put the army behind him and get on with his life. After his discharge, he rejoined Alma, who was now three months pregnant, and his son Michael, a frisky two, at the apartment in the St. James Towers in Brooklyn. Re-enrolled for night classes at St. John's Law School and back to work as a social worker, he felt ready for whatever might come next. Adulthood beckoned.

This time around, the social worker position was even more short-lived. Within a month, he was hired by the League, as the National Urban League is affectionately known among its staffers and officials. Family played a part as Gloria's connections helped her son land an interview with Mahlon Puryear, the League's deputy director.[1]

Brown jumped at the chance for a job at the venerable civil rights organization, unaware that the League was steering into some rough waters. Founded in 1911 to help ease the transition of Southern blacks migrating to Northern cities, the League was stepping up its activities in the nation's black ghettos, organizing community groups, developing grassroots leadership, and pushing for expanded government programs in education, health, and other social services. It was a marked change for the staid organization. Unlike the National Association for the Advancement of Colored People, which began a year earlier and reflected the activist approach of its guiding spirit, W. E. B. Du Bois, the League's founders were more in tune with the self-help and accommodationist philosophy of Du Bois's main rival, Booker T. Washington. While the early NAACP tended to attract lawyers and ministers, the League's early organizers were educators and social workers. While the modern NAACP challenged segregation through lawsuits, lobbying, and, to a lesser extent, organizing protests, the League, as a tax-exempt organization, saw its mission as providing job skills and refining the often rough-hewn ways of poor Southern blacks. Rather than protesting injustice through pickets and boycotts, the League used gentle persuasion to press companies to hire blacks. As Du Bois and other NAACP leaders urged their membership to take principled stands on national issues and confront inequities head-on, League affiliates attempted to mold the poor into well-scrubbed, morally upright, trained workers who would not embarrass the race. As a result, fairly or not, many in the civil rights movement considered the League an elitist, bourgeois charity run by black society's upper crust.

Worried about jeopardizing its nonprofit tax status as a social service charity, the League did not join suits to overturn segregation laws. It did not lobby for passage of antidiscrimination laws. It played no part in direct actions like the Montgomery bus boycott or the street protests in cities like Birmingham, Alabama, or Saint Augustine, Florida. At best, people thought of the League as a vital institution staffed by dedicated workers. "But they don't sit in; they don't march; they don't picket; they don't go to jail. They're not in it," said Julian Bond, a veteran of the civil rights protests in the South. "They do other things. They get jobs for people. They do job training. That's what they do. But they're not out here knocking heads, facing jail. They're not in that movement; the activist, confrontational movement."[2] In the heady days of the 1950s, the League seemed increasingly irrelevant to the raw issues of the times. Consequently, it received little attention and less money and ricocheted from one financial crisis to the next. When the new executive director took over in 1961, the League's budget was a modest $300,000.[3]

The new executive director, Whitney M. Young Jr., was a former dean of Atlanta University's School of Social Work. He realized that he had to get the League directly involved in the civil rights struggle or the organization would simply become irrelevant and die. So he went into action. He persuaded a reluctant board of trustees to be one of the sponsors of the 1963 March on Washington. He participated in the 1965 Selma-to-Montgomery march. "There's been this historical, continuing rap against the Urban League that it is a bourgeois, middle-class organization," said John Mack, a veteran Urban Leaguer who is executive director of the group's Los Angeles affiliate. "So part of what Whitney was trying to do was have the League become more aggressive."[4]

Brown joined the League at this turning point, although his first job description smacked of the old, conservative bureaucracy: job developer/ trainee adviser at an employment recruitment center in the Bronx. The center recruited job candidates from the neighborhood, provided them with some rudimentary skills, and found them work with businesses that were willing to provide on-the-job training. It was bread-and-butter Urban League work conducted under a contract from the federal government that paid all or part of the salaries for both League staff and job trainees. But Brown was not destined to spend long hours teaching black job applicants how to fill out a job application or show up on time for work. Puryear had other plans for him. It wasn't long before Puryear brought him down to the League's main office in midtown Manhattan and made him a special assistant to Young.

From the moment Ron Brown walked through the doors of the national headquarters everyone knew he was someone to watch. He had an aura about him. His by then well-known family connections, his brains, good looks, and the confidence he exuded let everyone know he was someone who would rise in the League hierarchy. The question was merely how fast. No one envisioned him as the group's next executive director after Young; at twenty-six years of age, he was much too young to be considered the crown prince. But the betting was that unless he made some serious missteps he would eventually reach the top spot. "He was clearly the princeling when he joined the League, and Whitney treated him as such," said a former League staffer. "Everybody knew that this guy was a little different from other people running programs." Professional staff soon began to trust his judgment. Young became not only a boss but a mentor. Puryear, always on the lookout for talent that could be developed, helped the young man out whenever he saw a way.

WITH PURYEAR'S OKAY, Brown left the office every day at about 3:30 in order to catch the subway to Brooklyn to attend classes and to study.[5] The campus was located in downtown Brooklyn, right across the street from the New York City Board of Education. It was an urban college, full of commuter students, devoid of dormitories or swaths of green. "We didn't have a blade of grass," said Bernard Gegan, a professor who taught there at the time.[6] They had small, cramped classrooms overlooking a busy street. Professors often kept the windows shut tight to block out the traffic noise, causing students to sweat in the un-air-conditioned classrooms from more than the difficulty of the lessons. "It was very much a blue-collar place," said Gegan. "People who were the first in their family to go to college would be the typical student."[7] Many, especially those attending in the evenings, held down full-time jobs. There were very few blacks at the law school, but there were some at a time when the elite law schools in New York, like Columbia or N.Y.U., didn't have any.

Even with Puryear's help, Brown struggled to stay current in his schoolwork and was not always the best prepared in class. But his maturity and military discipline made him a better student than he had been at Middlebury. "If you ever learn to study you're going to be a world beater," Mario Cuomo, who taught Brown in two classes at St. John's and who would later become a four-term governor of New York, once told him. Cuomo was understanding of Brown's and the other night students' difficulties when it came to class preparation. "If he was not always as prepared as we'd like a student to be it wasn't because he wasn't willing to work," Cuomo said. "He was an extremely hard worker. It's just that he was using up a lot of his energy doing other things that he was required to do just to survive as the head of a family."[8]

What Brown lacked in preparation he compensated for with wit and an ability to think quickly on his feet. "He had the ability to communicate, to explain, to persuade, and he did it always without raising his voice," Cuomo recalled. "Some people rely on passion, disputation, or even presentation. He didn't. He was always calm, soothing, self-assured, which created a kind of aura of confidence, which is invaluable if you're a lawyer, and certainly if you're a politician."[9]

Brown remembered Cuomo as a teacher who intimidated students. "But he did not intimidate me," he recalled. "We're both people who like to banter."[10]

Brown wrestled with the demands of work, school, and family, barely having time to do more than notice the rising unrest on America's campuses, the growing Vietnam protests, or the latest outbreak of black anger in the country's urban areas. In 1968, when Robert Kennedy fell mortally wounded on the campaign trail in Los Angeles and Martin Luther King died of gunshot wounds at the Lorraine Hotel in Memphis, Brown and Alma were horrified along with the rest of the country. But the spirit of the times came closer to home when Young, in response to the riots that followed King's assassination, announced a "New Thrust" in which the League would become even more aggressive in advocating for the urban poor. It was a bold idea for the League that matched the demands of the times.

YOUNG APPOINTED BROWN director of the Black Student Summer Program in May 1969, giving him the task of recruiting sixty students to work in fifteen League affiliates across the country. It looked like a fairly routine assignment at first. Launched the year before as part of Young's New Thrust effort, the program was paid for by corporate donations. The concept was to harness the activism and black consciousness rising on college campuses and direct those forces toward League activities. Students received a modest stipend of $85 a week, plus room and board and transportation costs to and from the cities where they would work. Young hoped Brown, then twenty-eight years old, would serve as a bridge between the students and the older, often staid League leadership and staff.

But in the volatile climate of 1969, reaching out to young people often had unintended consequences. Militancy was the watchword of the day, and black organizations could just as easily find themselves the targets of the direct protest as white ones. "All hell was breaking loose on campuses," said Charles "Chuck" Hamilton, who was elected to the League's board of trustees in 1968 as a junior at Harvard. "Between the civil rights movement and the war in Vietnam, everything had become much more polarized and black students had become much more militant. It was natural that that was going to feed into any forum that was dealing with issues of race relations and social justice."[11]

The inevitable confrontation between the students and the League leadership erupted on July 28, 1969, when twenty young firebrands—many of them students in Brown's program—staged a protest at the opening of the League's annual convention in Washington. The dissidents, aged eighteen to twenty-nine, many sporting huge Afro haircuts and wearing colorful dashikis, interrupted a speech by League president James A. Linen, president of Time Inc. For good measure they also threatened to disrupt Young's keynote speech, scheduled for the next night. Despite Young's assertion that the League's programs fostered "ghetto power," the protesters complained there were not enough poor people and young people in the League's hierarchy. Mike Morris, a student at Southern Methodist University, declared that the League was "just an extension of whitey's arm and whitey's mind."[12]

The dissidents submitted a list of demands, including greater representation of young people on the organization's board of directors and the setting aside of a percentage of League funds to be controlled by black college students without any oversight by League officials. The demands seemed unreasonable, but Young wanted to avoid the embarrassment of further demonstrations at the convention.

The protest put Brown in a tricky situation. "This was Whitney Young's showcase; his P.R. vehicle, and the last thing he needed was some young people raising hell," said Mack.[13] Brown obviously wanted to defend his mentor. But these angry young people included Brown's own charges. They, like the enlisted men in his army platoon, expected him to help them—or, at least, to not undermine them. It didn't help matters much that many of the protesters distrusted Brown almost as much as they did older League officials. Not only was he a League officer, he had been in the military. "They wanted to know what my real role was," Brown said years later. " 'Is this guy some kind of a CIA agent?' "[14]

The rebellion put to the test the negotiating and deal-making skills that Brown would later make his trademark. He shuttled back and forth, hammering out a compromise between League officials and the students' leaders. Brown convinced them to pare down their list of demands, dropping some, such as carte blanche control of some League funds. At the same time he promised to press League officials to give serious consideration to other items on the list, such as greater board representation. In the end, he put together a solution that guaranteed a peaceful conference.

Back at headquarters, Brown's legend grew. Word spread about his people skills and his ability to keep small brush fires from being fanned into major conflagrations. He developed a reputation for dealing with the League's internal politics and turf battles. "I can remember having arguments with other staff, and Ron was a master at mediating conflict," said Vi Kaufman, a former League official. "Everybody always seemed to leave happy. He might be giving away more than you intended to, but he made it sound so good and everybody's agreeing. Then you'd leave and you'd say to yourself, 'My God!' And you would call him and say, 'Ron, I agreed to that?' "[15]

In May 1970, Brown graduated from St. John's with a newly minted law degree and a promotion to head a new division of the Urban League called

Law and Consumer Affairs. The rise inside the League that many had predicted was now beginning to occur. In three years, Brown had gone from helping high school dropouts fill out job applications to running a summer intern program to managing a department that helped local affiliates recruit minority police officers and push for black ownership of cable television systems.

It was harder to tell if the League was rising as well. Two years after the announcement of New Thrust, the League was tottering financially. Local United Way charities, a traditional source of funds for the League's local affiliates, had reduced their financial commitments, partly from worries about the League's new activist direction. Young's weakness as a manager did not help matters. The biggest blow to the League's finances came from the Ford Foundation, which had strongly supported the grassroots efforts by local League affiliates in the first two years of New Thrust. Ford officials told the League that they were dramatically scaling back contributions, cutting them from $3.6 million in 1969 to $1.75 million in 1970.[16] In a November 1970 memo, the League's deputy executive director described the group's financial health as "bleak."

The reduction in the Ford Foundation's support staggered the League, hitting as much at Young's image as it did the organization's programs. With his reputation on the line, drastic action was needed, and on December 11, 1970, he made a desperate telephone call to Leonard Garment, a special consultant to then-president Richard Nixon. Young asked if Garment could arrange a meeting with top-level administration officials—including, if possible, the president—to discuss "new trends in the black community." In addition, Young shared with Garment the fact that the League faced a potentially fatal financial crisis and wondered if the White House could help it out. "The Urban League, itself, is apparently facing acute difficulties and needs help," Garment would later write in a memo to Nixon. "Young feels it will be to the Government's advantage not to let the Urban League go under."[17]

Garment arranged a meeting with Nixon, who had been subjected to tough criticism from black leaders over his proposals to weaken the Voting Rights Act, his judicial appointments, and his opposition to busing to achieve school integration. Nixon saw saving the League as a means of cleaning up his reputation among African Americans. "It served a very useful purpose," said Garment. "It was doing something that was needed and it was a way of cooling things a little bit because there was so much hatred of Nixon and the administration as being antiblack."[18]

At the meeting with Nixon and his cabinet on December 22, 1970, the administration was prepared to direct more funds to the organizations. "The word came down from the Oval Office, look, we're going to have a cabinet meeting; I'm going to invite Whitney Young and we're going to go right around the cabinet table and the agenda for the meeting is what can you do for the Urban League," said Bradley Patterson Jr., Garment's chief deputy.[19]

The cabinet officials pledged more than $21 million in contracts within a month of the meeting. With the League able to use 22.8 percent of federal contract funds for its own overhead, the meeting with Nixon stabilized the League for years to come. On the way out of the room, one of the League staff was overheard declaring, "It sure helps to go to the top."[21]

Young's strategem saved the League. But it had serious, long-term implications. A year after meeting with Nixon, about $8.3 million of the League's income—more than 55 percent of its revenue—came from Washington.[22] The sleepy little private agency was now for all intents and purposes a federal contractor. Young's gambit had made the organization subject to the vagaries and politics of the federal budgeting process. Given that fact, League officials would later determine it as imperative that the organization have a strong lobbying presence in Washington.

EVEN BEFORE the Nixon meeting placed the League on firmer financial footing, Ron and Alma felt confident enough in their personal financial position to buy their first home. They paid $41,500 for a white frame colonial house in Mount Vernon, New York, a suburb in Westchester County, just north of the Bronx. Built in 1920, the house was set back up a sloping front lawn facing a busy thoroughfare in a white neighborhood bordering Bronxville, a tony suburb. Its roomy backyard provided plenty of space for Michael and Tracey, who was born in 1967, to romp about. Taking title in June 1970, Ron and Alma had a good time fixing up the house, painting several rooms in bright, splashy colors.

The Brown family quickly settled into the comfortable suburban lifestyle of upwardly mobile young black professionals. Alma took tennis lessons at the local YM-YWHA and became active in the League of Women Voters. The couple hosted weekly sessions of a couples bridge club at their home and threw their first annual New Year's Day party for their pals from the city and their new friends from Mount Vernon. "It was a focal point; it was a gathering place," May Carpenter, who worked with Alma, said of the Browns' house.[23]

The Browns soon fell into a group of young families, both black and white, that shared several things. Nearly all were newcomers; nearly all had young children and were interested in local issues, primarily the public schools; nearly all were college-educated professionals; and nearly all had moved to Mount Vernon to raise their children in a racially integrated setting. They became friendly with each other at playgrounds and PTA meetings, and in the course of things often discussed the town's racially charged politics.

Mount Vernon was a racially divided bedroom community of about 72,700 people packed into a four-square-mile area just north of New York City. Whites made up about 65 percent of the population, with blacks comprising about 35 percent. The New Haven Railroad line bisected the city into a predominantly white North Side, where the Browns lived, and an overwhelmingly black South Side. In the years prior to the Browns' arrival there had been some attempts to break down the town's de facto segregation, most notably the opening of a unified high school in 1965 that replaced a largely black vocational high school on the South Side and a mainly white academic high school on the North Side. But by 1970, with continued white racism and the rise of the black consciousness movement, blacks and whites viewed each other suspiciously across the steel ribbons of the railroad tracks.

At the time the city was dominated by Republicans whose strength rested on the large number of conservative Italian American voters. Candidates without the blessing of the Italian Civic Association, a staunchly conservative group, had little chance of winning, and the Republicans ruled both the city council and the local school board with an iron hand. Still, the group of young professionals the Browns associated with decided to put up their own candidates for the school board and convinced a blue-collar, liberal Italian woman from the North Side and a black man from the South Side to run for the seats. Ron and Alma stuffed flyers into envelopes, went door to door leafleting, and helped to get out the vote on election day. To everyone's surprise both of the candidates won.

Flushed with victory, the group decided to get involved in the local Democratic Party. What they quickly discovered was that in 1971 Mount Vernon's racial divisions were reflected in the local party. The Democrats were split into two factions, black Democrats from the South Side and so-called Regular Democrats, mainly Jewish liberals, from the North Side. Though the two groups often cooperated, they neither trusted each other nor socialized together. The newcomers decided to form a biracial faction of Democrats to provide a bloc of swing votes on the local Democratic Committee. To denote the fact that they belonged to neither the black Democrats from the South Side nor the white Democrats from the North Side, they called themselves the "Non Group," a loose organization comprised of about forty members—about evenly split among blacks and whites.

The Non Group gave Ron a platform for his first foray into politics. The group was "intentionally, not just consciously, biracial," said Herb Reich, who was one of its leaders. "Mount Vernon was a biracial city. If you wanted to get anything done you had to have a biracial group."[24] Among the first things the group did was run candidates for the local Democratic Committee, a body that sets policy for the local party organization. In 1971, the Non Group fielded a slate of candidates in twenty-three of the city's fifty-four districts. Each district elected a pair of delegates to the committee, and the Non Group's pairs were, whenever possible, one white and one black. Among the candidates was Ron Brown, who ran with a young white woman. "Ron and I looked good together on the pictures for the flyers," said Marie McCarthy, Brown's running mate for district leader in one of the few racially integrated neighborhoods on the

North Side. "He was very slender, with kind of a little Afro and a beard and always the fashion plate. I tried to do my Jackie Kennedy imitation." The two always campaigned together, walking their district, arguing for the need for new blood on the Democratic Committee. "I remember him out campaigning and loving it," said McCarthy. "He loved pressing the flesh and he did it very well."[25] Brown and McCarthy won seats on the city's Democratic Committee, along with sixteen other pairs of candidates from the Non Group. It would be the only public elected office that Brown would ever win.

With their victories, the Non Group became the swing votes on the local Democratic Committee, forcing the contending blocs of white and black Democrats to compromise in order to get their support. The Non Group met regularly at the Reichs' home to plot political strategy, share political intelligence, and hash out a consensus on issues. Brown participated regularly, though not Alma, who, in addition to working in her own job as a counselor in a program for pregnant teenage girls, took the primary responsibility for raising the children.

With the fervor bred of commitment and friendship, the Non Group's meetings resembled encounter groups as much as they did strategy sessions. The group insisted on honest dialogue and the sharing of all they knew. Candor, sometimes brutal, was encouraged, if not required, and the discussions often became heated. Brown always remained calm, however. "Almost everyone else would, at some point, argue vociferously and loudly," said Herb Reich. "Not Ron."[26] Not that Brown never became angry during the sessions. He just never raised his voice. Geri Reich, Herb's wife, said she could tell when Brown was becoming annoyed. He would turn in his chair facing away from the group and sit at a right angle to the discussion. He leaned over, and seemed to withdraw into himself as he gathered his thoughts. Then, when he was ready, he'd turn back and speak softly—and rationally. "He didn't waste words," she recalled. "If we were in a meeting and someone took this stand and someone else took the opposite stand and things were jumping in the room, Ron wouldn't participate until he had it all set. Then he would have his say, which would summarize and continue with an idea of his own, taking some parts from what already had been said. He was a good conciliator."[27]

Early on, the group faced distrust and hostility from David Ford Sr., a powerful leader of the black Democrats from the city's South Side. He viewed the new group as interlopers whose commitment to the city was more dilettantish than long lasting. Ford could see the city's long-term demographic trends. Mount Vernon's black population was growing. As racial tensions rose, as they inevitably would, the college-educated professionals, black or white, who said they wanted to live in an integrated setting would do what everyone else often does. They would move on.

The Non Group delegated the business of dealing with Ford to Brown. In the racial atmosphere of the day it did not make sense to have a white emissary to the black Democratic leader. Beyond race, however, Brown displayed other skills that made him the right choice. According to Herb Reich, "He would come back and say, 'Here's what Dave says. Here's where I agree with him and here's where I disagree with him.' He was such a good reporter. He would bring things back accurately, and he not only told you what was said, he would also tell you the nuances, the things that aren't being said."[28] Brown was also able to gain Ford's trust and respect. "We developed a strong friendship that carried on through the years," Ford said. "If there was an issue, he would call and we would sit down and we would talk about it. Sometimes I understood where they were coming from and I went along. Sometimes I was adamant on what I had to do and he understood that."[29] Ford, who had his troubles with other Non Group members, found Brown smart and pragmatic. "I thought he was the best thing going. . . . He was levelheaded, very cool and very deliberative."[30]

For two years Brown and the Non Group were a moderating force on the local Democratic Committee. They helped forge consensus on zoning, parks, and educational issues. According to Ford, Brown helped keep the committee from splitting apart over its position on Vietnam and Ford's staunch support of the American war effort. But Ford had also assessed the group members correctly. They might have been passionate about local issues and local politics, but they were, in effect, transients who, as their careers took off, left Mount Vernon behind. "I remember Dave Ford saying to us, 'You people all have upward mobility and you will all leave and I will still be here,'" said McCarthy. "In a sense he was right. Four or five years later we were all gone, including Ron."[31]

HALF A WORLD AWAY in March 1971, Whitney Young drowned while swimming in the rough surf off the shore of Lagos, Nigeria. While his death sent shock waves across black America, insiders at the League absorbed the news without panic, though not without pain. On the plane carrying Young's body back from Africa, Bayard Rustin, head of the A. Phillip Randolph Institute, leaned over to Daniel S. Davis, a League official, and asked in his high-pitched, clipped English, "Tell me, Dan, who do you think will replace Whitney?" It did not take Davis more than a moment to answer, "Vernon Jordan."[32]

Though a search committee of the League's board of trustees looked at more than seventy prospects to succeed Young, most League staffers were not surprised when it selected Jordan. Despite his relative youth—he was thirty-six years old at the time—Jordan was a veteran of the civil rights movement and of black institutions. He was smart, striking, urbane, well-spoken, politically astute, and a proven fund-raiser, just what many in the League felt the organization needed for its image and its well-being in the 1970s. He was a protégé of Young's, someone the Urban League's executive director had once suggested apply to become his deputy. But later, sizing up Jordan's personality, Young changed his mind, at least for the moment. "I think we all consider you more likely a candidate for the executive director spot rather than the deputy," Young wrote Jordan. "But that isn't vacant yet!"[33]

Five years older than Brown, Jordan was born to working-class parents, the second of three sons, and raised in a public housing project in Atlanta. His father, for whom he was named, was a mail clerk at a military base. His mother, Mary Griggs Jordan, owned her own catering business and often prepared meals at Atlanta's fine white homes and clubs where relationships were forged and deals were made. She often brought Jordan and his brother Windsor along to help out, giving the young Vernon a makeshift fan to shoo away flies from the punch bowl. Among the affairs that Mary Jordan catered was the monthly meeting of the Atlanta Lawyers Club. Jordan, who was a teenager at the time, was intrigued by the sense of power and style these white barristers projected. "I liked the way they dressed," he once said. "I didn't like the way they talked, necessarily. I didn't like what they said. But I liked their demeanor, their decorum."[34]

Rather than having him attend one of the black colleges in Atlanta, the Jordans sent Vernon to DePauw University in Greencastle, Indiana, where he was one of only five blacks in a student body of 2,200 and the only African American in his class. Tall, handsome, and charming, Jordan worked his way through college, driving a bus for two summers for the Chicago Transit Authority, making $2.45 an hour and often working sixteen hours a day. "I loved driving the bus," he once told an interviewer. "The girls would get on a bus and give you their telephone numbers on the transfers."[35]

After graduating from DePauw, Jordan attended Howard University Law School, considered the best black law school and the training ground for civil rights attorneys like Thurgood Marshall. He knew at the time what he wanted to do. "In those days, civil rights law was at the cutting edge of change in the South," he said. "And the South was home, and I wanted to be home and be part of that change."[36] For a black lawyer in Atlanta, being on the cutting edge of the civil rights movement meant being affiliated with Donald L. Hollowell, a noted African American attorney who handled discrimination suits, death penalty cases, habeas corpus appeals, and anything else in the civil rights arena. "King is our leader," civil rights workers in Georgia used to sing at sit-ins. "Hollowell is our lawyer."[37]

Jordan began as a legal assistant in 1960, and was soon caught up in one of Hollowell's famous cases, the desegregation of the University of Georgia. Two black students, Hamilton Holmes and Charlayne Hunter, later famous as Charlayne Hunter-Gault, the television journalist, had been denied admission. Hollowell believed race was the reason, though university officials denied it. As Hollowell's law clerk, Jordan dug through thousands of pages of student records at the university's registrar's and admissions offices and found documents showing that a white female student whose circumstances mirrored Hunter's had been admitted while the black applicant had been rejected. With this newly found piece of evidence, the courts ordered the university to accept the two black students. On the day they were to register for classes, Jordan escorted Hunter onto the campus, where they were met by a howling mob of whites. "Vernon didn't seem to have any fear at all," recalled Horace Ward, another young lawyer in the firm who escorted Holmes that day. "He escorted Charlayne about the campus just like they belonged there."[38]

In the mid-1960s Jordan became field director of the NAACP's Georgia office. There he found himself at times in the middle of the tricky relationship between Roy Wilkins, the executive secretary of the NAACP, and Martin Luther King Jr. The two civil rights giants disagreed over strategy. Wilkins believed the struggle for civil rights was primarily a legal one that should be fought in the courts. He did not feel that mass actions like the Montgomery bus boycott that brought King to national attention—a battle that was ultimately won as a result of a Supreme Court ruling—would not do much to advance the cause. King thought the legal route too slow. Wilkins also considered King a young upstart and rabble-rouser who was stealing the thunder—and potentially the members—of the NAACP, a group that had labored hard in the vineyard for decades. As NAACP field director in Georgia, Jordan spent much of his time responding to entreaties from Wilkins, who wanted to make sure local chapters and younger members of the NAACP did not fall under King's sway.

Still, Jordan remained an activist. Perhaps his most important civil rights work, and certainly his most enduring, was with the Voter Education Project (VEP). Started in 1962 by the Southern Regional Council, an Atlanta-based civil rights group, it was intended to spur black voter registration in Southern cities, small towns, and rural areas. The idea was to create a large bloc of new black voters as a means of shifting the balance of Southern political power away from the segregationist leaders of the region's Democratic Party. The VEP would conduct registration drives, often finding local leaders to organize them. Private foundations would finance these efforts. And the FBI was supposed to provide security for the young field workers, which in the early days, under J. Edgar Hoover, it often failed to do.

Danger and disappointment radicalized many of the idealistic young field workers, especially those from the Student Non-Violent Coordinating Committee, who were the foot soldiers in the voter registration drives. One person who was not turned into a militant, however, was Jordan. "Vernon is not a radical," said James Gibson, a friend since childhood. "Vernon has never been a radical. Vernon is a middle-class guy who is a professional and is very skillful. He has values that connected him to the grass roots. But his style has always been establishment."[39]

Jordan first worked as deputy to VEP's first director, Wiley A. Branton, a resourceful lawyer from Arkansas who used any means he could, including a light complexion that allowed him to pass for white, as a way of rescuing his field workers who had fallen into the clutches of a backwoods rural sheriff. For his first years Jordan assisted with paperwork, recruited workers, and kept track of them in the field. Occasionally, Jordan operated as a field worker himself, journeying into small towns and trying to find a local person courageous enough to organize a voter registration drive, trustworthy enough to make sure that money sent to him or her for that effort would in fact be spent on it, and charismatic enough to get other blacks to join in.

It could be enormously nerve-racking and dangerous work to address small gatherings of black men and women in churches in small towns in the Mississippi Delta—or South Georgia or the Black Belt of Alabama—with the local sheriff standing outside waiting to follow you to where you would be spending the night. As was his fashion, however, Jordan somehow managed to break the tension. Frances Polly, an elderly white woman who often traveled to the same town as Jordan, recalled that "when six o'clock came, we would go to my room and open up the gin bottle."[40]

For a short time in 1965, Jordan was lured away to work for the federal anti-poverty program as a lawyer in the Office of Economic Opportunity. The work, part of the Johnson administration's War on Poverty, was nowhere near as stimulating as directing voter registration efforts in the deep South, and the results were not as tangible as looking at a report sent back by a field organizer declaring that the number of black registrants in some rural county in South Georgia had climbed from 500 to 3,000. But the pay at OEO was good—and it was regular. When friends would ask Jordan if he eliminated poverty yet, he would quip, "I have at my house."[41]

But in the autumn of 1965 Jordan replaced Branton as VEP's director. He was immediately faced with a major problem: the fact that VEP had less than $25,000 in the bank. Jordan's foremost task during this period was developing and maintaining a steady stream of funding from major foundations. He soon learned the lesson that white foundations didn't give money merely because they liked a black organization's history or its programs. They gave money to a black group because they liked the group's leader. If the leader didn't show probity, sound judgment, and charm, the foundations just as often took their money elsewhere.

"You could get a dog to run Yale and Yale will still get its money," Jordan said. "The foundations cared about these [black] organizations, but they also cared about who was running them."[42] In order to ensure donations, Jordan had to make sure he presented an image of mature, reliable, and nonradical leadership—a talent he developed as director of the VEP and honed to perfection in later years.

First under Branton and then Jordan, the VEP was enormously successful, registering thousands of blacks and in the process transforming Southern society perhaps more than any other effort in the civil rights movement. "It was the way to pry the can open," said Reese Cleghorn, a former VEP official. "You could integrate a store or a lunch counter, and most likely fail. But nothing that you did apart from voter registration was going to fundamentally alter the structure of the South."[43] Yet, while Branton and then Jordan were quietly transforming Southern politics and Southern society, most of the nation's attention was focused first on the Freedom Riders and King and later on the "revolutionary" rhetoric of Stokely Carmichael, H. Rap Brown, and the Black Panthers. "Vernon was doing *the* political work of the second half of the 1960s, the most enduring political work," said Taylor Branch, a former VEP field worker and the Pulitzer Prize–winning historian of the civil rights movement in the South.[44]

As those black voters took their places on the voter rolls, they flocked to the Democratic Party, creating a powerful bloc that, in later years, would have significant implications for the party and for Ron Brown.

With his ability to gain rapport with virtually anyone he met, Jordan seemed a natural for politics, and indeed, a number of people urged him to run for office in Atlanta. For a while he considered it, especially when the city created the new position of vice mayor. Blacks were becoming a significant political force in the city, and there was little question that a good black candidate could probably win a citywide office such as mayor—or even congressman. The prospect was raised to Jordan, and he announced in 1970 that he was going to run for Congress. But three weeks later he was offered the job of head of the United Negro College Fund (UNCF) and, following the advice of Whitney Young, opted for that instead. "He toyed with the idea, but he didn't do it," said Cleghorn. "I think he didn't ever want to be in that kind of conflict. He didn't want to be in the position to lose."[45] Jordan does not disagree with that analysis. He felt being the chief money man, a kind of chancellor of the exchequer, of then forty black colleges was more exciting than running for Congress. And, he felt, "It was also more certain."[46]

The choice for Jordan to head the Urban League seemed natural. The UNCF's headquarters in New York shared the same building as the Urban League, and he was an intimate of Young, who had helped persuade him to travel north to take the position. As head of the UNCF, Jordan brought in $9 million for the fund in 1970, a feat that impressed the League's trustees. And with his imposing six-foot, four-inch frame, deep resonating voice, and suave urbane demeanor, he looked and acted the part of the head of a sophisticated civil rights organization. "Vernon had leadership stamped all over him," said Davis. "He was a kind of larger-than-life personality. When he walked into a room, all eyes went to him."[47]

JORDAN'S SELECTION to head the Urban League began a complicated twenty-five-year relationship with Ron Brown. Jordan had met Brown when he moved to New York from Atlanta to take over the United Negro College Fund. He was impressed with the fact that Brown was going to law school—something that few members of the Urban League staff did. The two lived in Westchester County—Brown in Mount Vernon and Jordan in Greenburgh—and they struck up a friendship, much of it through games of tennis that Brown, a much superior player, generally won.

They were much alike: smart, handsome, polished, each the product of an education at a white college—Brown at Middlebury, Jordan at DePauw. Both were lawyers. Both moved comfortably in the upper strata of black and white society. Each radiated confidence. Each loved the trappings of power and living the high life. Each had winning ways with women. Each was fiercely ambitious. It was no surprise that they were drawn toward each other. It was also no surprise that they repelled each other. As both men blossomed and became celebrated trailblazers there were moments when Jordan and Brown seemed to be replaying the competition between F&Os—first and onlies—that Brown had experienced in college. "They respected each other; they got on each other's nerves," said James Hackney, who was Brown's counsel at the Commerce Department and his good friend. "They were close for a long time, and remained close, but at some point they both went their own ways. There was a rivalry there. For two people who spent as much time together over the years as they did, their relationship was very complicated."[48]

Under Jordan, Brown's already quick-moving career at the League shifted into a higher gear. In the beginning their association flourished. Jordan saw Brown as a talented and trusted adviser whose sound judgment was of particular value. "He was young and he was smart and he was quick and he was fast," Jordan said.[49] Trusting Brown, Jordan piled more and more responsibility onto his younger colleague, increasingly thrusting Brown into a more public role. If demonstrators picketed the Urban League offices, it was Brown, and only Brown, who was to meet and negotiate with them. When leaders of black organizations—some moderate, some radical—met at the National Black Political Convention in Gary, Indiana, in 1972, it was Brown who represented the League.

The relationship between Brown and Jordan was like that of siblings, with the older of the two recognizing the gifts of his younger brother and seeking to use those talents to his benefit, not unlike the relationship between John and Robert Kennedy. "At one point they had a great relationship and Ron was seen as Vernon's guy," said John Mack. "It was understood that he was the number two guy. He had that label and that position . . . Ron was like Vernon's alter ego."[50] The two also cut dashing figures: suave, well-spoken, and radiating a kind of cool dynamism that was a marked contrast to the aging leadership of Roy Wilkins at the NAACP. "When we saw him and Vernon together we'd just say, wow!" said Faith Williams, who worked in the League's public relations office. "We just felt so lucky working in an environment where our leaders looked so good and were so smart."[51]

In 1972, Jordan named Brown general counsel, reviving a position that had remained unfilled for years as all the organization's legal work had been farmed out to outside counsel. As the group's chief lawyer, Brown was ostensibly expected to advise Jordan and local affiliates on legal matters, mainly dealing with maintaining the group's tax-exempt status. He also would be expected to scrutinize contracts and review the group's insurance policies. Any more complicated legal work was still handled by Millbank and Tweed, the League's counsel.

In fact, Brown showed little interest in the run-of-the-mill legal chores. As general counsel, Brown was supposed to keep track of resolutions passed by the delegate assembly, the League's highest-ranking body, at the organization's annual conference and write them up into formal text. "Damn if the son of a bitch wouldn't come into my office and just dump it on me as if it was the most natural thing in the world," the official recalled, chuckling. "It really wasn't all that much work, and he'd do it in such a friendly way that I would go ahead and do it and give it to him. . . . The guy just oozed charm. But behind all this was the assumption that I would do it. And I know for a fact that I wasn't the only one that experienced that kind of thing. I was personally amused by it. But I also know from being around politicians that this is how politicians are."

Brown really was more *consigliari* to Jordan than general counsel to the League, generally delegating the detailed legal work to Andrew Adair, the only other licensed lawyer working for the League. "Ron was very lazy when it came to desk work," said Adair. "I don't mean that in a negative way. But Ron did not spend his energy sitting at his desk, or writing opinions about our insurance policies or writing memorandums. That was not his forte. He would rather spend his time strategizing on the direction the Urban League ought to be going. He would burn long hours doing that."[52]

Brown also provided legal advice to affiliates around the country, helping them negotiate with state and local governments. "He was so smart and could grasp things quickly. He was great at putting out all kinds of fires," said Robert Hill, the League's director of research. "He didn't just advise you, he'd get right in the middle of the fray."[53] But Brown's value to Jordan went beyond legal work or even League strategy. Jordan saw him as a link to the League's immediate past, someone who was known to many League veterans and whose presence reassured those concerned about the direction in which Jordan was taking the organization. "If you're a social worker, trained and experienced, you tend to always be a social worker," said Adair, "and you wondered why Vernon was going down the road of things like voter registration. Those were question marks for a number of senior Urban League executives."[54] Brown, however, was not allied with any of the factions within the League who were suspicious of the outsider Jordan and uncomfortable with the new, more political direction he charted for the League. "He was sufficiently young in the Urban League organization that he didn't belong to anybody," Jordan said. "He knew everybody and everybody knew him. But he was not in anybody's camp."[55]

Realizing that Brown seemed to understand Jordan and could easily relate to him, League officials used Ron as a kind of sounding board, a way to discern how a thought or proposed policy shift might be received by Jordan. Often heads of local affiliates and members of the staff found that the best way to get an idea to Jordan was to give it first to Brown. "When we sat around and did pie in the sky or what if, Ron's input would have greater weight," said Carol Gibson, who headed the League's educational programs. "You knew that you could take something to Ron and gauge his reaction. That might tell you a little bit about where Vernon might want to go."[56]

And Jordan did want to go into different places. Coming out of UNCF and the Voter Education Project, Jordan brought a new, much more political orientation to the League. In addition to naming Brown as general counsel, Jordan also created a major new program for the League, Voter Education and Citizen Participation. The goal was to register black voters, keep them informed of political developments, and mobilize them to cast ballots on election day. It was Jordan's new thrust for the League, one more in line with his outlook. Unlike Young, Jordan was not particularly interested in fostering ghetto economic development, which he felt the League did not have the expertise to carry out. Likewise, the social service programs run by the League held little fascination for him and were seen mainly as a means to keep the money flowing in from foundations and the government. What excited Jordan was the opportunity to play on the grand stage, to be the major spokesman for black America to both the private sector and to government. "Vernon is a controversial figure," said James Gibson, who has known Jordan since childhood. "I think he has been an enormously valuable figure. He is also a supreme egotist. So part of his value is that his ego drives him to do big picture stuff, or do things in a big picture style."[57]

It was a propitious time for the organization and the civil rights movement as a whole, a time that seemed to mesh with Jordan's particular talents. The outlawing of de jure segregation ended any obvious need for mass marches and demonstrations. Equally important, the Great Society programs launched by Lyndon Johnson and expanded by Richard Nixon and the Democratic Congress placed much of the responsibility for the next phase of the movement for black advancement—the push to reduce poverty and to guarantee blacks a larger stake in the economic system—squarely in the hands of the federal government. Further, there was a void in black leadership that Jordan was eager to fill. Martin Luther King Jr. had been killed in 1968, and no other charismatic leader had yet emerged to take his place. Even if he had not been aging and losing his grip on control of the NAACP, Roy Wilkins was too deferential to grab the mantle of the black leader.

"There was sort of a vacuum," Jordan recalled. "Given my background, I thought advocacy was very important. But I also understood the traditional role of the Urban League, and I thought you could combine advocacy and services. And that's what we did."[58] The way was open for someone as engaging, as charming, as political, and as driven as Jordan to emerge. "Vernon always wanted to be in the power broker seat for black America," said Adair.[59]

It was not all a matter of ego. It was also a matter of the group's survival. With the League already tethered to Washington as a result of Young's securing federal contracts from his meeting with the Nixon cabinet, Jordan was acutely aware of the need to maintain close contacts with the White House, the federal agencies, and Congress. It was a role he reveled in. "Vernon was much more of a political animal than Whitney was," said Daniel Davis, a former League official. "He came up through the Voter Education Project and he was a lawyer, whereas Whitney was a social worker and had a different orientation. Whitney was a great political person too. . . . But Vernon was a bit more attuned to the political angle and realized that this great power shift had occurred."[60]

The leadership of the modern civil rights movement was coming full circle. For virtually all of the century, the movement was, for the most part, run by black intellectuals and lawyers in the North. With the rise of King and the SCLC, attention and leadership had shifted into the hands of Southern ministers who preferred direct confrontation in the streets to political lobbying and legal challenges. But King's demise, the lack of a charismatic preacher to replace him, and the flood of black people onto the voting roles meant the leadership of the movement was coming back to its traditions. Politically savvy blacks in the North like Jordan and Brown—and later Jesse Jackson—were again taking charge.

Jordan invested an enormous amount of his personal time to ensure that the League stayed connected to the power centers in Washington, and made sure that journalists were made aware of his efforts. He cultivated the ties to the Nixon administration that had been begun under Whitney Young. He frequently visited the White House, regularly playing tennis with John Ehrlichman, Nixon's domestic policy adviser. Their correspondence is studded with warm personal references. "Dear John," began most of Jordan's notes. "Dear Vernon," Ehrlichman responded. "Warm personal regards," Jordan signed off on a January 5, 1973, note to Ehrlichman.[61] "I am looking forward to seeing you on the courts at 4:30 this Wednesday," Ehrlichman wrote in a June 26, 1972, note thanking Jordan for sending status reports of federally financed League projects.[62] For his part, Jordan clearly used his access to Ehrlichman to push the civil rights agenda, especially that of the League. He sent Ehrlichman suggested language for Nixon to use in part of his second inaugural address.

Jordan's closeness to the Nixon administration caused some grumbling within the League and among many blacks in general. But he knew the value of it. "Vernon used to always say, 'I don't want to have to communicate with this administration through the newspapers or through a third party,'" said Carol Gibson. "'When I'm upset about something, I want to know that I can dial the phone and they'll pick it up.'"[63] In what could have been an apocryphal tale, but still a telling one, that was often recounted by League officials, he was accosted one day in an elevator at the League's headquarters by an angry black man who demanded to know why he was cozying up to Republicans. Jordan reminded him of the importance of his efforts by asking the young man a question of his own: "What federal program are you on, brother?"[64]

But Jordan, no doubt, also knew that being based in New York his contacts with those in power in Washington were at best episodic. To protect the League's interest and maintain its high visibility as a civil rights advocate in what was becoming a media as well as a political capital, Jordan felt he had to have a more forceful Washington presence than what was being provided by the head of the Washington bureau. The incumbent in that position, Cenoria D. Johnson, was an icon of the Urban League, whose roots went way back to the kind of white-gloved volunteerism and black high society partying that had been the group's tradition. League veterans worshiped her. Many of the group's professional staff in New York, especially Jordan, considered her ineffective. "She was a wonderful woman," Jordan said. "She had just outlived her time."[65]

The solution was obvious. On July 23, 1973, Jordan named Brown the director of the League's Washington bureau. It was time now for his protégé to move on to a bigger stage.

CHAPTER SIX

HOMECOMING

S HORTLY AFTER ARRIVING in Washington in 1973, Ron and Alma paid $62,500 for a two-story, white-brick colonial house. It was set on a curving street lined with tall oak trees a few blocks from Rock Creek Park, a verdant swath running north and south that bisected the city into a largely white section west of the park and a majority black one east of it.

The house was located in Shepherd Park, a green, hilly eighty-block neighborhood best known for the Walter Reed Army Medical Center and for its sturdy brick or stone Colonial and Tudor houses. Well-tended azalea bushes that accented many houses burst each spring into vibrant red, pink, violet, or white blooms, amply justifying street names like Holly, Jonquil, Kalmia, and Geranium. Settling in, the Browns joined a growing cadre of well-to-do African American professionals in stubbornly integrated neighborhoods like Crestwood, Carter Barron, and Shepherd Park, whose relative affluence earned them the name the "Gold Coast."

As the second in command of a thriving civil rights group, Brown represented a fresh face, new ideas, and a sense of dynamic young leadership at a time of dramatic change in the nation's capital. In his absence, legal, demographic, and political change had washed over Washington. The Republican candidate for president in 1952, Dwight D. Eisenhower, pledged to end segregation in the city. A year later the Supreme Court ruled unanimously that Washington had to enforce a previously ignored 1873 law that banned discrimination in city restaurants, and in 1954 the D.C. schools were desegregated. The pace at which Washington's Jim Crow tradition fell away was breathtaking to some. "These years, 1951 to 1955, proved to be the most dramatic for the history of the city," the American Friends Service Committee reported excitedly in 1955. "In three years, the city made changes in its racial practices so rapidly as to be startling to even the most optimistic."[1] Six years later even the Washington Redskins, the last team in the National Football League without any black players, yielded to pressure from the Kennedy administration and signed Ron Hatcher, a black fullback from Michigan State.

But the end of segregation hardly ended Washington's racial problems. Poverty-level migrants from the rural South had poured into the city, continuing a trend that began during World War II. As African Americans flooded in, however, even those with the financial means were for the most part barred by racist real estate agents and mortgage lenders from joining the postwar trek to the suburbs. As a result, by 1960 Washington's population was 54 percent black; the capital was the first major American city in which blacks were the majority.[2]

In the scorching summer of 1967, when cities like Newark and Detroit went up in flames, President Lyndon Johnson, fearing the worst if the federal government failed to yield some control over Washington, pushed a bill through Congress granting a measure of home rule. The bill allowed for the appointment of a mayor and a city council, though Congress would retain the right to veto the city's budget.

These efforts, however, failed to prevent the racial conflagration that engulfed Washington in response to the assassination of Martin Luther King Jr. on April 4, 1968, hours after King had been gunned down in Memphis. The riot, Washington's first racial disturbance since 1919, raged for three days. Fires burned out of control along Georgia Avenue, close to where Brown's mother had grown up. The injured swarmed into Freedman's Hospital, where he was born. The mayhem was barely contained by 5,000 regular army troops and 10,000 members of the National Guard dispatched by President Johnson to restore peace.

Whites, frightened by scenes of rampaging blacks, fled in droves. By 1970 the city's population was nearly 70 percent black and 30 percent white, almost an exact reversal of what it had been when Brown was born. Socially and politically, Washington had become a bifurcated city—one part black, relatively poor, more permanent, whose political focus was local, and the other part white, more affluent, more transient, whose locus was the federal government. Ron Brown's time in Washington would span both worlds.

Coming home to D.C., he found old friends and an influential, ready-made black network. "Everybody kind of knew Ron Brown," said Marjory H. Parker, a former member of the city council. "His father and mother were Washingtonians. . . . His mother had relatives here. Washington was kind of a small town. Everybody who went to Howard and everyone who went to Dunbar [High School], you all kind of knew each other."[3]

The first person President Johnson appointed as the city's mayor in 1967 was Walter Washington, Bill's college roommate. Four years later the voters made Washington their first elected mayor. He was joined in city government by Sterling Tucker, the head of the National Urban League's Washington affiliate, who became president of the city council. It was into this close circle of influence that Ron moved in 1973. The black establishment heartily welcomed back its son, but its members were not sure yet what he was made of. And while taking over the Washington office of the Urban League automatically garnered him a measure of respect, he knew that making it an effective operation was quite another matter.

HOUSED IN a suite of offices near the National Theater, between the White House and the Capitol, the League's Washington bureau was widely regarded as a mediocre operation. Brown concentrated his energies on changing that view. Within a year he had replaced virtually everyone in the office with a group of smart, driven lobbyists. His hires might have been somewhat dilettantish on the details of federal programs, but they were good at keeping tabs on proposed changes in legislation and federal regulations. They could write succinct reports and knew how to maintain good relationships with the New York headquarters and with offices around the country. "We wanted to have an impact on policies as they were being developed in Washington," said Betty Adams, one of the key staffers in the Washington bureau. "We took advantage of opportunities to state our point of view, and of course, to disseminate information to our real troops, who were the local affiliates and the staff in the national office."[4] Brown made sure his staff was made up of people like himself: masters at the art of schmoozing.

His other task was to raise the League profile in Washington. Jordan already had access to the Nixon White House, so Brown's strategy was to make the League more of a player on Capitol Hill and with other civil rights groups. Almost immediately, he and his staff increased their appearances before congressional committees. For a House or Senate committee to consider a bill that might affect blacks and not hear the opinions of the League office, mainly via an appearance by Brown, became a rare event. "We testified more before committees," said Bill Haskins, a former League vice president. "We testified a *lot* more."[5] Brown became especially close to some key Democratic lawmakers, like Congressman Augustus Hawkins, chairman of the House Committee on Education and Labor, and Senator Edward Kennedy, who chaired the Senate Labor and Human Resources Committee. Both committees were key for policy reasons and because they oversaw the Labor Department, the chief source of federal contracts for the League.

Next, Brown made sure the League was much more active in the Leadership Conference on Civil Rights (LCCR), a coalition of civil rights groups, liberal religious organizations, and labor unions. At the time the coalition was undergoing growing pains. Groups representing Hispanics were clamoring for the civil rights movement to pay more attention to the plight of this fast-growing minority. Women's groups, like the National Organization for Women (NOW), also pressed for inclusion. Some black civil rights leaders, like Clarence Mitchell, the NAACP's longtime Washington lobbyist, were wary of allowing these groups a presence under the LCCR umbrella, believing that the coalition would be spreading itself too thin. Brown brought his talents as a negotiator and conciliator to bear, helping to keep the group together while balancing its members' sometimes different interests.

Finally, he urged the League's research department, which had been moved to Washington in 1969, to raise its profile. League research papers began to stream in to federal agencies, congressional offices, and other civil rights groups. In 1976, the League issued its first annual State of Black America report, which provided a snapshot of the financial, health, and educational status of African Americans, always making a point of how much blacks lagged behind whites. The research department gave an empirical basis for the League's policy positions. The research also boosted the League's reputation among federal agencies and other civil rights groups.

Everything that mattered in the organization's Washington office now played to Brown's strengths: interacting with lawmakers, working out differences between groups, speaking in public, and appearing on television. He was a quick study who could rapidly absorb the basics and the nuances of federal policy and could impress any congressional committee and the journalists, lobbyists, and administration officials who attended hearings. His aides would provide him with detailed briefing memos on any issue. In a day or two he was an expert, dazzling senators or congressmen with his seemingly intimate knowledge of arcane policy details.

The testimony, the stepped-up contacts with Democratic powers on the Hill, and the work with other groups, including unions, when combined with new programs to register and educate voters, caused some in the League to fret that the organization was getting too political, too partisan, and that its tax-exempt status would be jeopardized. But Brown knew just how far to take things, how far to go in testimony, which groups to align with and when— without giving the Internal Revenue Service a reason to question the group's tax-exempt status, known from the section in the tax code as a 501(c)3 designation. "He was very smart," Haskins said of Brown. "He knew what we could do and what we couldn't do. But he also knew that there were things that we should do, and he found a way to do them while, at the same time, protecting our 501(c)3 status."[6]

Brown was on the same wavelength as Jordan. He also had his boss's trust in his abilities. As a result, the normally tightly controlling Jordan gave him wide latitude. Alone among the League's national officers, Brown could make a major strategic decision without first running it by Jordan. Being good at both internal and external politics, however, Brown seldom charted a course that was too independent, even going so far as making sure Jordan saw all congressional testimony he was planning to give. "Ron had no real supervision," said Haskins. "As long as he didn't screw up too badly, nobody was going to jump on him."[7]

Brown had made a remarkable journey in a short period of time. Less than a decade earlier he was lamenting that he had sat on the periphery of the civil rights movement. By the mid-1970s he was at its core. As the movement left the streets and the lunch counters of the South and moved into the halls of Congress and the corridors of federal agencies in Washington, Brown stood at its center. Rather than reading about the struggle of African Americans in the pages of *Time* or *Newsweek* or *U.S. News,* Brown was helping to create the news that other people read about in newspapers and magazines. But as he moved into the heart of the struggle, events occurring thousands of miles from America's shores would soon threaten the very movement in which he had become a key player.

IN THE MID-AFTERNOON on October 6, 1973—barely eleven weeks after Brown took over the League's Washington office—222 Egyptian jets lifted off their runways to attack Israeli command posts and positions in the Sinai Desert. The raid marked the start of the Yom Kippur War, the fourth conflict between Israel and her Arab neighbors since the Jewish state's founding in 1948. Like the others this one would end with a resounding Israeli victory. But the war would have a lasting impact on the United States because it would help spur a huge change in the price of a precious commodity—oil.

On October 16, representatives of the Organization of Petroleum Producing Countries (OPEC) gathered in Kuwait City and agreed to a 70 percent hike in the price of oil to $5.11 a barrel. The following day, Arab oil ministers also met in Kuwait City and voted to impose an oil embargo on the West as a means to force it to put political pressure on Israel. More important, the Arab oil ministers, including representatives of Saudi Arabia, the world's second-largest oil producer after the Soviet Union, also agreed to cut their production, a move that served to bolster the price hike that had been decided the previous day. The two actions were separate. One, the embargo, was a political move to pressure Israel's allies. The other, the price hike, was a response to market conditions. But they were inextricably connected. "Suffice it to say that the new Arab-Israeli war probably stiffened the resolve of the Arab price negotiators," said the *Middle East Economic Review;* ". . . also, the cuts in output will incidentally serve to push up oil prices still further."[8]

The oil price hike hit America like a thunderbolt. Much of the country's postwar prosperity had been built on the availability of cheap oil. It had helped make American workers the most productive in the world, resulting in higher incomes and a rapid improvement in their standard of living. The dramatic gains of the civil rights movement took place during the strong economic growth of the 1950s and 1960s. Financially satisfied, whites confronted by Martin Luther King's moral crusade and chastened by the appalling violence in the South could afford to feel tolerant and support the drive to end segregation. Government programs to improve the economic plight of African Americans, like Lyndon Johnson's Great Society and Richard Nixon's Philadelphia Plan, which for the first time encouraged companies to grant a preference to blacks in hiring and promotion, also met relatively little resistance.

Suddenly that prosperity came to an end. Starting in the last quarter of 1973, productivity rates—measurements of an average worker's output that are affected by factors such as the costs of materials and energy—slowed dramatically. Both the flattening out of productivity and the inflation that shook the economy—itself caused in large measure by the oil price increases—had a devastating effect on all workers. Businesses shed jobs, moved operations overseas where costs were cheaper, and held down wage hikes. Incomes stagnated and in some cases declined, especially among those in the working and lower middle classes. The average white male worker earned nearly $27,000 annually in 1973. By 1980 his earnings would drop to $24,636 when adjusted for inflation.

This economic trauma had a corrosive effect on the civil rights and political environment in which Brown worked. The nation turned rightward. Whites became more conservative, less prone to support civil rights initiatives, more wary of allowing their taxes to fund expensive domestic programs designed to aid minorities. Prior to the oil price hikes, the movement's thrust was to win basic rights and expand opportunity. After the hikes, it became a matter of simply holding on.

The macroeconomic changes in the U.S. economy meant that just as Brown was becoming a frontline player, the modern-day civil rights movement was coming to an end.

RON BROWN WAS HAVING his own microeconomic struggles. During his time in New York, he had been named to the boards of directors of a number of New York City–based organizations. Among them were the Association for Homemakers Service, the Fortune Society (a group that lobbied for prison reform), the American Civil Liberties Union, and the National Committee on the Employment of Youth. Unlike the organizations on whose corporate boards Vernon Jordan served, these were nonprofit organizations that did not pay board members. Indeed, most had to stretch funds even to pay travel expenses for their directors to attend board meetings.

Brown continued to serve on these boards after his move to Washington, and in some cases he billed the League for his travel to New York to attend their meetings. The League, however, balked at such payments, and in late December 1973, it bounced a reimbursement request he had submitted for travel to New York for the Homemakers Service meeting. At the time Jordan made it clear that he thought Brown's board obligations were a distraction. "It is my feeling that as you become increasingly involved in Washington, it will be difficult, just from the viewpoint of time, to come to New York for meetings of such varied organizations as the Association for Homemakers Service, the Fortune Society, the American Civil Liberties Union and the National Committee on the Employment of Youth," Jordan wrote to him.[9]

Jordan wanted Brown to continue as chairman of the board of the National Alliance for Safer Cities—a group that would keep him in contact with politically powerful big-city mayors—and was willing to have the League pay for Brown's travel to attend meetings of this organization's board. But Jordan did not want the financially strapped League underwriting Brown's expenses to attend other groups' meetings. "It had been my impression that more of them would be able to pay for travel for their board members," Jordan wrote. "If they cannot, and if they feel it is important to have representatives from the [Urban] League, the answer would seem to be to suggest someone from the New York–based [Urban League] staff."[10]

Jordan's attitude incensed Brown. He countered that, while his travel forms did not always reflect it, he often conducted League business when he traveled to New York for board meetings. In an angry, three-page memo to Jordan, Brown wrote that he considered his board work for other organizations "important not only to me personally but important to the National Urban League as well" and said there were several of these organizations "from which I cannot in good conscience withdraw."[11] Brown did offer to resign from the Fortune Society board, and, both employing a bit of sarcasm and tweaking Jordan's goal to maintain contacts that would help raise money for the League, Brown also offered to step down from the Association for Homemakers Service: ". . . although I love to serve with all those rich ladies, I will refuse this request if you so desire," he wrote.[12]

"What is of greatest concern to me about your memorandum is the implication that my involvement with boards of other organizations somehow reflects improper use of my time to the detriment of the activities of the National Urban League and the Washington Bureau," Brown fumed. "I would like to assure both you and [League Deputy Executive Director for Administration Alexander] Allen that I am fully aware of the problems of use of time and establishment of priorities."[13]

In the end, the League agreed to pay for Brown's travel to attend meetings of boards where he served as chairman—the National Alliance for Safer Cities and the National Committee on the Employment of Youth. But the League would not pay for Brown to travel to meetings of the boards of the ACLU, the Fortune Society, and the Association for Homemakers Service. It could not be determined how happy Brown was with this compromise, but it is doubtful he was very pleased. He believed in the work of these organizations. But beyond that, Brown was smart enough to understand the advantages of remaining involved with these boards. Membership on boards was a major way to network and to get oneself known to movers and shakers. Even if the board was for a nonprofit organization that did not pay directors' fees or reimburse expenses for board service, one's presence often meant contact with other board members who were corporate executives or rich socialites who were doing volunteer work. With companies always on the lookout for talented blacks to broaden the diversity of their boards, membership and competent work on the board of a nonprofit organization could catch someone's eye and lead to being named to the board of a Fortune 500 corporation, where some real money could be made. It also had not escaped Brown's attention that Jordan was urging him to give up a position with the ACLU, a group whose board Jordan had strongly recommended Brown join in the first place.

It was galling to Brown for Jordan to try to keep him off the boards of nonprofit agencies when Jordan, as president of the Urban League, had been invited to sit on a number of corporate boards. Most of these boards paid handsomely for doing little more than showing up at meetings.

Brown swallowed whatever resentment he felt about the tussle over his board memberships and threw himself into his work. While he was making a name for himself in Congress and with other civil rights and liberal groups, he maintained a strong relationship with the executive directors of the local League affiliates. Many of these affiliates contracted directly with the federal government to run programs, and therefore they often needed to keep in touch with the League's Washington office to ensure continued federal support. He was also more familiar to them than Jordan, who was deemed by many of these powerful local affiliate heads to be an outsider. And Brown was accessible. While some directors of local affiliates sometimes had a hard time getting Jordan to return their telephone calls, Brown was always eager to talk to them and to pass on to Jordan their views, concerns, and complaints.

There are some in the League who suggest that Jordan began to feel jealous of his younger subordinate as Brown expanded his influence and reputation in Washington. There is little evidence that was the case, however. Brown's work in Washington boosted the League's—and therefore Jordan's—name and image. If Jordan was displeased with Brown's efforts, he certainly did not show it. He continued to pile additional responsibilities on Brown. In August 1976, he made him deputy executive director for programs and governmental affairs, placing him on a par with only two other League officials and just below Jordan himself.

IN FEBRUARY 1976, less than three years after Brown had moved to the capital, Walter Washington named him a trustee of the new University of the District of Columbia (UDC). The school was formed from the merger of three colleges, Federal City College, Washington Technical Institute, and the District of Columbia Teachers College, with the hope that it would become a low-tuition, high-quality school for the working class and the poor on the model of City College and the City University of New York. The board subsequently elected Brown to be its first chairman, in part because they recognized his talents as a leader, and also because he had no ties to any of the three institutions, which jealously guarded their shrinking turf as they were being subsumed into the larger UDC entity. Brown frequently appeared on television or in the newspapers to explain the school's problems and confidently predict their resolution. He impressed people with his cool demeanor and his quick, well-formed responses. People in the political world marked him as a comer.

Soon other organizations sought his talents as a leader. In 1976 he assumed the job of legislative director of the Leadership Conference on Civil Rights and set about transforming that position. Though it was the leading lobbying voice for civil rights, the Leadership Conference for years had been run somewhat high-handedly by a group of white men such as Joseph Rauh, Arnold Aronson, Marvin Caplin, and William Taylor, most of whom came out of the labor movement. While their commitment to civil rights was unquestioned, they tended to make all the strategic decisions for the coalition, often without any meaningful input from the other groups. "It was the most powerful civil rights organization in Washington, but the whole hierarchy, except for Clarence Mitchell, who by that time was so ill he was not around, was white and Jewish and former labor people," said a black civil rights activist who worked closely with the Leadership Conference in the late 1970s. "That was the leadership. It also included the NAACP and the Urban League. But the NAACP and the Urban League weren't calling the shots."

Several lobbyists for other civil rights groups—especially women like Elaine Jones of the NAACP Legal Defense Fund, Antonia Hernandez of the Mexican American Legal Defense Fund, Althea Simmons of the NAACP, and Laura Murphy, a young staffer for the American Civil Liberties Union—felt their views and ideas were ignored. Often they were reluctant to attend Leadership Conference meetings since they believed they were not being taken seriously. But they felt compelled to go for fear of the decisions that might be made in their absence. "Elaine, Althea, Laura, and myself, we were the broads who kept things going," said Hernandez. "But we would get together internally and say, 'Oh God, what shit are they up to now?' "[14]

Taking over as chairman of the group's legislative committee, Brown changed all that. "With Ron it was very clear: 'I'm legislative director, I'm it. You deal with me,' " Hernandez said. "So now the other guys had to work with him. Ron was deferential to some degree. But it was not their game, no longer just their way of thinking and decision making."[15] He sought advice from most of the groups' representatives, making extra sure to get the input from blacks and Hispanics who were active in the coalition. "We were empowered by this man," said one black lobbyist. "He really helped give minorities who were participating in a secondary role in the Leadership Conference first-tier treatment because he would treat us with respect. So if Joe Rauh ignored a suggestion that little, twenty-five-year-old Laura Murphy made, Ron would pick it up and say, 'Hey, wait a minute, that's a good idea.' "

THE ELECTION OF Jimmy Carter in 1976 opened up enormous opportunities for talented people like Ron Brown. Carter owed much of his victory to solid black support, especially in the South, and black leaders demanded that the new president appoint African Americans to cabinet and subcabinet positions. Carter responded by naming more than 150 African Americans to cabinet and subcabinet jobs, including ten ambassadorships, five U.S. attorneys, twenty-eight federal judges, the ambassador to the United Nations, the secretary of the army, and the solicitor general.

Among those rumored to be in line for administration jobs were both Jordan and Brown. According to Jordan, Carter offered him a number of "cabinet-level positions," including secretary of health and human services and secretary of housing and urban development. But Jordan declined. Meanwhile, a number of civil rights groups and labor unions touted Brown for chairman of the Equal Employment Opportunity Commission (EEOC).

Established in 1965 to handle complaints of job discrimination, the EEOC was a bureaucratic mess by 1977. The agency started off with marquee leadership. Its first chairman was Franklin D. Roosevelt Jr. But in its early years it suffered from revolving door leadership—the EEOC had eight different leaders in its first twelve years as chairman after chairman threw up his hands in despair over the agency's slow-moving and tangled bureaucracy, bad management, and poor morale. By early 1977 the EEOC had a backlog of more than 120,000 cases that were not even close to being settled. Anyone filing a complaint alleging discrimination in hiring or promotion could expect to wait a minimum of three years before the case was resolved.

Though he told friends he would like a job inside the new administration, Brown had not specifically thought about EEOC, according to Carol Gibson, former director of educational programs for the League. She said that Brown told her it was Jordan who put the thought in his head. Gibson recalled that Brown once related a conversation to her in which he asked Jordan if he was interested in a job in the administration. Jordan said no.

"Had you ever thought about EEOC?" Jordan then said to Brown, according to Gibson.

"No, I hadn't," Brown replied.

"Well, why don't you think about it?" Jordan said.[16]

With this nudge from his boss, Brown began a quiet campaign for the job, feeling sure that he had a strong supporter in Jordan.

Brown, however, had a formidable rival: Eleanor Holmes Norton, the thirty-nine-year-old chairwoman of the New York City Human Rights Commission, an agency that handled local employment discrimination complaints. Norton had great credentials. A graduate of Antioch College and Yale University, where she received a master's in history as well as a law degree, Norton possessed a sharp and penetrating mind. Although shy of her fortieth birthday, she was a veteran of the civil rights movement, having done organizing work in the South with SNCC. Active in the women's movement, she had the solid endorsement of feminist groups. And as head of New York City's Human Rights Commission under Mayors John Lindsay and then Abraham Beame, she could boast of administrative experience in enforcing antidiscrimination laws as well as an ability to negotiate the rough politics of affirmative action in a city where blacks and Jews played major political roles. "One advantage I had over Ron was simply I came out of the belly of the civil rights movement," Norton said. "Ron was somewhat younger, and had not been on the front lines."[17]

It was a tough competition. Still, Brown had the backing of organized labor, a powerful group in the Democratic coalition. The AFL-CIO pushed hard for him, having gotten to know him from his work at the Leadership Conference, a group that was essentially bankrolled by the labor movement. Labor also found Norton objectionable because of her ties to feminist groups and leaders such as Bella Abzug, the congresswoman from New York. Many labor leaders were still smarting from their exclusion from the Democratic National Convention in 1972, when they had been ousted by many blacks, feminists, and other liberals who insisted on a larger share of delegates. Union leaders were eager to show political muscle and get their man appointed to chair the EEOC. "They felt strongly that Ron was their guy," said Landon Butler, a former Carter aide who was involved in choosing agency heads. "Eleanor had much more support in the liberal wing of the party. She was more closely associated with the feminist liberal wing, and from labor's point of view, that was anathema."[18]

With two important Democratic constituency groups—women and labor—touting different candidates, the incoming Carter administration had a dilemma. Brown believed the support of Jordan would prove to be critical to his chances, figuring that with Martin Luther King dead, Roy Wilkins of the NAACP aging, and Jesse Jackson just beginning to emerge as a national figure, Jordan was considered *the* preeminent civil rights leader at the time. He also felt confident that Jordan would back him for the job. After all, he told friends, it was his boss who had suggested he seek the position in the first place.

But Brown had not counted on the tenacity of Norton, who was also a friend of Jordan's. She had frequent contacts with Jordan in the New York social scene, and she and her then-husband, Edward, were frequent guests at the Jordans' home for dinners and parties. Norton, unlike Brown, did not assume that the existence of a friendship equaled automatic support from Jordan. She lobbied Jordan intensely. "Eleanor Holmes [Norton] made a strong political pitch for that position," said Andrew Adair, the associate director for programs at the League. "She would call Vernon every day and say, 'Vernon, I've got to have that job. I've got to have that visibility.' Ron sat back and assumed that Vernon would make the pitch for him."[19]

It was clear to Jordan and others that Norton was the better qualified of the two. Her position as head of the New York Human Rights Commission, where she had reduced a backlog of cases similar to the one plaguing the EEOC, meant that she had experience in managing a large bureaucracy. In contrast, Brown had never run anything larger than the Urban League's Washington office and a training school for Korean soldiers. The combination of a superior résumé and heavy politicking worked, winning for Norton first Jordan's support and ultimately the job.

As always, Brown was gracious in defeat, calling Norton to congratulate her and to say he harbored no hard feelings. "When it was all over, he called me up and said—I'll never forget the words—'You are a tough momma,'" Norton said.[20] Inwardly, however, Brown seethed both from the defeat and from what he considered Jordan's betrayal. "He was very, very disappointed when Vernon supported Eleanor," said Carol Gibson.[21] Brown placed a high premium on loyalty. And in this first test of the trait, Jordan, whom Brown thought was his friend, had failed. "That was the first thing that really was a dagger in the heart of Ron," said John Mack, the head of the Los Angeles affiliate to whom Brown unburdened himself. "After all, he was Vernon's guy, and he figured that . . . there was no way in the world Vernon would not support him. . . . But in terms of defining moments and events, this was devastating to the relationship. I don't think Ron ever forgave Vernon for it."[22]

Jordan strongly disputes this version of events. According to him, Brown, not he, initiated the talk about the EEOC position. "Ron came to me and he said, 'I would like to be the head of the EEOC,'" Jordan recalled. "I said I would look into it and see what I could do." Exploring the possibility with Carter administration officials, Jordan said, he discovered that Norton had the inside track for the job because of her experience. "I had talked to the Carter people. It was very clear that they wanted Eleanor and only Eleanor," Jordan said. "He came to see me and, in effect, said, 'How's the EEOC thing going?' I said, 'It's going to Eleanor.' He was visibly disappointed about it." But, Jordan said, Brown did not display any resentment or state that he had viewed his boss's actions as disloyal. "He didn't stop doing his work," Jordan said. "He didn't stop doing a good job. He did not stop being my friend. . . . The notion that I somehow betrayed him because Eleanor had gotten the job is bullshit."[23]

Jordan is correct about a critical element in the saga: the Carter administration never seriously considered Brown for the job. From the start, Carter's aides considered Norton the superior candidate, though they felt intense pressure from labor to reject her. For a while, the administration thrashed about looking for a compromise candidate who would mollify labor while bypassing both Brown and Norton. But in the end Carter's aides could not find anyone else with the credentials who would be acceptable to civil rights groups. Reluctantly, Hamilton Jordan, Carter's chief of staff, recommended Norton for the job. He also suggested that Carter confer with George Meany, the head of the AFL-CIO, and grant Brown a face-saving interview. "There are so few people in this country that have had direct EEOC experience and have done it well and want this job. I'd recommend that we appoint Eleanor Holmes Norton, but that you discuss it personally with Mr. Meany," Jordan wrote the president. "Also, I would suggest that you spend 5 minutes interviewing Ron Brown who is their candidate. It will save us a lot of grief."[24]

Brown probably never learned of these behind-the-scenes machinations. He did not know that he really lost out because of lack of credentials, not lack of support from Jordan. He had probably overestimated Jordan's ability to influence the Carter administration when it came to appointments. But with his ego bruised from losing out, he apparently needed a villain. Jordan fit the bill. Over the years rumors would abound within the Urban League that Jordan had blocked Brown from becoming the head of the EEOC. Those rumors did not spring to earth spontaneously like Aphrodite emerging from the head of Zeus. They had a source. Its name was Ron Brown, and he complained loudly and often to people like Mack and Gibson of betrayal by Jordan.

As Brown tended to his wounded pride, he began scanning the horizon for new opportunities. He first saw his chance in local Washington politics.

IN 1977 the District of Columbia prepared for its second mayoral election since the granting of home rule. Like the first election, the contest laid bare some of the overarching themes that would define local D.C. politics for years—the power of the still overwhelmingly white business establishment, and the city's racial and class divisions.

As it had for years, Washington's black population remained sharply divided along class lines, with upper-middle-class blacks often viewing with disdain their lower-class brethren clustered in some of the city's poorer neighborhoods like Anacostia. "Bamas" these poor blacks were often called, reflecting the fact that many were recent migrants from the rural South. The dislike was returned in equal measure by the city's poor, who, like their economically better off brethren, often saw things in terms of skin color and were resentful of the light-skinned "bourgeois" blacks of the Gold Coast. "It was a segregated city among blacks," said Calvin Rolark Jr., editor of a weekly newspaper. "The lighter-skinned blacks didn't associate with the darker blacks, and the Howard University blacks didn't associate with anyone."[25]

Four years earlier Walter Washington had barely defeated Clifford Alexander, a former secretary of the army, in the Democratic primary. (With Democrats holding a nine-to-one edge in registration, a win in the primary was tantamount to victory in the general election.) Alexander ran a strong race, but

Washington won on the strength of support from the business establishment, which was familiar with him from his tenure as the appointed mayor, and from segments of the city's poor black neighborhoods who saw Alexander as the epitome of the upper-crust Gold Coast Negro.

By fall 1977 members of the city's business community had grown disenchanted with Washington. They thought he lacked drive or verve. Moreover, they feared another emerging politician—Marion Barry. A member of the city council who had worked in the South with the Student Non-Violent Coordinating Committee, Barry was an effective grassroots organizer in some of Washington's poorer neighborhoods. He had won election to the D.C. Board of Education and to the city council. But some of the more elitist blacks saw him as a country bumpkin whose fracturing of the English language, womanizing, and street hustler style would be embarrassments to the city.

Casting about for an alternative to Barry, Vincent Cohen, who was Alexander's campaign manager in the 1974 race, and John Hechinger, head of a string of hardware stores in the area, thought of Ron Brown. He was smart, handsome, and well-spoken. He had good credentials with the nation's establishment civil rights groups. He had performed well as chairman of the UDC board. He was obviously someone the Carter administration thought highly enough of to consider for EEOC chair. "He was a natural," said James Gibson, who was an adviser to Barry but came to admire Brown. "He had the poise. He had the skills to walk about publicly. He had a knowledge of the town. He moved easily in the national Democratic and liberal political world. He knew the advocates who were interested in cities."[26]

The idea of running for mayor intrigued Brown. He began sounding out potential political and financial backers. Over lunch with Milton Coleman, the *Washington Post*'s city hall reporter, he took note of the dissatisfaction many people were feeling with Barry, Washington, and Sterling Tucker, the president of the city council and another potential candidate. As the two men chatted over their meal, Brown made the case for his candidacy, suggesting that his Urban League work made him much more of a heavyweight with folks on the Hill and in the White House than Washington, Tucker, or Barry.

"Do you think the president would call Walter Washington on urban policy?" Brown asked. "He'd call me on urban policy."[27] As the waiters cleared the table, Brown warmed to his subject. He conceded that he wasn't as well known. But he argued that contributors and other political operatives should at least hold off committing to the other candidates until they had a chance to look him over. "I see no reason for anybody to rush to judgment," Brown said. "We've got ten months or more before the primary . . . I see no advantage, except to the three 'out front' candidates, of choosing up sides now."[28]

At best, Brown's "candidacy" was a quixotic impulse, one that had no serious chance of success. He had middle-class friends and some well-connected pols whispering in his ear. But he did not have enough name recognition or a record to really attract the interest of wealthy donors or a mass following. "I don't think he was a well-known personage in the city," said Hechinger. "I don't think very many people locally knew who Ron Brown was."[29]

Brown's best shot was for Washington not to seek reelection, as had been rumored. In a three-way race, he believed he could have locked up the support of those disenchanted with Tucker or Barry. But, when it looked more and more likely that Washington would opt to try for one more term in office, Brown's fledgling effort was doomed. On February 13, 1978, he summoned reporters to inform them that he was abandoning a candidacy that he had never officially announced.

"As many of you know, rumors and speculation have circulated as to my political plans," Brown said, failing to mention that it was he who was the source of the rumors and speculation. "I have carefully weighed the pros and cons of seeking the office of the mayor, and have decided that I will not now seek that or any other elective office."[30]

MONTHS AFTER Brown had tested the tricky local politics of Washington, D.C., new trouble erupted in the often-contentious relationship between blacks and Jews. The flash point this time was the Reverend Andrew Young, Carter's ambassador to the United Nations.

Young, a former top lieutenant to Martin Luther King Jr. in the Southern Christian Leadership Conference and a former Democratic congressman from Atlanta, had been a key strategist in Jimmy Carter's 1976 election campaign, helping deliver the black vote in the South to the Democrat. He had been rewarded with the appointment of U.S. Ambassador to the United Nations. The posting was a breakthrough position for African Americans, placing a black man outside the traditional box of cabinet positions like health and human services or housing and urban development. As such, Young was seen by many black people as a pioneer and a symbol of what one of their race could accomplish if the door would only swing open. He was a hero to them. But to some in the Carter White House, the civil rights icon was out of his depth at the U.N. and was becoming a political liability.

In late August, Israeli newspapers revealed that Young had met briefly with Zehdi Labib Terzi, an official with the Palestine Liberation Organization (PLO), at a Manhattan apartment the month before. At the time, it was official U.S. policy that no administration official have any contacts with the PLO, which the government considered a terrorist organization. Conservatives and officials of some Jewish organizations called for Young's resignation. On August 15, he complied.

Young's resignation—in essence, a firing—tore the scab from what was the festering sore of black-Jewish relations. Bitter name-calling followed with often anti-Semitic rhetoric emanating from some black activists. Leaders of national civil rights organizations like Jordan and Benjamin Hooks, who had recently taken over as head of the NAACP, tried to walk a fine line. While in agreement with the general principle that black-dominated civil rights organizations should not be patronized by Jewish groups, they had to ensure that emotions did not get out of hand so that an irreparable rupture did not occur. At the same time, they did not want to come off as too conciliatory and risk being pilloried as Uncle Toms.

A week after Young's resignation, some two hundred civil rights leaders met at the NAACP headquarters near Columbus Circle in New York City to air their grievances and plot how to keep the black-Jewish unrest from sundering the movement. Tensions ran high. Many of the participants felt a need to maintain ties with Jewish organizations. But they also wanted to show more autonomy. The participants announced that the meeting would serve as a "Declaration of Independence" of black civil rights groups from too much Jewish influence. They produced a statement noting the contributions of individual Jews and Jewish organization as part of the liberal coalition but going on to declare that "within the past 10 years some Jewish organizations and intellectuals who were previously identified with the aspirations of black Americans for unqualified educational, political and economic equality with all other Americans abruptly became apologists for the racial status quo."[31]

The meeting poured propane on the smoldering resentments between many blacks and Jews. The situation wasn't helped when Jesse Jackson, Joseph L. Lowery (the head of Martin Luther King's old group, the Southern Christian Leadership Conference), and other black leaders journeyed to the Middle East and publicly embraced Yasir Arafat, leader of the Palestine Liberation Organization, the very group with whom Young had made his politically fatal encounter. Some black leaders began to backpedal.

Jordan and Hooks had to figure out how to distance themselves from what they felt was irresponsible behavior on the part of radical black nihilists. In a speech to the National Conference of Catholic Charities, in Kansas City on October 14, Jordan struck back. "Black-Jewish relations should not be endangered by ill-considered flirtations with terrorist groups devoted to the extermination of Israel," Jordan said. "The black civil rights movement is based on nonviolent, moral principles. It has nothing in common with groups whose claim to legitimacy is compromised by cold-blooded murder of innocent civilians and schoolchildren."[32] A week earlier, Hooks had assailed the "headline-grabbing" actions of black leaders who had traveled to the Middle East and met with Arafat.

On the day Jordan gave his speech, a delegation of black civil rights leaders left for Israel. The trip was organized by Bayard Rustin, director of the A. Phillip Randolph Institute and one of the strongest defenders of the Jewish state among black leaders. Rustin, who once compared the PLO with the Ku Klux Klan, had been dismayed by the confrontational tone coming out of the

August 22 meeting at the NAACP headquarters. The junket was sponsored and paid for by Histadrut, the Israeli labor federation; the group was not visiting any other country in the Middle East. Clearly, the trip was to be a public signal to Jewish groups in America that some civil rights groups remained strongly pro-Israel.

The trip carried its own risks. Segments of the black community denounced Jordan for criticizing fellow black leaders in his desire to maintain good relations with Jewish liberals. The day after Jordan's speech, a group of black New York ministers, led by the Reverend Wyatt Tee Walker, a noted civil rights figure, released copies of an open letter to Jordan that declared that his speech had "brought an end to the masquerade of the Urban League as a civil rights organization and of you as a civil rights leader."[33] Such concerns about Jordan's speech were even held within the League. "I'm not going to suggest that there was a big-time rebellion or insurrection," said John Mack. "But at least some people were questioning the wisdom of it. Now, we didn't go public and call a press conference to blast our leader. We kept it in the family."[34]

Jordan signaled how important he considered the trip by dispatching Brown, one of the League's top officials, as his representative. It is not clear whether Brown agreed with the idea of the junket or with Jordan's attempts to mend fences with Jewish groups. But he went uncomplainingly. "It may have been the case [that he went] out of loyalty to Vernon," said Mack, "and one thing about Ron, he was loyal."[35]

From the start, there were tensions within the delegation, different opinions on how much support to express for Israel, how much condemnation to express of the PLO, and what to say about black leaders who had met with Arafat. The Jordan speech had raised the ante, ensuring that the group would be hounded by journalists throughout their trip. As the black leaders gathered at Kennedy Airport in New York, they had to run a gauntlet of reporters to reach the El Al Airlines departure lounge. Sharp differences among trip participants soon emerged. William Pollard, head of the civil rights division of the AFL-CIO and the head of the delegation, said forcefully that the trip was not a repudiation of the August 22 Declaration of Independence from Jewish influence. For his part, Rustin used the occasion to disassociate himself from the August 22 statement, stating, "As far as I'm concerned there were a number of things that came out of the August 22 meeting that I want to repudiate, but that is Bayard Rustin [speaking], not this group."[36] Before boarding an El Al jet, the black leaders closeted themselves in a private departure lounge in order to cobble together a joint statement. They emerged a short time later to say they had not reached agreement on what to say.

Once again, the trip highlighted Brown's skills as a mediator. The delegation contained several forceful personalities, and their disagreements went beyond policy disputes. Rustin wanted to use the junket as a way to announce

publicly that there were some blacks, like himself, who had unquestioning support of Israel. Pollard felt Rustin was going too far and was jealous that Rustin
was garnering the lion's share of the media attention. Brown found himself
constantly mediating between the two. In the private lounge at the El Al ter-
minal, for example, Brown argued forcefully that the group not engage in
public squabbling over their different positions regarding other black leaders'
contacts with the PLO. Others concurred. "We agreed not to criticize Jesse
Jackson for meeting Arafat," said John T. Smith, an official with the United
Steel Workers Union and a member of the group.[37] Arriving in Tel Aviv, the
group issued a statement that they had been able to agree upon during the
plane trip.

The statement, according to Smith, reflected the compromise path Brown
had worked out. The group stated their trip should not be read as a repudiation of "other groups that preceded us," but insisted that "just as Israeli citizens
differ on questions of strategy and tactics in these matters, so do black Americans also hold a variety of views on the problems affecting the solution in the
Middle East."[38] The group expressed support for Israel's right to exist within
secure borders. The delegation also said it believed that "Palestinians, like all
other peoples, should have the right to self-determination."[39] Finally, the group
said they were "deeply committed to continue and to strengthen the special
and historic relationship that Blacks and Jews have [maintained] in the United
States."[40]

In Israel the group visited Yad Vashem, the memorial in Jerusalem to the
six million European Jews killed by the Nazis and their allies during the Holo-
caust. Rustin openly wept when inspecting photographs of Nazi atrocities.
They also toured the Golan Heights, stayed in a kibbutz, dined with a moderate Palestinian labor leader, and met with Prime Minister Menachem Begin.
Despite the covenant not to criticize black leaders who had met with Arafat,
Rustin continued to take potshots at Jackson, Lowery, and Walter Fauntroy, the
nonvoting congressional delegate from the District of Columbia who had also
met with the PLO head. "I cannot embrace the PLO without embracing the Ku
Klux Klan, and the Red Brigades, and the Baader-Meinhof group in Germany,"
Rustin said in a speech on the second day of the group's tour. "The uniqueness
of black people has been their nonviolence and we will not permit Jesse Jackson or Lowery or Fauntroy to rob us of this."[41]

While agreeing with Rustin on his strong support of Israel, Brown stressed
in interviews that the rights of Palestinians were not incompatible with the
right of Israel to exist. It was a masterful performance. Brown kept dissention
within the delegation from spilling out into public view. He tried to spread
around the role of group spokesperson in order to soothe the bruised egos of
those who felt that Rustin was hogging all of the press. Brown also maintained
peace during those moments when meetings with Israeli officials became

somewhat testy. "Even in our discussions with Israeli leaders, Ron was a great guy for leveling things off," Smith remembered. "When he felt there was a sharpness being used in verbal exchanges, he would have something to say that relaxed the air."[42]

But working behind the scenes, and as the number two man in the Urban League, living in Jordan's huge shadow, Brown did not have enough stature to ensure that the trip and his role in it would be remembered. It would soon be forgotten by all except his close friends and associates. Yet it would be resurrected, at least privately, by Brown when he ran for chairman of the Democratic National Committee and needed to deflect the charge leveled by some Jews that he was too close to Jackson and, therefore, was possibly anti-Semitic. That would be years later, however.

RETURNING TO the United States, Brown once again began thinking about how to escape the League. One problem was money. Brown was acutely aware of the amount of money Jordan was making in his position, and he felt that he was being cut out of the action. The fortune Jordan was earning from sitting on boards could not be anything but a stark contrast to the penury Brown believed the League displayed toward him when it wouldn't pay for his transportation to attend a few meetings of the nonprofit boards that he sat on. There were other opportunities, like giving speeches, where extra money could be made. But Brown felt that even here he was being blocked by Jordan.

"I remember one time, Ron came to me and said, 'Does Vernon ever give you any speaking engagements?'" said Bill Haskins. "I said, 'Yeah,' and then he said, 'I mean *paid* speaking engagements?' I said no, and then he said, 'Me neither. He's always sending me some damn place where I can't make any money.'"[43]

Jordan was also larding additional responsibilities on him. The position of deputy executive director entailed staying in New York for extended periods each week, a burden that Brown felt was wearing him down and further angered him toward Jordan. "That built in a natural strain because Ron had to commute to New York; two or three days a week he was there," said Clarence L. Barney, the former chief executive officer of the League's New Orleans affiliate. "He confided in me that he was mad as hell about that."[44] Once again, Jordan disputed this view. "He loved it," Jordan said. "He never complained."[45]

More responsibilities, not enough income, and feeling that his way to the top of the League was blocked by the presence of Jordan, who, after all, was still a young man and showed no intentions of moving on, Brown was becoming increasingly restless at the League. Running for mayor had been symbolic of the larger problem for Brown. More and more he was beginning to feel that the universe defined by the Urban League was too small and too confining. As important as he might have considered the work, it was too one-dimensional, and he began to yearn to break out of the world of social service work. "One reason I was anxious to leave the Urban League was [that] I was tired of being limited by a small pond," he said in an interview. "You know, I was an expert on all things black."[46]

The vehicle for his release turned out to be Ted Kennedy.

Less than three weeks after Brown returned from the Middle East, Kennedy announced his intention to run for the Democratic nomination for the presidency. As he set up his campaign operation, at least one of his lieutenants, Peter Edelman, began making the case that it needed a high-ranking, highly visible black. "When Ted Kennedy asked me to come into his campaign and run his issues staff in the Washington headquarters, I just felt that one thing I was going to contribute, if nothing else, was to make sure that there would be both an African American and a woman—I'm talking about both of those— in senior substantive positions," said Edelman.[47] Brown seemed a natural choice. Edelman knew him slightly, and knew Jordan even better—Edelman's wife, Marian Wright Edelman, was a veteran civil rights worker and had known Jordan from their days in the South. So it did not seem that it would be difficult for Brown to break free from the League in order to work for the campaign.

The siren song of the Kennedy campaign exerted a strong pull on Brown. Here was his chance to break out of the confining world of the Urban League and swim in a bigger sea. Brown was also unhappy because Jordan had recently installed John Jacobs, a veteran League official from St. Louis who would later head the organization, as his executive vice president and had ordered all top League officials, including Brown, to report to him. Brown, used to having direct access to the top man, felt slighted. "He was unhappy about that, and I said, 'Ron, that's the way it's going to be,'" Jordan said.[48]

Several of Brown's colleagues, include Andrew Adair, Carol Gibson, and Bill Haskins, say that Brown requested a leave of absence to work for the Kennedy campaign and that Jordan turned him down. Jordan denies this. "These guys came to see me and said, 'We want to talk to Ron Brown about coming to work for Kennedy. We want to hire him full-time.' I said, 'You'll have to talk to Ron Brown. If that's what he wants to do and this was the time to do it, that will be his decision. . . . I never had a conversation with him about a leave of absence. . . . My conversations with him after I told him what they were talking about was whether or not that was a good thing for him to do." Jordan said he told Brown that it was.[49]

The issue of League officials' wanting to take leaves to run for public office was not a new dispute within the organization and had caused Jordan some consternation about what such political activity might mean for the League's 501(c)3 tax exemption. All across the country political careers were opening up for African Americans, especially as the nation's urban centers became increasingly black. League officials like Livingston Wingate, the head of the League's New York City affiliate; T. Willard Fair, head of the Miami affiliate; William Johnson of Rochester; and Norman Rice in Seattle were clamoring to run for public office. Many of them already had high name recognition, and many of them felt they could accomplish more in public office than they had been able to as leaders of a nonprofit social service agency. Jordan felt besieged. He was constantly telling them that if they ran for office they would have to leave the League. "There was a written policy. You couldn't serve God and man at the same time," Jordan said. "Livingston Wingate wanted to run against [New York Congressman] Charlie Rangel. I made him resign. T. Willard Fair, he couldn't run. I said no. Norm Rice . . . had to quit the Seattle Urban League so he could run for the city council 'cause I said, 'You cannot work for the Urban League and serve in political office. We're a 501(c)3!' "[50]

Despite Jordan's assertion that he blithely told Brown it would be fine to work for Kennedy, he knew that it meant losing his talented Washington office director. An Urban League official running for the school board was one thing. Having the head of your Washington office helping a high-profile candidate try to unseat a sitting president was something else altogether. What if Kennedy was to lose? How safe would the League's federal government contracts be with a reelected Jimmy Carter in the White House, mindful of how Jordan's trusted aide had tried to defeat him? Jordan had already felt pressure in New York when Wingate was defeated by Rangel in 1972. "When he lost, he came back," Jordan said. "And the politicians in Harlem called and said, 'Wingate can't come back to the Urban League.' . . . They didn't only want to defeat him, they wanted to crush him."[51] And make no mistake about it, Jordan thought Carter would whip Kennedy. "Vernon said several times in staff meetings, 'He's not going to win anyway, and then you're going to be out in the cold,' " said Robert Hill.[52]

Hill and others felt that Jordan had another reason for not wanting to let Brown go. Brown was an effective number two, a person he could trust in the most important League job after the presidency of the organization, a person who made the League—and, by extension, Jordan—look good. He simply did not want to lose that. "Vernon didn't want Ron to leave because he didn't want to lose an effective director of Washington operations," said Hill. "Vernon is selfish, sell-fish!"[53]

For Brown, the relationship had deteriorated. He felt he had worked hard and effectively for the League but his boss and mentor seemed to choke off every opportunity. He had not backed him for EEOC; he had not paid him enough or given him opportunities to make a decent outside income; and he had installed John Jacobs as the number two man at the League, effectively closing off the possibility of Brown's succeeding Jordan. Brown decided that to reach his potential he had to get out from under Jordan's long shadow. So he left, causing what would be a rift in the two men's relationship that lasted for years; some say it never healed.

"When you add up these events on a cumulative basis it did have a devastating impact on the relationship," said John Mack. "After a while, from Ron's point of view it was, on one hand, you're my man, my main man. And then whenever these opportunities presented themselves to him, Vernon was not supportive. He was, if anything, blocking—from Ron's point of view—blocking his chances to advance, to move on to the next level and to develop his leadership skills."[54] Some who knew both men say the split was inevitable. Brown had become too ambitious and Jordan too controlling for the big-brother-little-brother relationship to last.

PART THREE

THE VIEW

(1980–1988)

CHAPTER SEVEN

KENNEDY

A LEXIS HERMAN sat in the living room of her apartment near the Mall and spoke of her friend Ron Brown. She was dressed casually, her beige skin tone accented by burnt orange slacks and an orange-and-white shirt. Decades away from her native Mobile, Alabama, had only slightly lessened her broad Southern accent. The year since Brown's death had not worn away the sadness in her voice when she talked about him.

The two had met in 1973 when he was at the League and she was in Atlanta running a program to provide employment training for black women. They became fast friends. Eventually, both would make a leap into the wider world of white politics. Brown would go first, acting for Herman and scores of other African Americans as a kind of scout, veering off onto a new path, taking chances, and then beckoning those behind to come along. Sometimes, Herman said, she wasn't sure whether Brown had taken the right route, and she warned him to watch his back. The road had its perils.

She particularly remembered her wariness when he signed on with Ted Kennedy. Like Vernon Jordan and most other prominent black leaders and politicos, she doubted that Kennedy could topple an incumbent president. "I felt that whatever shortcomings Carter had, we had access to Carter," said Jesse Jackson later. "And to support Kennedy in that situation was too great a risk."[1]

Brown's decision to buck the trend meant that he entered the Kennedy camp with little external support. With virtually all black leaders backing Carter, he could hardly call on them for help should the going get rough. Without mentors or people to watch his back, he would have to fight his battles on his own. It was a gamble to leave the black world of federally funded programs, and he knew it.

In the autumn of 1979, however, linking up with Edward M. Kennedy seemed more of a sure bet than a roll of the dice. When the 47-year-old Massachusetts senator announced on November 7 that he was challenging Jimmy Carter, the Democratic incumbent for his party's presidential nomination, Camelot seemed to be reborn. Political reporters and party leaders saw a juggernaut in the making. "You had to be in Washington in the summer of 1979 and be a Carter partisan to be absolutely shell-shocked [by] the Beltway consensus that the nomination was Kennedy's for the asking," Tim Kraft, the campaign manager for Carter's reelection effort said later.[2]

The presidency of Jimmy Carter was in tatters. Inflation raged out of control, and Carter had responded by flip-flopping on economic policy—first ignoring advice to institute a program of fiscal austerity, and then, belatedly moving toward one. His folksy, down-home style, never popular with the establishment in Washington, was wearing thin in the rest of the country. The leading Republican contender, the former governor of California and a former actor, Ronald Reagan, looked like a political lightweight. So it seemed to many a pundit that Kennedy had a lock not only on the Democratic nomination, but on the presidency as well.

When Ron Brown joined the campaign on December 3, he gambled on the conventional wisdom and the strength of his bond to the Kennedy camp. Kennedy's interest in civil rights issues and his chairmanship of the Senate Judiciary Committee, where many civil rights battles were fought, had brought him into increasing contact with Brown. The two men had hit it off, and their relationship evolved beyond that of a lobbyist and a member of Congress into one of friendship. The Browns became part of the Kennedys' social circle, and Brown himself was a tennis guest at the home of Ethel Kennedy, Ted Kennedy's sister-in-law, and the widow of former Attorney General Robert Kennedy.

"There's nobody who I like better or have more personal regard for than Teddy," Brown would say later. "In some ways we're very much alike—we joke around and tease one another. I'd like to think we take work seriously without taking ourselves too seriously."[3] Their casual camaraderie had grown into a full-blown professional commitment that would change Brown's life.

IN EARLY December, Kennedy's staff made a public show of making it appear that Brown would not be pigeonholed into working only on "black" issues. Kennedy brought him along on an early campaign swing through New Hampshire, site of the pending February 26 primary and a state with a minuscule black population. But at the Kennedy campaign national headquarters in an abandoned Cadillac dealership near Georgetown—an office immediately dubbed "Cadelot" by the staff—everyone knew Brown had been recruited to help the campaign organize the black vote.

Brown's title was Deputy Campaign Manager. It meant little. His job was no different from other representatives of minorities and constituent groups, like Fernando Chavez, son of former farm workers union leader Caesar Chavez and Joanne Hawes, a former Hill staffer and official with the National Women's Political Caucus. They were all hired to be the liaisons to particular groups, and at the start, their roles were narrowly defined: do outreach and symbolize to these minorities and women that the Kennedy campaign cared about them.

But don't foolishly think the title actually confers power. As usual, Brown did not complain.

How could he really? He had never worked on a presidential campaign. He had no political experience and therefore could not demand entrée into the inner circles of top Kennedy decision makers. Despite Brown's desire to move beyond the small pond of black affairs, the label "black expert" remained firmly affixed to him.

Brown, Hawes, and Chavez soon began grousing that the campaign assigned a small number of staff for their work and they were given precious little resources to organize and motivate their respective voting blocs. "A lot of it was just frill with no substance," said Chavez. "I think the campaign tried to make an attempt. But it really didn't come close to doing what it could have done."[4] With his own personal pipeline to the candidate and skill at office politics, however, Brown quickly began to accumulate clout.

He was diving into an operation where the internal office politics were as ferocious as the external battle between Kennedy and Carter. The campaign was a hotbed of cliques that competed fiercely with each other for their boss's approval. So he built alliances with people like Hawes and Chavez. He argued that rather than fighting over the small crumbs the campaign allocated for minority outreach, they should plan and carry out joint events and operations. He dispensed advice freely, instructing Chavez and Hawes on how to maneuver within the campaign and how to win—or lose gracefully—the inevitable skirmishes over policy and politics. He advised on the little things that confer status and power inside a campaign, telling colleagues like Hawes and Chavez to make sure they sat near—or even better, next to—the candidate on the campaign plane. He instructed them to maneuver close to the candidate during photo opportunities. Such minor details of positioning may seem small and petty but in the Kennedy campaign—and probably every campaign—they carry signals both on the inside and the outside of how seriously you are to be taken.

Brown made it clear to his colleagues that he had three basic goals and everything he did was geared to achieving them. "One, you're trying to do as much as you can for the campaign, for the candidate," Chavez recalled Brown telling him. "Two, you're trying to do as much as you can for your respective community. And three, you're trying to do as much as you can, to some extent, for yourself."[5]

Brown worked hard at advancing all three.

He seemed to be enjoying himself. One day, he found out that Oren Teicher, a young aide, hailed from Westchester County. Teicher had dealt periodically with David Ford, the Democratic Party chairman in Mount Vernon whom Brown had charmed years earlier. In a leisure moment, Brown and Teicher spent time reminiscing about the crusty old Democratic boss.

Among the denizens of the cubicles at Cadelot, Brown's popularity grew. Every day he found time for a good joke, a warm smile, and an encouraging word. Still, people noticed that he was not afraid to utter a cross word or take somebody in the campaign to task. But even when Brown showed annoyance, he seemed to find the sport in it. Antonia Hernandez, a young Kennedy staffer whom Brown knew from the Leadership Conference on Civil Rights, recalled the time when an arrogant and snobbish campaign aide refused to greet or even acknowledge a group of supporters Brown was escorting through Cadelot. Brown seemed unfazed by the snub, and kept his group going. A short time later he returned, turned to Hernandez in the next cubicle, and flashed her a surreptitious wink. It was a gesture of solidarity—and of fun. It said that we're in this together and there's no need to cower before the rudeness of smart alecky white guys with a sense of entitlement. "It was a 'just watch this' kind of thing," she recalled.[6]

Then he confronted the rude staffer.

"It's these people that make it possible for you to be where you are," Brown told the ill-mannered aide in a measured but firm tone that left no doubt of his seriousness. "And it's that attitude that's going to cost you. It doesn't take much to have a little courtesy."

If Brown worried about his lack of campaign experience, he did not let it intimidate him. He had common sense, good instincts, and confidence. He was not above bluffing his way through situations where he lacked knowledge. "I remember one time I was having some difficulty because I didn't know something," Hernandez said. "Ron said to me, 'What's the matter? If you don't know it, fake it. They don't know it either—and they don't know that you don't know.' "[7] With this sense of bravado, Brown soon established himself as a comer within the campaign. He may have been faking it at the beginning, but he knew he would figure things out quickly.

What advanced Brown in the Kennedy campaign, however, was more than his personality and street-smart approach to office politics. It was his effectiveness in adroitly positioning himself with both the campaign and the black community. Brown was fully aware he was the campaign's token black. Within that role he was able to gain the trust and respect of the Kennedy senior staff by acting as the go-between with the black community, not its advocate. He transmitted the concerns of black politicians to the campaign and helped the senior staff figure out how to address those concerns. He was not, however, the person inside the campaign demanding that it do certain things for black people.

"Ron would always come in and always make it clear that he was the representative of the Kennedy campaign to the group and not the other way around," one observant campaign staffer said privately. "That didn't mean he wasn't a black person. It's just that he wasn't the one who was on the attack. . . . It was always, 'This is the concern that so-and-so is raising over here. Here is what he has over there. Here is the analysis of the situation and here is my judgment and recommendation.' "

Brown did not rant if the campaign did not take a position that had been demanded by a particular black leader or constituency group. That was not his style. He empathized with the problems—be they financial, philosophical, or political—the campaign might have acceding to a request. It was an ability that not all the liaisons to constituency groups possessed, and that ability was one of the reasons, in addition to what was considered his political judgment, that Brown rapidly penetrated into the inner sanctum of the campaign.

As he was working his way in, however, the campaign itself was sinking.

TWO EVENTS that actually occurred before Brown signed on had seriously wounded the campaign. On November 4, 1979, three days before Kennedy announced his candidacy, Islamic militants in Iran seized the American Embassy in Tehran and took a number of Americans hostage. The invaders, staunch followers of the Ayatollah Khomeini, a militant Islamic cleric, demanded that President Carter turn over the deposed Shah of Iran, the hated autocrat, who after his abdication had come to the United States for medical treatment. The militants who took over the embassy later released some of their hostages. But fifty-two Americans would remain captive for more than a year.

The Iranian hostage crisis completely shook up the presidential contest. As is often the case when the country seems under siege, the public rallied around the president as the most tangible symbol of national honor and sovereignty. In the early stages of the crisis, Carter took decisive actions, such as freezing Iranian assets, that for a time allowed him to shake off the image of an irresolute leader. Carter also used the crisis as justification for adopting a "Rose Garden Strategy," refusing to leave the confines of the White House to campaign and rebuffing all requests from Kennedy to debate him. With lives hanging in the balance, Kennedy and other candidates, including Republicans, refrained from sharp criticism of Carter's handling of the crisis.

But on a December 2 television talk show in San Francisco, Kennedy ignited a firestorm of criticism when he said that the Shah of Iran "ran one of the most violent regimes in the history of mankind" and that he "stole umpteen billions of dollars from his country." Despite the truth of Kennedy's comments, the Carter campaign turned on him for voicing views that mirrored those of the hostage takers. "It was nothing really attacking Carter directly, and yet it was played up as though somehow Kennedy had attacked America," said Tom Quinn, campaign manager for California governor Edmund G. Brown Jr., another Democratic presidential aspirant.[8]

Kennedy's woes were not all foreign imports. The second event was manufactured very close to home. On November 4, the same day the Iranian militants stormed the American Embassy in Tehran, CBS News broadcast an interview Kennedy had given to correspondent Roger Mudd. In it, an obviously fatigued candidate gave stunningly inarticulate answers to such basic questions as why he wanted to be president, stammering and fumbling over words and phrases, hesitant with answers, and punctuating responses with strings of "uh's."

The interview was devastating to Kennedy's image. "Whether people saw it or not, they heard about it," Paul G. Kirk Jr., a Boston lawyer who became Kennedy's campaign manager, said of the Roger Mudd interview. "As a result, if they saw a network clip that showed some less-than-articulate statement, then, I think, there were perhaps a few that said, 'Well, we've read about this fellow and he hasn't lived up to expectations.' "[9]

The twin blows punched the air out of Kennedy's campaign. He had based his appeal on the issue of leadership. Yet, Carter's early handling of the Iranian crisis stole that issue away from him. Meanwhile, the subtext of his campaign—that he was the heir of the urbane, glittery Camelot of his brothers—was undercut by the Mudd interview. Deprived of these dual themes, Kennedy had little else. His politics were not that different from Carter's. He had voted with the president 84 percent of the time during the previous Congress.[10] Lacking a reason he could give Democratic and Independent voters to abandon a beleaguered president, Kennedy's campaign collapsed. In early November, right after Kennedy entered the campaign, an ABC News/Louis Harris poll gave him a commanding lead over Carter of 46 percent to 32 percent among Democrats and Independents.

By the end of December, after Brown had gained stature and trust within the campaign, Kennedy trailed Carter badly in the same poll.

Brown was among a number of top Kennedy aides who gathered with the candidate at Kennedy's home in West Palm Beach, Florida, on the day after Christmas 1979 to assess the damage and brainstorm ways to right the listing ship.

Brown and the campaign's other brain trusts lounged on lawn chairs in Kennedy's yard chewing over the hard reality that the theme of providing a leadership alternative to Carter—the issue on which Kennedy had staked most of his appeal—was not working in light of the hostage crisis. While the candidate's young son, Teddy Jr., who had lost a leg to cancer, gamboled about on an artificial limb tossing around a football, the strategists wondered if Kennedy should try to differentiate himself from the president on the basis of issues. Such a course contained dangers. Kennedy's major differences with the president tended to place him solidly on the left, especially his advocacy of wage and price controls and gas rationing as a response to the continued inflation and the energy crisis brought about by the fall of the Shah. Kennedy's advisers were concerned that if their candidate defined himself more clearly voters might find that definition too liberal for their tastes. "Clearly, there was some concern about moving in that direction," Brown said later. "Others thought that we couldn't sit around and wait for the Iranian crisis to end; it was paralyzing the campaign."[11]

The West Palm Beach meeting did not result in any marked change in Kennedy's strategy. After listening to some back-and-forth from his advisers, Kennedy opted to stay the course, maintaining, at least through the Iowa caucuses the following month, the tactic of trying to sell himself as a leadership alternative to Carter, rather than to take on the president based on ideological differences. "The West Palm Beach meeting was not a decision meeting," Brown said. "It was kind of an input meeting, a discussion meeting."[12]

It was for Brown, however, a breakthrough meeting. Participants could not recall exactly where Brown stood on the issue at hand, whether he contributed any specific advice, and, if so, whether his counsels were heeded. Still, the fact that he was included in the gathering of the campaign's top officials meant that Brown had quickly moved beyond doing "black issues" and was accepted as one of the campaign's top strategists. Up until that point, Andrew Young in 1976 had been the only African American to reach the heady heights of being a serious inside player in a major presidential campaign. Whatever Brown contributed to the Kennedy campaign during the West Palm Beach meeting and beyond paled in relation to what the campaign contributed to his knowledge and his development as a political heavyweight.

It was one of the few times in history that a black person had what Alexis Herman called "the view."

"The view on the inside," she said. "You may not be at the table, but you're in the room. You could at least hear the discussions. You could understand what, for most of us, up until the 1980 experience, was hearsay. It was somebody else telling us. The closest would have been Andy Young with Jimmy Carter in '76, in terms of a real insider who could kind of go toe-to-toe with the boys. You go back to any other presidential campaign. You take Humphrey, you take Johnson, you take Kennedy in '60, the black infrastructure was dealing with black politics, the black vote. You did not get the broader view. That's what I mean, the view. The view for me is the bigger picture. It's not that slice that deals with black people and what are you going to do about the African American vote. That's what 1980 did for Ron. It gave him the view."[13]

For the moment, however, Brown's view resembled the scene from the bridge of the *Titanic*.

THE MAJOR BLOWS in January came from an issue that Kennedy felt he had laid to rest: Chappaquiddick. In early January, a new poll indicated that the public, far from having forgotten about the 1969 incident or forgiven Kennedy his role in it, still harbored doubts about his behavior that night. As Carter's standing improved as a result of the hostage crisis, more and more people were giving Kennedy's performance at Chappaquiddick a closer look—and finding it wanting.

By mid-January a *Des Moines Register* poll that earlier had Carter and Kennedy in a dead heat now showed the president leading the senator by a margin of 57 percent to 25 percent among Iowa Democrats. Less than two weeks later, Carter trounced Kennedy in the Iowa caucuses, besting his rival by a margin of more than two to one. For all intents and purposes, the Kennedy campaign, which had started out with an aura of inevitability, was finished. "This was the shortest campaign in history," said Tony Podesta, a Kennedy aide. "It was like there were ten million people backing us on November first. And then by the first of February it was all over."[14]

Podesta exaggerated only slightly. The loss in Iowa was stunning and virtually fatal to Kennedy's campaign. "Most of us did not anticipate the dimensions of the Iowa loss," Brown said later. "So then you were in a crisis kind of situation after that, after that loss."[15] Supporters, especially labor leaders, governors, mayors, senators, and members of Congress who had urged Kennedy to run, now were nowhere to be seen. Their abandonment stung Brown, who had a regard for loyalty.

"I can describe, certainly my own disappointment as being very profound then, about so many people, both elected officials and others, who I knew had come to him in the summer and had urged him to run and who were not to be heard from when they were most needed," Brown recalled. "We went to talk to some of those people; they either wanted to remain silent or had decided to support the president. . . ."[16]

A week after the Iowa caucuses, Kennedy's campaign was down to $200,000 of the $4 million it had raised. The campaign laid off some of its paid staff and gave up the expensive jet it had chartered.

Kennedy's defeat in Iowa prompted changes more profound than letting a few staffers go and stepping down in the quality of his chartered jet. The loss forced him to undertake the approach that had been considered and rejected at the West Palm Beach strategy session in December: a full-throated frontal assault on Carter's record in an attempt to differentiate the challenger from the incumbent. In a speech at Georgetown University on January 28, Kennedy assailed Carter's foreign and domestic policies. The candidate accused the president of overreacting to the Soviet thrust into Afghanistan. He called for the United Nations to set up a commission to investigate the crimes of the Shah and to negotiate the release of the American hostages. He also sharply criticized the Carter administration for letting the Shah enter the United States for medical treatment. On the domestic front, Kennedy proposed an immediate six-month freeze on wages and prices, followed by mandatory wage and price controls. He also called for gas rationing to help wean the country off its dependence on Middle East oil.

Kennedy's speech had two goals. He wanted at long last to distance himself from the president and provide reasons for people to vote for him beyond the Kennedy name and the mushy concept of "leadership." He also sought to reassure donors, potential volunteers, the press, and the public at large that he had no intention of abandoning his quest to unseat Carter, at least not yet.

The Georgetown speech was a pivotal moment for the Democratic Party. It was clearly a decision by the candidate to veer to the left in order to differentiate himself from Carter. It also polarized the Democratic Party. The campaign had always been a personal struggle between two men and two camps that did not like each other. The Ivy League Brahmins who surrounded Kennedy looked down on the Southern Bubbas who backed Carter. The Carterites returned the enmity in full measure. White House Press Secretary Jody Powell often sneeringly referred to Kennedy as a "spoiled, fat, rich kid," while Kennedy's supporters would speak in private of Carter as that "redneck Southern Baptist."

With the Georgetown speech and Kennedy's swing to the left, regional and ideological divisions augmented the personal antagonisms. Carter was the leader of the centrist wing of the party, representing, for the most part, white Southern Protestants. Kennedy carried the standard of the liberal Northern wing that was much more black, Hispanic, Jewish, Catholic, and trade unionist. For the first three years of Carter's presidency—and the first three months of the 1980 primary campaign—these cleavages had been papered over. From the moment Kennedy left the podium at Georgetown these racial, religious, and regional differences engulfed the Democrats. They would haunt the party—and bedevil Ron Brown—long after the 1980 campaign.

At the time, however, Kennedy's speech failed to reignite his faltering campaign. Despite hailing from nearby Massachusetts, he was beaten by Carter in the New Hampshire primary. Carter also overwhelmed the challenger in Florida, Alabama, and Georgia, and then trounced him in Illinois. The string of steady defeats spawned talk within the campaign that the candidate would drop out.

But Brown had become a true believer. He argued in private councils that Kennedy ought to hang in there. "I believed very strongly that Kennedy needed to persist in that campaign, that he couldn't run when it was easy and get out when it got hard," said Robert Shrum, Kennedy's chief speechwriter. "If we really meant what we said when we went into the campaign for specific reasons, then those reasons had to keep us in the campaign even though we were in great difficulty. . . . Ron agreed with that, and I thought he was very wise."[17]

Despite such gallant talk, Kennedy limped into New York for the state's March 25 primary. Carter appeared ready to deliver the knockout blow. "Basically, the feeling was if we lost New York as badly as we were projected to, the bottom was really out," said Kirk.[18]

The pressure was not on Kennedy alone. Brown was assigned to travel to the Empire State; his assignment was to help the campaign bring out the vote among blacks concentrated in New York City and its suburbs. It was another homecoming of sorts for him. He had left New York seven years before to make his mark in Washington. Now he was returning as the top black in a campaign that was opposed by most of the black leadership in the city and the state. Not only would the eyes of the Kennedy campaign be on him, so would those of New York's black political establishment, including Vernon Jordan, his mentor, who lived in New York City and who had warned him against signing on with the Kennedy campaign. Brown was not facing an impossible task, however. Despite the opposition of black leaders, polls consistently had shown that rank-and-file black voters favored Kennedy over Carter. The key in New York then became translating this support into a solid showing at the polls by boosting turnout.

Arriving in the city, Brown convened a meeting of the small number of black politicians and union leaders who had endorsed Kennedy to discuss ways of increasing black interest in the primary election. He was a familiar figure to many of those who attended. Several knew his family from the days when Bill Brown managed the Hotel Theresa. Among those who came was a new generation of black politicians, like David Dinkins, who would later become mayor of New York City, and Bill Lynch, a young strategist.

The participants at the meeting decided to have Brown make a large number of campaign appearances in black areas in New York City, Westchester, and other parts of the state, where he spoke in black churches and at meetings of black social clubs. He cut a radio spot that was played widely on black radio stations. The subtext of Brown's appearance was that while Carter had fired Andy Young, the top-ranking black in his administration, Kennedy had placed an African American into the hierarchy of his campaign. "Getting his name out there as the deputy campaign manager was a big deal at the time," said Lynch, who later became Dinkins's chief of staff.[19] Brown also convinced the Kennedy camp to dispatch family members like Sargent and Eunice Shriver to campaign extensively in black areas. What impressed Lynch during the campaign was Brown's ability to comfortably speak before a black audience and then abruptly switch style and focus when meeting with white strategists for the campaign.

"He was the ultimate crossover guy," Lynch recalled. "He could go into black churches and relate to people in the church. He could relate to black people on the street. And then I would watch him in meetings hold his own with white politicians."[20] Brown's efforts in New York paid off. Kennedy prevailed in the March 25 primary largely based on his carrying New York City by 62 percent and close-in suburbs by a two-to-one margin. It was a victory that was built in large measure by a heavy turnout of black voters. The challenger also won the Connecticut primary held the same day.

The upset wins in the New York and Connecticut primaries would have momentous consequences for Kennedy—and for Brown.

For Kennedy, the victories in one of the country's major media centers gave his faltering campaign a huge psychological boost. Coming back from the brink, the wins gave Kennedy sufficient hope to carry him through the final brace of primaries in California, Ohio, and New Jersey in early June. In a sense, the twin victories blinded Kennedy and his top advisers to the ultimate futility of their task. Despite the wins, they had little chance of catching Carter. The president's victory in the Illinois primary earlier in the month had given him a nearly insurmountable cushion of more than 150 delegates. Kennedy would have to win more than 60 percent of the remaining delegates in order to have a shot at the nomination.

The New York primary gave Brown the chance to prove both his loyalty and his worth. His work in helping to organize the critical black vote impressed people in the campaign with his political skills and engendered enough trust for him to be given increased responsibilities in the months ahead. The extension of the campaign also meant that Brown would have more of an opportunity to cement his relationship with Kennedy. Brown could only guess at that point what that relationship might mean for his future, but he believed in the candidate, and it was obviously worth building up in any way possible.

After New York, Brown witnessed the transformation of Kennedy's effort from a campaign to a "cause." Campaign officials and the candidate himself often used that term to describe why they were staying in the race even though they had little or no chance of securing the nomination. "It became a political campaign of principle," said Carl Wagner,[21] director of field operations for Kennedy's campaign and someone who was to play an enormous role in Brown's life. The focus was now on getting a chance to present Kennedy's message to voters and to gain a measure of respect from an adversary who was running away with the nomination. But remaining in the race would have disastrous consequences for the Democrats in 1980. Brown witnessed that firsthand and would remember eight years later, when he was an adviser to another charismatic Democratic insurgent—Jesse Jackson—whose effort was as much a "cause" as it was a campaign.

On June 3, the final day of the primary elections, three large and vote-rich states—California, Ohio, and New Jersey—held their contests. It was a critically important day for the Kennedy campaign. The question was no longer denying Carter the nomination. Carter was only a few delegates short of the number needed to assure his renomination, and the odds were good that he would win at least one primary—probably Ohio—that would put him over the top. But if Kennedy wanted to maintain enough of an aura of momentum to stay in the race until the convention, he needed wins in California or New Jersey, if not both.

Prospects in California looked good. The state had never really taken to Carter. In 1976, Governor Edmund G. (Jerry) Brown had swamped Carter in the primary 59 percent to 20 percent, and Carter had lost the state to Gerald Ford in the general election. Three weeks before the primary, a poll by the respected pollster Mervin Field showed Kennedy leading Carter among Democratic voters 42 percent to 39 percent. And several weeks earlier Jerry Brown, who once again had run for the Democratic presidential nomination, had dropped out of the race, leaving another slice of the anti-Carter vote free to migrate to Kennedy. Indeed, Kennedy felt so confident of taking the delegate-rich state that in May he said that if Carter agreed to debate him before the June 3 primaries, and the president won the most delegates that day, he would drop out of the race.

Still, California's Democratic electorate contained its own pitfalls and presented a daunting set of challenges. California's Democratic Party mirrored the state. It was riven along racial and ethnic lines, with blacks, Hispanics, and whites at times as distrustful of each other as they were of Republicans. There was also the state's famous geographic split, with Democrats from Northern California and the Bay Area looking askance at those in the huge megalopolis of Los Angeles and San Diego in the south.

The Kennedy campaign needed a peacemaker and conciliator in California, someone who could keep the headstrong state political leaders from calling Kennedy's headquarters in Washington and requiring national campaign staffers to spend precious time patching up squabbles rather than concentrating on places like Ohio or New Jersey, where the races were much closer. "At the time, California, Ohio, and New Jersey were all on the same day," said Wagner. "I had to have people in those states who could handle themselves and could handle other people because the Kennedy campaign had attracted to it some very distinct and unique people; people of very strong will. . . . I was sitting there in the campaign needing a manager for California. And I had people in California of rather substantial will, folks like John and Phil Burton, Willie Brown, Maxine Waters, Nancy Pelosi, John Tunney, George Miller, the AFL-CIO, and Caesar Chavez—you know, an easy group of people to reach consensus with who agree on everything all the time and would defer to you in a minute."[22]

Wagner was being facetious, of course. Of those he mentioned, the Burtons and Willie Brown were powers in the state legislature, Waters was an outspoken city councilwoman from Los Angeles, Pelosi and Miller were members of Congress, Tunney was a former member of the U.S. Senate who had been Kennedy's law school roommate, and Chavez was a legendary union leader. None was a shrinking violet. "It was a formidable and volatile coalition," said Wagner. "It was multiracial, multiethnic. You had the politics of North and South, major donors and the Hollywood crowd, and a wide range in terms of class and income. The breadth of the coalition was tremendous. The question was could you keep it buckled together."[23]

Wagner also had another problem. Unable to pay many of its permanent workers very much, if at all, the cash-strapped Kennedy campaign did not have a large stable of experienced campaign managers to call on. Going out into the field and working a state at this stage in the campaign was a risky affair. Something unforeseen could always occur, and a primary that appeared to be in the bag could be lost. Those who stayed at the national headquarters had the luxury of not being clearly identified with a state, should the effort there turn sour. What's more, since Kennedy's campaign was based in Washington and Massachusetts, those in the headquarters had the satisfaction of going home to their own beds every night. Given the precarious state of the campaign's finances, people in the field were likely to be bunking on the sofa of some supporter or sharing a queen-sized bed in some no-star motel with another campaign worker.

"There was this A.P.B. that went out for anybody who could, should go out into the field," said one campaign worker. "Let me say that a number of the prima donnas at the deputy campaign manager level and above did not move out into the field."

Technically, Brown was not part of the campaign's political wing, those operatives who coordinated campaigns in different states. But with few people left to turn to, Wagner decided to take a chance on Brown. One day, Wagner walked into Brown's cubicle and asked him if he would go run California for the campaign.

"How do you do business?" Brown asked him.

"I do business on the basis of a handshake," Wagner replied.

"Fine. Where are the tickets?"[24]

Brown's willingness to take on California, a state he knew little about, helped solidify his relationship with Wagner. It was a friendship that would benefit Brown enormously in the future.

NEVER BEFORE had a campaign selected a black person to be its top dog in any state. Some within the campaign reacted with a measure of consternation, some with a measure of pride. Everyone was surprised. "The notion that someone who is black should be put in charge of a state, especially one as large and as critical as California, was revolutionary," said Podesta. "I mean, there was sort of the feeling, that, you know, this is a good thing. This is a very smart guy who's terrific and it's good that this campaign is breaking down barriers and stereotypes and putting somebody like that in charge of this big state. . . . So it was a pleasant surprise. But it was a surprise nonetheless."[25]

For Brown, California provided more than an opportunity to prove his value to the Kennedy campaign and to show off his skills. It would be another of his coveted firsts.

Brown's selection also surprised many of the high-powered Democrats in California who had never heard of him. Coming from out of state and with no major victories in past campaigns hanging from his belt, Brown was viewed warily by a number of the honchos of the state's Democratic Party. But Brown quickly won over many of his doubters, both by his political wisdom and by his low-key, cooperative personality.

He recognized early on the key role of John Tunney, who, in addition to being one of the state's well-known Democrats and the Kennedy campaign's California chairman, also had a friendship with the candidate that went back years. Brown made sure he played tennis regularly with the former senator, socialized with him, and listened to his concerns. "That was something that Ron Brown was unbelievably good at doing—stroking people," Tunney recalled. "I felt that he was stroking me, too."[26]

Tunney could be valuable. If problems arose in the campaign, Brown could ensure that the word got directly to Kennedy through the candidate's old friend from law school, rather than having to worry that a message might fall through the cracks of the campaign bureaucracy. "Here he was dealing with an extremely close friend of Kennedy's who was a former senator himself," Tunney said. "Obviously I was a person with a direct channel to the candidate, and [Brown] made it very clear to me that he wanted various things brought to the attention of the candidate. Perhaps, at least in the beginning, not so much towards the end, I had greater access on a daily basis than he did."[27]

Brown was not a nuts-and-bolts guy, skilled in the art of campaign logistics. So, Wagner dispatched Oren Teicher to California to handle the day-to-day operations. "He didn't really know a whole lot about the technical stuff, buying a voter list, organizing a phone bank," said Teicher. "That clearly was not his forte. But the hard stuff in politics is people. Anybody can learn how to call up the phone company and order twenty phones. All of the so-called political skills are learnable."[28] Brown's lack of campaign experience prompted Wagner to send out a host of talented and experienced political operatives, virtually all of them white, to help in organizing the campaign in different parts of the state. At first Brown resented the intrusion, believing that the higher-ups in the national office did not trust him to carry out his mission. Yet, according to Wagner and Teicher, Brown grew to accept the value of surrounding himself with talented people. His ego might have suffered at times, but the lesson he learned about the value of delegating authority to people who could do the job—and, in the end, make him look good—was one that he would carry with him through the rest of his career.

Brown and Teicher set up shop on the top floor of an aging office building in Los Angeles. The site, which had been Jerry Brown's former California campaign headquarters, sat amid low-end retail shops, street vendors, and derelicts in the garment district. As Teicher organized the logistics, Brown did as many media interviews as he could handle, providing an image to liberal segments of the party of a Kennedy campaign so enlightened that it had an African American running its state operations. Brown also worked to knit together the agendas and personalities of Kennedy's big-name supporters.

Far and away the most difficult part of Brown's assignment was working out Kennedy's schedule when he campaigned in the state. Everyone wanted a piece of the candidate's time. And figuring out which requests to honor involved navigating through California's political rapids. An appearance by the candidate conferred a measure of power and respect. The group that got him did so because he recognized its political importance. Thus, labor leaders, blacks, Hispanics, environmentalists, women's groups, Hollywood fund-raisers, state political powers, and all the rest cajoled, implored, or threatened when it came to making their case for Kennedy's time. Brown had to figure out ways to satisfy as many demands as possible. "California is lots of different states," Teicher remembered. "In Southern California, the question was, Do you do a black event or a Hispanic event? A west side event or an Orange County event? A labor event or a women's event? This was a substantial piece of what the disputes and arguments were about."[29]

As was his style, Brown somehow managed to satisfy everyone—or figure out a way to placate them. "Most of the people left conversations with Ron Brown thinking that he agreed with whatever you wanted to do," Teicher recalled. "That was his personality, and in that environment, it was the kind of personality you needed to thrive."[30] Indeed, he thrived so much that Wagner joked that two weeks after Brown got to California he "started getting phone calls from people in California, some of them important people, some of them rank-and-file Democrats wanting to know whether it was true that Ron Brown was moving to California to run for governor. I said, 'Of course.'"[31]

Even as he navigated the tricky waters of California politics, Brown had a more tangible problem—lack of money. The campaign had been essentially broke for some time. As a result, it could not pay for some of the basic requirements of a political effort, such as airing television advertisements. Two weeks before the primary, the national headquarters sent Brown a tough new commercial that featured actor Carroll O'Connor, a craggy-faced Irish American who played the bumbling, soft-hearted bigot Archie Bunker in the hit television show *All in the Family*. Zeroing in on Carter's record on the economy, O'Connor sought to equate him with Ronald Reagan, the bête noire to liberal Democrats who normally vote in primaries, saying, "Carter equals Reagan equals Hoover equals Depression."[32]

By any measure, it was a hard-hitting commercial. But Brown had virtually no money to get it on the air. Entreaties to the national headquarters for money to buy air time had brought the response that the cupboard was bare. Brown had to figure out how to raise the money himself in California or figure out another way to get the message out. As the primary drew near, Brown sat in a hotel bar one night with Adam Clymer, a *New York Times* reporter, lamenting his plight. As Clymer and Brown discussed the commercial they suddenly hit on an idea: why not call a news conference and show the advertisement to reporters, especially television reporters? The local television stations might then broadcast the commercial that evening, giving it air time at no cost to the campaign. Brown followed up on the idea. Indeed, he traveled around the state, holding news conferences at which the advertisement was shown. He boasted at these press conferences that he had an advertising budget of $195,000, enough to ensure that residents of the state would see the commercial a number of times, including 172 times on the seven local television stations in Los Angeles. In fact, he had nowhere near that amount, and unless a person tuned in to his or her local news program that night he would never see the Carroll O'Connor commercial. Still, Kirk said, "he saved the campaign some dough, but still got the message out that the ads were supposed to convey."[33]

Soon, Kennedy operatives in other states, who also faced tough financial straits, were copying Brown's tactic. "It worked so well that [Paul] Tully did it in Ohio and I did it in New Jersey," said John Sasso. "He'd send us the tapes on the plane, and we'd hold our press conferences. . . . I was amazed. It was like front-page news day after day."[34] In later years, Brown's ploy would become standard practice for many campaigns. But in 1980 it was revolutionary. "Everybody's caught on to that scam by now," said Shrum. "But in those days they didn't know anything about it. [Reporters] said, 'Kennedy's going on TV,' and played the spot. . . . I'm not sure we got that many points, but we at least got it shown once on all the news programs."[35] Whether Brown's ploy actually made any difference in the final result is difficult to tell. But the tactic became part of Brown's story. Proof positive of his political smarts.

Even as he struggled with limited funds, Brown did not lose his trademark sense of humor. Shrum recalled one campaign swing when Kennedy did a round of interviews in the morning in San Francisco, was scheduled to fly along with his entourage, including Brown, to Arizona for a fund-raiser, and then fly to Los Angeles for a major speech. On the way to the airport in San Francisco, Shrum suddenly realized that he had left the only copy of Kennedy's speech at the television station where the candidate had last been interviewed. He and Brown dashed back to the station to retrieve the speech but did not make it back to the airport before the campaign party took off. Rather than panic, Brown suggested to an agitated Shrum that the two of them have a leisurely lunch and then fly down to Los Angeles to meet Kennedy there. On the tarmac at LAX, Brown surprised Kennedy, who had not realized that Brown and Shrum had not been with him in Arizona, "Where have *you* been?" Brown demanded in mock anger.[36]

Brown also had a hand in another event that was revolutionary for any presidential campaign in 1980—a fund-raiser sponsored by gay political activists.

Kennedy had been invited to address a May 24 fund-raiser at the home of Clyde Kairns, a gay political activist who lived in the Hollywood Hills. At the time gay rights was a nascent issue, and the idea of a presidential aspirant embracing this cause was not readily accepted. The invitation spawned a lively debate among Kennedy's top campaign people, with some advisers concerned that such an appearance might cost the candidate votes in more conservative states like Ohio. "In 1980, it wasn't all that common, and people got a little weird about it," recalled Kathy Garmenzy, a former Kennedy staffer who worked in the California campaign. "Ron just chilled all that out."[37] Brown was among those who felt that the issue was about discrimination and that Kennedy needed to come down in support of gay rights. Kennedy agreed, and as was his style, he made light of the possible repercussions, making an oblique reference to his reputation as a womanizer. "Don't worry about it," Kennedy said to an adviser. "It's the upside of my downside. Nobody will think I have a personal interest."[38]

Brown was able to hold the Kennedy coalition together, and in the end Kennedy beat Carter handily in California, 44.8 percent to 37.7 percent. Never mind that Carter was in trouble from the start in the state. Never mind that the president had focused more of his resources in Ohio, a state that was much more winnable for him. Brown had managed a winning campaign in what was emerging as the most politically important state in the country. Not only that, he had won the plaudits of the state's top Democrats, people who would be invaluable to him in his later career. The California primary was in every way a watershed for him. He was more than just a player. "California made him a confident player," said Wagner. "He played with the biggest guys in the political world and performed extraordinarily well. I think Ron always thought he could be a player. But to play on the biggest court in American politics and win had to have an enormous impact on his confidence."[39]

For the Democratic Party in 1980, June 3 was one of the worst days imaginable. Carter handily won primaries in Ohio, New Mexico, West Virginia, and Montana, garnering enough delegates to clinch the nomination. At the same time Kennedy beat Carter in New Jersey, Rhode Island, South Dakota, and, of course, California. The victories built sufficient momentum to allow Kennedy to consider staying in the race through the convention that August in New York City.

The results of the June 3 voting presented Kennedy with the same dilemma that had gnawed at the campaign since the first loss in Iowa four months before: to stay in, carry his "cause" forward, and risk being seen as a spoiler, or admit defeat and start the process of unification. There were more than ample reasons to pull out. Party elders, sensing that Reagan might be a more formidable adversary than first imagined, tried to persuade Kennedy to give up his pursuit of the nomination. Polls also showed that despite the challenger's supposedly momentum-generating wins in the final round of primaries, Democrats still preferred the president by a two-to-one margin. Even two thirds of the Democrats who voted for Kennedy in California thought Kennedy should abandon his campaign for the sake of party unity, according to a *Los Angeles Times* exit poll.

Several days after the June 3 primaries, Kennedy called his top campaign advisers, including Brown, back to Washington to confer on what to do. Carter had been trying to reach Kennedy to invite him to meet at the White House. There, the president hoped to convince Kennedy to drop out so that the two could emerge united. At the first meeting of Kennedy's advisers at his Senate office, the group debated whether to pull out, though some argued that before withdrawing Kennedy needed to have the debate with Carter he had long sought. They felt that such an action could keep things in flux in the hope that a miracle might occur. "There were people who thought that was anywhere from impolite to insane," said Shrum. "There was a strong division of opinion and people who said, 'We've made the best run at it that we can, why don't we figure out how to honorably end this thing.'"[40]

According to Shrum, Brown strongly favored demanding a debate and not dropping out. "Ron and I and several other people felt we had to come up with a way to keep the challenge alive," Shrum said. "He strongly spoke in favor of it."[41] Others who attended the meeting do not recall which side of the issue Brown took. Kennedy listened to his advisers go at it for a time and finally picked up the telephone himself and called the White House to accept Carter's invitation.

Kennedy met with Carter at the White House and proposed a deal similar to the one he made before the June 3 contests. If the president debated him and the polls afterward showed no change in Democratic voters' attitudes, the challenger would drop out of the race. With little to gain from such a debate, Carter declined. Kennedy then met reporters in the driveway outside the White House and vowed to stay in the race. "I am a candidate for the nomination," Kennedy told reporters, "and I'm going to continue to seek the nomination."[42]

The decision begged a question: why? To what end? The rules of the Democratic Party—specifically, number F(3)c of the party regulations—stated that any convention delegate that was pledged to a specific candidate had to vote for that candidate on the first ballot. Since Carter had more than enough pledged delegates to win on the first ballot, there was no way Kennedy could capture the nomination.

The group met again, this time at Kennedy's home, to kick around the pros and cons of continuing the race. "Kennedy was trying to decide whether we were fooling ourselves since we knew we didn't have the votes," said Kennedy aide Richard G. Stearns.[43] With rule F(3)c, which the Kennedy staffers dubbed the "Robot Rule," sitting like a guard post in the middle of any road Kennedy would have to travel to get the nomination, the candidate and his advisers—including Brown—made a fateful decision. They would campaign to change the rule. Their public rationale was that why should a delegate elected in, say, March have to honor a pledge to a candidate in August? After all, political and economic conditions change, and the candidate who looked so wonderful in the snows of New Hampshire might look less attractive in the harsh summer in New York City, where the Democrats would be holding their convention. In fact, they adopted the strategy because they had run out of other ideas. After nine months of campaigning and thirty-five primaries, Kennedy had not dented the incumbent's lead. Seeking a floor fight on rule F(3)c would allow Kennedy to carry his campaign on to the convention, where they hoped to be able to generate a groundswell of support for him among the delegates. "It was about the only thing left that we could think of," said Stearns.[44] It was also a long shot.

Given the futility of the enterprise, the decision to carry on the campaign was puzzling. There was little doubt inside the campaign that forcing a fight all the way to the convention was divisive and could, in the end, hurt Carter's chances in the general election campaign against Reagan. Yet the Kennedy forces, Brown among them, persisted. There is no evidence that Brown—or anyone else—during this period had the foresight to stand back, assess the damage a continued Kennedy campaign was doing, and argue that the candidate should fold his tent for the good of the party and to keep the hard-edged Reaganites out of the White House. "We were asking people to join in a mass political suicide on the floor of Madison Square Garden," said one Kennedy insider. "It was all very interesting political business. But here's the question that I don't understand in retrospect: what did we think we were doing?"

Carter shares some of the responsibility for Kennedy's persistence. After he clinched the nomination, the president did little to extend an olive branch to the Kennedy campaign. Two weeks after the primary, rather than seek compromise, the Carter camp used its political muscle to turn aside virtually all platform proposals made by Kennedy, especially those regarding the economy. Said one Kennedy staffer, "Their attitude was that they were the conqueror and anything we proposed they were going to challenge."

In addition, the Carter forces took a tough stance on the fight over the Robot Rule, declaring that they would yank the credentials of any of their delegates who voted to overturn it. Had the Carter forces compromised, Kennedy's continued challenge would have been vulnerable to the charge that it was nothing more than an ego-driven effort that would do little except help elect Reagan in the fall.

"We were helped by the strategy," Brown later said of the hard-line efforts of the Carter camp.[45] Podesta agreed. "Carter was stupid, I think, to fight about it," said Podesta. "I mean, if he had let us win the rule change, everybody would've had the free conscience to vote for whomever they wanted—and they would have voted for Carter."[46]

Still, throughout the latter part of June, July, and early August, Brown and other Kennedy aides traveled around the country meeting with supporters to convince them to come to New York to fight for the change in the rule or to get the full convention to adopt Kennedy's minority platform planks. "Ron's job was to juice people up," said a senior Kennedy aide. It might have been an ill-fated exercise, but it was also the type of challenge that was fun and meaningful to liberal Democrats, many of whom had been eager participants in the antiwar and labor movements and were always spoiling for a good fight.

"I remember one rally in Michigan," the staffer said. "Ron had all these people cheering about going on to New York. They were cheering about how they were going to fight F(3)c, this credentials fight which they didn't understand. They didn't know what he was talking about. They didn't care. It was, 'Here we go! Let's get 'em!' It was quite terrific."

Kennedy's strategy had its predicted results. The convention at Madison Square Garden was chaotic. On the eve of the gathering, Kennedy pointedly refused to get out of the race, going so far as to release a list of seven Democrats he might consider as his vice presidential running mate. When Carter gave some ground on platform issues, most notably agreeing to a plank that opposed the use of high interest rates to fight inflation, Kennedy still refused to withdraw. On the second day of the convention, Carter's forces prevailed in the vote on rule F(3)c, thereby effectively ending Kennedy's challenge. Finally, recognizing that his beloved "cause" was at an end, Kennedy withdrew.

But far from being gracious in his withdrawal, Kennedy refused to say he would campaign for the president. In his keynote speech he concentrated his attacks on Reagan and the Republicans, rather than on Carter. But after Carter's acceptance speech, Kennedy virtually snubbed the titular head of his party. Appearing onstage after the president concluded his remarks for the traditional show of unity, Kennedy stalked around the podium for several minutes, reveling in the applause and forcing Carter to pursue him back and forth on the stage like a love-starved puppy seeking approval. The image of an incumbent president chasing after a rival he had just defeated infuriated Carter's backers and contributed to the impression of the president as weak and undeserving of respect—themes that Reagan would use with great effectiveness in defeating Carter.

Kennedy's insurgency, his obstinate refusal to withdraw when it looked hopeless, and his sore loser behavior at the convention, sparked intense debate within the Democratic Party during 1980 and beyond. Carter partisans accused the senator of engaging in a nihilistic effort that might have felt good during the primaries and the convention but in the end contributed to the party's loss of the presidency and the Senate in the Reagan landslide. Some of Kennedy's backers disagreed, asserting that it was Carter—and specifically his economic policies, which they said caused double-digit inflation and double-digit interest rates—that lost the election.

In the wake of Reagan's victory in November, some of Kennedy's backers engaged in a bit of soul-searching. "Yes, we believed that Carter's support was soft," said Antonia Hernandez. "And yes, they were terrible to us and yes we could cite stories and chapter and verse about how we were abused by the Carter people. But it was, like, did we contribute to what eventually happened in '80?"[47] Said another Kennedy campaign official: "We knew what we had done. We lost the presidency. We got Ronald Reagan. I think those of us who participated in the '80 effort, fun though it was at the time, couldn't help but understand in retrospect that it was not a good way to win a presidential campaign."

Among those who came to that conclusion was Brown.

"He was keenly aware of it," said Alexis Herman, "and we talked about it, so much so that we would get down to the minutest details about staged walk-outs, doubts about whether Kennedy would appear on the stage that night with Carter, and all the drama that was going on behind the scenes to make sure that Kennedy was on the stage with Carter."[48]

There would be other years when Brown would contribute more directly to Democrats, accomplish more directly for candidates, gain more fame for himself as a political player. But there is little doubt that 1980 was an important milepost. The year before, he had been a black official of a civil rights organization, little known outside a small—though influential—slice of the black community. By the end of the 1980 primary campaign he had emerged as a national player. Not only had he seen the "view," as Alexis Herman termed it, he had rubbed shoulders with and gained the respect of one of the most important and powerful groups of Democrats, Kennedy's close aides. Although Kennedy lost the battle, his forces eventually won the war and took over the Democratic Party. Thus, wherever Brown turned when it came to party business in later years, he almost always found Kennedy people.

But 1980 was about more than just proving his ability and meeting the right people. For Brown, the view he saw included witnessing what a difference it made to Democrats when disparate elements of the party could be knit into a successful coalition, as he did in California. And it was about seeing what happens when ideological fervor and personal ambition are allowed to split the party. The party lost. Reagan swamped Carter in November and the Republicans captured the Senate.

These were lessons Brown would not forget.

CHAPTER EIGHT

THE PLAYER

BROWN HAD STAKED a lot on the Kennedy insurgency. Its demise now severely limited his job options. He couldn't go back to the National Urban League, where Vernon Jordan had warned him about the foolishness of hitching his career to the Kennedy bandwagon. He was approaching forty, and had spent his entire adult life working in nonprofit agencies, government jobs, and campaigns. Tracey, now twelve, had started at the National Cathedral School, where tuition ran $3,500 per year. With Michael in private school, too, and Alma's job at the Labor Department likely to disappear if Carter lost the election, Brown's money situation was not great. He was worried.

But with Kennedy in his corner in a town where networks are key, Brown's worries soon turned into expectations. Stephen Breyer, Kennedy's chief counsel on the Senate Judiciary Committee, had been nominated to the federal bench. Kennedy promised Brown that he would be Breyer's successor. The deal was that Brown would work as a consultant for the committee until the Senate confirmed Breyer, then he would take over Breyer's old job as chief counsel, one of the most prestigious staff jobs on Capitol Hill. Kennedy's promise all but wiped away Brown's anxiety.

Brown moved effortlessly into the committee staff. "Everyone thought he was a decent, nice, pleasant person who was really a pleasure to be with," recalled Breyer. "He really made you feel better about yourself."[1] Anticipating adding another notch to his belt of African American firsts, Brown felt confident enough about his future on the Hill to turn down an offer to be executive director of the Leadership Conference on Civil Rights. Though it was the top staff job for the country's leading civil rights coalition, he looked at it as a step backward. He wanted to stay in touch with civil rights work; he did not, however, intend to return to it to make a living.

But in politics, voters have a habit of ruining the best-laid plans. In this case, the Republicans, holding tight to Ronald Reagan's coattails, captured the Senate in November. Suddenly the best job Brown could hope for in the long term was counsel for the committee's Democratic minority, a less prestigious job with much less power and much less appeal.

"It was going to be an uphill battle with the Republicans controlling the Senate," recalled Breyer, who later became a justice on the U.S. Supreme Court.

"It's much different being in the minority. In the majority, you tend to set the agenda. When you're in the minority, you have to react to an agenda set by others."[2]

Brown held the chief counsel's job for a short time in late 1980, during the Senate's lame duck session after the election. He was prepared to accept the party's minority position.

But when the Senate returned in January, Kennedy stepped down as the ranking Democrat on the Judiciary Committee. The move essentially left Brown out in the cold. Kennedy did move him over to his personal staff as his staff director for a time, but it was clear to Brown that he needed to look for other work.

Brown took a deep breath, preparing to face the job market. But he did not have to pound the pavement alone. Kennedy picked up the telephone and made several calls around town to help his protégé land a job. It didn't take long for him to persuade Charles Manatt, the new chairman of the Democratic National Committee, to hire Brown as the DNC's full-time general counsel in March 1981.

To Brown's dismay, that job lasted only a few months. Manatt had neglected to tell him that he had also promised the same job to someone else. The double-dealing was not unusual for Manatt, a fast-talking lawyer from California with a reputation for telling one person one thing and then telling someone else the exact opposite. "Inside the DNC it was well known at the senior level, and Ron and I even talked about it," said Gene Eidenberg, who was Manatt's chief of staff. "If he tells you one thing today, you'd better check around and find out who else has heard something 180 degrees different because we're going to end up having to patch it up."[3] But Brown checked whatever anger he must have felt. Manatt was a valuable ally, and now he owed him a favor.

Manatt was, in fact, eager to have Brown on board in some capacity. He told Brown he would appoint him a deputy chairman of the DNC, which, despite its name, was a part-time staff position. He also told him that it was in his best interest to look for full-time work outside the committee with one of the city's big law firms. "It wasn't that I didn't want him full-time," Manatt said. "It was that I thought that at the age of forty he ought to be in the private sector."[4]

Manatt might have been following his own agenda, but Brown agreed with his logic. "I had to think about practical success as well as psychological success," Brown later said.[5] He gave both Manatt and Kennedy the go-ahead to contact Washington law firms on his behalf.

THE FIRM OF Patton Boggs & Blow did not have a long history in Washington. Its roots went back only to 1962. Under the direction of James Patton and George Blow, the firm achieved a modest level of success. Things really took

off, however, after 1966, when the original partners were joined by a gregarious scion of a Louisiana family and the man to whom Kennedy placed a telephone call on behalf of Brown—Thomas Hale Boggs Jr.

Patton came from the CIA and Blow from the wealth and privilege of the
Virginia horse country. Tommy Boggs was the son and namesake of Thomas
Hale Boggs Sr., a gregarious, back-slapping congressman from New Orleans
who rose through the ranks to become the House Majority Leader in 1971.
"My sister Barbara used to say that some people have antiques and jewelry
around the house," Tommy once said. "We had the Kennedys and Humphreys
and Rayburns."[6]

Politics seemed to run through the Boggses' blood. Tommy Boggs's great-
great-great-great-great-grandfather, Thomas Claiborne, had been elected to the
House in 1793, and he had other ancestors who served in the House from
Virginia and Tennessee. His father was a power within the Democratic Party,
and after his death in a plane crash in 1972, Hale Boggs's widow, Lindy Boggs,
succeeded him in the House. Boggs's older sister, Barbara, announced in 1982
that she would run for the House, then withdrew from that race to campaign,
unsuccessfully, for the Senate. Boggs's other sister, Cokie Boggs Roberts, immersed herself in covering politics as a radio and television journalist. Tommy
Boggs was interested enough in politics to try his hand at running for a House
seat from Maryland in 1970. He lost. "The best thing that ever happened to me
was that I got beat when I ran for Congress," he later said.[7]

The loss freed him to pursue a career influencing lawmakers rather than
trying to become one. "Interviewing with a lot of law firms, I quickly saw that
they had very little knowledge of how Congress worked," Boggs recalled. "And
in those days there were just a handful of lobbyists, anyway—virtually none in
any of those firms except for Clark Clifford—so I saw a need and I knew that
I wanted to represent companies with problems in government."[8]

In the decade following his election defeat, Boggs helped Patton Boggs &
Blow establish itself as a high-flying Washington law firm specializing in international transactions, litigation, and lobbying—especially lobbying.

"Customarily, if we have a client who has a problem with the government, we'll try to lobby the executive branch to persuade them," explained
Timothy May, Patton Boggs's former managing partner. "Failing that, we might
go to the Hill and try to get Congress to legislate what we want or put something in an appropriations bill that would prevent the agency from doing what
we don't want it to do. And failing that, we'll sue 'em. And, yeah, we've done
all three of those many, many times."[9] Big-name companies like Patton Boggs
charged their business clients for each step along the way, billing (in today's
dollars) upwards of $500 an hour for everything from creating ersatz grass-
roots organizations to making arguments before the Supreme Court.

At first, the large, traditional law firms in Washington viewed the new firm
as a pariah. There seemed something terribly déclassé about lobbying. But

Washington was undergoing profound changes in the way it did business. After Watergate exposed the public to secret backroom deals and suitcases full of money for presidential candidates, Congress was forced to diminish the power of committee chairmen and get rid of closed committee meetings where legislative horse trading often occurred. Congress also placed strict limits on the amount of money individuals and political action committees could contribute to candidates. These changes had a host of unintended consequences. A new breed of professionals rushed in to influence government: high-priced lobbyists wearing Gucci loafers and Armani suits, and representing the interests of big business. By 1980 there were more than 9,000 lobbyists in law firms that specialized in the practice.[10] There were also political consultants, direct mail specialists, media strategists, and professional organizers of so-called grassroots campaigns.

"In the old days, if you wanted a levee in Louisiana you voted for a price support program for potatoes in Maine," Boggs once told an interviewer. "Nobody knew what was going on. Now, all of a sudden, there's this tremendous need for a public rationale for every action these guys take."[11] And given the fact that the process was so public, that rationale had to be grounded in substance—or at least the appearance of it. The lobbying specialists jumped in to fill the need.

Providing lawmakers with a supposedly substantive rationale for decision making was one thing. Being able to cut through the Washington clutter to gain the attention of legislators was something else. "The substance don't do diddly-squat if you don't have the access," Chuck Fishman, a Democratic lobbyist, once said.[12] What gave the lobbyists access was money, of course, not anything so crass or stupid as direct bribes or payoffs. In Washington, "money" meant the contributions politicians needed to run their new, television-oriented election campaigns. And because of the new limits on campaign contributions, this money had to be raised differently.

"[No longer could] the Speaker of the House simply say, 'Take care of this young congressman from Texas—he's very good on your issues, Gulf Oil Company,'" Boggs explained. "Now the guy has to call fifteen thousand people to raise $1.5 million. . . ."[13]

Boggs, a rectangular-shaped man with a large head and a mass of dark curly hair, was a master at the aggressive fund-raising tactics that pulled together donations from corporate political action committees, business executives, and wealthy individuals. "Tommy Boggs practically invents a fund-raiser for someone and then he invites the member of Congress to attend," said Thomas "Lud" Ashley, a former Democratic congressman from Ohio. "There are half a dozen law firms in town that do that—raise money and lobby. . . . Either they go to the members and offer to raise money, or the member goes to them and says, 'I'd appreciate it if you will handle my Washington fund-raising,' and the collection is all taken care of for the member."[14]

As the firm's reputation as a fund-raiser extraordinaire grew, Patton Boggs and Blow's influence on Capitol Hill rose. In the 1970s Boggs helped convince Congress to provide loan guarantees to bail out a bankrupt Chrysler Corporation. Over the years, the firm's clients have read like a who's who of corporate America—American Express, Bear Stearns, the Chicago Board Options Exchange, MCI Corp., M&M Mars, the Dole Food Company, and the Major League Baseball Players Association. The silver-plated client list boosted the firm's prestige, and Boggs's ability to generate business enhanced his power within it.

Though Patton Boggs—the company changed its name in 1994, when Blow retired—was known over the years as a Democratic lobbying house, its main ideology has been making money. Boggs argued that the Chrysler bailout was needed to protect the American automobile industry from foreign competition, but the firm later turned around and represented the Automobile Import Dealers Association, a group representing Japanese car companies. "We basically pick our customers by taking the first one who comes in the door," Boggs once told an interviewer.[15]

It was no secret that Washington lobbyists, lawyers, media strategists, and other information and influence specialists earned six-figure incomes and drove expensive cars—such as Lexus and BMW—in the 1980s. Far removed from the rest of the population, white or black, they lived in tony Washington suburbs like McLean and Potomac and owned summer homes on Maryland's eastern shore or in the Blue Ridge Mountains of Virginia and West Virginia. They vacationed in Aspen and Vail in the winter and the Dordogne in the summer.

Meanwhile, productivity rates once again lagged in the 1980s. Incomes grew during the economy recovery of that decade, but almost all of the growth was concentrated among the 20 percent of the population earning the highest salaries, and much of that among the top 5 percent of earners. At a time when the average American worker still struggled, lobbyists could manipulate the public but could not empathize. They were a class separate and distinct.

When he received the call about Brown from Kennedy in the summer of 1981, Boggs was intrigued. He had seen Brown around town—mainly as a Kennedy aide—and, like most people meeting Brown, immediately noticed his assets. As a potential partner he brought a number of pluses. He knew the people on the Judiciary Committee, at least on the Democratic side. He knew his way around the Hill. He obviously was a favorite of Kennedy, who was still a power in the Senate despite the Democrats' minority status.

Topping it all, Brown was black. At the time, Patton Boggs had no black partners—indeed, there were few blacks among the high-powered lobbying firms. Given the firm's high political profile in Washington, an overwhelmingly black city, and among Democrats, who have such a large African American constituency, Boggs and other partners knew that would not do. "I would say there were a number of us around here who were very anxious to have this law firm diversify," he recalled.[16] There might have been a number of Patton Boggs partners who felt that way, but the decision to bring Brown on board was essentially Boggs's.

Brown accepted Patton Boggs's offer. It was the kind of place where he thought he could thrive. He easily identified himself with people who were successful because of brains, sweat, and charm. But these people inhabited a world unlike any, black or white, that he had known before.

"I was thirty-nine years old then, and had never practiced law, and was walking into a major law firm as a partner," he later told an interviewer. "So it was like proving yourself all over again."[17] He might have presented a facade of self-assurance to most of the partners, but Boggs himself noticed how Brown's left leg would bounce up and down on the ball of his foot while he was seated, or how he would rock up and down on his heels and toes when standing. Boggs would soon recognize these as signs of uneasiness, even when Brown's voice remained level and his face placid.

Patton Boggs could be a tension-producing place. The firm did more than pioneer a more highly aggressive form of lobbying. It was on the cutting edge of a change in the way Washington lawyers got paid. Big-time Washington law firms generally paid their partners according to the whims of their firm's executive committee. Compensation could just as well be based on office politics as on how many hours a partner actually billed. "In the old days, two or three guys would sit around in a room and decide at the end of the year how much money each partner would make," Boggs recalled.[18] Especially galling was the fact that senior partners often got a much larger share of a firm's earnings based on nothing more than their longevity with the partnership, rather than legal work performed.

At Patton Boggs, partners would receive a fixed percentage of the group's earnings based on the amount of legal work each did and the amount of business each brought in. The firm used a rigid mathematical formula that did not vary from year to year to determine each partner's yearly revenue. A partner received 38 percent of the amount he or she billed to a client for work conducted on that client's behalf. An additional 28 percent of the billing was paid to the partner who recruited the client, whether or not that partner actually did any work for that client. The formula was immutable. It applied to everyone. "If you've been here twenty years, you don't necessarily make any more money than somebody who's been here a year," said Boggs. "We don't reward people because of tenure."[19] If a partner had a good year, the sky was the limit. If he or she had a hard time finding clients, tough luck.

For the first time in Brown's career, there were no office politics or traditions of compassion to fall back on. At Patton Boggs, as the saying went, you eat what you kill. "For a bunch of liberal Democrats we surely believe in the free enterprise system," said one partner. "Socialism is not an ethic at Patton Boggs." It is the kind of law firm that attracts a particular breed of lawyer—a hungry go-getter who has more than a little confidence. This type of person does not panic if he or she has a bad year, and is sanguine enough to know that earnings will pick up the following year.

It is also a cutthroat firm. Since money could be made by generating business and not having to do the subsequent legal or lobbying work, a premium was placed on rain making. In Washington's small and clubby legal and lobbying world, where several lawyers might have a relationship with a corporation's Washington representative, it was sometimes difficult to sort out which Patton Boggs lawyer was actually responsible for bringing in a new client. Bickering between partners over who should get the credit, known at the firm as "attribution," was constant. Lawyers skilled in a particular field like taxes who actually did the grunt work would demand a share of attribution from partners who brought in the business. Those partners skilled at seeding the clouds would refuse. Those less accomplished could not afford to for fear that the client would bolt if he or she could not get the firm's top legal dog, say, in taxes or federal regulations.

So Brown, the newcomer, had reason to be nervous. None of his prior positions had connected him to the old boy network of the corporate world. Nor were large companies eager to place decisions involving millions, or perhaps billions, of dollars in the hands of a lawyer with little legal experience and few long-term relationships with members of congressional tax-writing or business regulatory committees. And there were few large black-owned businesses—let alone enough in need of legal work in Washington—to give Brown or any other black lawyer a national client base.

Still, Boggs was eager to see his only black partner succeed, and having more work and potential clients than he knew what to do with, threw business Brown's way at the beginning. "[Boggs] was only carrying on in the sense that he was principally providing the work for Ron to do," said Timothy May. "But that wouldn't be uncommon in the case of someone who comes from the government. The probability is that everybody who comes to us from the government, because they have no clients, is going to be working on some of Tom's clients when they first arrive."[20]

Among the first major clients he steered to Brown was a consortium of Japanese electronics firms. The companies were worried about a new proposal to place a tax on the sale of all videocassette recorders and blank videotapes. The idea was to compensate Hollywood producers for copies of movies that were being made by people with the videotape cassette recorders. Such copies took away a source of revenue from the sale or rental of movie videos. The movie companies also wanted to be able to place strict controls on the rental of movie cassettes from video stores, including setting the price for rental of each cassette.

A coalition led mainly by Sony and Matsushita, the two largest makers of VCRs; the Japanese Electronics Industry Association; its American counterpart; and video store owners came together to fight the movie industry proposals. But at the beginning they were being outfoxed by the movie industry—and the recording industry, which joined the battle to try to get the tax extended to audio tape players and audiocassettes. Possessing years of Washington experience, movie and recording industry lobbyists knew their way around the Hill. They could produce big-name celebrities who told star-struck lawmakers how much the American film and recording companies were threatened by videocassette and audiocassette machines, most of which were being made by that hated foreign economic rival, Japan. "They would bring in Beverly Sills, Charlton Heston, and the classic Washington celebrities," said one person involved in the coalition. "We'd have nobody but a bunch of Japanese executives who didn't speak English very well."

In near desperation, the coalition, which went by the name of the Home Recording Rights Coalition, decided it needed more experienced and more professional lobbying help. In late 1981, William Tanaka, a Japanese American lawyer who was the Electronic Industry Association of Japan's Washington representative, suggested the group hire Boggs to help with the campaign to halt the royalty on VCRs and tapes.

Boggs parceled out the account to Brown because Brown had relationships with people on the Senate Judiciary Committee, the panel that handles legislation that deals with copyright issues. Not everyone was pleased with the choice. Brown was set to travel to Japan for his first meeting with executives from the electronics company. But before he left Boggs got a call from Tanaka. Broaching the matter as delicately as he could, Tanaka suggested to Boggs that the firm send someone else. The Japanese, he suggested, were not the most tolerant people regarding race, especially when it came to the competence of black people. Boggs, probably from a mixture of being offended and a realization that if he pulled the rug out from under Brown he would probably lose his only black partner in a welter of bad publicity, told the lawyer Brown was going anyway. When Brown returned he had doubled the amount the consortium had originally agreed to pay Patton Boggs. "So they may not have liked African Americans, but they sure liked Ron Brown," Boggs said.[21]

In the ensuing nerve-fraying battle for hearts and minds on the Hill, Brown constantly counseled the coalition to define its opponents before their opponents defined them. Along with two other lobbyists, Bob Schwartz and David Rubinstein, who worked for other law firms, he provided political advice and served as go-between and conciliator. He calmed tempers, smoothed bruised feelings, and figured out who worked best with whom and who didn't.

"There was no question that Ron served as a mediator," said Nancy Buc, a lawyer who represented Matsushita. "That was his personality. He was really good at it. He was terrifically skilled at getting everybody calmed down, never getting ruffled and never giving up."[22] He was adept at it even though constant fighting within the group sometimes drove him to distraction. Buc recalled that Brown, weary of all the infighting, once left a meeting and walked around and around the block while he calmed down.

Brown held the coalition together, and the bill setting a tax on VCR and blank cassette sales was defeated. The coalition also beat back the proposal to allow movie companies to control the distribution and price of movie cassettes. The actions cleared the way for the widespread sale of VCRs in the United States, something that was not yet considered a safe bet.

COMPARED TO the Japanese coalition, the Democratic Party looked even more out of control. Brown had accepted Manatt's offer to make him a vice chairman of the Democratic National Committee, but the DNC was in shambles. Jimmy Carter had suffered a humiliating defeat. The party had lost the Senate. It was riven with internal divisions caused in part by a proliferation of racial, ethnic, and gender caucuses. Changes made in the early 1970s in the rules for nominating the party's candidate had increased the influence of minorities and women. At the same time they reduced the influence of elected officials and unions within the party, spawning anger and alienation among those groups. Bad blood still lingered between Carter and Kennedy, and those two wings of the party, distrustful and wary, felt their struggle for the soul of the Democrats would be renewed in 1984, when everyone expected that Kennedy and Carter's vice president, Walter Mondale, would slug it out for the party's nomination.

Manatt needed a staff that incorporated all the warring factions and candidates. Brown represented Kennedy. Gene Eidenberg, the chief of staff, was a former Mondale aide. Joel Bradshaw and others were close to Gary Hart, a senator from Colorado who was expected to run. Brian Lunde, another senior staffer, came out of the Kentucky organization of Governor John Y. Brown, a rising star whose wife, Phyllis George, a TV personality, gave the Democrats some much-needed glamour.

In July 1981, shortly after Brown came on board as deputy chairman, Manatt set up the party's Commission on Presidential Nomination. Known as the Hunt Commission after its chairman, James B. Hunt Jr. of North Carolina, the panel's assignment was to rewrite the party's rules. From the start, the Hunt Commission's task was fraught with risks. Complicating any effort to revamp the party's rules was the looming presidential contest. The Mondale and Kennedy camps wanted to make sure that the panel's work would be advantageous to their candidates. But more critically, the entire initiative was intended to increase the power of elected officials and union leaders. That meant diminishing the clout of minorities and women, who had only just recently gained more leverage with the party. Manatt inserted Brown into this potential maelstrom by putting the Hunt Commission under his jurisdiction.

By now Brown was seasoned at keeping all parties at a table and preventing blowups. He kept an eye out for the interests of Kennedy, his mentor, and for minorities and women. He also worked hard to come up with compromises to keep the commission from degenerating into factional squabbling, displaying a remarkable ability to anticipate objections by one faction or another even before an offending issue was raised. Whenever his gut or his political intelligence told him that a proposal was likely to be too inflammatory, Brown would come up with compromise ideas. His reasoning was that it was easier to prevent a fight before public positions were taken than afterward.

Brown realized now that the issues the commission grappled with were perennial ones. They would come up again and again. As he and the DNC staff grappled with these and other issues, Brown began to get a sense of the committee's limitations, possibilities, and importance. Impressions of what the DNC and its chairman could be were gleaned from long discussions over lunch or drinks after work with people like Eidenberg. The two men spoke of the need to build the DNC infrastructure and political expertise so that it could better help the party's presidential nominee. They talked of the importance of forging close links with Democratic congressional leaders and how Manatt, a Californian, did not have the respect of major figures on Capitol Hill. Most of all they talked about how an effective party chairman could help unify the disparate party, be a major spokesperson, and help promote the values of the party. Mostly, it was just talk between two men who weren't really in a position of power voicing ideas of what could be. Neither, especially Brown, was in any position to take any action. But ideas could be filed away for some time in the future. Who knew what could happen?

"Ron was a sponge during this period," said Eidenberg. "He was not the prime decision maker or the driver of the process. . . . But he wanted to be in that play, not because he would single-handedly rewrite the rules. He wanted to be there because it was part of his learning period."[23]

After the Hunt Commission issued its report in 1982, Brown began reducing the amount of time he spent on DNC business. The committee had been taking up huge amounts of his time, and, given the compensation structure at Patton Boggs, that meant his income from the law firm was suffering. He had to keep his priorities in order, and the paying job came first.

Brown was by no means poor. But the image of Brown as a rich, wildly successful lawyer was a myth—at least at the beginning. In 1985 he earned more than $343,000, making him one of the higher-paid partners at Patton Boggs. But prior to that came relatively lean years—by the rarified standards of big-time Washington lobbyists. According to Rob Stein, who would become one of his closest associates, Brown was making only between $200,000 and $300,000 early on. That, in Stein's view, made Brown "a guy who didn't have that much money, no real money until 1985-86."[24]

To be sure, it was a lot of money for the average person, but Brown was not exactly an average man. Like his income, his already high expenses kept rising.

In late 1981, Ron and Alma purchased a new house in a new development called Chatsworth in a predominantly white neighborhood west of Rock Creek Park. The new place was a significant step up from the old house in Shepherd Park, requiring the Browns to take out a $250,000 mortgage at a time when interest rates hovered around 12 percent. Worse yet, Ron could not sell the Shepherd Park house for some time, forcing the family to pay two mortgages for most of 1982. Big bills were, in fact, fast becoming as much a way of life for Ron Brown as they had been for his father.

By the time Michael entered college, the Browns owned two residences, including a vacation home in West Virginia. They also owned a Cadillac and a Jaguar, the latter of which was an unending source of grief and was constantly in the shop. They fancied expensive clothes. They threw lavish parties and took exclusive vacations. Ron strove mightily to keep up with his peers in both the black and white elites when it came to appearances and entertainment.

"If I'd buy a pair of Guccis, Ron would have a pair of Guccis," Boggs joked years later. "I'd buy a Hartmann suitcase; Ron would get a Hartmann suitcase. I'd get a Jaguar. Ron got a Jaguar."[25] It wasn't merely that Brown was a dandy and a social climber infused with a desire for conspicuous consumption. Friends say his spending was driven by a more practical motive.

Brown believed in the importance of projecting an image. In order to play the part of political strategist or corporate lawyer one had to look and act the part. How could he ask major corporations to take him on as their lawyer if he looked like a struggling attorney just barely hanging on in the corporate world? It was a lesson he had learned at the knee of Bill Brown, who always stressed the need of not looking "like an ordinary Negro."

"I think Ron put himself under some pressure to have his material life reflect a level of accomplishment and success that was consistent with the upwardly mobile circles he was in," said Stein.[26] Brown's well-tailored suits told the story. Most were, in fact, bought off the rack in high-end stores in New York. Brown then would take them to a talented and inexpensive tailor he found in the city who would alter them to fit him like a glove. The result: a $600 or $700 suit ended up looking like it had cost $2,000. When reporters would later notice and friends would later kid him about his expensive wardrobe, he did not disabuse them of that notion. If keeping up appearances was a struggle for Brown, he wasn't about to show it.

ANOTHER trait linked father and son, a powerful attraction to women. In 1983 as Ron was walking down one of the halls at the law firm, he almost literally ran into a woman named Nolanda Hill. It was an encounter that would lead to a thirteen-year association that enabled him to gain a greater measure of control over his finances, if not his life. Hill would become Brown's friend, business partner, financial consultant, benefactor, and, by some accounts, lover.

Years later, Hill remembered. "The first time I ever saw him, our eyes locked and that was it," she recalled. "The first time I met him we knew we had each found the other half. We became really good friends, pals."[27]

"I was madly in love with Ron, for years," she added. "And he was my best friend. He was my everything."[28] She would also almost be his undoing.

She was born Nolanda Butler in 1944 in Dallas, Texas, the daughter of a service station operator and a schoolteacher in nearby Irving, where farmers grew vegetables on the Trinity River's bottomland. She was the middle of three girls and was the favorite of her dad, Noland Butler, after whom she was named. He gave her a love of baseball and football, and taught her how to shoot rabbits, squirrels, quail, and doves on the prairie land between Dallas and Fort Worth. She learned to sing and play the piano from her mother, and in high school and college she and her sisters formed a singing group, the Butler Sisters, "the New Sound from the Old South," that performed at rodeos, church socials, and military bases, and even made some television appearances. The Butler Sisters' work sparked in Nolanda an interest in television. Nolanda felt the medium's power and potential. She also noted that all the decision makers were white men. She figured that with a combination of brains, drive, and judicious use of feminine wiles she could find a place for herself in this expanding new world. "Television is going to change the world," she remembers saying to herself. "It's got everything you need—sight, sound, motion, and stupid white men."[29]

When the Butler Sisters broke up in the late 1960s, Nolanda decided she wanted to learn about television. She read everything she could lay her hands on and got a job at a UHF station in Dallas. While working there she met and became involved with Sheldon Turner, the general manager of the station, a man twenty years her senior. In 1971 Nolanda divorced her husband, whom she had met in college, and married Turner, who taught her the intricacies of the television business. But working for a TV station was not enough for Nolanda. In the 1970s, under prodding from Nolanda, she and Turner acquired the license of a UHF station in Dallas. "UHF was just getting off the ground, and I decided that's my place right there," she said. "There's no way on this earth that a poor girl from Irving was ever going to get into the completely male-dominated, newspaper-dominated television business. And it was obvious to me that unless you were in ownership you would never get past being the babe at the front desk."[30]

As she and Turner were trying to make a go of the station, her personal life became entangled with her career. During the 1970s she hired a young lawyer named Billy Hill Jr. to represent the business. The business needed help obtaining financing, and Hill had ties to the local banking industry. In return for his help, Hill gave him a 15 percent stake in the business. She also became romantically involved with him, and in 1976 she divorced Turner to marry Hill. It was her third marriage, part of what was an emerging pattern of mixing profit and pleasure.

After years of struggling, fortune smiled on the Hills and Turner, who, despite the divorce, remained part of the station's ownership. In 1983 Metromedia Broadcasting bought the television station for $15 million. Nolanda Hill was suddenly rich and could pursue her dream of owning a television station in Washington, where she could showcase a woman's ability to make it in the broadcasting world. That year, Hill traveled to Washington for a symposium on American Women in the Telecommunications Marketplace. While there, she tagged along with her husband, who had business to discuss with his lawyer at Patton Boggs. As the two men conducted their affairs, Hill grew bored and wandered the law firm's halls—and met Ron Brown.

There was perhaps no more controversial figure in Brown's life. She has been labeled untrustworthy, a gold digger, neurotic, a habitual liar. "She used and abused Ron," said Bart Fisher, a former Patton Boggs lawyer who handled some of her legal work.[31] Friends of Brown have argued that even if she felt a romantic attachment to him, the feeling was never fully reciprocated. One thing is clear. She was able to worm her way close to him and, either from love, her ability to bedazzle, or a kind of mutual exploitation, form a bond with Brown that survived sometimes heated admonitions from his friends that nothing good would come of it. "Ron was a very astute guy, good at reading people, and he totally missed her," said one of his advisers. "It was the only thing we ever fought about."

The relationship evolved slowly. Hill retained Patton Boggs as her lawyer and, as a result, spent a lot of time hanging around the firm's offices. Proximity was key. "I was his friend before we were sexual," Hill said. There were telephone calls throughout the day, lunches when time would permit, little gifts like a book of Emily Dickinson verse. The intimacy, sexual and otherwise, did not start for several years. But when it did, she said, for the rest of his life they shared everything, not just their bodies but their inner thoughts. She said, "I knew about all his closets, his different compartments."[32] Hill insists that she gained a level of trust that was unknown among Brown's friends—and, she said, even his wife. According to Nolanda, he opened up with her, broaching subjects such as his wife, his family, his thoughts on other people (including the famous ones he worked with), his finances, and eventually his other women and his sense of himself.

"He was insecure. He was very often afraid," she said. "He had perfected—he had created—a persona that he almost took off and hung up on a hanger when he got behind closed doors, when he didn't have to be on."[33] Her view, while plausible, is impossible to confirm.

Whatever success Hill had in getting close to Brown stemmed from both her strengths and his weaknesses. She was a bright, beguiling woman who spun off an air of assured competence in a man's world. "When she's calm . . . she's a very impressive woman," said one Brown adviser. "I've been around her when she's been a very impressive woman. . . . She appeared to have an extremely bright future." But friends and associates of Brown say finances played a major role in cementing the relationship. In their own way each saw the other as a meal ticket.

OF NECESSITY, Brown was absorbing Patton Boggs's eat-what-you-kill philosophy. It was a matter of survival at the firm. Patton Boggs had no monopoly on greedy or rapacious clients. But the firm's philosophy of essentially taking on anyone who walked in the door with money meant that a share of its business was conducted on behalf of controversial figures. If a lobbyist wanted to make it big, he or she could easily end up representing some unsavory clients. Such was the case with Brown when he agreed to represent the government of Haiti in 1983.

Brown could hardly have chosen a more worrisome client. Haiti was a mass of contradictions and problems. Poor, proud, and troubled, it was the second country to gain independence from a European colonialist and the oldest independent black nation in the Western Hemisphere. At the same time it had a checkered history of brutal regimes and American intervention in its domestic affairs, including an occupation by U.S. Marines from 1915 to 1934. For more than fourteen years it had been ruled with an iron fist by François Duvalier, known as Papa Doc, who maintained power through manipulation of voodoo religious imagery and the Tonton Macoutes, a private army that brutally repressed any dissent. After his death in 1971, Duvalier was succeeded by his nineteen-year-old son, Jean-Claude, who was called Baby Doc and whose rule, while not as harsh as his father's, nevertheless stifled the development of democracy and siphoned off the aid that was meant for Haiti's poor.

In October 1983 the Duvalier government decided it needed help in Washington and hired Brown to represent it. It was to be one of the most controversial moves of his career, spawning sharp criticism from political adversaries, biting jibes from friends, and acute embarrassment. It proved impossible to explain how someone who was steeped in the civil rights movement could ethically represent one of the most repressive regimes in the Western Hemisphere.

During his lifetime Brown would say that he represented the Haitian foreign ministry, with whom he had signed the contract, and not the Duvalier family. In her book, Tracey L. Brown claimed that at the time her father was hired by the Haitian government the country received no foreign aid from the United States because of its human rights record—a fact that she said her father deplored as punishing the people for the actions of their rulers. Ms. Brown said her father tried to convince the Haitian government to improve its treatment of its citizens so that the U.S. government "would perceive it differently and be more inclined to grant aid."[34]

The assertion that Brown merely represented the foreign ministry and not the Duvalier family is a distinction without a difference. The family *was* the government. Jean-Claude Duvalier held the title of president for life and was an all-powerful figure. His authority did not somehow stop at the gates of the foreign ministry. What's more, throughout 1983 and 1984 Brown met with Justice Department officials and members of Congress to discuss the case of Franz Bennett, a Haitian citizen who had been arrested and convicted for cocaine trafficking in the United States.[35] Bennett was the brother of Michele Bennett Duvalier, Baby Doc's wife, who, according to congressional sources, was "hell-bent" on securing his release.

The claim that Brown was simply trying to get U.S. aid restored to Haiti in order to alleviate the suffering of the Haitian masses is simply wrong. American aid had not been halted at the time of Brown's hiring and would only be suspended for a few months in 1986 when the Reagan administration sought to pressure Baby Doc to step down. During Brown's time as a lobbyist for Haiti, he was able to increase U.S. aid from $38 million a year to $55 million. He argued that Haiti's record on human rights was not as bad as it seemed and the country was deserving of the aid. He also lobbied that the aid should be funneled to the Duvalier government and not through private programs, an arrangement that the Duvalier government pushed for very strongly. Channeling aid through the government, however, increased the likelihood that the funds would be diverted into the pockets of Duvalier and his cronies, rather than benefiting the people.

Brown employed his considerable knowledge of how Congress works and which arguments to use with different groups. To members of the Congressional Black Caucus and its pointman on Haiti, D.C. delegate Walter Fauntroy, Brown stressed that, while still atrocious, human rights in Haiti were improving. On the other hand, when dealing with the State Department, Brown's tack was more that of a clear-eyed legal adviser seeking ways to keep a modicum of good relations between his client and the Reagan administration. "He did not blow smoke at me and come in to see me and say, 'Gee, human rights in Haiti are just hunky-dory and there really is no problem,'" said Richard Howill, who was assistant secretary of state for the Caribbean. "He didn't come in and try to snow me with things that he knew that I clearly would not buy. It was come in and try to get an honest appraisal of what U.S. policy was, what the parameters were; ask questions that were intelligent and straightforward and could be used by him to tell his client what he probably had to do to achieve certain goals."[36]

Still, to some of those Brown dealt with, it was also clear that the Duvalier government was being less than candid with Brown, deliberately keeping him in the dark about instances of repression. Stephen Horblitt, Fauntroy's chief adviser in Haiti, recalled one meeting with Brown in which the lobbyist was asserting that the situation in Haiti was ameliorating. When Fauntroy showed him evidence of recent arrests and allegations of torture, Brown was surprised. "He was taken aback," Horblitt said. "He wasn't taken aback because we said it. It was because he didn't know about it."[37]

Brown sought to increase U.S. involvement in Haiti, organizing trade missions to the country for American corporations. These involvements could boost employment through the provision of low-wage jobs, in a country where joblessness reached as high as 50 percent. In what would be a precursor of his philosophy in later years, Brown believed that linking Haiti's economy with that of the United States would increase America's leverage on the Duvalier regime to institute political reforms. But it cannot be denied that these increased investments would also enrich Haiti's elite class, who were the owners of the country's businesses. Brown tried hard to burnish Haiti's tarnished image among American government officials and in the news media. In a report sent to Duvalier in November 1983, Brown claimed to have achieved some success.

"Despite the unfair image of Haiti portrayed by the American media, and despite the opposition expressed by some members of Congress, I can assure you that today, as never before, a growing number of people—both members of Congress and government officials—stand ready to defend the interests of Haiti," he wrote.[38] Brown also boasted that his political connections would help ensure that Haiti's position vis-à-vis the United States would improve. ". . . in order to assure the protection of Haiti's long-term interests, it is essential that we maintain good relations with presidential candidates," Brown wrote. "To that effect, while we've always maintained excellent relations with the government of President Reagan, we've set out to establish contacts with virtually all the Democratic candidates, thereby ensuring access to the White House regardless of who wins in 1984.

"My current role as deputy chairman of the Democratic National Committee has served us well in these efforts, while my contacts with my counterparts in the Republican Party assure continued access and excellent relations with the government of President Reagan."[39]

Brown was under no illusions about the people he was working for. He knew that work for a regime like Baby Doc's was, at best, a temporary affair. Sooner or later the government would be replaced, probably through a coup, or would demand of him something that he could not in good conscience do and he would be fired. He used to joke that with such an end being inevitable, timing on his part was everything. "His number one rule was he knew he was eventually going to get fired," said Bob Schwartz, a lawyer who worked with Brown on other issues in Washington and with whom he often discussed his work in Haiti. "The second rule was don't get fired while you're in the country because you might never get out."[40]

But Haiti was the source of enormous frustration as well. According to Schwartz, Brown spent a lot of time trying to convince the Haitian government to improve its treatment of the Haitian people and create enough stability to lure foreign investment. "He went on and on about if they would just get their act together a little bit politically, what a terrific place for foreign investment Haiti was," Schwartz said.

"You know that Ron wanted to do well for himself. But he also wanted to do good for people. . . . Whether he was fooling himself or he genuinely believed it—and I think he genuinely believed it—he also saw the possibility of taking a black population that had nothing and was being exploited and to actually help attract investment and things that would be of permanent value long after Duvalier was gone. That was certainly the way he talked to us about it."[41]

But Brown never had the chance to reach that goal. In late 1985, protests against Baby Doc swept across the country, presenting the most serious challenge to the thirty years of iron-fisted rule of the Duvaliers. The protests were met by a mounting police crackdown, which prompted the Reagan administration to suspend that portion of U.S. aid that was not channeled through private charitable and development organizations. Many in the country's business elite, especially those who were close to Baby Doc's father, grumbled that the son's rapacious ways—and especially those of his wife's family—were jeopardizing their standing with foreign donors, who supplied about 40 percent of Haiti's budget. For the first time the Reagan administration began to distance itself from Baby Doc. The government clearly was tottering.

Brown stepped up his lobbying in Washington, focusing almost exclusively on the issue of restoring foreign aid payments to Haiti. He received assurance from state department officials that the Reagan administration would restore aid as long as the Duvalier regime promised that aid would, in fact, be distributed, and would not be diverted into the pockets of Baby Doc's cronies.

In fact, the Reagan administration did not turn back on the aid spigot, but it didn't matter. Unbeknownst to Brown, he was at the time being used as little more than a puppet in a diplomatic shadow play, someone to draw public attention while the real drama was taking place in the dark. As the situation began to spiral out of control in Haiti, an intimate of Baby Doc made a "back channel" approach to the State Department with a deal. The dictator would agree to leave if the United States could guarantee his safe passage out of the country and a relatively comfortable exile. Fearful that the hard-liners in Baby Doc's cabinet would stage a coup if they knew he was secretly negotiating his departure, the State Department was only too happy to continue negotiations with Brown to create the impression that they had not abandoned the Duvalier government. "Anybody looking from the outside would think that the front channels were going just fine," said Howill, referring to his talks with Brown. "So we may have bent over a little ourselves to accommodate certain things in order to create the conditions under which [Duvalier] could leave."[42]

Baby Doc did, in fact, agree to depart, fleeing Haiti with his wife on February 7, 1986, aboard a U.S. military transport plane. Even after he was long gone, the youthful president for life was a millstone around Brown's neck—and, if Boggs is to be believed, around the neck of the law firm. "If we had it to do over again, had known the complications of Haiti, we would have rejected it," he later told an interviewer.[43] In that light, some of Brown's colleagues at Patton Boggs have sought to explain his representation of the Haitian government as the kind of mistake a lawyer makes in the early part of his career before a stable of more established and more respectable clients is built up. "I'm sure Ron always regretted that he took it on, too," said Timothy May, referring to the Haitian account. "But he was just getting started, and you take the clients you can when you're just getting rolling."[44]

But Patton Boggs did not reject the Duvaliers at the time. The account was seemingly a profitable one for Brown and the law firm at the time. Justice Department records show the firm billed the Haitian government more than $500,000 during the period Brown represented it. In later years, however, Patton Boggs lawyers not only say the account was more trouble than it was worth, they insist that the government of Baby Doc stiffed the firm for $60,000 in unpaid bills. Nor did Brown express much ambivalence to friends about his client. According to at least one of Brown's former friends, when the subject was broached he would dismiss it with a quip. "Socially, at parties, we kidded him about working for this butcher," the old friend said. "He'd laugh about it and say, 'Hey, he pays his bills.' "

IN 1984 yet another woman entered Brown's life and stayed. Lillian Madsen, an artist, worked in the cultural attaché's office in Haiti's embassy in Washington. Though married to a wealthy Haitian of German extraction, Madsen had moved to Washington to be near her daughter, who was attending private school in Virginia.

By any measure, Madsen was stunning to behold. The daughter of a white Spanish father and a black Haitian mother, she had clear golden skin, long flowing blond hair, light brown eyes, a petite though well-proportioned figure, a full sensuous mouth, and a gleaming smile. "They went out and they flipped for each other," said a friend of Madsen's. "He dated her till the day he died."

According to those who knew him well, Brown developed a lasting sense of responsibility toward Madsen, comforting her after her daughter was killed in a car accident in later years. He also was, according to Madsen, a kind of father figure for her son, who later joined her in Washington. "He was like a mentor," Madsen said. "He gave advice and encouragement. He was always there for him."[45]

Said one Brown intimate, "There's no question that he had an important relationship with Lillian. There was far more to their relationship than that this was just his squeeze. He had almost a family sense about Lillian." That sense of responsibility, however, would cause him immense difficulties in later years. Indeed, it would set in motion a process that brought on extreme legal difficulties and stood in the way of his achieving his ultimate dream.

Yet, even as his relationship with Madsen deepened, Brown's friends insist that he remained a loving husband to Alma and a devoted father to his children. "Alma was the queen," said a friend. "And he cherished his children." Maintaining these two emotional ties was, according to friends, a prime example of Brown's ability to compartmentalize his life, creating distinct cells in which he devoted his time, energy, and love in (perhaps) equal measure to whomever and whatever was contained in each.

AT PATTON BOGGS, it is a short leap from seeding the clouds to thinking about creating them yourself. An entrepreneurial spirit was encouraged. Patton Boggs lawyers were constantly involved in side business deals—creating and managing their own companies. Unlike other partnerships that discourage this sort of thing out of concern that all of the law firm's partners might be liable for the actions of a business owned by one of its partners, Patton Boggs took no position on this issue. Thus, many of its partners—including, ultimately, Brown—were constantly balancing their obligations to the firm with their own business deals.

"There is more of that going on there than probably any major law firm in town," said a veteran Washington lawyer. "Ron wasn't atypical. When he got there, he figured out this is the way to do it. His entrepreneurial fires were certainly stoked. You get into an environment, you often assume the contours of that environment."

Brown, however, had no experience in the intricacies of setting up and running a business. He was neither a tax nor a corporate lawyer. He was a lobbyist. He knew how to put coalitions together, to work the Hill, to schmooze and glad-hand. He knew when and where to apply political pressure points. He did not know how to set up corporations or read a balance sheet.

Nolanda Hill did, and to many people that seemed to be the hold she had on him. "She was a very smart, manipulative woman," said Stein. "She made him feel that she could make him rich while he was off doing his stuff. She could help manage his money and build his wealth. So he was indebted to her. She didn't blackmail, but she created a perception of dependency. He wasn't very smart in business. The truth is, he didn't know business. He didn't care much for the details of business."[46]

Brown discovered business opportunities mainly as a result of two factors: his political contacts and his race. He was able to parlay both into business ventures, some more successful than others. In 1984 the executives of the Public Employees Benefit Services Corporation, which went by the acronym PEBSCO and was based in Columbus, Ohio, delivered an opportunity almost too good to be true. The company administered special retirement programs for municipal workers. Though Brown had little or no knowledge of investment instruments or fund management, he had contacts with big-city mayors all over the country. As a result, he could help PEBSCO win lucrative contracts in Atlanta, Philadelphia, New Orleans, and Washington.

"That whole business is relationships, and Ron had relationships with a lot of people," said Mark Koogler, who was the lawyer for PEBSCO at the time. "You talk about this and people say, 'Okay, something's dirty here.' But that's not it at all. . . . He had the relationships with people which allowed PEBSCO to be in a position to sell themselves. . . . Then it was up to PEBSCO to prove that it should get the contract that was being bid."[47] Brown soon formed his own company called Capital/PEBSCO and entered into a joint venture with PEBSCO to market and administer these investment plans in a number of cities. He also obtained an insurance license, making him eligible to earn a broker's commission from the sale of these plans. PEBSCO would turn out to be one of the few business opportunities that Brown would ever make money on. By 1992, the year before he became secretary of commerce, Brown was making between $50,000 and $100,000 annually in dividends from Capital/PEBSCO and another $40,000 from PEBSCO in consulting fees for helping it obtain contracts with other cities.

Brown's success with PEBSCO was a direct result of various governmental affirmative action policies. As PEBSCO sought to obtain business from various cities, the company's interests were well served by Brown's contacts and by the fact that he was black. Several of the cities, including Atlanta and Washington, where Brown helped the company win contracts, required that city vendors enter into joint ventures with minority firms or have minority subcontractors. Brown's pairing of his own Capital/PEBSCO with PEBSCO also helped on that score.

"I think he saw a growing niche market that he was able to capitalize on," Koogler said.[48] There was a kind of moral symmetry in Brown's being able to help enrich himself as a black front man for a white company. Arguably, being able to capitalize on his race in getting municipal contracts was no more than compensation for the racism that kept him from getting private clients. If affirmative action simply made one already well-to-do black man that much richer, then so be it. He was probably comfortable with the thought that he, after all, had done his part for civil rights and was still supporting the cause. Others would now have to put themselves on the line to lift the downtrodden out of poverty.

As it turned out, a relatively young former lieutenant of Martin Luther King Jr. was doing just that. A preacher with a peripatetic agenda, Jesse Jackson was still making poor people his priority. In the late 1970s, while Brown was building a reputation through the Urban League, Jackson was traveling the country, appearing in dingy auditoriums in crumbling ghetto schools with a revolutionary message to young black kids—that they were worth something. He exhorted them to stop taking drugs, becoming pregnant, and dropping out of school; instead they should bear down and work hard.

"Just 'cause you were born in the slums doesn't mean the slums were born in you," he would shout, rattling the rafters and pumping up the hopes of black youngsters. Jackson's message to black kids to take personal responsibility for their own salvation excited more than just students and teachers in tough inner-city schools. News reporters and politicians alike responded to his fervor. At last a compelling black figure, other than the leaders of the anti-Semitic Nation of Islam, was speaking of black effort, not white guilt. CBS-News's *60 Minutes* ran a segment on Jackson. The federal government gave his organization more than $4.5 million in grants to take his campaign nationwide. Jackson became a national figure by using his oratory to inspire blacks to register and vote.

Along the way, he also discovered he liked political activity. Some of his aides, most notably Frank Watkins, Jackson's long-serving white acolyte, pressed him to reach for the Democratic presidential nomination. Since the passage of the Voting Rights Act of 1965, the number of black registered voters had jumped from 6 million to 10 million, largely through the efforts of groups like the Voting Rights Project under Vernon Jordan. Jackson had a ready-made constituency yearning for a way to express its pride in its hard-won accomplishments and aching to flex its political muscle. Even if he did not win the nomination, he could energize this constituency and forge it into a major bloc that Democratic Party leaders would have to heed in the future.

But Jackson found that his vision of racial pride, self-help, and solidarity was hard to sell. While grassroots voters flocked to his banner, his candidacy was not greeted with great enthusiasm among established politicians and leaders, including Ron Brown. When Jackson asked Brown to support his bid for the nomination, Brown turned him down, arguing that he could not take much time from his legal work at Patton Boggs to do much campaigning on Jackson's behalf. Brown was doing no worse than most of the black middle class and the political elite. Andrew Young, Jackson's colleague at the Southern Christian Leadership Conference, had also declined to endorse Jackson. So had Coretta Scott King, Martin Luther King's widow, and Coleman Young, Detroit's first black mayor. Most thought Jackson's campaign was a long shot, and the front-runner and eventual nominee, Walter Mondale, had a solid record on civil rights.

The failure of the country's black political elite, especially Brown, to sign on to his crusade stung Jackson. "Jesse was hurt because he knew that Ron would have lent a certain credibility to his campaign that no one else would," Representative Mickey Leland, a friend of both men, said years later.[49]

That disappointment could still be heard in Jackson's voice more than fourteen years after his 1984 campaign. "I felt those who didn't support us in '84 missed a great opportunity," he said when asked about Brown's decision not to back him. "I thought they played it safe."[50] He had a point.

For while Brown did not find time to work on behalf of Jackson, his schedule did permit him to insert himself into another political race that year.

IN 1984 Lindy Boggs faced her stiffest challenge since she was elected to Congress from New Orleans eleven years before to succeed her husband, Hale. Her challenger in the Democratic primary, Israel Augustine Jr., seemed formidable. He had been drafted to run by a group of black ministers, and he had the endorsement of the city's three black city council members. "Chuck" Augustine, as he was known, was a lawyer. He once served as legal counsel for the Southern Christian Leadership Council, where he had been friends with Martin Luther King. He had been the city's first black criminal court judge, and in 1981 he had been elected to the state court of appeals.

Augustine's strength, however, flowed from more than his résumé. It also stemmed from the changes in the district. New Orleans, like other cities, had experienced dramatic white flight from its urban core during the 1970s. As a result, black political activists had successfully won a federal lawsuit brought under the Voting Rights Act that forced the Louisiana legislature to redraw the lines of Boggs's congressional district. Blacks were now 56 percent of the registered voters in the newly configured district, and with the quiet, unassuming, and solid Chuck Augustine in the race, many political commentators predicted that 1984 would produce the state's first black representative in Congress in more than one hundred years.

Into these racial crosscurrents waded Ron Brown—to campaign in support of Boggs. Brown traveled at least once, and possibly several times—no one can recall with certainty—to New Orleans to publicly endorse Boggs and, according to some local activists, privately try to reduce support for Augustine. He met with local activists and black businessmen, and according to Clarence Barney, head of the National Urban League affiliate in New Orleans, tried to discourage them from backing the black challenger. "He represented some realities to them, playing pretty hardball, that had everyone taking a look at whether this lady who had represented us well was someone we really needed to displace," Barney said.[51]

The question of whether it is better for black people to be represented by a black freshman or an established white person with more influence and clout has been a real dilemma for years. Sincere people have come down on either side. What raised eyebrows about Brown's involvement, however, was that he had so little connection to the race. He had never lived in New Orleans.

Even Boggs's campaign manager, Terry Alarcon, acknowledged that his presence there was "unusual." By 1984 Brown had cut back his work at the DNC to concentrate on his law and lobbying work. And even so, DNC officials generally remain neutral in primary contests or nonpartisan elections, as this was, where the top contenders were both Democrats. Given Brown's dependence on Lindy Boggs's son, Tommy, to send business clients his way, it is hard to escape the conclusion that Brown's politics in this instance put personal advantage first.

This was, in fact, in keeping with Brown's actions during this period of his life. He had become a player, the type that was becoming more and more common on the Washington scene—smart, driven, politically astute, increasingly wealthy, and out for himself. In the years since he had left the National Urban League and had toiled for Ted Kennedy's beloved "cause," Brown had taken on a brutal dictator as a client, worked to defeat Louisiana's first serious black congressional candidate in nearly a century, and had at least one extramarital affair. Friends had always said that Brown had an uncanny ability to separate his actions into different psychological compartments so as to ignore his sometimes contradictory behavior. As he became more and more of a player, that ability must have been working in overdrive.

But with a man like Brown, whose life was one constant motion forward, nothing stays the same for long. In 1984, Jesse Jackson represented too much of a risk and too small a dividend for Brown's portfolio. By 1988 everything had changed.

Gilbert Dawson Brown Jr., Ron Brown's paternal grand-father. *(Charlotte Stewart)*

Nancy Nickens Brown, Ron Brown's paternal grandmother. She died when he was still an infant. *(Charlotte Stewart)*

Gilbert Dawson Brown Jr. in his later years seated during a family gathering. At right is Gloria Osborne Brown feeding the infant Ron Brown. *(Charlotte Stewart)*

A young Ron Brown along with his father, Bill Brown (right), hold two unidentified children. *(Charlotte Stewart)*

Ron Brown from the 1962 edition of the Middlebury College *Kaleidoscope*.
(Public Affairs Middlebury College, Middlebury, Vermont)

Outgoing Democratic National Committee Chairman Paul Kirk Jr. holds the hand of Ron Brown, the new chairman, after his appointment to the post in Washington. *(AP/WideWorld Photos)*

Then governor of New York, Mario Cuomo (left) joins hands with Ron Brown, chairman of the Democratic National Committee, and New York mayor David Dinkins as they announce New York City's selection as the 1992 Democratic Convention site. *(AP/WideWorld Photos)*

Ron Brown, the chairman of the Democratic National Committee, reads the paper at breakfast at the Capitol Hotel in Little Rock, Arkansas. With him is Alexis Herman, then a top DNC aide. *(Jim Estrin/New York Times)*

President-elect Bill Clinton gives Democratic Party chairman Ron Brown a hug after announcing Brown as his choice for Commerce secretary, during a press conference in Little Rock, Arkansas, December 12, 1992. *(Reuters/Jim Bourg/ Archive Photos)*

Ron Brown with South African president Nelson Mandela in Capetown during a November 1993 visit. *(Ronald Bell, Commerce Department)*

Ron Brown with children on a trade mission to Africa. *(Ronald Bell, Commerce Department)*

Members of the military stand guard at the casket of Commerce secretary Ron Brown in the lobby of the Commerce Department in Washington on Tuesday, April 9, 1996. Brown's body was laid in repose at the department before the funeral services. He was buried in Arlington National Cemetery. *(AP/WideWorld Photos)*

President Bill Clinton grieves with the family of Commerce secretary Ron Brown during a ceremony at Dover Air Force Base in Delaware, where the remains of thirty-three Americans, including Ron Brown, who were killed in a plane crash in Croatia were returned home, April 6, 1996. Seated, left to right: Clinton; Brown's wife, Alma; son, Michael; and daughter, Tracey. *(Reuters/Mike Theiler/Archive Photos)*

(Ronald Bell, Commerce Department)

CHAPTER NINE

JESSE

BEYOND THEIR race, gender, and age—they were born only sixty-eight days apart—Ron Brown and Jesse Jackson had almost nothing in common. Widely separated by class, upbringing, style, and outlook, they had traveled starkly different roads in life.

When Brown was born at Washington's Freedman's Hospital, Gloria Brown was attended by the best doctors, nurses, and medical technology available to African Americans in Washington in the 1940s. Jackson came into the world in a small, wood frame house along a dirt road in a working-class black section of Greenville, South Carolina. His mother, Helen Burns, sweated through labor on a metal frame bed in a dimly lit room, a small electric heater providing the only comfort against the chilly night.[1] Only sixteen years old and unmarried, she was urged to stifle her cries of pain so as not to alert the neighborhood that a baby was on the way. Her family's shame and embarrassment went far beyond the mere fact of the baby's illegitimacy. The baby's father, Noah Robinson, lived next door with his wife and three stepchildren. "My father wanted a man-child of his own," Jackson said later, looking back on his own conception. "His wife would not give him any children. So he went next door."[2]

Jackson spent his childhood coping with poverty and the legal segregation of the South. His stepfather, Charles Jackson, whom his mother married when young Jesse was three years old, first worked as a shoe shine attendant at the local barbershop and later as a janitor cleaning offices in downtown Greenville. Young Jesse went to all-black schools where he earned academic honors and starred as quarterback on the high school football team, gaining a football scholarship to the University of Illinois.

He felt lost and angry on the overwhelmingly white campus at Champaign-Urbana, where, he said, white football coaches, disdainful of blacks as leaders, refused to let him play quarterback. Angry over the slight, Jackson left, transferring after his freshman year to North Carolina Agricultural and Technical State University, a mostly black school in Greensboro. After graduation, he studied at the Chicago Theological Seminary and was ordained to the ministry of the Baptist Church. In 1968 he became the associate pastor of Fellowship Baptist Church in Chicago and soon after cut his teeth as a confrontational activist with Martin Luther King Jr. and the Southern Christian Leadership Conference.

Brown and Jackson had been antagonists nearly as often as they had fought side by side. In 1979 Brown had been part of a delegation of black leaders who traveled to the Middle East to show strong support for Israel and to endorse the U.S. policy of shunning contact with the Palestine Liberation Organization. Jackson, on the other hand, had argued for a policy of engagement with the group. Years later Jackson and several of his key lieutenants were still smarting from the explicit and implicit criticism they had received from black leaders—and they lumped Brown into this category—for meeting with PLO leader Yasir Arafat. "It was more of the elitist, Washington-based politics that was heavily dependent on funding from Jews," said Lamond Godwin, a Jackson intimate.[3]

Jackson had also faulted Brown for being a part of Ted Kennedy's insurgent 1980 campaign. "The Kennedy-Carter battle in the primaries helped to lay the groundwork for Reagan's victory, and Ron was in the Kennedy machinery," Jackson said. "We were on different sides in that battle."[4]

Some people in the Jackson camp blamed Brown for Kennedy's endorsement of Jane Byrne in the 1983 Democratic mayoral primary in Chicago. She was running in a three-way race against Richard M. Daley, the son of the former mayor, and Harold Washington, the black congressman from the city's South Side. It mattered little that Kennedy was repaying a political debt to Byrne, one of the few Illinois Democrats who had backed his 1980 campaign, or that he was trying to line up support in case he decided to run for the Democratic nomination in 1984. Some of the racial purists in the Jackson camp felt Kennedy should have backed Washington, the eventual winner, or stayed out of the race altogether. "That infuriated us and infuriated the black community," said Godwin. "Ron was with the Kennedy people. He was not with us. . . . I don't think he was happy about it, but I think he was like most Washington-based people—arrogant, posturing for what they thought was going to be the bigger battle between the Kennedy and the Mondale forces, and then just taking us for granted."[5] And, of course, Brown was one of a number of black officials who declined to endorse Jackson's bid for the Democratic presidential nomination in 1984.

All these differences reflected the ultimate distinction between the two men: Jackson was a political outsider leading the irregulars who were storming the citadel; Brown was one of the few blacks inside the castle keep, and he sought to make changes in more subtle ways. Jackson insists that he bore no malice toward Brown, though at times he seems to border on it. "Ron and I remained mutually respectful," he says. "We were just on different sides politically. I was not in the structure he had found a comfort zone in. I was in another structure."[6]

When Brown's and Jackson's different roads converged in 1988, it was more than just a momentary merging of two careers.

IN 1988, unlike 1984, the Democratic field had no established front-runner with long-standing civil rights credentials at the start of the primary campaign. The field was clear. Jackson began lining up the support of black leaders. He won endorsements from mayors of Chicago, Newark, Washington, D.C., New Orleans, and Oakland, as well as from a majority of the Congressional Black Caucus, including Charles B. Rangel of New York and Brown's old friend David Dinkins, the borough president of Manhattan. Black politicians had kept Jackson at arm's length in 1984. But he had run well in their cities and districts, and their doubts were overcome by the push from below. How, they were being asked by their constituents, could they justify not backing Jackson? Black politicians—and not a few white ones—comforted themselves with the knowledge that minister Louis Farrakhan, the fiery leader of the Nation of Islam who played a highly visible role in Jackson's 1984 effort, said he would not publicly support Jackson this time around. With Farrakhan, a black separatist with a history of anti-Semitic rhetoric, out of the picture, climbing aboard Jackson's bandwagon was suddenly much easier.

In May 1987, when Gary Hart, who had run second to Mondale in 1984, withdrew from the race, it left Jackson atop the polls, mostly on the basis of name recognition.

For all of the promise, his effort still had plenty of problems. As of September 30, 1987—less than two weeks before he was to formally announce his candidacy—Jackson's campaign was in debt and looked to be falling far short of the $3 million it had hoped to raise by the end of the year.[7] Jackson needed the money to hire staff and to mount a radio and television advertising blitz to move his campaign beyond his base of black voters.

The campaign also suffered from Jackson's habit of being a hands-on manager, making many of the critical scheduling, staffing, and tactical decisions himself rather than delegating them. "There is a part of him that really is a frustrated campaign manager," said Robert Borosage, who was Jackson's main issues adviser. "He likes to do the politics. So instead of the great, sweeping moral statements which we wanted him to do and he knew he should do, he always wanted to get into the nuts and bolts of the politics, which is actually not his strength."[8]

Many on the staff—if not Jackson himself—recognized that the campaign needed a veteran and respected campaign manager and campaign chairman. In late 1987 those duties were being handled by Richard Hatcher, the mayor of Gary, Indiana. "Dick Hatcher was as decent a man as has ever been in politics, but he couldn't hold it together," said Steve Cobble, who became Jackson's chief delegate counter during the campaign. "He couldn't raise the money. We were seriously in debt at the end of the summer of '87. He was too close to Jesse. He had trouble telling him no."[9]

As Jackson continued courting prominent black politicians to endorse his candidacy, he found a reluctance on the part of some to sign on unless he could assure them he would hire an experienced manager who would ensure there would be no repeat of the chaotic, shoestring effort of 1984. Willie Brown, the powerful Speaker of the California Assembly, whom Jackson wanted as his campaign chairman, was adamant on this point. "I did not want the responsibility of also trying to run the campaign," Willie Brown recalled, "and the only way to make sure that did not happen was that you had a talented staff person."[10] Jackson's lieutenants and others involved in the campaign approached several experienced political operatives, including Robert Beckel, who managed Mondale's campaign in 1984; Carl Wagner, who was Kennedy's director of field operations in 1980; and Eugene Duffy, an aide to Atlanta mayor Maynard Jackson.

In the autumn of 1987 Willie Brown and Maxine Waters, a member of the California Assembly, also approached Ron Brown. "He had the obvious skills," Willie Brown said. "He had the establishment connections, which is what the Jackson campaign needed, and he had the savvy of knowing how to run campaigns. He had worked for Kennedy and had been successful at that. He had been a party insider for a long time. And he was an African American."[11]

He was also not interested in the job. Unwilling to give up his job at Patton Boggs and fearful that he would not be able to exert influence over the mercurial Jackson, Brown spurned the offer. He did, however, agree to serve on the Jackson campaign's steering committee, and he later contributed $1,000 to the campaign. "He did not want to be in the position to try to control Jesse Jackson," Willie Brown said. "He was of the opinion that Jackson was not a part of the regular political process, and Ron wanted always to be in the regular political process. He was not about protest."[12]

Brown had reason to be concerned. Jackson was a headstrong candidate whose impromptu actions were often taken without consulting anyone. Harnessing such a wild political stallion would be difficult, and since part of Jackson's strength was in fact his unpredictability, it might even be counterproductive. Also, many of Jackson's close advisers only wanted a manager to run the office, handle fund-raising, and file qualifying petitions for state primaries. The strategic decisions would be made by the candidate and a small coterie of Jackson intimates. "We wanted somebody in a figurehead position," said Godwin. "We were always going to control the thing with an inner circle group. And Jesse runs his own campaign."[13] Such an arrangement was hardly attractive to Brown.

Brown had another reason for turning Jackson down—he didn't think the candidate had much of a chance. There seemed little point in undertaking a highly visible role for a long-shot campaign that could very well split the party along racial lines. "I think at this point Ron was not sure it wouldn't be a repeat of '84," said Alexis Herman. "We used to say in '84 that it was a crusade, not a campaign. I'm not sure he believed that this time it would be a real campaign."[14] What would be the point, Brown felt, of cutting into his legal and lobbying practice for that? "I wasn't ready to stop what I was doing to run a campaign that clearly wasn't going to win," Brown recalled. "My commitment wasn't deep enough."[15]

Brown's refusal did not sit well with Jackson. To him it was a reflection of the disdain with which Washington insiders like Brown viewed his campaign. "He didn't believe the '84 campaign was politically practical and he felt the '88 campaign would do worse than '84," Jackson said, still bitter. "He thought we had been lucky. He underestimated our campaign. He misread it. He played his cards too close to his chest because the people with whom he related most closely, they didn't believe in the campaign, didn't believe in me, were afraid of the issues that we raised."[16] Jackson never expressed such sentiments publicly at the time. He might have been miffed at Brown but he still had use for him.

Shortly after Brown's refusal, the Jackson campaign hired Gerald Austin, an experienced political operative from Ohio, who had successfully directed two campaigns for Richard Celeste, the governor of Ohio. He was a quiet and hardworking man, who Jackson's inner circle believed would stay out of the limelight and would not try to outshine the candidate. He was also white and Jewish, which would help provide an image of a racially diverse campaign. However, he had no relationship with Jackson. Indeed, he was hired by Willie Brown without ever having met the candidate.

The potential danger that could flow from this lack of any solid relationship between Jackson and Austin was lost in the glow of Jackson's surprisingly strong start. Much to the dismay of many Democratic Party professionals, Jackson as a candidate was more exciting than the rest of the Democratic field put together. His fiery oratory on the stump outclassed all others. He enthralled crowds by his passion and his ability to wield the language as a sword, deftly using down-home metaphors as a way to make complex subjects understandable to a wide audience.

But Jackson brought more than just oratorical flair. He brought an unabashed populism that scorned corporate greed, called for tax hikes for the wealthy, social spending for the poor, retraining of laid-off workers, a reduction in military spending, and a halt in the shifting of jobs out of the country. "Let's stop mergin' corporations and purgin' workers," he thundered. "Let's reinvest in America!"

In the political climate of the 1980s it was a revolutionary message and—to the country's elites—a dangerous one. It went beyond the politics of race and straight into the politics of class. The broad economic malaise that began with the oil price shocks in 1973 had been exacerbated by the quadrupling of oil prices following the fall of the Shah of Iran in 1979. The sluggish economy continued to squeeze the middle class and decimate the poor. Even as corporate profits soared during the 1980s, productivity remained flat, as did incomes when inflation was taken into account. Industries like auto, steel, and heavy manufacturing were restructuring and letting go thousands of workers. Farm foreclosures spiraled as agriculture became increasingly concentrated in the hands of a few gigantic corporations. Imports were seen as taking workers' jobs. Any significant rise in pay that occurred took place among the top 20 percent of income earners, those with college and postgraduate degrees. And even there prosperity was even more heavily concentrated among the top 5 percent. Those members of the elite like Ron Brown who sat at the table of power wielded economic and political clout far beyond their numbers.

Jackson stunned the political world with strong showings in the early races, garnering nearly 10 percent of the vote in the Iowa caucuses and the New Hampshire primary, a spectacular show for a black candidate in states with tiny African American populations.

Jackson scored well on Super Tuesday, March 8, running first or second in sixteen of the twenty-one primaries and caucuses held that day. Weeks later he shocked the Democratic political establishment by winning the Michigan caucuses with an astounding 55 percent of the vote. Suddenly people began to think the unthinkable, that Jackson might actually win.

Throughout the winter and early spring, Willie Brown privately pressed Brown to reconsider his earlier refusal to be Jackson's campaign manager. Austin would continue in his role, Willie Brown told him, but the campaign needed a Washington presence. Brown resisted the pressure, though he played an increasingly active role behind the scenes. When Patton Boggs business took him to a particular part of the country he would call the campaign to see what needed to be done—schmoozing with potential contributors, stroking politicians whose endorsements were needed, mediating between warring factions of Jackson's coalitions.

Though he was doing much better than anyone had expected, and far better than any black candidate ever, the image of Jackson as a serious contender was a mirage. Notwithstanding Michigan, his proportion of the vote was not really growing. Meanwhile, white candidates fell by the wayside. Former Arizona senator Bruce Babbitt quit after New Hampshire, as did Illinois senator Paul Simon for all intents and purposes. Super Tuesday ended the campaign of Richard Gephardt, a Missouri congressman. Tennessee senator Al Gore was knocked out in an ugly New York primary during which Mayor Ed Koch, a Gore supporter, raised the issue of Jackson's alleged anti-Semitism and declared that Jews "would have to be crazy" to vote for him. The divisive New York contest left only Jackson and Michael Dukakis, the governor of Massachusetts, in the race. There was little doubt who would win the battle.

"I recognized that after New York we were finished," said Austin. "After New York it became a two-person race. When we would get 37 or 38 percent of the vote in a three- or four-person race, we'd win. Well, now we'd get 38 percent and get beat 62 to 38. . . . Dukakis had spent his money early because he needed to be the last white guy standing. He accomplished his goal."[17]

For nervous party officials, the situation was trickier than just that. Jackson had amassed enough delegates to be a force at the convention in Atlanta. He and his constituents could make specific demands, probably changes in party rules, no doubt specific planks in the party platform. His constituents might demand that Jackson be the party's vice presidential nominee—a prospect leading party strategists believed meant certain defeat of the ticket. From the party's point of view, dealing with the expectations of Jackson's still overwhelmingly black base—blacks were still the party's most loyal voters— would require extraordinary skill in a manager. In 1984 Bert Lance, a former intimate of Jimmy Carter, had become one of Jackson's advisers mainly at the behest of the Mondale campaign, which hoped Lance would be a moderating force. Four years later the stakes were even higher. Dukakis might actually win in the general election if the party remained united, and Jackson was dealing from a position of greater power than he had in 1984. A key go-between needed to be found.

The push for an interlocutor did not come solely from nervous party professionals. Some of the more established black politicians within Jackson's camp recognized early on the potential for trouble. They felt that Austin might not have what it took to avert disaster. They also recognized the political capital that would be squandered in a fiasco.

"At some point right after Super Tuesday, Jackson and I had a conversation about the need to start having a plan for the convention," Austin said. "At that point it was based upon the fact that we would be major players and that the convention piece of this thing would be important so we ought to start planning on it immediately. He said at that time he wanted Ron Brown to run his convention operation."[18]

Selecting Brown, a Washington insider with strong ties to the party regulars, would send a powerful signal of Jackson's desire to at least consider coming into the tent and not splitting the party, even though Jackson had said he had never left. What better person to negotiate peace than a person whose ties to the Dukakis camp were about as close as his connections to Jackson's? Coming out of Massachusetts, Dukakis was surrounded by veterans of Ted Kennedy's 1980 campaign. John Sasso, Dukakis's closest political confidant, worked with Brown in 1980. Susan Estrich, another old buddy of Brown's from the Kennedy campaign, was Dukakis's campaign manager. She still talked regularly with Brown, asking his advice on a host of campaign issues. The Dukakis high command also included Jack Corrigan, another old Kennedy hand. What's more, Paul Kirk, the chairman of the DNC, who would no doubt play some role in brokering agreements between the Dukakis and Jackson camps, was another of Brown's compatriots from the 1980 campaign. The Jackson people were well aware of the Kennedy connection between Brown and the Dukakis staff and felt it would help them in negotiations. Had the Democratic front-runner been anyone else it is highly likely they would not have pushed Brown so hard to be Jackson's convention manager.

"The reason Ron Brown was selected to run the [convention] in 1988 was quite simple, because in '88 the Kennedy people [were winning] with Dukakis," said Lamond Godwin. "Massachusetts, Harvard, Boston, the Kennedy School, that crowd. Ron Brown was the top black Kennedy guy."[19]

At a fund-raiser at a Georgetown club Jackson once again approached Brown, tapping him on the shoulder as Brown was engaged in another conversation and telling him it was "time to bring the first team in."[20] Still he hesitated, spending a week telephoning party leaders, asking them whether he should take the job. The response was an enthusiastic yes. Party strategists wanted Brown on the inside of Jackson's camp to at least "control" the sometimes-obstreperous candidate. "Everybody said, not just 'Do it,' they begged him to do it," a former Kennedy aide later said.[21] On May 16, Jackson named Brown as head of his convention operation.

Why did Brown change his mind? There is little doubt that the relentless pressure from Jackson and Willie Brown probably wore down his resistance. Also by May, Jackson had proved himself to be a viable candidate and a formidable presence in the race and within the party. Never had an African American reached such political heights. There was more than pressure from Jackson and Willie Brown weighing on Brown. He had a chance to be part of history. Brown had missed the heavy action of the civil rights movement. He had missed Vietnam. He wasn't going to miss this. "It was like somehow we had broken through and that it was incumbent on those of us who had experience, who had been around the block once or twice, to step up and help Jesse in a real way," said Herman. "So I think Ron saw a historic opportunity and wanted to be part of it."[22]

He also saw a chance to help his party avoid a disaster. Brown had been down this road before. Substitute the word "crusade" for "cause." Replace the concept of having "a seat at the table" with that of "wanting our voices to be heard." Compare the idea of hard-core black support with that of bedrock liberal support, and the Jackson campaign against Dukakis was a rerun of the Kennedy insurgency against Carter eight years earlier. Brown had witnessed what a fractured convention had done to the Democratic Party's prospects in November 1980. He knew how much that had contributed to Ronald Reagan's win that year. He was determined to do what he could to make sure history did not repeat itself in 1988. "Ron was the right choice in '88 for Jackson, in part, I think, because of his 1980 experience," said a former Kennedy campaign aide who worked for Dukakis. "Nobody underestimated the costs of those kinds of fights. We had done it. We knew how easy it is once they've started for bridges to be burned. We knew how to do it. We also knew what it cost." Brown knew it well. He told his son, Michael, and his daughter, Tracey, that the reason he got involved in Jackson's campaign was because he "saw a train wreck about to happen."[23]

Nowhere was the feeling of relief felt more strongly than within the Dukakis campaign. The presumptive Democratic nominee had the most to lose from a convention full of discord. Going into the convention, Dukakis led Vice President George Bush in the polls, and the Democrats were salivating at the prospect of recapturing the White House. An ugly face-off with Jackson at the convention could jeopardize Dukakis's chances, especially since it might alienate black voters. At the same time, many people in the Dukakis camp felt that appearing to kowtow too much to Jackson would anger many white, centrist Democrats who had bolted the party in recent years. They felt that Mondale had made that mistake four years prior and that it had cost him votes among white suburbanites. "By and large, the attitude among the white folks in the Dukakis campaign with respect to anything having to do with Jesse was fear and trepidation, if not loathing, because of the simple calculation that Jackson had the ability to destroy Dukakis's chances in November," said Christopher Edley, Dukakis's issues director and one of the few high-ranking blacks in his campaign. "And they didn't have a clue—that's a bit of an overstatement—they didn't know quite how to deal with it."[24]

Suddenly, here was Brown, a known quantity to many high-ranking Dukakis people, being named as Jackson's convention manager. He was black, he was familiar to them, he was known to be "reasonable." He must have seemed like a gift from God. "I remember telling people in the campaign, 'This is a win-win. Ron is a player. Ron is a mainstream Democrat who will play a constructive role. This is really good news,'" said Edley.[25]

If Brown's appointment was greeted with relief among many in the Dukakis camp, it ironically met with dismay among some of Jackson's more radical followers. "That's Baby Doc's lawyer!" Frank Watkins, a longtime Jackson aide, recalled thinking when he heard about Brown's appointment. Brown's establishment credentials, so much a salve to Dukakis, made some people on Jackson's staff feel confused, distrustful, and even angry about having him lead their charge into Atlanta. Given the differences between their ideology and Brown's, some Jackson advisers questioned just who this guy was going to be working for. "The campaign was over and here we were at the convention deciding how we were going to come together for the general election campaign," said Godwin. "The Dukakis people, the Massachusetts crowd, send Ron as their emissary, as the guy who would get us on board and deliver us."[26]

Saving the Democrats from themselves could also help Brown fulfill the last piece of advice he had given Fernando Chavez eight years earlier—doing what you can for yourself. Brown was well aware of how much the gratitude of party regulars would boost his own political and professional career.

Tommy Boggs advised him that his work for Jackson, should it result in a peaceful convention, would further Brown's and the firm's contacts in Congress and result in more business for Patton Boggs.[27] Also, the role of the peacemaker would further Brown's standing in the party, and who knew where that could lead an ambitious party insider?

"I don't think Ron Brown would have taken the job to begin with, on reflection, unless he had an agenda in mind," said Willie Brown. "He did not take the job for money. He did not take the job for any great love of Jesse Jackson. He didn't take the job as a racial statement. He took the job as a political animal—and a political animal usually has an agenda."[28] In Brown's case, the agenda included the possibility of becoming party chairman.

Brown had actually been thinking about running for chairman of the Democratic National Committee for months—indeed, some Washington political insiders say, for years. Brian Lunde, a former DNC chief of staff, recalled lunching with Brown during 1985 when Brown politely but deftly grilled him about the latest developments inside the committee. Lunde had the distinct impression that Brown was keeping tabs on the committee's work in order to prepare himself for running for chairman of the DNC at some point in the future. Indeed, talk of a Brown chairmanship was bubbling around the DNC during the mid-1980s, at least according to Brown. ". . . there was talk about me running during the time that Kirk was chairman," Brown later said. "Every time I'd walk in this building between '85 and '88, some would say . . . 'You gonna be the next chairman?' "[29] Friends like Yolanda Caraway, who was also working in the Jackson campaign in 1988, had been urging him to seek the position long before the Democratic convention in Atlanta in July.

Right after the California primary in June, several Jackson campaign officials met at Brown's office at Patton Boggs, and a number of people raised the issue with him. Some made the point that the convention would be a showcase for Brown, heightening his visibility among party officials and political reporters, always looking for a fresh face. Should Dukakis falter in the general election, the DNC's chairman race would be wide open and, given the increased clout the Jackson forces anticipated gaining within the party, Brown would have a shot. "We have more strength than we ever had on the DNC," Steve Cobble, who kept track of delegates for Jackson during the primaries, told Brown. "You could do this,"[30] Brown said nothing in reply but leaned back in his chair and flashed a knowing smile.

At the time, such an assessment might have seemed like pure whimsy. Dukakis was leading Bush in virtually all public opinion polls, and pundits projected his lead would widen after the Democratic convention. It is generally the prerogative of sitting presidents to choose the party chairman, so if Dukakis were to win he would probably select Sasso, his trusted adviser, or maybe even persuade Kirk, the incumbent chairman, to stay on.

But Cobble and others in the Jackson camp were not convinced of the inevitability of a Dukakis win. They had taken the measure of the Massachusetts governor as a presidential candidate during the primaries and found him, and his campaign operation, wanting. By their reckoning, Jackson's strong showings in the South on Super Tuesday and in places like Michigan exposed Dukakis's weaknesses. They were not so sure he would be able to take out the presumptive Republican nominee, Vice President George Bush. "Those of us inside the Jackson campaign were not sure he was going to walk the distance," Cobble recalled of Dukakis. "We were not picking out our chairs inside the White House. We were thinking this guy could get beat."[31]

The idea of being party chair had obvious appeal to Brown. He eagerly wanted to become the first of his race to head a major political party. It would also place him at one of the power centers of American politics. But the price to be paid for the seat at this particular table was a peaceful convention. And as the summer of 1988 wore on, there were precious few signs that accomplishing that task would be a breeze.

IN THE WEEKS before and after Brown's appointment, Jackson peppered the Dukakis campaign with demands and dropped hints that the convention might be a rowdy affair. He renewed his complaint about the unfairness of the party's rules for the primaries. He grumbled that the system of selecting superdelegates—generally party regulars, such as senators, House members, governors, and mayors, who generally disliked and distrusted him—and the winner-take-all primaries meant that his number of delegates did not reflect his proportion of the vote. He scorned Dukakis—though he later muted this criticism—for not being sufficiently distinct ideologically from Bush. He and his lieutenants suggested that they would press for approval of a number of divisive platform planks like those urging tax increases on the wealthy, calling for a unilateral freeze by the United States on the development of nuclear weapons, and supporting a Palestinian state. Perhaps most ominous from Dukakis's standpoint, Jackson broadly suggested that the Massachusetts governor name him as his vice presidential running mate. "I've earned consideration," Jackson said.[32]

Jackson's demands placed Brown in a politically awkward position. Though Jackson would, by the end of the primaries, have garnered 6.6 million votes, Brown was not sure that was enough strength to force his will on the convention. The only way that could be done was by threatening to be a disruptive force in Atlanta. That, of course, would be a repeat of the 1980 convention. To avert that, some—even some of those who considered themselves Jackson's supporters—felt that Brown would have to negotiate as much with his own candidate as he would with Dukakis. "Jesse was pressing for recognition of his success at securing all those votes," said Willie Brown. "And obviously there is no room in the world of politics for that. In the world of politics either you win or you don't win. Your total number of votes don't count for very much. Jesse was convinced that they should. . . . He pressed for that, while Ron, being the pragmatic person that he was, knew that it didn't count for very much and was trying his best to interpret that appropriately for Jesse."[33] Whatever he felt about Jackson's demands, Brown, always the good lawyer, represented his client's case as best he could. There was, according to people in both camps, never a wink and a nod from Brown, never an unspoken message that Dukakis shouldn't take seriously what he said on behalf of Jackson. "I was not serving multiple masters," Brown said later.[34]

It was a job that was not made any simpler by the ineptness of the Dukakis campaign in trying to woo Jackson. Since the end of the primaries in June, Jackson had been publicly suggesting that he wanted to be in the running for the second spot on the ticket. And the Dukakis camp, fearful of alienating Jackson, encouraged Jackson in this dream, even going so far as to interview him along with other candidates for the job. It was all shadowboxing. Dukakis and his campaign strategists had no intention of selecting Jackson as a running mate, calculating that whatever he might bring to the ticket would be more than offset by defections among centrist whites, especially in the South. Brountas insists that during this vice presidential minuet he informed Jackson it was unlikely he would be on the ticket. Still, Brountas pledged that the civil rights leader would be informed personally of Dukakis's final decision. Paul Brountas, a Boston lawyer and Dukakis's campaign chairman, had told Jackson that he would not be learning the news thirdhand or from the newspapers. Someone from the Dukakis campaign would call him first. On July 12, less than a week before the convention was to begin, Dukakis named Senator Lloyd Bentsen of Texas as his running mate. But notwithstanding Brountas's promise, no one bothered to tell Jackson of the choice before it became public.

Politics is a business populated by people with prickly egos. And there is perhaps none more prickly than Jesse Jackson's. When he heard about the choice of Bentsen—from a reporter, no less—he blew up. To Jackson, making the selection without consulting him and letting it leak out before telling him were signs of disrespect, and he voiced his disappointment in starkly racial terms. "It is too much to expect that I will go out and be the champion vote picker and bale them up and bring them back to the big house and get a reward of thanks while people who do not pick nearly as many voters, who don't carry the same amount of weight among the people, sit in the big house and make the decisions," he said during one speech.[35]

Brown seemed to share Jackson's anger. He called his old friend, Susan Estrich, who was Dukakis's campaign manager, to vent and to find out how such a thing could have happened. "I had never heard Ron so mad," Estrich recalled. "He was furious. He called me just furious. How could I have done this? 'How could you guys have done this?' "[36]

Whatever the reason for Dukakis's failure to reach Jackson, Brown knew that it would make having a peaceful, unified convention that much more difficult. He stressed to Estrich that he would do his best to lower the temperature in the Jackson camp. But the price for peace had gone up. "I can't put a lid on it completely," he told Estrich. "You're going to have to give more."[37]

A few days before the convention Brown called Brountas and suggested that the two of them meet in Atlanta just prior to the convention to try to work out some of the points of contention. "Why don't you and I go down to Atlanta early?" he asked Brountas. "Why don't we get together before everybody arrives and see where we're headed and whether we can resolve differences amicably so that the party won't suffer from a split?"[38] Dukakis, who received a chilly reception when he spoke to the National Association for the Advancement of Colored People a day after the Bentsen fiasco, agreed.

Before meeting Brountas, Brown flew to Nashville to meet with Jackson. The reverend was leading a bus caravan from Chicago to Atlanta, a two-day event that irked the Dukakis camp, which felt it was done to upstage the Massachusetts governor. The bus tour had stopped for the night in Nashville. Jackson was meeting with those he liked to call the "Family"—people like Rangel; Waters; Hatcher; former Manhattan borough president Percy Sutton; and Joel Ferguson, a Michigan business executive—to plot out strategy for the convention. In preparation for the meeting, Brown had Borosage and Harold Ickes, another key staffer, draft an options memo for Jackson, laying out the range of things that could be demanded of the Dukakis campaign at the convention. The memo listed a number of things that a second-place finisher traditionally would ask for. A key demand was a prime-time speech by Jackson at the convention. According to Borosage, Jackson was not happy. "I don't want this memo out," the candidate said. "Get all the copies and tear them up. I don't want the press to see them. I don't want this to be a discussion about this stuff. I want it to be about a seat at the table. That's what the family wants, a seat at the table."[39] Others soon chimed in, agreeing with Jackson. Borosage recalled, "He wanted the discussion with Dukakis to be about being a respected person at the table helping to plan the fall campaign and that's what we should be talking about."[40]

Brown was taken aback by this outburst, and Borosage, who witnessed it, thought it was crazy. "I'm thinking this is horseshit," he said. "Let's figure out what we should ask for." But he noticed that while Brown seemed somewhat shocked and perplexed by the reaction in the room, in the end he knew who he was working for. He listened closely at what was being said and did not try to argue people out of it. "Ron was a sophisticated guy, so he endorsed the conclusion of the meeting and he kept moving," Borosage recalled.[41]

It was broiling hot on the Saturday before the convention when Brown and Brountas met in a suite at the Peachtree Plaza Hotel in Atlanta. Brountas came alone. Brown was accompanied by his son, Michael, then 23, who for the most part stayed out of the room but popped in periodically to see if the two men needed refreshments or anything else. After several hours of talking, they settled what the parameters would be for negotiations on most of the issues, just how "a seat at the table" for Jackson was defined. Notwithstanding Jackson's outburst in Nashville, they discussed items contained in the options memo Borosage and Ickes had prepared. Would Jackson get a prime-time speech? When would it be? What would he say? Would he be provided sufficient (in Jackson's eyes) money and resources during the general election campaign? How large a staff would he have? Would he have his own campaign airplane? What type? Where would he campaign? How often? Who would decide that? Who from Jackson's staff would work in Dukakis's campaign hierarchy? How much power would he or she have to make decisions? "Obviously, the requests were far more than we were willing to accept," said Brountas. "But on the other hand, we provided enough so that he could be effective if he were out campaigning for us, and we didn't want to put some straightjacket on him either and say, 'Okay, you've got to come to us with each weekly budget.'"[42] Brountas and the Dukakis camp also wanted assurances that if an agreement was reached and difficulties cropped up in the future, those problems would be worked out amicably—and in private. They wanted to make sure that Jackson would "work effectively without having all sorts of antagonistic meetings all the time."[43]

The two men left the other issues such as changes in party rules and platform debates to be worked out during the convention by other negotiators. They knew the big issues were Jackson's role at the convention and in the campaign, so that's where they focused. Brown knew there might be problems in other areas, but once he and Brountas had cut a deal on these two big issues everything else would fall into place, no matter how much incendiary rhetoric was uttered, even from him. "What was interesting to me was that, after we spent some time together and essentially agreed on a course of action, Ron indicated that I would take some heat from him publicly," Brountas said. "But the important thing to remember was what he and I had agreed on that day would actually occur."[44]

A few days later, after Jackson's bus caravan arrived triumphantly in Atlanta and Dukakis and Bentsen flew into the city, the principals met. After several hours of talks, Jackson and Dukakis essentially ratified the agreement that had been reached by Brown and Brountas. There were some minor adjustments, and Jackson, mindful of how much Dukakis needed to be seen as independent, wanted to make sure that the agreement did not look like a concession. "Now, you can't give me anything or the press will burn you," he told Dukakis. "So we have a unity convention, a unity press conference with you and Bentsen. I endorse the ticket. You say nice things about me. I say nice things about you and Bentsen. We put hard feelings aside and you don't give me anything."[45]

The script was followed to the letter. At a press conference held on July 18, the opening day of the convention, Dukakis and Jackson announced that they had reached agreement to cooperate in the general election campaign. Though the two men presented an image of unity, Dukakis avoided any commitment to include Jackson's policies in the platform or the runner-up's followers on the DNC or in a Dukakis administration. The two men said that their campaign staffs would be integrated for the fall election. But Dukakis insisted that he and Jackson were creating a "coalition," not a "partnership."[46]

There were, as Brown had predicted, some bumps that had to be smoothed out during the convention. Some were small. The Dukakis camp—either by accident or as a deliberate attempt to retaliate against Jackson—failed to provide enough passes for Jackson's supporters. They often got a hard time when it came to the signs they were allowed to bring into the hall. Some issues were larger. Intense and delicate negotiations took place over a plank put forward by the Jackson forces supporting the creation of an independent Palestinian state. There were also intense talks surrounding changes in the rules for selecting delegates to future conventions and the makeup of the DNC. Dukakis aides also were concerned about what Jackson would say in his keynote address and wanted to vet his speech. He refused. These sticking points created some tense moments between the two camps and, at times, between Jackson and Brown. "To watch Ron maneuver through all of that was always a magnificent sight," said Mario Cooper, the producer on the podium at the Atlanta convention. "It's Atlanta, ninety-some degrees, 98 percent humidity, and Ron does all this and shows up in his high-collared shirts and perfectly tailored suits. He was amazing to watch."[47]

ONE PERSON who reveled in Brown's performance in Atlanta was his father, who attended the convention. Bill, once a magnet for attention during his days as the manager of the Hotel Theresa, was now a pallid shadow of his old self. His bail bondsman business had failed. His marriage to Peggy had ended in divorce. Even the Theresa, the site of his magical years, was gone, converted into an office building.

For a time, Bill struggled to hold on to the image of a bon vivant ladies' man. Martha Lewis, who, as an attractive young woman, had been a regular at the Sunday parties hosted in Bill and Gloria's apartment at the Theresa, recalled a brief fling with him in the mid-1980s. The relationship did not last long. "I had forgotten that about forty years had passed, and, although Bill looked good, I didn't really realize he had as many health problems as he had," said Lewis. "He had had a couple of heart attacks, and was really not in good health. So we remained good friends. But the romance didn't go very far."[48]

But Bill could still live vicariously through the success of his only child. Escorted by Percy Sutton, the former Manhattan borough president and an old friend from Harlem, Bill was able to see his son at work up close. He nearly burst with pride as he watched the son he had nurtured, sent to the best schools, and launched into life become a man who had now surpassed him in nearly every way. Two months later Bill Brown would die of heart failure.

TO THE PRESS and some party insiders, the biggest victory that Ron Brown was able to win for Jackson seemed to be the end of "winner-take-all" primaries. During the primaries, Jackson was insistent that he was being cheated out of delegates by the system. He believed that his delegate tally would have been higher if delegates were awarded based on the proportion of the popular vote each candidate received. At the convention, Jackson was adamant that the winner-take-all system be junked. What Jackson—and perhaps Brown as well—did not know was that he was pushing on an open door. As a liberal reformer, Dukakis also disliked winner-take-all elections. Moreover, Dukakis and Tad Devine, a Washington lawyer who negotiated the issue for the Massachusetts governor, felt that allocating delegates proportionately actually would help an incumbent president—which Dukakis hoped to be—ward off an insurgency. "A winner-takes-all system favors left-wing or right-wing insurgent candidates," said Devine. "It allows you to win all of the delegates with a plurality of the vote. When we put this system together we were essentially insuring that if Dukakis wins the election there would be no challenge to him in 1992 . . . the big giveaway—proportional primaries—was, at the time, viewed as a huge capitulation to Jackson. It was part of this idea that we're giving up too much. In my mind we were giving up nothing."[49]

Though Brown did achieve victories for Jackson, he at times sought to limit the potential damage of some of Jackson's actions. After a deal was cut with the Dukakis camp to enlarge the DNC so that Jackson could appoint more of his supporters to it, Jackson wanted to select, among others, Jim Zogby, the leader of the Arab American Institute. The group was best known for pressing the United States to take a more evenhanded position of Middle East issues and was strongly supportive of an independent Palestinian state. Brown felt that Zogby, as one of the best-known of the Arab American activists, would attract too much criticism of the DNC from Republicans seeking Jewish votes. He asked Zogby to reconsider taking the position. "Are you sure you want to do this?" he asked Zogby. "You'll be a lightning rod."[50] Zogby caught Brown's drift. He decided to yield his seat to another Arab American activist who held the same views but had a much lower profile. When Jackson found out what had happened he was furious, but he did not countermand Brown's maneuver.

At times during the convention Brown seemed to be dancing as hard as he could, doing a waltz with the Dukakis camp and a fast tango with the Jackson forces, all the while networking for himself.

Alexis Herman recalled that one day she and Brown were chatting in his hotel suite. The subject came up of the attempt during the 1984 convention by the Mondale forces to replace the chairman, Charles Manatt, with their own man, Bert Lance. That had thrown the convention into turmoil for a short time, but the problem was finally resolved, with Manatt staying on. Who knows, Brown said, if there was a wrangle over the DNC chairmanship at this convention, perhaps someone might put his name forward as a compromise candidate.

Hearing Brown muse about seeking the chairmanship, Herman had a feeling of déjà vu. Here he was, once again entertaining the idea of running for a political position. She felt she was hearing the same blue-sky fantasizing that was the sum total of Brown's effort to run for mayor of Washington, D.C. Whimsical thoughts, not to be taken seriously.

"Yeah, right," she replied sarcastically.

Brown feigned offense at the put-down. Placing one hand on his hip and affecting a hurt tone, he asked playfully, "You don't think I could be chairman of the party? You don't think I could be chairman of the party?"

"Yeah, sure, Ron," Herman said, keeping her sarcastic tone.[51]

But it was not all fantasizing, and it was not all joking. Not wanting to wait until after the general election, the Jackson camp took a chance on getting Brown named party chairman during the convention. Kirk, the incumbent chairman, recalled that during the convention Jackson and Brown were at one point arguing for him to be dumped as party chair and replaced by Brown. The idea was resisted by the Dukakis camp, which was more than pleased with Kirk and was fearful that to acquiesce to such a demand would make Dukakis look like a weak Jackson lapdog. "They were trying to figure out what are the prices here that have to be paid," said Kirk. "This issue was put on the table and [Jack] Corrigan and those guys said absolutely no."[52] Corrigan, who served as Dukakis's field director during the 1988 campaign and was one of the chief negotiators with the Jackson campaign, also recollected that the Jackson camp floated the idea of replacing Kirk with Brown. "The way I remember it, it came up in a conversation, and we said, 'Come on, we're not going to do that,' " Corrigan recalled. "And that was the end of it. It wasn't something they pushed. Maybe it was just a trial balloon."[53] The demand that Kirk be replaced by Brown was also confirmed by a close associate of Brown's who recalled that it was "part of the negotiations."

In the end, Brown kept his faith with Jackson and his word to Brountas. The Jackson people got what they were after: increased influence within the party and changes in the rules that they felt would help Jackson should he decide to run again for president. The Dukakis camp got what it wanted: a peaceful, unified convention. The Democratic nominee left Atlanta with a huge boost and a lead of seventeen points over Bush in some polls. "People on the floor of the convention were seriously thinking about where they were going to work in the White House," said Cobble.[54]

Their optimism would not hold, however. After the convention Dukakis sat on his lead, spending weeks in Massachusetts attending to the business of state government rather than going out on the road campaigning. As a result, Bush was able to regain the momentum and come blazing out of the Republican National Convention a month later with a targeted media campaign that sent Dukakis reeling. As Dukakis saw his lead melting away during the sultry month of August, he began to lose faith in his top campaign team, including Estrich. He began to ignore the advice of his political team, avoided meeting with the news media, and isolated himself in the Massachusetts statehouse. As Estrich's influence waned and Dukakis grew more petulant, campaign officials began to search for a replacement. Among those they approached was Brown. "Ron, at that point, had a better relationship with Dukakis [than Estrich]," a former top Dukakis aide told me. "He had a better shot because he was fresh meat."

Brown declined. "He had just finished Jackson," said a top-ranking Dukakis aide. "He was burned out. It didn't surprise me that he didn't want it. I think he was smart." He was smart, some people in both the Jackson and Dukakis camps said, not only because he realized that Dukakis was becoming a difficult candidate to handle. He was also smart because he had seen the Democratic nominee at close quarters and knew the kinds of blunders he made. "Ron had the measure of this man," said a senior Dukakis official. The convention had been a triumph for Brown. Being too closely affiliated with a losing Dukakis campaign would only tarnish that glitter. Why bother? If down deep Brown felt the campaign was not salvageable, it would be better to handle the mundane assignments he might be called upon to do and wait things out.

On the Friday before Labor Day, Dukakis called John Sasso, his trusted adviser, who had been forced to resign nearly a year before. Could Sasso come back and help right the listing campaign? Sasso, who was vacationing on Martha's Vineyard, agreed to meet with Dukakis at his home in Brookline. Once there he agreed to return to see what he could do to fix things.

Near the top of Sasso's priority list was patching up the relationship between Dukakis and Jackson. "As we started to talk that weekend about what we needed to do to get back on track, having Jackson campaigning enthusiastically for the ticket was clearly one of them," Sasso said, referring to his meeting at Dukakis's home.[55] Four days after he received the plaintive call from Dukakis, Sasso met with Jackson, Brown, and Percy Sutton at the Stanhope Hotel in New York. In a stormy, four-hour session, Jackson complained bitterly that, in his zeal to win over white middle-class voters, Dukakis was not fashioning a message that would appeal to the core Democratic constituencies—minorities, working-class people, women, and the poor. The civil rights leader also angrily grumbled about the campaign's penury when it came to providing resources for his efforts. Sutton, according to Sasso, acted like a Greek chorus.

Sasso did not take the criticism lying down, firing back at Jackson for putting Dukakis—as he did Mondale four years earlier—in a difficult position. Neither candidate, Sasso said, deserved such a fate. "I watched him in two presidential campaigns, with Walter Mondale and Mike Dukakis, two men who, whatever else you might say about their strengths or weaknesses as presidential candidates, were deeply committed to civil rights, to inclusiveness," Sasso said. "And I thought that he, at times, went out of his way to make them appear weak. And I told him so, very directly."[56]

Tempers flared. Voices were raised. Whenever things threatened to get out of hand, Brown stepped in. Remember, he continued to remind them, their common enemy was George Bush. They should keep their focus on beating him, not beating up each other. At the same time he kept reminding Sasso of Jackson's importance in motivating core Democratic voters in a way that no one else in the party could. In the end, Sasso agreed to increase the amount of funds Jackson received to campaign and conduct voter registration drives. And Jackson was back on board. Brown agreed to move to Boston to be a senior adviser on the campaign, attending the daily meetings of the top Dukakis advisers, making sure there was input from Jackson in those sessions and that the reverend was kept apprised of the decisions.

"I think Ron's job was seen by everybody as making sure that the party stayed together, and he got enormous credit for it," said Cobble. "But I don't think Jesse would have picked him if he wanted to bolt. He would have picked somebody with much more edge to them who would have been much harder to deal with than Ron."[57] Both Jackson and Dukakis were political grown-ups. They knew how important peace was. But both could be stubborn and petulant, and both could easily be trapped in their obstinacy by their need to show their followers that they were not weak. Even those who understand the need for peace often need a mediator to help them achieve it.

Brown remained faithfully on task. The perception that he had momentarily saved the day was firmly rooted in the minds of many Democratic activists and in the public at large. "The '88 campaign gave him the visibility," Jackson said. "More people learned that Ron existed between June and July and then between July and November [1988] than in any previous part of his life."[58]

PART FOUR

THE DEAL

(1988–1996)

CHAPTER TEN

THE RACES
WE WIN

T UESDAY NIGHT, November 8, 1988, was a particularly dreary evening for the would-be revelers jammed into a ballroom in Washington's Capital Hilton Hotel. The crowd, mainly young, second-tier staffers from the Democratic National Committee and the Michael Dukakis campaign—the bigwigs were drowning their sorrows in Boston—as well as congressional aides, friends, lobbyists, and assorted hangers-on, sipped drinks, chatted in groups, and watched television monitors display the familiar but still-depressing news: another crushing defeat for the party's presidential nominee. Seated at a table, Will Robinson, a burly Dukakis staffer whose girth, beard, and long brown hair gave him an air more akin to a Hell's Angel than a political operative, caught sight of Ron Brown about to exit the room. Spying Robinson, Brown slid into a chair next to him.

"What d'ya got?" Brown asked Robinson, who had been monitoring vote trends during the evening. "Gimme spin. Gimme spin."

Robinson filled Brown in on the details of what was shaping up to be a forty-state blowout by George Bush over Michael Dukakis. Brown listened intently but was not satisfied. "Give me good news," he demanded. Robinson noted that the Democrats were likely to increase their majorities in both the Senate and the House and that Dukakis's tally in the Electoral College would exceed Walter Mondale's four years earlier. Keeping his voice level to mask his disappointment, Robinson noted that Dukakis had gotten a higher total of the popular vote than any of the party's recent standard-bearers. Brown nodded and left, seeking out the ubiquitous reporters and camera crews. As he rose to go, however, he casually tossed off a thought that was clearly on his mind as the news of the Dukakis defeat rolled in and was also one of the reasons he was so eager to get his face in front of television cameras that evening.

"I'm thinking of running for chair," he said. "I want to talk to you about it."[1]

Dukakis's disastrous loss provided Brown with an opportunity, just as people like Steve Cobble had predicted it would. Now he moved quickly to make the most of his chance. His desire to be party chairman stemmed from the same drive and the same yearning to play on a bigger stage that had caused him to leave the Urban League nine years before. But, according to associates, his view of the party unity he had helped forge in Atlanta was also a motivation. If he could help construct a bridge between Dukakis and Jackson and help unify the party for at least a fleeting moment at the convention, could that spirit of cooperation be infused into the structure of the party?

TEN DAYS AFTER Dukakis's defeat, the Democratic state chairmen held their annual meeting, that year at the Tapatio Cliffs Hotel in a suburb of Phoenix. Amid the Spanish tiling and yucca plants, party officials could schmooze, drink, hold regional caucuses, and, as had become their custom, wring their hands over what had gone wrong in the presidential election. So with Brown's candidacy for the chairmanship the subject of speculation in the press thanks to judicious tips he had planted among political reporters, he went to Phoenix to make the rounds, glad-handing, smiling, cajoling, gathering support for his upcoming run.

His potential candidacy was not exactly greeted with open arms. "Ron was one of the most charming people in the world and really knew well how to deal with people," said Alice Travis-Germond, a raspy-voiced, chain-smoking party activist from California who became one of Brown's close advisers. "But there was some skepticism about whether or not he was the right person for this job."[2] It was the "wrong time" he was often told.

Outside a small circle of close friends and advisers, few people in the party felt that Brown had any chance at all—and many felt the effort would do more harm than good. Brown's highly visible role as Jesse Jackson's convention manager might have won him plaudits at the time. Now it threatened to become a liability. Some political pundits noted that by virtue of his second-place finish in the primaries, Jackson was a potential force in the 1992 race for the Democratic nomination, a prospect, some argued, that would be enhanced with Brown at the helm of the DNC. The idea of Brown as a stalking horse for Jackson had a number of Democrats worried.

Many in the party felt Brown's candidacy for the DNC's top job would tear the party along its racial fault lines and call attention to Jackson's influence within the party. What was the point of going through all that for a candidate who, in the end, would probably lose? It was all downside, with no prospect of a reward in the end. "I love Ron, but he was seen as a Jackson person, and I felt the committee was not going to elect Jesse Jackson's guy," said Brian Lunde, who was to manage the campaign of Brown's chief rival for the chairmanship.[3]

Even Alexis Herman was doubtful. She had seen how difficult it was to achieve and maintain a partnership with the Dukakis campaign, and she felt that the Jackson forces were not so much accepted within the party as merely tolerated. She felt someone identified with those forces did not have much of a chance of winning the chairmanship. Herman told Brown she would help his campaign where she could, but with her own business to run she would not get fully involved in his race. "I wished him well, and I wanted to believe in my heart of hearts that it would happen," Herman said. "But I didn't think so. So I told him, 'I'll do my part by helping you raise some money to get started to let you hire staff. And then I'll let you go off on this dream chase.'"[4]

The problem, it was said, was more than Brown's race. Many polls suggested that the public had soured on liberalism. Some Democrats feared that the Republicans would have a field day pointing out that the Democrats' top official was a protégé of liberal Ted Kennedy, an acolyte of liberal Jesse Jackson, a veteran of the liberal National Urban League—and an African American to boot.

But fortune favors bold people who take the plunge when others urge delay or caution. Brown chose to not focus on race or public opinion polls. He grasped that a race for the chairmanship of the Democratic Party is not like a general election contest. Rather than having to appeal to a wide range of voters, he would be campaigning for the hearts and votes of the 404 members of the DNC, a body dominated by the liberal wing of the party. If voters had rejected left-leaning politics, the DNC had not.

Brown also anticipated a relatively weak field. Two of his opponents, former congressmen James Stanton of Ohio and Mike Barnes of Maryland, drew little support outside their home states. Southern conservatives led by Senator John Breaux of Louisiana favored James Jones, a congressman from Oklahoma. But Jones never expanded his base outside of the South. Brown's chief rival was Richard Wiener, the chairman of Michigan's Democratic Party, who had also served for four years as head of the Association of State Democratic Chairs. Well liked within the party, Wiener figured he could count on support from the state chairmen. But image was not his strong suit. A short, bespectacled man with a tinny voice, Wiener and charisma were mutually antagonistic concepts.

Observers expected the newly formed Democratic Leadership Council (DLC), a group of centrist-to-conservative Southerners that wanted to move the party to the right, would fight against Brown's candidacy. But in the midst of attempting to establish a new think tank, and disdainful of the liberal and incestuous politics of the DNC, the DLC kept its distance. "We had a point of view, but we weren't going to fall on our swords about it," said Al From, the DLC's executive director. "We got out there in 1984 and we couldn't get anybody that we wanted to even think about running. And then we thought about it and determined that even if we did, we basically had no votes on the DNC, no way to influence the race."[5]

The DLC's decision to sit out the race was also influenced by the ambivalence of one of its founders, Bill Clinton, the governor of Arkansas and the group's incoming chairman. Contemplating a run for the Democratic presidential nomination in 1992, Clinton did not want to antagonize any of the contenders in the chairmanship race whose help, or at least neutrality, he might later need. "I remember calling Clinton and him calling me back from Kentucky one night," said From. "It became very clear that he was not going to take a position on the race. . . . He made it very clear that he wasn't going to jump on the bandwagon of a candidate."[6]

But it did not escape the notice of some people that having Brown as chairman could be a way of "handling" Jackson. Blacks and other minorities had become an important voting bloc within the party. The Jackson forces had increased clout within the committee—African Americans held 78 seats, and Hispanics occupied 19 seats on the 404-member committee—thanks largely to the concessions Brown had won in negotiations at the convention. Once more, the price of admission to the table of power was, in part, Brown's perceived ability to cool out the rabble-rousing Jackson.

At one meeting of Brown's campaign strategists Steve Cobble was asked if Brown could win the race on the basis of support from Jackson alone. "No," Cobble replied. "He's going to get half the committee votes on the basis of Jackson votes. He's going to get the other half from establishment white players who think he's the one that's got to be the liaison with Jesse. He's the one who's got to tell Jesse that he can't be on the ticket in '92, if it comes to that. They'll want Ron to deliver that message, not some white guy."[7]

BROWN ANNOUNCED HIS candidacy on December 6 at the Democratic National Committee headquarters, a squat, beige building a few blocks southwest of the U.S. Capitol. Reporters gathered to hear the announcement.

He called himself an "independent, mainstream, progressive" Democrat. Then seeking to straddle the party's ideological divisions, he said, "We can, I believe, safely ignore the advice of those who tell us almost daily that we need to change the ideals, the ideas, the principles on which our party has been built. . . . One thing this country certainly doesn't need is two Republican Parties."[8]

The reporters pounced on Brown's tap dance.

"Mr. Brown, what is a mainstream, progressive Democrat?" was the first question.

"How does being a liberal relate to being a mainstream, progressive Democrat and how does that relate to getting votes?" was the second.

At that point, Brown tried to turn the discussion away from ideology and toward his ability to work with other party leaders. "Frankly, the ideology of the chairman of the party doesn't matter much," he said. "The ideological direction of the party is going to be set by the Congress of the United States—

George Mitchell, Jim Wright, Bill Gray, Tony Coelho, Tom Foley, other leaders of Congress."[9]

Brown also deflected questions about his ties to Jackson. "I am nobody's candidate. I am my own man," he said.[10] He insisted he would be neutral in the 1992 presidential nomination race; declared that he would not write off any section of the country, including the South; and estimated he already had "pretty close to 120, 130" votes on the committee.

"It's a good thing nobody asked him for a list," said Carl Wagner, his old friend from the 1980 Kennedy effort, whom Brown had chosen to manage his campaign.[11]

BROWN HAD scant time and little cash to make those numbers real and to expand upon them. First, he needed money to pay for staff, office equipment, and telephone lines; to charter airplanes and rent cars and hotel suites. Rob Stein, a Washington lawyer who worked mainly with nonprofit corporations and had known Brown from previous DNC work, signed on to help organize the finances. Fund-raisers were thrown by Patton Boggs, by a number of the firm's clients, and by other Democratic contributors.

Signaling the emergence of African American entrepreneurs as political players, fund-raisers were also put together by record industry mogul Clarence Avant; by Bertram Lee, a Washington businessman who would later become the first black to own a major sports team, the Denver Nuggets in the National Basketball Association; and by an up-and-coming black lawyer in Los Angeles named Johnnie Cochran. In all, Brown raised about $300,000 to fund his race, an extraordinary amount to compete for the votes of about four hundred people over a sixty-day span.

Normally, the DNC chairman's contest is a cloistered affair, a game of small-scale face-to-face politics in which candidates buttonhole each member of the committee individually, either in person or by telephone, and persuade him or her of their qualifications, and their ability to do the job—a kind of New Hampshire primary writ small. The DNC members—the voters in this particular election—include the chairperson and vice chairperson of the party in each of the fifty states, at-large members who are voted into the DNC by other committee members, and people who are appointed to the body by mayors, governors, senators, and House members, generally as a way to pay off a political debt to a wealthy benefactor or an interest group or a union. The committee itself has no real power. The committee staff, led by the chairman, carries out specific tasks like conducting voter registration drives or raising money. The party's platform is decided every four years by the party's presidential nominee and is ratified at the convention. As was made plain during the 1988 convention, the brokers in presidential campaigns—in that case, Michael Dukakis and Jesse Jackson—hashed out the rules for conducting primaries.

DNC members have little to do except be flown to annual meetings, where they are put up in posh hotels and have their food and drink paid for and their opinions ignored by the party professionals. Their say on who will be the chairman of the party comes only as a result of defeat. If the party's presidential nominee wins the White House, he selects the next DNC chairman. If the nominee loses, which had become habitual for the Democrats, the DNC members suddenly become important for a fleeting two-month period. In that short life span of significance, they want to be courted, and courted heavily.

This was the type of campaign in which Wiener's chief strategist, Brian Lunde, specialized. A tall, blue-eyed Kentuckian who looked like he had just stepped off the set of a 1950s sitcom set in Middle America, Lunde was the former executive director of the DNC. That put him on a first-name basis with nearly all members of the committee. He had successfully managed Manatt's and Kirk's bids for party chair. Lunde had also run the 1988 campaign of Senator Paul Simon, a political liberal from Illinois, for the Democratic presidential nomination, so he had good contact with the party's left wing. Lunde's presence, along with Wiener's ties to state chairmen, made Wiener the front-runner at the outset . . . if the contest went according to normal rules.

So, Brown and his strategists decided to change the rules. In addition to fighting mano-a-mano for each individual committee member, Brown and Wagner devised a strategy to go after endorsements from big-name governors or senators and have them put pressure on the DNC members from their states. The campaign figured out who was the dominant player in each state, whether it was the state's senator, governor, labor leader, or a member of Congress. Having established the state's kingpin, the campaign then figured out how to get to that person in a way that would not only win his or her vote but bring every one else in the delegation along. "There's no way in the world Ron was going to beat Rick Wiener with an inside campaign, not a chance," said Wagner. "The only way we were going to do it was strategically pick up the strongest political personality in their state and have them bring the whole state delegations along. . . . In essence, we made them our brokers."[12]

The strategy altered how the game was played. It was also a recognition of how much the party had changed. Power in the party no longer flowed up from the local level. It trickled down from Washington or Albany or Sacramento or Harrisburg. The days were long gone when local party bosses called the shots. By the time of the 1989 race for the chairmanship, the dependence of local Democratic leaders on senators, House members, and governors who controlled the flow of government funds from Washington and state capitals had shifted the locus of power within the party. Like Willie Sutton, Brown and Wagner decided to go where the money—and, with it, the power—was.

The campaign set up shop in a small office provided rent-free by Patton Boggs in its building near Georgetown. The campaign "war room" was on the fourth floor, a few floors below Patton Boggs's offices, so Brown could do his legal work during the day and pop down to the headquarters to strategize with Wagner, talk over fund-raising efforts, and meet with the scheduler. On evenings when Ron was in town he sat in his shirtsleeves in his law office, his left leg bouncing up and down on the ball of his foot, calling DNC members around the country, often staying until eleven o'clock to catch people on the West Coast.

The drill seldom varied. He worked his way through one of four loose-leaf binders, each representing a region of the country. Each page was devoted to an individual committee member: name, address, telephone number, connection, if any, to Brown, and other relevant information such as whether the person was a labor official, a liberal, a conservative, or a moderate. Each person was assigned a number from zero to five. Zero meant the person had publicly committed to Brown. One meant he or she would support him but was not yet ready to say so in public. Two meant the person leaned in Brown's direction. Three was uncommitted. Four, leaning toward someone else. Five, had endorsed someone else. While Brown chatted up his target, an aide sat by looking up the telephone number of the next person to be called and, as Brown finished up one conversation, placed the next call. The aide also listened intently to Brown's side of the conversation to glean hints of what the other person was saying. Brown invariably felt the chat went swimmingly, and he had to be nailed down on how far the committee member actually had agreed to commit.

"He loves me," Travis-Germond remembered Brown sunnily commenting after most calls. "I think he's going to be with us."

"Yeah," she would reply. "Now, what did he actually *say*, Ron?"[13]

Whether making his pitch to marquee Democrats or to rank-and-file DNC members, Brown deemphasized ideology and concentrated on the need to build the DNC into a first-class political operation that could elect a president in 1992. "The strategy was saying, 'Don't be worried, I'm not the wicked witch of the left. What I am is a nuts-and-bolts person who wants to build a strong party organization that can elect Democrats,'" said Mark Steitz, an operative Brown had met during the Jackson campaign and who would become a close aide.[14] Although his presentation tended to make the point, Brown also hit hard on the idea that he could be an effective, articulate spokesman for the party, a talent lacking in the low-key, sometimes dour Kirk, and one that certainly was not Wiener's strength.

Targeting the big-name Democrats, stroking the DNC members, playing down ideology, playing up strengths of style and presence: as a strategy, it all made sense. The only difficulty was that it wasn't working—at least at the start.

Getting the endorsements of top Democrats turned out to be not as easy as Ron hoped. Kennedy, whom Brown considered a key component of the strategy, waffled at first. However, after Jackson called him at Brown's behest and applied some arm-twisting, he came around. Soon thereafter former Arizona governor Bruce Babbitt, who had run unsuccessfully for the 1988 Democratic presidential nomination, declared he was for Brown. A former civil rights worker in the South and a popular governor, Babbitt's endorsement carried some cachet. But he also was looked upon in many Democratic circles as somewhat of a maverick. A lanky, deep-voiced Westerner who used to joke that he had a "face made for radio," Babbitt had run poorly in the primaries, mainly on a theme that the Federal government needed to tackle its budget deficit, a message that had fallen flat with the Democratic electorate. He also came from a small, Republican-leaning state. His endorsement was considered by some in the Brown camp as courageous, but it didn't bring much with it. Kennedy brought more prestige, but given Brown's close ties to the Massachusetts senator, his endorsement surprised no one.

The endorsements of two other big-name Democrats, Bill Clinton and Mario Cuomo, eluded Brown. The disappointment among some in Brown's camp was profound. Wagner's association with Clinton went back to anti-Vietnam War protests in 1969. But the complications of possible presidential runs overrode old relationships. "If we get Cuomo—we had Jackson and Kennedy—and if we get Clinton, we've covered ourselves," said Cobble. "Carl thought that was going to happen, and they were very dismayed when Clinton told them that he couldn't do it. I remember Carl being thunderstruck that Clinton wouldn't step forward on this. I was basically disgusted 'cause I had no personal allegiance to him. I felt, what a wimp!

"And then Cuomo did the same thing!"[15]

Cuomo said he felt signing on with Brown at an early stage would cause more speculation about his own presidential plans and could end up hurting Brown's chances. But he said he would be happy to throw a fund-raiser for his former law student. "I said, 'Yes, I'll help you, but I'll tell you, Ron, we have this problem,'" Cuomo recalled. "'If I come out and endorse you that will be bad for you. People will think I want to run for president. They'll say we're friends. They'll say I want you as chair because I want to run for president. . . . There's no point in your having that as a burden.'"[16]

BY MID-DECEMBER some of Brown's supporters felt the chairmanship was slipping beyond his grasp. Wiener issued press releases almost daily announcing two or three committee members who were climbing aboard his train, creating the impression that he was on a roll. Meanwhile, Brown's campaign refused to say how many votes it could count on. "We are within striking distance," the campaign said lamely. But Brown, ever the optimist, never wavered in his belief that the strategy would pay off in the end. "I don't think Ron ever doubted that he was going to get Kennedy, Cuomo, Bradley, and Clinton," said one of his advisers. "I think the question was when and how. I think Carl was very frustrated 'cause Carl thought it would happen sooner and easier. But it was taking longer than we anticipated."

Then the campaign got its first real breakthrough with a telephone call from Bill Bradley.

As a professional basketball player with the New York Knicks in the years before he became a United States senator, Bradley had had more experience with African Americans than the overwhelming majority of white lawmakers in Washington. He had traveled with blacks, showered with them, won with them, lost with them. He had a sense of their pride and aspirations that few whites had experienced. He also had a reasonable comfort level with the one black Democrat who seemed to be affecting everyone: Jackson.

Five months earlier, in Atlanta, Jackson had held the thousands of people in the Omni Arena and the millions who watched on television spellbound with his address to the Democratic convention. The speech was a compilation of themes and images of his standard stump speech, and his delivery at the convention was, compared to past performances on the stump, below par. But to many who had never heard Jackson up close and in extended form it was a powerful performance that solidified his reputation as far and away the best orator on the political scene. In his peroration, Jackson became deeply personal, seeking to inspire poor young blacks in the inner cities by recalling his humble origins.

"I understand," Jackson said, seeking connection. "I am the son of a teenage mother, who was the daughter of a teenage mother. I understand. I was not born with a silver spoon in my mouth. I understand.

"Born in a three-room house. Bathroom in the backyard, slop jar by the bed. I understand."[17]

Bradley, seated in the New Jersey delegation near the podium, was visibly moved. The next day he showed up at the convention wearing a red-and-white button that read "I understand."

When the Brown campaign first approached Bradley for an endorsement, the New Jerseyan gave a noncommittal reply, saying nothing more than he wanted to "think it over." He called around seeking assurances that Brown was not a radical or too tied to Jackson. Among those who gave him such assurances was Eleanor Holmes Norton, Brown's former rival for the chairmanship of the EEOC. A day or two later as Bradley sat with a group of other Democratic senators in the Senate cloakroom, the topic of the DNC race came up. Bradley became uncomfortable with the tone of the discussion. He decided at that moment that he would have to do more than just don a button.

"I remember sitting in various Senate discussions where people were talking about Brown's prospects and whether he should be the chair and I thought I was in a room of baseball owners talking about whether Jackie Robinson should join the Dodgers," Bradley recalled.[18]

Bradley contacted Brown and told him he was going to endorse him for the chairmanship. He also called the chair of the New Jersey Democratic Party and the other DNC members from his state and persuaded them to back Brown. "Bill Bradley was extraordinary," said Wagner. "Bradley was there at the starting gate with everything he had and delivered the entire New Jersey delegation for us."[19]

December must have been the month of epiphanies. As the Brown camp was digesting the good news, suddenly Cuomo changed his mind and decided to join up. He said that his road to Damascus ran through the editorial board of the *New Republic,* a right-of-center Democratic publication that is best known for its staunch support for Israel and its staunch opposition to affirmative action. According to Cuomo, at one point during a luncheon meeting with the publication's editors the discussion turned to the DNC chairmanship race and several people suggested that, because of his links to Jackson, a victory for Brown would hurt the party. Cuomo said he was incensed. Leaving the meeting, he immediately placed a call to Brown. "I've changed my mind," Cuomo said. "I don't like this. I'm not good at this—doing it, not doing it, being careful. What is that? So let's just go for broke."[20]

AT THE COMMITTEE'S Midwest regional meeting in Chicago on January 7, the Brown forces put on an impressive display of organization, the type of meticulously planned, staff-heavy effort Brown would later become famous for. Delegates, media, and others arriving for the meeting at the Hilton Hotel near O'Hare Airport were handed copies of an editorial in that day's *Chicago Tribune* endorsing Brown's bid.

The Brown campaign drew the number 4 out of a hat, meaning he would be the fourth speaker in the main hall where delegates, reporters, and others were gathered. As the managers of other campaigns stood in the back of the room listening to the candidates' remarks, David Mercer, a young African American who served as Brown's Midwest coordinator, began sending up large blocs of state delegations to Brown's suite. While the other candidates were speaking, Brown could make his pitch. Mercer hogged the only telephone in the hall, giving political intelligence to Christine Varney, a Washington lawyer who was working on Brown's campaign, or Alice Travis-Germond about the delegation that was on the way up: who needed special stroking, where the chair of the delegation stood, what was his or her relationship with the rest of the state's DNC members. Mercer's operation allowed Brown to address some delegates more than once. "So by the time he got down to the main hall he had already talked to each delegation," said Mercer. "So when he was talking in the main room, it wasn't a persuasion thing, it was more of a vision thing."[21]

After the addresses, the DNC members and others were invited to the candidates' suites for drinks and further socializing. Brown's campaign made sure there was an extra room where the candidate could bring a wavering committee member for private persuasion. "Basically, our strategy was work, work, work, work, and lower the temperature of the Southerners," said Steitz.[22]

The next day, Brown and the other candidates made their pitches before the assembled Southern chairmen at their regional meeting in an Atlanta airport hotel. Brown's presentation did not go over well. Using what had become his basic stump speech, Brown told his life story, about growing up in Harlem and his work with Kennedy. "In other places, this was helpful," said Travis-Germond. "Here it got polite applause."[23] After his remarks, the Brown entourage repaired to its suite to receive DNC committee people and other interested parties for a series of one-on-ones with the candidate. Few bothered to come. Campaign aides furiously worked the halls trying to get people to drop by for a tête-à-tête with their candidate. For the most part they failed. Brown and the staff spent several hours virtually alone amid their drinks, pretzels, and chips, at first wondering where everybody was, then engaging in gallows humor, and finally getting angry. Some Democratic activists did show up, but often they would not cross the threshold into the suite, preferring to engage in brief talks by the front door. "It was devastating," said Travis-Germond.[24] Driving home from the airport with Travis-Germond, after the Brown entourage had returned in Washington, Varney broke down in tears.

Jim Brady, the Louisiana chairman and one of the more vociferous Brown critics, does not recall people refusing to meet with Brown. But he admits that he and his colleagues did not approach the meeting in Atlanta with open minds. "Ron left disappointed that he was not able to sell himself," he said. "I think he may have even perceived that he didn't get a fair enough opportunity. Maybe too many of us went in there with closed minds against him. There's probably some truth to that. But I don't think anyone treated him unfairly there. We may have gone in there with one opinion and came out with the same opinion. We didn't sway."[25]

True to form, Brown did not lose his temper in front of his staff. Instead, he tried to make them feel better by relating the tale of being refused service at a Virginia restaurant on his way to Fort Eustis back in 1963, and by maintaining his eternal optimism. "He tried to comfort those around him and say, 'Look, I've gone through this before, it's okay,'" said one of his associates. "This is not going to get in the way. I've dealt with this all my life, and it's never held me back and it won't now." But back in Washington, amid his black friends, with whom he tended to feel more comfortable, his anger came out. "They don't want to give me a fucking chance," one friend recalled him railing.

Brown wasn't the only one having difficulties with Southerners. Wiener was running into major problems on both sides of the Mason-Dixon line. As he saw Brown's strategy of picking up endorsements from high-profile Democrats starting to bear some fruit, Wiener attempted to emulate it. But the Michigan chair did not have the power of personality to win over big-name

Democrats, particularly since his own governor, James Blanchard, wouldn't endorse him. "It killed him," said Lunde. "People said, 'If you're so good, why isn't your own governor for you?'"[26]

One reason was that labor—or, more specifically, the United Auto Workers, the key institution in Michigan's Democratic politics—was also not for Wiener. And, once again, the influence of a prominent African American was a key ingredient. Among the emerging powers in Michigan's Democratic Party was Joel Ferguson, a wealthy black business executive who owned several television stations, apartment houses, and office buildings—and was a member of the DNC. Ferguson had run Jackson's victorious campaign in the 1988 Michigan caucuses. He was also a longtime friend of Brown who had known the candidate from when Brown worked for the Urban League. Ferguson used his influence to arrange a meeting between Brown and Frank Garrison, president of the Michigan AFL-CIO. Impressed by Brown, Garrison then convinced Owen Bieber, head of the United Auto Workers Union, a major power in Michigan politics, to back Brown. Bucking the two biggest labor leaders in his state was not something Blanchard felt he could do. As a result the governor never publicly endorsed Wiener.

Wiener also faced equally acute problems in the South. At the beginning of the race, the chairs of the states of the old Confederacy had, through a series of conference calls, decided that they would endorse a candidate only as a bloc. The idea had been cooked up by the chairmen of Alabama, Florida, Louisiana, and Texas as a way to maximize their influence with the incoming chairman when it came to the allocation of resources for the next presidential race.

But the Southerners couldn't agree on which of the DNC candidates to back. Bob Slagle, the affable chairman of Texas's Democratic Party, supported Wiener, while others, including Brady, were behind Jones. Committed to unite behind someone but unable to agree on whom, the Southern chairmen just sat there, a large, unmovable mass that helped slow Wiener's momentum and gave Brown—the candidate most of the Southern chairmen did not want—time to gather more support. "We started out of the blocks with massive DNC numbers, and every day there would be a new telegram come in our mailbox—four new members endorse Wiener, the next day eight, the next day five," said Lunde. "He had the momentum thing going. . . . But we knew a couple of things others didn't know. The Southern bloc; we knew we were going to ram up against that wall at some point, and sure enough we did."[27]

On January 17, eight days after the Southern chairmen's meeting in Atlanta, Lunde sent Brady a confidential memo stating that he believed only Wiener or Brown could be elected, and imploring the Southerners to back Wiener. "After six weeks of active campaigning, Jones, Barnes, and Stanton are not competitive," Lunde wrote.[28] In Lunde's view, the dithering by the Southern chairmen was keeping alive the hopes of some candidates—particularly

Jones—who had no chance. Also, the endorsement of Wiener by the Southern chairs would help bring on board moderate Northern governors like Evan Bayh of Indiana and Bob Casey of Pennsylvania. "They were using the Southerners as an excuse while they tried to figure out their politics," Lunde said.[29]

In his memo, Lunde also alluded to the racial implications of the Southerners' failure to unite behind any candidate. "There is little doubt that the longer [S]outhern leaders delay a commitment to Rick Wiener, the more likely they will be seen as a stop Brown movement," Lunde wrote. "This, in turn, could escalate national press attention on the election and increase tension within the committee."[30] Lunde's pleadings had no impact. The Southerners couldn't decide. "The problem was some of those Southern chairs didn't think Rick could win," said Slagle.[31]

The inertia of the Southerners and failure to win the support of Blanchard were fatal to Wiener's campaign. With the Michigan chair stuck, and Jones, Barnes, and Stanton not generating any enthusiasm, Brown's candidacy, which had looked like a long shot only a month before, was starting to seem more viable. "We hit a wall probably I'd guess forty votes short of what we needed, maybe fifty," said Wiener. "We had far more than anybody else had walking in, but not enough to get there."[32]

Lunde's prediction about moderate Northern governors soon came to fruition. Shortly after Lunde sent his memo, Brown met with Pennsylvania governor Bob Casey in a motel in Alexandria, Virginia. Casey did not know Brown, and his politics were much closer to those of Jones's than to Brown's. But he was considering an endorsement on the basis of a recommendation from James Carville, a consultant who had managed Casey's two gubernatorial campaigns (and would later be one of Bill Clinton's chief strategists in 1992). "I was largely relying on what Carville was telling me, having had confidence in his judgment," Casey recalled.[33] The two men talked for the better part of an hour, mainly about the direction of the party, the need to avoid factional differences, and invariably Jesse Jackson. "The Jackson phenomenon had been a very difficult thing to deal with," Casey said. "African American voters had always been a natural part of the coalition, and there was some tension there. Brown was an obviously skillful and resourceful and adroit person. I felt he would be in a position to moderate some of the positions between the Jesse Jackson wing of the party and the more centrist faction. I felt he would be a stabilizing influence."[34]

Brown's rivals had other explanations for Casey's movement toward Brown. For some big-name Democrats, the DNC chairmanship race was a throwaway bone, an endorsement that was of no great importance since, at that time, few people considered the committee itself of much relevance. But these Democratic figures were aware of the symbolic importance many of their black constituents would place on an African American's gaining the position. So some leading Democrats no doubt figured, why not support

Brown? "We were told—and this may not be fair to Ron—but there was a sense, especially in Bradley's case, and also in Casey's, don't you guys understand, these guys get to do their black thing with Ron," said Lunde. "We got that from Casey's staff people. Don't you guys get it? He's fixing his black problems in Philadelphia."[35]

Whether Lunde's view is an accurate one, or merely the rationale of a losing campaign, the Casey endorsement helped place another important brick in the wall of support that Brown was erecting. The Pennsylvania governor was the Democratic Party's most visible anti-abortion spokesman. Though Brown was himself solidly pro-abortion rights, getting Casey's backing allowed him to further his case that he could build bridges between those in the party with wildly different positions on important emotionally charged issues.

A JANUARY STORY in the *Jewish World* newspaper posed the question, "Will Jews remain comfortable in their traditional political home, the Democratic Party? . . . Centered around Jesse Jackson's presidential bid last year, that question is resurfacing as Ronald Brown, a former Jackson campaign strategist, is trying to win the chairmanship of the Democratic National Committee . . ."[36] Perhaps nowhere within the Democratic coalition was it more important for Brown to build bridges than between himself and Jews. If he could not show viability among this mainstay of the Democratic left wing whose financial support of the party was critical, his claim to be a unifying candidate would fall flat. Throughout the race, the theme of a potential schism between blacks and Jews was a staple of both the mainstream and the Jewish press. The fact that Wiener was also Jewish further inflamed the passions surrounding the race.

The Brown camp picked up reports of a "whispering campaign" among some politically active Jews that if Brown was elected they would stop contributing to the party. The rumors infuriated some people in the Brown campaign. "It was a horrible, racist, disgusting thing to be saying," said Rob Stein, "and it was wrong. I viscerally knew it was wrong."[37] When they first got wind of the sub-rosa denigrations, Brown and his strategists debated how they should respond. Some of his advisers argued that they should get a number of prominent Jewish leaders to hold a press conference supporting Brown and denouncing those spreading the stories of impending Jewish defections. Brown nixed that strategy. In his view, a public show of Jewish support would only inflame the issue. Reporters would start asking other prominent Jewish leaders where they stood on the Brown race. Some Jewish opponents with legitimate policy differences with Brown might draw denunciations or demonstration from blacks, and Brown would be asked to respond. A public fight could easily widen the very racial split that Brown said he could bridge.

Instead, he counseled that a better strategy was holding quiet, private meetings with influential Jewish Democrats in strategic places like California.

If they were impressed with him, they would tell their friends. It was only natural, and he would ask them to. And their friends would tell their friends. And so on. It wasn't a large universe that you had to influence. Word of mouth could do it. "Ron said there's only one way to deal with a whispering campaign," said a campaign aide. "You whisper back." Brown's response also stemmed from his nonconfrontational style and his unwillingness to publicly show anger. "He had the most inhuman threshold of anger I've ever seen," Stein said. "This was like any problem, any challenge to be overcome. . . . The man just said, 'Figure it out. Let's figure out how we're going to deal with this.' "[38]

Through friends in the Jewish community, Stein set to work on organizing a series of meetings with prominent Jewish leaders to both allay their fears and to get financial support. The contributions were less important, Brown and his strategists figured, than the fact that some major Jewish donors were comfortable enough with the candidate to back him financially. "What we wanted to do initially was to get some checks in so that we could say, if we had to, those [reports that Jewish donors would withhold money] are crazy, we're getting support from important people in the Jewish community," Stein said.[39]

At the same time, Steve Grossman, a businessman from Boston who was a prominent Democratic fund-raiser and a leader of the American Israel Public Affairs Committee, a major pro-Israeli lobbying group, had also heard the whispers. Grossman, who did not know Brown, nonetheless feared a black-Jewish split within the Democrats and decided to find out more about him. He called both Kennedy and Cuomo. "Tell me about Ron Brown," he asked. The recommendations he got from both were sufficient for him to speak with the candidate for forty-five minutes by telephone. During the call Brown related his past trips to Israel, declared he was not a stalking-horse for Jackson, and laid out his ideas for revitalizing the party. Grossman was convinced. He wrote Brown a check for $10,000 and promised help in contacting Jewish opinion leaders and some of the Jewish members of the DNC.

"I felt that after forty-five minutes we knew each other, that we both were very much in synch in terms of what the party needed and how important it was to end this adversarial relationship that had grown up during the '88 campaign," Grossman recalled. "That was something Ron was dedicated to working to overcome. I was struck by how clear it was that he was the right person to do it by virtue of his life experiences and how unfair and grotesque it was that a small group of people, for reasons that had nothing to do with reality but had to do with perception, had begun this whispering campaign."[40]

Grossman and other Jewish leaders contacted Stanley Hirsh, president of the Jewish Federation Council of Greater Los Angeles, to set up a meeting with Brown and prominent Jewish leaders in Los Angeles the next time Brown was out there. "Ron was a formidable salesman," said Hirsh, who brought together ten leaders of the Jewish community in Southern California to meet Brown for breakfast at his private club. After the meeting, Brown asked Hirsh how it went. "You hit a home run," he replied.[41]

A FEW DAYS after he announced that he was running for the chairmanship, Brown met with Rochelle Horowitz, the political director of the American Federation of Teachers (AFT), at the Washington Court Hotel to sketch out his ideas and solicit her support. Labor leaders, like many other Democratic activists, were in a sour mood following the 1988 loss. The Dukakis campaign not only had blown a large lead, it had ignored both them and the DNC political machinery that labor had helped to fund. Though the labor movement had only 41 seats on the 404-member DNC, its clout with Democrats far outweighed those numbers. Labor is the only large institution that is a consistent backbone of the Democratic Party. Though the party would later seek to gain more political contributions from rich individuals, which usually meant wealthy business executives, it was labor that provided the financial underpinnings of state and local parties, supplied workers for campaigns, and paid for many "independent" expenditures—television campaigns, telephone banks, and get-out-the-vote efforts.

To party activists, especially labor, the Dukakis campaign came to symbolize the arrogance of presidential campaigns in general. The national committee's essential function was to help raise money and to put on a national convention. Once the nominee was crowned, the party apparatus was cast aside by a presidential campaign that felt it knew best. "That would have been fine if they had won," said Joan Baggett, political director of the Bricklayers Union. "But they didn't win, and people felt very burned by the process."[42]

Brown understood the frustration. Over breakfast with Horowitz, he made the pitch that under him the DNC and the party mechanisms would not be thrown overboard the next time around. "Ron was very insistent that he was going to be elected chairman and that he was going to serve a full four-year term and that any presidential candidate would know that he was going to be chair during the general election," said Horowitz. "He was going to prepare the party for the general election and it was not going to be thrown aside."[43]

Horowitz was excited by the vision that Brown had outlined. But when she returned to her office later on she received a sober reminder of how difficult it might be to put Brown into a position to carry it out. "The first conversation I had I remember saying, 'Ron Brown's going to run for chair,'" Horowitz recalled. "And the person said, 'What! He's representing Jesse Jackson!'"[44]

In addition to Horowitz and Baggett, Brown picked up the support of officials of other unions, like the Communication Workers of America and the America Federation of State County and Municipal Employees, that were powers within the Democratic Party. The trade unionists set about trying to figure out how to gain Brown the endorsement of the AFL-CIO. That goal was not easy. The building trades unions, including bricklayers, carpenters, plumbers, and others, backed Stanton, and John Perkins, the powerful director of the AFL-CIO's Committee on Political Eduation, the federation's political arm, quietly supported Wiener. "At the time he met with me I figured he had a less-than-even chance of getting the chairmanship and a less-than-even chance of getting the support of labor," said George Gould, the political director of the National Association of Letter Carriers, whom Brown tried to woo.[45]

Figuring the way for Brown to dispel the preconceived notions some labor people had about him was for them to view him up close, Baggett, Horowitz, and the others convinced the AFL-CIO leadership to set aside a day when the political directors of a number of powerful unions would be able to meet with all the candidates person-to-person. "Wagner said to me at one point, 'isn't it wonderful to have a campaign where you don't have to worry about your candidate embarrassing you,' " said Horowitz. "That was true about Ron. You never had to program him. You never had to worry that there would be some silly gaffe. He'd walk into a room and he'd leave it with more people supporting him than did when he arrived."[46]

Even with Brown's impressive showing in his interviews with political directors, Brown's labor allies still had to convince the Political Works Committee, a body made up of the heads of the sixteen most politically active unions, to back him. Given the opposition from Perkins, who wielded considerable influence within the AFL-CIO, that was not a sure thing. The committee's endorsement was crucial since AFL-CIO president Lane Kirkland had already determined that the organization as a whole would follow the committee's recommendation. Knowing of Perkins's opposition, Brown's supporters hoped that, at best, the Political Works Committee would opt to not support any candidate, as seemed likely.

On the morning the committee met, Perkins confidently told Wiener that labor would stay neutral in the race. "We didn't have a majority [on the committee]," said Horowitz. "We never had a majority. We had, at best, five out of sixteen unions. And even if you added up the numbers we didn't have it by membership. So what some of us figured would be the best thing to do was prevent anybody else from getting the endorsement."[47]

That was not good enough for Brown, however. He wanted to create an impression of his candidacy as an unstoppable juggernaut. That would force his rivals from the race. A decision by the Political Works Committee to remain neutral would not do that. Only an endorsement would. He instructed his allies to press the committee to make a decision.

The committee met on January 11. Albert Shanker, the president of the American Federation of Teachers, could not attend the meeting, so Horowitz went in his place. The discussion lasted several hours. Horowitz noticed that the Brown supporters, like herself and Gerald McEntee of American Federation of State, County, and Municipal Employees (AFSCME), were making a forceful presentation. "The others were not strong," she recalled. "Some people were for Wiener, some were for Jimmy Jones. But it was only the Brown supporters who knew why they were doing it."[48] Luckily for Brown on the day of the committee meeting, the building trades unions, which were opposed to Brown, were having their annual convention in Florida, and with the exception of Jack Joyce, head of the bricklayers' union, none of their leaders bothered to show up. Joyce made his pitch, but "one person presenting the case for the building trades against Ron Brown and for Stanton was not nearly as heavy as if there were five or six building trades national union presidents sitting at the table," said McEntee.[49]

The lack of strong support for any other candidate appeared to carry the day. Kirkland interrupted the discussion to say that he "sensed" that there was a consensus for Brown and thus the committee would recommend his endorsement. The committee never took an official vote. Horowitz was stunned. She and McEntee looked at each other, unsure how to respond. "We just said, 'Okay,' and the other people didn't protest," Horowitz said. "They didn't say no."[50]

Horowitz rushed to call Wagner at Brown's campaign headquarters. "I was hysterical," she recalled. "We all were astounded. I think he made me say it to him three times. Ron has been endorsed by the AFL-CIO!"[51] Wagner reached Brown at the airport in Indianapolis, where he was holding a meeting with aides to Governor Bayh. Wagner kept his message short and to the point: "You've got it. You've just won it. You're the party chairman."[52]

LABOR MIGHT HAVE clinched it, but there was still an endgame. Barnes quit a week after the AFL-CIO endorsement and threw his support behind Brown. Jones, sensing the race slipping away, approached Wiener with a proposal that the two of them share the position, that Jones would be the overall chairman, while Wiener would actually run the DNC. Wiener turned him down. Finally, Jones sent members of the DNC an Evans and Novak column that played up Brown's connection with Jackson. Another piece of campaign literature carried a black-and-white picture of Jones's face on the front, cropped at midforehead and mid-nose, leaving his light eyes and pale skin as the only visible features. The effect of the photograph was to identify him only as a white man. "How will our party be perceived?" read the caption.[53]

James Baker, the chairman of the Alabama party, was asked by a reporter what he would do if Brown was elected. "You can't secede from a national party, but frankly, I would," was the answer.[54]

Such a racially charged sentiment evoking the Civil War stunned Brown. "Do you believe this?" he asked his friend Alexis Herman when he read the quote. "Man, it's only the DNC chair. You'd think I was running for president of the country."[55] For someone who said he was well acquainted with racially insensitive conduct, Brown could display a remarkable naiveté, according to some of his friends. It allowed him to see racism only in the abstract or as something that burdened other people. When he felt its brunt, he was genuinely surprised. "Ron knew there was racism in the world," said Horowitz. "But, every so often, when it got turned against him, he would be shocked. It would be, 'My God, he did it to *me.*'"[56] Some Southerners laughed off Baker's remarks. "The Southern chairs thought that was pretty outrageous," said Slagle. "I don't know of any of them who thought that it wasn't nuts. And they certainly didn't want to be associated with it."[57]

One person who was affected by the comment was Wiener. Sensing that he had no chance to win, and seeing that the race was taking an ugly turn, he decided he would bring it to a close. "I sat there thinking, I'm capped; I'm not moving," said Wiener. "I've got one or two things I can do. I can either try to ride fears based on statements like that, see if I can win it anyway and probably not be successful. Or I can do the right thing. And the right thing for me at that point in time was to bring closure to the race."[58]

Before he withdrew, Wiener had one last ploy. His campaign approached Breaux, Jones's biggest patron in the South, and told him that if Jones didn't get out of the race in the next twenty-four hours Wiener would drop out and endorse Brown. The deadline came and went and the Wiener camp heard nothing. "I wanted him to get out because he couldn't win and I could," Wiener said. "But he was absolutely convinced that if he was still standing at the end he was going to win."[59]

On January 25, a little more than two weeks before the DNC was to meet in Washington and fifty days after Brown had announced his candidacy, Wiener withdrew from the race and threw his support behind Brown. Stanton quickly followed suit, and on January 30 Jones pulled out, still warning that the party was too much in the control of northeastern liberals who had backed Brown. "The Democratic party could go the way of the British Labor Party unless we make some very fundamental changes in our message and in our image," he said in departing.[60]

On February 9, 1989, the Democratic National Committee met in Washington and unanimously elected Brown chairman. The world's oldest political party, whose roots went deep in the slaveholding and segregationist South, and the same party that, since the mid-1960s, had been in the forefront of the fight for black equality, had become the first major political party in a Western democracy to be headed by a person of color. Dressed in his traditional dark suit, white snap-collar shirt, and expensive tie, his smile as bright as the gold cuff links he wore, Brown noted in his acceptance speech this latest advancement of a people and a country. "There is no need to dwell on, but we cannot ignore, the history of this moment," he said. "In choosing the first American of

African descent to lead one of America's major political parties, you have made history.

"I know some people are wondering just what kind of history we made," he went on. "Let me speak frankly. I did not run on the basis of race, but I will not run away from it. I am proud of who I am. And I am proud of this party, for we are truly America's last, best hope to bridge the divisions of race, region, religion, and ethnicity. Our strength is our diversity, and so is America's."[61]

Brown went on to remind those who had chosen him that they had not merely made a symbolic gesture, a feel-good vote in the name of racial pride or white guilt. He would and should be judged not on the basis of color and precedent but by performance and results. He had no doubt what the evaluation would be.

"The story of my chairmanship won't be about race," he said. "It will be about the races we win over the next four years."[62]

This race displayed the tactics he would employ as the DNC's new chairman: a well-thought-out strategy, a clear-eyed assessment of his strengths and weaknesses, a well-executed plan that still allowed for improvisation, the gathering of solid professionals, and the development and articulation of a solid message. With unerring optimism, luck, and a strong belief in himself, Brown had prevailed even when friends, enemies, pundits, and political wise men said he could not. As he coasted to victory in the final weeks he could not help being satisfied with what he had accomplished—for now.

"I remember when it was clear he was going to win, he loved teasing me," said Alexis Herman, who had dared to doubt her friend. "He loved telling me, 'Told you so. Told you so.' "[63]

CHAPTER ELEVEN

SUCH A BLOODY MESS

I N THE DAYS following his election, Brown was all over the news. He was interviewed on the weekday morning television news programs, made the rounds of the Sunday morning talk shows, and was profiled in a raft of flattering newspaper and magazine articles. It was a stunning amount of press coverage for a chairman of a political party's national committee. Prior to Brown it had taken months of cajoling and pleading by the DNC senior staff to get one of the Sunday public affairs shows to interview Paul Kirk or to book a speech to the National Press Club for Charles Manatt. Brown was different, a star from opening day.

"There's no question that being chairman of the Democratic National Committee is a lot more important than it was three months ago," Brown said, assessing his sudden fame. "A lot of people didn't care much about it before. People certainly didn't know who the party chairman was before. I think everybody around the world knows who the party chairman is now."[1]

Race, obviously, made a difference. Black pioneers still made good news copy—a testament to how little progress blacks had made in breaking into the top echelons of society. In some ways, Brown was the Jackie Robinson of American politics, bringing bona fide skills and charisma to the field. He also filled a void for the Democrats. With Michael Dukakis defeated, the party had no acknowledged leader. The Democrats' congressional leaders—House Speaker Jim Wright and Senate Majority Leader George Mitchell—were virtual nonentities outside Washington and their home states. Ted Kennedy had withdrawn from the national spotlight, and the only other potential Democratic superstar, New York governor Mario Cuomo, remained a relative recluse in Albany, far away from the media spotlight. Handsome, telegenic, with a ready smile and a quick wit, Brown seemed perfectly suited for television. With the rest of the party leadership seeming to be all gray men in blue suits, Brown cut a dashing figure. While others seemed to melt into the TV studios' backdrops, Brown exploded off the screen.

He was, as always, keenly aware of his image. Even before the DNC election, but when his ascension to the DNC chairmanship seemed assured, *Time* magazine decided to make him the subject of a major profile. The article was to be written by Walter Isaacson, a rising star at the magazine who would later become its managing editor. Brown cooperated fully, giving Isaacson loads of time and access. The story, slightly edgy but overwhelmingly fawning, was all set to go for the January 30 issue. There was, however, a problem with the main photograph.

A few days before the story closed, Brown met Neil Leifer, one of *Time*'s most creative photographers, in Rock Creek Park for what was supposed to be a photo shoot for the main portrait. It was a bright, sunny winter day when Brown pulled up in his car at the designated spot in the park, hopped out, and was greeted by the sight of Leifer, his lighting gear set up, standing next to a tethered donkey. He calmly told Brown of his intention to shoot the incoming chairman of the Democratic Party atop the beast.

"Let me get this straight," Brown said to Leifer. "You want me to sit on that donkey? No way, not a chance."[2]

Motorists zoomed by on Rock Creek Park's winding road, on their way to work or to visit the monuments downtown, as Leifer drew on his power of persuasion to convince Brown, dapper in a conservatively cut suit and white shirt with his signature collar pin, to hop aboard a donkey. None of the pleadings worked.

"Neil, this is an important post," Brown told him. "I don't want to do anything that could be interpreted as being undignified. I'm happy to cooperate. But I'm just not going to do it." Referring to the new chairman of the Republican National Committee, Brown said, "When you show me a picture of Lee Atwater squeezing an elephant's balls, I will get on that donkey."[3] Leifer finally gave up and found an alternative. He posed Brown at the entrance to the Supreme Court, standing between two large white columns. The photograph bespoke a kind of strength and endurance and placed Brown in a setting of established power. Brown loved the shot. So did his family.

Brown needed to be nimble in his dealings with the press. Reporters relentlessly threw tough questions at him, and even if the questions became somewhat familiar, they never became comfortable. What did he think his election meant for race relations? How would he unify the party? Was he a stalking-horse for Jesse Jackson? One set of questions presaged queries that would relentlessly dog him later in life. Noting his lobbying work at Patton Boggs and the fact that he had been a registered agent of foreign governments, *Washington Post* reporter David Broder asked Brown, two days after his election, how he would deal with this potential conflict of interest and whether he would sever his ties to his law firm. "I'm doing exactly what every other chairman of a national party has done in recent years, including the most recent chairman, Frank Fahrenkopf, of the Republican National Committee," Brown shot back. "I would expect to be judged by the same standard that others have been judged by."[4]

The idea of Brown's allegedly profiting from public and political office, and his demand that his business dealings be viewed in the same way as those of his white contemporaries, lingered in the air throughout his time at the DNC. He could not have been surprised. Brown was a smart enough student of the Washington environment to know that the city's landscape had been radically altered since the Watergate scandal fifteen years earlier. The fame accorded Bob Woodward and Carl Bernstein, two *Washington Post* reporters whose early coverage of the Watergate break-in had led to the toppling of President Richard Nixon, had spawned a more aggressive press that salivated at the thought of knocking off the high and the mighty. Where reporters had been much more indulgent of the financial, ethical, and sexual transgressions of politicians in the past, they now engaged in a serious game of "gotcha," seizing on the slightest hint of impropriety and relentlessly hammering the alleged miscreant. Brown now had a seat at the table, but along the way the room's décor had changed. A prying, assertive press corps now occupied a permanent place in the corner, ready to jump on anything that suggested wrongdoing, large or small.

He might have been aware of the new climate, but attitude and economics argued against giving in to the notion that he should quit Patton Boggs and concentrate solely on his job at the DNC. Others before him had not done it. And with an annual salary of only $65,000 from the DNC chairmanship, he could ill afford to give up his legal practice. Also, while others might have tempered their behavior, anticipating intense media scrutiny, Brown was unwilling to give his detractors any signs of doubt or weakness. He maintained his supreme faith in his ability to talk his way out of trouble. He adored press attention. But he could not bring himself to, in his view, grovel for it, or even modify his ways to get it, something his friends felt angered the press all the more.

"He had this willingness to stand up to people and not to give in, which pissed people off, especially the elite press in this town, who always thought he was an unsavory character," said Mark Steitz. "When they started calling him unsavory he didn't immediately say, 'Oh, I'm so sorry, oh, I'm so sorry, oh, I'm so sorry.' He said, 'Go fuck yourself; I'm as good as you are.'"[5]

Brown suspected white reporters of engaging in a racial double standard. No doubt some did. But such a view only helped blind him to the need to be more careful in his business dealings. Publicly, Brown avoided whining that he was being picked on because he was black. "For the most part he reacted with a resolute confidence that there was just nothing to [allegations of impropriety]," said Mario Cooper, the DNC's deputy chief of staff. "And . . . he always wanted to be careful not to fall into the trap he often thought African American leaders fell into, which is blame everything on racism. He did feel he had done nothing that was out of the ordinary, nothing wrong, and certainly what was done was in line with previous chairmen and people of his stature who happened to be white."[6]

Make no mistake about it, Brown was eager to taste whatever material benefits came with the job. A few days after his election he met with Paul Kirk, his predecessor as chairman, for a briefing. It was Brown's first opportunity to question the outgoing chairman on matters such as finances, personnel, and other issues surrounding the job. But those were not the initial things Brown asked about. "What are the perks?" Kirk recalled Brown asking. "Are there any clubs you get to join?"[7] The questions stunned Kirk, who suddenly became worried about the future of the DNC. He obviously did not know about the third leg of the advice that had been conveyed to Fernando Chavez years before during the Kennedy campaign: make sure you do well for yourself.

There were deals that would raise eyebrows later on. In December 1988, in the midst of his campaign for the chairmanship, Brown was part of a group of black investors who paid $42 million to purchase WKYS, a local Washington, D.C., radio station, from NBC. The group's company, Albimar Limited Partnership, was a partnership whose major stake was held by Albimar Communications, Inc., a corporation founded by Bertram Lee and in which Brown owned a 10 percent share. At the time of the purchase of WKYS, the federal government maintained a program that gave tax breaks to companies that sold radio or television stations to minority companies. By selling WKYS to Albimar, NBC saved about $15 million in federal taxes. There was nothing illegal about the deal, but once again it highlighted the two sides of affirmative action. By giving such a tax break to the seller the government gave NBC enough financial leeway to extend a $10 million loan to Albimar for the transaction. Arguably, the program allowed black investors, who were notoriously short of capital, the ability to play with the big boys when it came to buying radio and television stations. But it was another example of an affirmative action program benefiting African Americans with means, in this case Lee and his partners, including Brown. Lee had also raised funds for Brown.

Hard questions about Brown's ethics, however, lay in the future. His immediate concern was figuring out how to meet the one standard by which any DNC chair is judged: winning the White House.

HIS FIRST DAY on the job, Ron Brown gathered the DNC staff into the committee's large conference room on the first floor. His mantra was the presidency. Important mileposts, mainly the congressional elections of 1990, had to be passed. But it was the 1992 presidential election that he wanted the staff to think about every day. "Ron was very clear, from day one," said Steitz. "He wanted to do one thing and one thing only. He wanted to elect a president."[8]

Considering the circumstances, Brown's confidence seemed little more than school yard bravado. History had not smiled upon the Democrats recently. The party had lost five out of the previous six presidential elections, their longest losing streak since the Civil War. At the presidential level, where voters tend to voice their opinion of a party's overall philosophy, the party was mired among the high 30 or low 40 percent of the voters. Only Jimmy Carter in 1976 was able to break the losing streak—and just barely, eking out a win with 50.1 percent of the popular vote.

Many political pundits pronounced that the Republicans had a "lock" on the Electoral College. The South, once a bastion of Democratic strength, now seemed cemented in the Republican column in presidential elections. Combined with traditional Republican strength in the Rocky Mountain states and strong Republican states like Indiana and New Hampshire, the GOP could virtually count on 219 of the 270 Electoral College votes needed to elect a president. Making things even more tricky for an African American chairman, a number of pundits and party insiders argued strongly that the Democrats' problems were bound up in race. In short, they believed the party was too closely identified with black people.

When Lyndon Johnson signed the landmark 1964 Civil Rights Bill he is reputed to have said that he had just lost the South for his party. Twenty-two years later his prediction seemed to have proved all too true. With the exception of Carter in 1976, no Democratic presidential candidate had carried the once solidly Democratic South since Johnson in 1964, primarily because of the defection of white Southerners. But the exodus of whites from the Democratic Party was not just a Southern phenomenon. Since Johnson, no Democratic nominee for president—again, with the exception of Carter in 1976—had been able to capture as much as 40 percent of the white vote nationwide. Studies were pointing to the principal reason for this loss of white support: white voters were beginning to view the Democratic Party as too beholden to minorities, principally blacks. Whether the issue was busing to achieve school integration, affirmative action that involved giving blacks preference in employment or college admissions, welfare, or crime, whites seemed increasingly to see the Democrats as giving away the store to blacks. And it was whites who made up key elements of the party's New Deal coalition—Southerners, blue-collar Northern ethnic voters, rank-and-file union workers, and liberal Jews—who were more and more attracted to this view. In 1985, following Ronald Reagan's trouncing of Walter Mondale, the staff at the DNC hired CRG Communications Corporation to conduct a marketing study of attitudes among Democratic voters and small-scale contributors. Using data from focus groups in six cities—Boston, Philadelphia, Orlando, Dallas, Minneapolis, and Los Angeles—the company's report provided shocking and scary news for the Democrats. On domestic issues, the party was often described as coddling black criminals, giving away money to lazy black welfare recipients, and taking away jobs from whites and handing them over to less-qualified blacks.

Economic trends fueled much of the anger of whites, many of whom had been battered by the loss of manufacturing jobs and the stagnation in hourly income that had been abiding features of the economy since 1973. Even as the upper tiers, both black and white, did well during the 1970s and the 1980s, median income among white males stagnated. Whites knew that college was the way to a better life for their children, but tuition costs were skyrocketing, and they worried that their kids would be denied admission to good schools because of affirmative action. In their worry and anger, they did not look upward at the elites and the tax breaks they were getting, but downward at the poor, whom they saw as recipients of government "giveaways." And for many working-class whites, "the poor" meant black people. Seizing on the anger and worries of white voters, the Republicans had made serious inroads into the Democrats' traditional base of blue-collar workers, primarily on the issues of taxes, busing, crime, welfare, and affirmative action. Brown, however, was determined to change the message and, along with it, the Democrats' fortunes. But first, he had to have two things: a modern, professional political operation and money.

For years state and local political machines, congressional leaders, and presidents, all jealously guarding their own political power, kept both the RNC and the DNC from amassing any political clout. Politically emasculated, the committees' staffs for many years served as a dumping ground for incompetent party hacks no campaign operation worth its salt wanted. "A second-rate answering service," Ray Bliss, who became RNC chair in 1965 in the wake of Barry Goldwater's crushing defeat, sneeringly described his committee staff.[9] Bliss began to change things. Then came Bill Brock, a former Tennessee governor who became RNC chairman in 1976. Brock invested every dime he could lay his hands on into a direct mail program, building a mammoth base of small donors while ignoring the pleadings of some Republicans who wanted to spend the money helping candidates during the 1978 midterm elections. The investment paid off. By the 1979–1980 election cycle, an investment of $12 million brought in a gusher of $54 million in direct mail donations, helping the Republicans to outraise the Democrats by a margin of nearly five to one.[10]

Brock didn't stop with just raising money. Under him, the RNC identified "winnable" congressional districts, developed a sophisticated research operation, recruited and trained candidates and their campaign managers, provided financial assistance to candidates, and aired national advertising campaigns such as one urging voters to "Stay the Course" and not abandon Republicans in the 1982 congressional elections. The revitalized RNC was a major factor in Ronald Reagan's 1980 victory over Jimmy Carter and helped the Republicans avert substantial losses in 1982, when the country was in the midst of its most serious economic downturn since the Great Depression.

The DNC's operations also improved during the 1980s, first under Charles Manatt and then under Paul Kirk. Manatt refinanced the committee's debt, freeing up more funds for day-to-day operations. Both men invested heavily in new computers and beefed up the DNC's direct mail fund-raising. Still, the DNC was completely outclassed by the RNC and could provide nowhere near the help to its presidential candidates.

Defeat had taken its toll on the committee by the time Brown took over. Resigning itself to irrelevancy, the DNC had turned inward, as interested in the development of the party platform, rules for the selection of delegates to the convention, or which ideological camp would win the election for party secretary as it was in winning campaigns. "The Democratic National Committee was, to a large extent, entertainment before Ron Brown," said Jim Ruvolo, who was chairman of the state party in Ohio. "We fought each other. We entertained ourselves. And America ignored us."[11]

For political operatives the DNC was a nonentity. Campaign managers, pollsters, media consultants, direct mail experts, field organizers, and fund-raisers handled the party's real action. They developed a message and handled telephone banking and get-out-the-vote efforts. They figured out targeted media buys or a strategy to get publicity on television or in the newspapers. They did the work. Many of the campaign operatives did not know what the DNC did. "As long as I have been in politics, hating the DNC has been a badge of honor for a field-worker," said Mark Blumenthal, a Democratic pollster. "The first campaign I worked in somebody told me, 'Those who know, do. Those who don't, do the DNC.'"[12]

Yet the 1988 election had shown the value of a strong national committee to a party's candidate and, again, how thoroughly outclassed the DNC was. Between January 1987 and June 1988—even before each party's presidential candidate was officially nominated—the RNC had spent more than $2 million on polling, determining the strengths and weaknesses of potential Democratic candidates. In the same period the DNC had spent $16,000. In 1988, the RNC budgeted $1.2 million for research and, including volunteers, had more than one hundred people combing through public records and newspaper clippings to dig up dirt on Dukakis. In contrast, as late as April 1988, the DNC opposition research department consisted of one director and two college students.

In the spring of 1988, when it looked like Dukakis would secure the Democratic nomination, the RNC operation sent five young operatives to Massachusetts, where they combed through twenty-five years' worth of the *Boston Globe,* the *Boston Herald,* the *Phoenix,* an alternative weekly newspaper, and the *Lawrence Eagle Tribune.* They even went through the Brookline City Council minutes going back to 1949. The sleuths unearthed intriguing and potentially explosive tidbits, like Dukakis's veto as governor of a bill requiring teachers in Massachusetts to lead their classes in the pledge of allegiance to the flag, and the former governor's continuation of a program—started by his

Republican predecessor—that allowed convicted felons, including murderers, to have weekend furloughs from prison. Republican operatives at first did not realize how potent an issue they had in the prison furlough program. But when they learned—ironically enough, from Democratic candidate Al Gore, who raised the issue in a debate during the New York primary—that while out on one of these weekend passes a black convicted murderer named Willie Horton had broken into the home of a white Maryland couple, pistol-whipped the man, tied him up, and raped his fiancée, they knew they had struck gold. And while Republican operatives denied that their use of the issue was racially motivated, the race of the victims and the perpetrator gave the issue more political juice.

By May, the Bush campaign, using issues dug up by the RNC's research department, had conducted focus groups and determined the saliency of some of these issues, especially Willie Horton. They were ready, in the words of Bush's campaign manager, Lee Atwater, to "scrape the bark off" Dukakis.[13] Even before Dukakis's nomination Atwater and his colleagues had decided in which parts of the country to use particular anti-Dukakis messages. They emphasized the veto of the pledge of allegiance among blue-collar ethnic voters in Illinois, Wisconsin, and Michigan. They targeted commercials highlighting Dukakis's failure to clean up the polluted Boston Harbor in environmentally sensitive states like California and New Jersey. Texas would receive much of the commercials and mailing highlighting the Democrat's anti–gun control positions. And they planned the Willie Horton commercial for the racially polarized South. "By the time you get to the convention, they had their whole plan set," said Steitz. "They walk into their convention, knowing they're going to use Willie Horton, and knowing exactly where they're going to use him."[14] Dukakis never knew what hit him. "It's like the San Francisco 49'ers versus Silo Tech," Charles Manatt said of the difference in talent and ability between the Republican and Democratic committees.[15]

Whatever Brown felt about the morality of the Republican tactics, he could not help but admire their effectiveness. And he wanted to put together the kind of hard-hitting, savvy political team at the DNC that could emulate them. "We can no longer try to beat professionals with amateurs," he said in a speech a month after his election.[16]

The professional that Brown got was Paul Tully.

SEASONED PROFESSIONALS of both parties considered Tully to be perhaps the best political strategist among Democratic operatives. He also was probably the most eccentric. Obsessed with presidential politics, he had worked in every primary or general election campaign since 1968. The list of candidates he served reads like a who's who of liberal Democrats: Eugene McCarthy, Robert Kennedy, George McGovern, Mo Udall, Ted Kennedy, Walter Mondale,

Gary Hart, Michael Dukakis. Some campaign pros considered presidential politics a specialty. For Tully it was everything. "The man, literally, lived his life in four-year cycles," said his friend Steve Rosenthal, who worked with him at the DNC. "He spent the two years after the presidential campaign trying to figure out why we didn't win. And then he spent the next two years trying to figure out how we were going to win."[17] He pursued his goal to the exclusion of everything else—money, career, appearance, love, home life, his health, and, ultimately, his own life. So well respected was he in Democratic circles that his presence alone would infuse credibility into a campaign. "I remember conversations of how pleased people were," said Jonathan Sallett, a former aide to Gary Hart, recalling the time when Tully joined Hart's abortive campaign in 1988. "People said, 'This is for real—we have Paul Tully.'"[18]

What was real for Tully were presidential campaigns. Congressional, mayoral, and gubernatorial races were mere means toward his ultimate goal of putting a Democrat—and as liberal a Democrat as he felt the country would accept—into the White House. "He used to joke that I was spending too much time with the midgets, meaning the congressional races," said Mark Gersh, a close friend who is director of the National Committee for an Effective Congress, a research company that advises Democrats. "The presidency was the real game."[19]

Tully, whom Brown hired as the DNC political director in April, grew up the child of an Irish working-class plumber in the tract housing blandness of Levittown, New York. Both he and Brown came out of the politics of the Democratic left, Brown from the liberalism of the black middle class, Tully from the union movement. His father was a charter member of the Steamfitters Union and held an office in the same local that produced George Meany, the legendary AFL-CIO chieftain.

Their politics were similar; their appearances and work habits were markedly different. Brown was meticulous in his dress, all the way down to removing the last stray thread or unwelcome piece of lint from his well-tailored suits. Tully could care less. His curly and unruly dark hair was as restless as he was. His cheap suits looked like he was recycling them out of his clothes hamper—masses of wrinkles, spotted with stains from the twenty cups of coffee he consumed daily, and littered with the ashes from the Marlboros he chain-smoked. "I can make a twelve-hundred-dollar suit look like it came from Sears faster than anyone I know," he told his friend Harrison Hickman, a Democratic pollster.[20]

He was a nocturnal beast, working all night or reading ten to twenty newspapers or magazines before falling asleep, generally at two or three o'clock in the morning, then dragging himself out of bed and into the office around noon. "Oh, I see Paul is here with us this morning," Brown used to cheerfully tease a bleary-eyed Tully when he got it together enough to make the morning DNC senior staff meetings. "Good morning, Mr. Tully."[21] Tully would usually answer with a grunt. A big man, he had been a defensive line-man on Yale's football team. But the lack of exercise and the heaps of junk food he had consumed over the years had long since turned the muscle mass of a football player into layers of fat. His father had died from a heart attack at a young age, and virtually everyone, including Tully himself, was aware that he was a ticking time bomb. "Clearly he was on a one-way trip to oblivion, and he probably knew it," said Gersh.[22]

It didn't seem to matter. Nothing seemed to matter to Tully except presidential politics. Money didn't matter. His salary of $57,000 as political director was far less than a person of his talents could earn doing political organizing for one of the big lobbying firms. He had tried marriage once, and subsequently had several relationships; none achieved any permanence. He had entered several business partnerships to do political consulting. Those also fell apart. He was always broke and always on the move. "He was a nomad," said Gersh. "He didn't have a regular job anyplace. He would go from campaign to campaign."[23]

He could be as volatile as he was single-minded. If he felt someone was thwarting his drive to put a Democrat in the Oval Office, Tully would turn into Washington's version of Mount Saint Helens: fuming, shouting, cursing, turning beet red with anger. On the way back from a contentious meeting with Senate Majority Leader George Mitchell's staff in which Tully managed to offend nearly everyone, Joan Baggett, the DNC's congressional liaison, turned to him. She said pointedly that she was going to ask Brown for a restraint for Tully, the type with a built-in gag that had stifled the Hannibal Lecter character in *Silence of the Lambs,* a popular movie at the time. Tully just glowered at her.

Tully's undiplomatic behavior constantly forced Brown to fill in the craters that had been blasted by his political director's verbal grenades. Brown did so deftly—and, just as important, shielded Tully from many of the petty political fights in which a DNC political director traditionally becomes enmeshed. Brown did not want Tully diverted from the goal of winning the White House. "Whenever it would look like it would blow up and Tully would storm and stamp and pout because he was being dragged into something that took him away, Ron would always side with Paul, keeping him on task, letting him remain focused," said Steitz.[24]

Brown did so because Tully was *very* talented. His specialty was in discerning voter behavior and figuring out how and where to apply pressure to change that behavior. Throughout the country, businesses, whether their products were dog food or programming on cable television, were becoming experts of market segmentation. They conducted research to determine which demographic niche would be most receptive to their offering and figured out a strategy to reach it. Tully understood the fragmentation of the American marketplace. His genius was figuring out how to appeal to different segments in a way that would allow him to stitch them together into a whole.

He would spend weeks poring over opinion surveys, exit polls, and voter performance in a particular state, precinct, or congressional district. He would use census data and marketing surveys to track changes in educational and income levels in an area; look at hobbies, church attendance, types of stores in a neighborhood. He was a numbers cruncher, but he was also a statistician who understood history, human psychology, philosophy, economics, mass media, and marketing. "I used to have a professor who said that politics was an art, not a science," said Jill Alper, who was a twenty-three-year-old staffer on the DNC under Tully. "That's how Paul practiced it." And he was relentless, always studying, always analyzing, always trying to figure things out. "Paul spent hundreds and hundreds of hours going over that stuff so that he knew the behavioral research, the voting records, and the demographic analysis," said Rob Stein. "He could massage it for any state and come up with an analysis based on both historic data as well as his projections of what was going to happen depending on who was going to be running."[25]

Everyone thought that Tully was brilliant—that is, if you could figure out what he was talking about.

Perhaps because he immersed himself so completely in the minutiae of politics, or perhaps because his mind often raced ahead of his vocal cords, Tully would often lapse into a cryptic shorthand that was barely comprehensible to most people. It was as if his work habits, his loner personality, and the volumes of data he had crammed into his brain had rearranged the neurons in the part of the cerebral cortex that produces speech. The result was a new language—Brown and Alexis Herman, who came on board as Brown's chief of staff, called it "Tullyese"—that only he could understand. Mike McCurry, the committee's former communications director, remembered Tully wandering into his office one day to show him graphs and charts depicting trends in voting behavior in a congressional district in both presidential and congressional elections and how those patterns changed depending on the issues candidates used. Tully, stabbing his fingers at the charts, gave an explanation that, as McCurry recalled, was something akin to: "See, you got eighty effort, eighty-four effort. Move. Flip. Move. Flip. Eighty-four, eighty-eight. Pattern! Pattern! See? There. Boom! Effort, effort. Move, move, move. Pattern!"[26]

"When I first met Paul, I thought I was the stupidest person in the world. He would be saying things and I had no idea what he was talking about, and I was imagining that everybody else in the room was following him with precision and clarity," said Stein. "Then I found out that nobody else understood him either. I felt so much better."[27] In the early days of their partnership Brown would sit placidly listening to Tully make presentations in meetings. Afterward, he would call Herman, who was also at the meeting. "Did you get it?" he would ask. "Explain it to me."[28]

In the end, the two men understood each other very well. Each possessed his own set of skills. Each one's talents enhanced the other's. Both shared the vision of electing a Democratic president, but it was Brown who kept it alive through his ceaseless cheerleading and leadership. The data supplied by Tully allowed Brown to show the vision to be more than a wishful fantasy; he could say that it was rooted in fact. "Paul was very much an anchor of Ron," said Herman. "He was the reality check of how we get there."[29] Brown never claimed to be an expert in the nuances of survey research. Indeed, Tully, aware of his verbal limitations, took pains to make sure Brown grasped the concepts he and his team demonstrated in their data. "Ron was not always comfortable looking at numbers," said a member of Tully's team. "We actually spent a great deal of time thinking about how to present some very complex research in a way that Ron would be comfortable with and not lose patience." If during a presentation Brown's left leg started bouncing up and down on the ball of his foot, they knew they had failed.

Tully could supply facts, figures, and projections. But he could never form them into an articulated whole or go out and sell the concept to the disparate elements of the Democratic Party that needed to be knitted together and rallied behind it. Brown excelled at the kind of external persuasion and internal politicking that would be needed. "Ron was the key voice articulating the substance of what Paul saw was the challenge for the Democratic Party," said a top DNC staffer. "Without Ron, Paul would have just been another political numbers cruncher."

Recognizing each other's strengths and shortcomings, they did not trip over each other. Each understood his role and its importance. Neither feared that the other sought to usurp it. "The fact is, one of the best things Ron Brown did, one of the smartest things Ron Brown did, was bringing [in] Paul Tully and letting him do his job," said Steitz. "He did not try to do Paul Tully's job. He did not get in the way of Paul Tully's job. They had a very explicit agreement. Ron does all the external stuff. Ron gets all the good face time. For Paul it was, 'Mr. Chairman, you go out there and look good, sir. I will stay here and just do the work.' Ron would laugh and say, 'As long as we win, Paul.' "[30] Brown and Tully shared an intense drive to win. They were not about fighting the good fight or making some ideological point. They were about getting into the winner's circle.

Brown stocked the other top DNC jobs with professionals. He persuaded Herman to give up her consulting business—she at first thought it would be for only six months—to become his chief of staff. He retained McCurry as the committee's communications director. McCurry was well respected and well liked among journalists for his sharp analysis and flippant tone. He also had plenty of experience in presidential politics, having worked as press secretary for Lloyd Bentsen, the Democratic vice presidential nominee during the 1988 campaign. The top research job went to Steitz, an economist who worked for the Congressional Budget Office and a veteran of the campaigns of Gary Hart and Jesse Jackson. Steitz, like Tully, was a bundle of nervous energy.

Brown also appointed Jack Martin, a veteran political operative who worked for Bentsen, as a "senior adviser," and persuaded Melissa Moss, a highly respected fund-raiser with the Democratic Leadership Conference, to be the DNC's finance director. The appointments were designed to do more than just bring seasoned political operatives into the DNC. They were also meant to knit the disparate elements of the party together. Herman and Steitz came out of the Jackson camp. Martin, an aide to Bentsen, was considered a link to Democratic leaders in the Senate. McCurry and Moss came out of the DLC, which some considered a rival committee to the DNC. And, of course, Brown himself was a link to Ted Kennedy.

With Tully and the others on board, Brown now had a well-balanced professional team; it was no guarantee of victory in 1992. For his team to be effective, Brown needed money, and he would need it early.

BETWEEN JANUARY 1987 and June 1988, the RNC had hauled in $49 million compared to the DNC's $13 million. That had allowed the Republicans to fund a sophisticated research, polling, and message development operation that had put together a general election strategy that could be handed to their candidate as soon as he had nailed down the nomination.

That's what Brown wanted to do. He dispatched Rob Stein to do a thorough analysis of the DNC's finances and how much he could expect to raise in the next few years. He also hired an outside consultant to assess the state of the committee's direct mail fund-raising program. The two reports he received contained a dollop of good news.

In the final months of the 1988 campaign when money was rushing into DNC coffers, Paul Kirk had squirreled enough away to leave Brown a $5.4 million surplus. As a result, Brown did not have to worry about keeping the DNC's doors open for the first few months. Also, the committee's direct mail fund-raising lists and operations were in relatively good shape. An investment of several million dollars would be needed to keep in touch with these potential small donors, but it would not be a crushing expense.

There was also a heap of bad news. Based on recent history, Stein felt that the committee could probably raise an additional $8 to $10 million in 1989, compared to the Republicans' $30 million. Given that it would probably cost around $7 million for fund-raising and administrative expenses, the committee would be left with only about $1 to $2 million to use in some of the campaigns that would take place in the fall. "There was no money," Stein said. "It was horrendous. . . . I would say, 'Look you've got one of two political parties in what is arguably the greatest country in the world and it has less money on an annual basis than the Children's Defense Fund, People for the American Way, the American Civil Liberties Union, and about fifty other organizations on the right and on the left. What's wrong here? What's wrong with this picture?' "[31]

The committee's precarious financial situation was made even trickier by Brown's contentious relationship with Robert Farmer, who was elected DNC treasurer at the same time Brown won the chairmanship. Farmer came into office following his triumphant performance as treasurer of Dukakis's campaign, which, for the first time, matched the Republicans in fund-raising. Perhaps sensing his special status, he had refused to endorse Brown's candidacy for chairman even after all Brown's rivals had dropped out of the race. Shortly before the DNC meeting in February, when it was clear that both he and Brown would win their positions, Farmer met with Brown to lay down a set of demands. "He walked in and he literally had a list of what he wanted," said Stein, who attended the meeting at the Patton Boggs office in New York.[32] Brown waited patiently for Farmer to finish, then leaned forward and said, "Bob, I think you ran for the wrong office. You should have run for chair."[33]

Discord between these two huge egos could have spelled trouble for the Democrats, especially among major donors. There had to be at least an outward show of peace. The two men's staffs worked overtime to make sure there was no big blowup. "To the naked eye, I would say that 99.9 percent of the people had no knowledge that things started off a little bumpy," said Gary Barron, who was Farmer's deputy in the Dukakis campaign. "They were extremely deferential and cordial in public. It was very theatrical how they would introduce each other—bow and salute—almost operatic."[34]

In his refusal to accede to Farmer's main demands—Brown named his own finance director and his own vice chairs—lay an important lesson. The new chairman might be an affable, seemingly easygoing individual, eager to please, eager to negotiate, eager to settle differences. He might delegate much of his responsibility to subordinates and manage with a light touch. But in the end he believed he was the ultimate authority, and he would not give up power easily, even to someone as pivotal as Bob Farmer. In the end, Ron Brown was the boss.

But boss of what? Unless Brown could raise funds he would be head of the political equivalent of a hot dog stand rather than an election powerhouse. Brown soon found major Democratic donors to be in a cranky mood. In the final months of the 1988 presidential campaign Farmer had squeezed Democratic donors very hard. Some 270 contributors had, under relentless pressure from Farmer and his aides, donated or raised $100,000 each. Having had their arms twisted to give and then watching the Democratic standard-bearer go down to defeat, Democratic fat cats felt burned out and abused. "People had given more money than ever before," said a former DNC official familiar with the fund-raising. "The party had raised more money than ever before. And it was a huge disappointment that Michael Dukakis was not elected president of the United States. People felt, many of the donors felt, that they had gotten their hopes up quite high, only to have them squashed. So they were not much in the mood to give to the institution."

In February, not long after he assumed office, Brown organized a meeting of about 120 of these large Democratic fund-raisers, known as Trustees, at New York's Waldorf Astoria Hotel. He had heard from Farmer and through his own contacts about how angry some of them were, and he felt a meeting might help clear the air and could be a start on the road to regaining their trust and support. "These were people who felt they had been turned upside down and their pockets emptied," said Rob Stein, "and for that they had gotten very little responsiveness or care and feeding or appropriate acknowledgment. They were angry, really angry."[35]

Shelia Davis Lawrence, wife of Larry Lawrence, owner of the Hotel Del Coronado in San Diego, stood up and challenged Brown. At these meetings Shelia usually sat quietly, deferring to her husband. But since he was not there at the moment, she decided to speak for him and, as it turned out, for nearly everyone else in the room. "You keep asking for money, taking, running away, never listening to anything that we have to say. . . . It won't fly," she said. "We're fed up; we're tired of this party not being run like a business. . . . We're not stupid and we're tired of losing."[36]

The crowd was more than just a gaggle of disgruntled fat cats. Most were new donors whom Farmer's operation had brought into the Dukakis campaign with no long-term allegiance to the DNC. Many were Jews whose knowledge of Brown did not extend much beyond his association with their perceived nemesis, Jesse Jackson, and Brown's victory over Rick Wiener, his Jewish rival in the race for the DNC chairmanship. It was not a crowd waiting for Brown with open arms.

Throughout the session, Brown displayed the people skills that were his patented strength. "The time to get the best out of Ron Brown is to throw something at him—verbally, in writing, or on TV," recalled Barron. "In a case where people were mad, or concerned or challenging, that's when Ron Brown shined. He was the best on his feet. I've never seen anybody who could handle situations better on a spontaneous basis."[37] The competitive drive among highly successful men and women can manifest itself in many ways. Some try to impress by being the brightest person in the room. Many are driven to show they can be the toughest *hombre* on the planet. In a nondescript meeting room in the Waldorf Astoria, Brown's most impressive attribute was on full display. Through the force of his will he would make people like him. Liking him, they would trust him. Gaining their trust, he could lead them. "It was a situation made for Ron because that was what he loved," recalled Stein, who, along with Tully, Farmer, and Barron, had accompanied Brown to the meeting. "He loved turning things around."[38]

Standing in front of the group, the only hint of nervousness his pacing back and forth, Brown listened patiently as the donors castigated the Democrats in general and the DNC in particular. He did not argue with the conclusions, make any excuses, or try to defend the Dukakis campaign. He would not criticize his predecessors in the DNC or Dukakis's fund-raisers or strategists. He just listened—intently, thoughtfully, as if the person speaking was making the most important point in the annals of political history. Then he presented his vision of what he wanted to do as DNC chairman—elect a president in 1992. Given the experience these donors had just gone through, Brown knew it would take a lot to get their support again. Still, he asked.

"I'm asking you for nothing less than a leap of faith," he said. "There is nothing that I can say to you today that is going to convince you that my words will come true. . . . Stay with us. Test us as we go along. Be tough on us. But stay with us."[39] It was a disarming performance, one that turned anger into a grudging willingness to give the new guy a chance.

The then-governor of New York was the featured speaker at the dinner following the Trustees' meeting. On his home turf, and sensing the frustration of an audience of unrequited donors, Mario Cuomo knew just what buttons to push, and he pressed them deftly. He spoke of their role as contributors, but instead of appealing to their narrow political views or their crass commercial self-interest, Cuomo based his appeal on religious and moral principle. He invoked the Hebrew concept of *Tzedakah,* charity, stunning a number of Jews in the room who had never heard the term used by a Gentile. He told the audience that their role had deep religious significance, that in the true nature of giving they were sharing resources and providing sustenance for institutions of democracy. "You could have heard a pin drop," recalled Stein. "People who felt horrible about themselves and horrible for being suckered into something that had been such a loser, all of a sudden began to feel as though they were saints."[40]

Like the others in the room, Brown sat transfixed by Cuomo's performance. "We talked about it for several days afterward because you don't experience those kinds of moments in politics very often," said Stein. "Political practitioners generally aren't philosophers or theologians or people who touch others' souls. And he had a way, in that moment, in that one evening, coming out of that difficult day, of making all of us feel as though we were engaged in an endeavor that had soul to it, that was godly."[41] As he sat and listened to Cuomo's magnificent oration, Brown could not help but feel proud that his mentor and law professor was coming to his aid. He also could not help but see that in Cuomo he had a man who could help him realize his dream of winning the White House in 1992. The brooding New York governor had riveted the nation with a brilliant speech at the 1984 Democratic convention. But he had inexplicably passed up the chance to run for his party's nomination four years later, a nomination many thought was his for the asking. Now Cuomo's gravitas reinforced Brown's resolve to unify the party.

Brown's unanimous election as DNC chairman barely papered over the party's ideological, regional, and racial rifts. In truth, Democrats seemed on the verge of tearing themselves apart in a round of soul-searching and finger-pointing. Racial politics, in particular, seemed to be ubiquitous. Two reporters,

Thomas B. Edsall of the *Washington Post* and Peter Brown of Scripps Howard, each working on a book about how race was defining American politics, saw this trend working to the Democrats' disadvantage. The Supreme Court rulings making it harder for minorities to win job discrimination cases in the federal courts had spawned a new debate over affirmative action and "quotas." Many in the party felt that the new debate and the Democrats' defense of affirmative action were driving white middle-class and working-class voters even further away. Republicans, under their new chairman, Lee Atwater, were talking about trying to entice more middle-class blacks to switch their traditional party affiliation, forcing the Democrats to fight harder to keep blacks—and, some Democrats feared, alienating even more whites. Many voices within a conflicted Democratic Party seemed to be calling for the party to choose between loyal black voters and fleeing white ones. "It was part of a whole school of thought that is still alive . . . that asserts that there is really no issue in politics other than race," said Steitz.[42]

Beyond schisms based on race and political philosophy, Brown had to contend with state and local party officials who felt ignored and abused by national party leaders. He also had to deal with congressional party Brahmins who felt they need not be concerned with what the people at the DNC did— indeed, what Democratic candidates in neighboring congressional districts did.

At one point during 1990, a Labor Party member of the British Parliament visited the DNC office and was briefed by Tully's deputy, Will Robinson, on the DNC's plans to convince Democratic candidates at all levels to work together. Robinson spent hours explaining the mechanics of how these coordinated campaigns would work and how the DNC was trying to convince Democratic candidates to cooperate. The visitor was baffled. If they don't go along with the program, he asked, why doesn't the DNC just kick them off the ticket or out of the party? That's what they do in the United Kingdom. Well, Robinson explained, the committee didn't have the power to do that. If it tried, there would be such a rebellion that the party would be torn apart.

As he left, the Brit could be overheard telling a colleague, "Poor chaps. They're in such a bloody mess."[43]

It hadn't taken Brown many days on the job, however, to realize that racial politics saturated the mess he had inherited, and his first clue came from an unexpected source.

FROM LATE JANUARY, when it became clear that Brown was going to win the chairmanship, Jesse Jackson had watched his former aide with a mixture of pride and dismay. As a civil rights advocate who sought to open doors for black people, Jackson could not help but feel a sense of accomplishment over Brown's success. But at the same time, there was a strong feeling among Jackson supporters that Brown, who had never been considered one of them, was only advancing because of the strength of the Jackson forces within the party.

"Some of our people thought that Ron got a free ride," said Lamond Godwin, a close adviser to Jackson. "He wasn't in the campaign. He just showed up at the convention, gets all of this publicity and credibility with blacks because of his association with us, and then winds up being the beneficiary of our increased influence inside the party."[44] Worse still for some, including Jackson, at the moment of his triumph Brown appeared to be distancing himself from Jackson. In speeches and interviews, Brown emphasized his independence. He never denigrated Jackson in any way, but he continued to make the point that he was his own man and would act in the best interests of the party no matter whom that might offend.

Jackson knew full well that he was the person from whom Brown was supposed to be independent, and felt it smacked of ingratitude. The civil rights leader in Jesse saw Brown succumbing to a classic divide-and-conquer strategy of finding an acceptable alternative black leader. "The people whom he defeated often became his chief sponsors," Jackson said. "We defeated the monied forces. . . . They had no juice. He was our candidate, and there was this major move to co-opt him, take him from us, and with that, our political strength.

"My constant appeal to Ron was, 'Please, don't go for that. We're a team, together. It's like you take the one home that you brought to the dance.' [But] he was going for too much of it."[45]

The preacher in Jackson saw Brown as Esther, the biblical maiden who remained queen only by denying her Jewishness. Jackson decided to cast himself as Mordecai, her uncle, who stood at the city gate in sackcloth and ashes to remind Esther of her heritage. A few days after Brown's election, Jackson wrote him a stinging letter. In caustic language, Jackson accused Brown of forsaking him and of forsaking black people, without whom he would never have reached the exalted position he now held. "Jesse Jackson took no prisoners in the letter," said Nolanda Hill, with whom Brown shared it. "It said, 'You are a traitor'—he used the word traitor—a disgrace. He used some other less complimentary language."[46]

The letter angered and hurt Brown, aimed, as it was, at a vulnerable spot in his psyche—his racial identity. In public settings, he spoke of himself as a proud black man. That was true, but to Nolanda, the views he expressed of black people could at times be cutting. Brown's black friends say they strongly doubt any notion that he was anything but a proud African American, even though the mistress with whom he shared Jackson's letter was white. Hill's perspective gives rise to a more nuanced view of Brown's racial self-image, however. Being whipsawed by people who wanted to force him into a particular mold was the price Brown paid for living in two worlds—one black, one white. He had just come through a bruising campaign for DNC chair, the subtext of which was that he was too black. Now the country's most prominent civil rights leader was suggesting he wasn't black enough.

Brown never responded to Jackson. That did not mean, however, that he would not have to deal with him again—and soon.

On February 28, a little more than two weeks later, the stage was set for a confrontation on Jackson's turf. Richard M. Daley defeated Eugene Sawyer, Chicago's black mayor, in the Democratic mayoral primary. The win set up a three-way race in the general election between Daley, a white Republican, and Timothy Evans, a black alderman who was running as an independent. Evans was trying to recapture the aura of Harold Washington, the black South Side politician who had broken the grip of Chicago's white Democratic machine and become the city's first black mayor in 1987. Evans had the backing of many of the city's black political figures, most notably Jesse Jackson. The race drew national attention since a win by Daley would make Chicago one of the few major cities to elect a white mayor after having a series of black ones. The symbolism of a Daley win was even more stark because he was the son of former mayor Richard J. Daley, "the Boss," the man who symbolized Chicago machine politics, a politics that had seldom looked out for the interests of the city's black residents. Since Daley had won the Democratic primary fair and square and was the party's official candidate, the question was whether he would get the support of the party's newly elected chairman. "It was far from a foregone conclusion that Rich Daley would win at that point," said David Wilhelm, a Chicago political operative. "And it was a racially charged city. Mayor Sawyer had probably gotten 97 percent of the black vote in the primary, and Daley had gotten probably about 97 percent of the white vote. So it was an extraordinarily racially charged atmosphere."[47]

Even before Daley won the nomination, and even before Brown won the DNC race, Brown said that he would endorse whoever was the party's nominee. He insisted all along that it was not a close call. He was head of the Democratic Party. His job was to help elect his party's candidates. Democrats, Brown said, "would be appalled if the chairman of their party did not support the nominee of the party in major races."[48]

But words would not be enough. Observers in both the party and the press wanted to know if Brown would travel to Chicago to make a personal endorsement of Daley. There was no question that Brown would endorse Daley. "The question was how would he do it," said William Daley, the candidate's brother and political adviser. "Would he do it by press release? Would he do it by an offhanded remark to someone? Would he do it by coming out? What was going to be the forum?" The Daley campaign obviously wanted a strong endorsement, up close and personal. And they let Brown know that.

Meanwhile, Jackson and his supporters were equally adamant—both privately and publicly—in urging Brown to stay away, sometimes couching their demands in the crudest racial terms. "When Ron Brown brings his Oreo you-know-what into Chicago, I'll guarantee I'm going to help organize a reception party for him at the airport and to follow him all the way to some white hotel to denounce his coming in," said Gus Savage, a black congressman from Chicago who had a history of making outrageous statements.[49] If Savage was the most public and the most trenchant in applying pressure, there were others who quietly tried to persuade Brown not to travel to Chicago. "I did not make a big public issue [out of it] because when we get people in positions of power we must not limit them in their jobs," Jackson said. "Yet you must remind them of the forces that are their most loyal forces."[50]

Despite Brown's sanguine comments that the endorsement was a straightforward matter, it was not an easy decision to go to Chicago. "[T]here was a lot of back and forth, discussions with the senior staff, plus people calling in [saying] don't come, it's too divisive, leave it alone, you don't need to start off this way," said Alexis Herman.[51]

In the raw racial politics of the Democratic Party, Brown's decision became a litmus test of his leadership. "One of the questions going into his chairmanship was whether he was a factional representative or was he going to be a strong, party-wide voice," said David Axelrod, a Chicago Democratic operative who was Daley's media adviser. "And this certainly would be one indication."[52]

There was also a sense at the DNC that Brown's rivals in the centrist DLC were lying in wait, hoping to see him trip up, or expecting him to prove his loyalty to the party by endorsing Daley. "That was the most difficult thing for him politically because all of them wanted to say, " 'See, we've found the guy who will stand up to Jackson. He's our type of guy. He's not a lefty. He's not theirs. He's ours,' " said Steitz.[53]

In the end, Brown did travel to Chicago to campaign for Daley—not once but twice. He was the target for some pointed barbs for the speedy in-and-out-of-town nature of his first trip, when he made only one public appearance with Daley. He was the object of pickets during his second trip when he attended a so-called Unity Dinner organized on behalf of all Democratic candidates, including Daley. Some black activists, like Lu Palmer, a Chicago radio commentator who led the march protesting Brown's presence at the dinner, accused him of violating his people.

But he came. And he gave a sufficiently strong endorsement of the candidate at a press conference for Daley's campaign to use his remarks in a commercial that aired on radio stations with largely black audiences. The decision to go to Chicago represented Brown's view that for black people to be successful in the political game and to maximize their influence they had to adopt a strategy of moving beyond a purely racial outlook that, while ego gratifying, can be marginalizing. He was, in essence, imploring black people to politically make the same transition that he had. Unquestionably Brown knew that race is a factor in American politics and American life. But he felt that polarization along racial lines was most damaging to minority voters, and that minority candidates and minority voters needed to broaden their base.

In the early months Brown tried to steer a middle course as chairman; he was mindful of the need to be seen as sufficiently independent of the body's liberal wing as represented by Jackson, but careful not to be viewed as the lackey of the party's moderate faction. He also wanted to begin moving the party's message toward the political center. Brown clearly took to heart the polls and focus groups that said the Democrats were too liberal on issues like crime and national security and that Democrats knew only how to tax and spend the people's money and were not good stewards of the economy.

"We need to demonstrate anew that the party of Kennedy and Johnson knows how to deliver on prosperity, and that the party of Roosevelt, Truman, and Johnson knows how to defend the peace," Brown said in a speech shortly after his election. "And we need to say flat out that there is no one tougher than the Democrats when it comes to protecting our children against drugs, when it comes to protecting our citizens against crime."[54]

This message caused a considerable amount of dismay among many of Brown's former colleagues in the civil rights movement and in the Kennedy and Jackson campaigns. But it was a shift many Democrats felt was needed and one that only someone with Brown's impeccable liberal credentials could pull off. "Ron understood exactly where you had to take the party and where the party was going," said Susan Estrich. "I honestly believe that the party would have gone further in a right-wing direction had it not been for Ron."[55]

Pushing the image of the party toward the political center, Brown had demonstrated that he had ideas. By not caving in to racial politics in Chicago, he had gained credibility as a leader. Now he needed wins.

CHAPTER TWELVE

THE PLAN

INDIANA'S Fourth Congressional District was an unlikely place for the stone to be rolled away from the Democrats' sepulcher. Flat and fertile, it was a predominantly rural district where Bible Belt values and rock-ribbed Republicanism grew as abundantly as the area's crops. In 1989 minorities made up 4 percent of the district's population and Democrats seemed nearly as scarce. "It's got Fort Wayne, where they roll up the sidewalks at nine-thirty every night," said Jeff Eller, a Democratic strategist who is a native of the state. "It's a city that has more churches than any other city in Indiana. It's a typical Midwestern conservative district."[1] The party had not held the Fourth's House seat since 1976, when it was first won by Dan Quayle, and there was little thought that that particular state of affairs was going to change.

In March 1989, however, the district held a special election to fill the House seat left open when Dan Coats, a conservative Republican, was appointed to the Senate seat vacated by Quayle when he became George Bush's vice president. The race pitted Dan Heath, the former chief of staff to Paul Helmke, the Republican mayor of Fort Wayne, against Jill Long, a college professor. Virtually all political strategists and pundits viewed Long's chances as something akin to those of the Christians versus the lions in ancient Rome. Even the operatives at the Democratic Congressional Campaign Committee in Washington, whose role it is to support Democratic candidates for the House, were pessimistic. "I got a call one day from the DCCC," Eller recalled. "They said, 'You know anybody who wants to go to Indiana to do a race that we can't win?'"[2]

At the same time, however, a number of people at the Democratic National Committee's political ship, including Will Robinson, decided to monitor the election. Intrigued by the optimism of the campaign, he convinced the DCCC to hire a twenty-three-year-old operative named Jill Alper and send her out to the district to do some field organizing. Alper, who had worked with Paul Tully during the Dukakis campaign, was eager, she came cheap, and Robinson felt she could pick up some valuable experience.

"We kept polling and we kept sending the data back," Alper recalled. "But the people at the DCCC didn't think the race could be won. But Will and Paul and Ron thought it could."[3]

Convinced by Alper's reports from the field and the polling data, Brown, Tully, and Robinson began talking up the race in Washington, creating enough of a buzz in political circles to help convince the DCCC to take another look at Long's chances. "The DCCC wasn't going to get into the position where its supposedly sick cousin, the DNC, was going to do more in a race than they were," said Robinson.[4] Eventually the DCCC sent in more troops, more money, and convinced labor unions to kick in some bucks as well. In the end, Long won by a scant 1,772 votes.

Not even Brown's biggest fans claim that the DNC's people arrived like superheroes at the eleventh hour to save Jill Long's campaign by themselves. Politics is much too complicated a business to be viewed through such a simplistic lens. Long ran an extremely effective campaign. The DCCC was, in the end, the entity that raised much of the outside money she needed. Still, it was the constant optimistic hawking by Brown, Tully, and Robinson that helped convince the unions and the DCCC to give Long a second look. "If you look at our numbers and look at voter registration, we're a Republican district," said Inga Smulkstys, who was Long's campaign manager. "Probably to the day of the election, we had a lot of skeptics out there. If Ron Brown, as chairman, wanted to be a skeptic, too, it would have been very difficult for us."[5]

A week later, the Democrats were crowing again, this time when Glen Browder, Alabama's secretary of state, crushed Republican state senator John Rice in a special House election in Alabama—a race that was supposed to be a signal of growing Republican strength in the South. Three weeks later, Democratic candidate John Vinich ran surprisingly well before finally being defeated in a special House election in Wyoming to fill the seat being vacated by Dick Cheney, who was joining Bush's cabinet as secretary of defense.

In the grand scheme of things, winning two out of three relatively insignificant House elections is hardly the stuff of legend. But it is difficult to underestimate the importance of these early races at that particular moment for Brown. As the new kids on the block, he and his team at the DNC felt they had something to prove, and that they needed to prove it quickly. He placed a lot of stock in creating an image—in this case, an aura of professionalism that would produce victories for Democrats. He couldn't afford to wait for that image to evolve over time. He needed people to view him and the DNC as winners right away. "People were going, 'What kind of chairman is Ron Brown going to be? Who is this team at the DNC?'" said Mark Steitz. "We were telling everybody and their brothers that we're campaign people, that we're not interested in the . . . internal party political battles of the past. We're interested in winning elections. So the first opportunities to be credible in any way, shape, or form were those special elections. Of course, we took them seriously."[6]

"Frankly, we've started down the road already—early on, and it was not unintended—to be assertive and state clearly what kind of role we intend to play," Brown said. "You have a choice, and the choice is whether you want to step up to the plate and play or whether you don't. And I think the way you conduct yourself from the beginning sets that tone."[7]

The early wins, however, were merely a temporary high, a quick snort of a fast-acting but quickly dissipating narcotic. He knew well that once the giddiness of the moment wore off he would need a long-range strategy. He still had to convince the skeptics among contributors, politicians, operatives, and political reporters that he had a plan to win the White House. Equally important, he needed to show that the Democratic National Committee had a strategy to elect Democrats up and down the ticket in the intervening years in order to give the party an organizational base in the states that would make the job of capturing the presidency a real possibility.

The road map Tully envisioned and Brown embraced called for conceding the once solidly Democratic Deep South to the Republicans, though the Democrats would still fight for border states like Tennessee and Kentucky— and in Florida, where transplanted retirees from the North leavened the rise of Republican conservatism. In the South's place Tully plugged in the western states—Oregon and Washington, which Dukakis won despite being blown out nationwide, and California, Colorado, and New Mexico, which he barely lost. "The West clearly is not owned by the GOP," Brown said as 1989 was drawing to a close.[8] With 20 percent of the Electoral College votes, California was the key. "The phrase we used to use again and again and again was a Lee Atwater quote, which was 'Give me California and the Iron Triangle [Illinois, Michigan, and Ohio] and I'll give you a president,'" said Steitz.[9] To Tully, the influx of Hispanics and Asians into Southern California was lessening the conservatives' grip in places like Orange County and giving the party a chance to win the state. With the probability that the state would get more congressional seats— and therefore more Electoral College votes—as a result of the 1990 census, California's importance loomed that much larger.

The new road map also allowed the Democrats to move beyond its most nettlesome problem—race. How to knit together a party that seemed to be dominated by minorities, especially blacks, whose icon was Jesse Jackson, and white Southern centrists symbolized by the Democratic Leadership Council was the subject of endless and enervating debate. Pundits gave the impression that the Democratic Party was hopelessly doomed by its racial dynamic. "These were people who were so blinded by the subject of race that they were incapable of seeing the underlying economic and geographic solutions to the party's problems," Mark Steitz said of such pundits.[10]

Shucking the South—and with it the region's overarching emphasis on race—permitted the Democrats to develop a more future-oriented message that emphasized subjects like the economy, education, the environment, trade, and personal freedom. It was a message that meshed well with Northern liberalism. "Liberalism is not such a dirty word in the Far West and the North," noted two perceptive political scientists in early 1989. "A combination of liberal social policies (day care, environmentalism, not criminalizing abortion, respect for civil liberties) and/or liberal economic programs (money for education, health care, housing; a more progressive tax structure) would be well received."[11] Or, as Ann Lewis, a veteran Democratic operative, put it more succinctly, "If you understand that the votes are in Washington, Oregon, California, and the West, you stop trying to figure out which candidate you need to appeal to Mississippi and Alabama."[12]

Tully and Brown, nevertheless, urged the party not to neglect what had become its base among minority, mainly black, voters in Northern cities. Dukakis, in his zeal to pursue suburban voters who had been deserting the party in recent elections, had neglected the party's urban base. He campaigned almost exclusively in the suburbs and kept big-city mayors at arm's length. As a result, in 1988 the Democratic candidate garnered fewer votes than Mondale had four years earlier in every city east of the Mississippi with the exception of Cincinnati. With the population of cities shrinking, some strategists felt little could be gained by spending lots of time and money chasing the urban vote. But Tully and Brown argued that large margins of victories in cities made it that much easier to carry states.

The centerpiece for Brown's and Tully's strategy for winning California, the cities, and even suburban swing districts was devised by Tully. They called it the coordinated campaign. It was a plan to tie the presidential campaign in 1992 to the campaigns of Democratic candidates for the Senate, the House, governors' mansions, and state legislatures. The idea was to create interlocking campaigns in each state that would combine the various Democratic candidates' tactics, resources, and manpower into a well-coordinated, seamless campaign that would carry Democrats to victory across the board.

"At its core it is essentially a business-oriented idea—eliminate duplication and increase efficiency," said Steitz. "It was to political campaigns what mergers are supposed to be for banking."[13] It was hardly a new concept. What was new about Brown's and Tully's scheme was its scale and its timing. They wanted to have coordinated campaigns established in all fifty states by 1992. Indeed, they hoped to have them set up in a majority of states well before the next round of Democratic presidential primaries, with an interim goal of having them on the ground and working in twenty-five to thirty states by the 1990 midterm elections. "I'm talking about preprimary, before you know who the nominee is, everybody getting together and agreeing on a plan," Brown later said. "It's never been done on a broad scale in Democratic politics."[14]

As Brown tried to sell the plan's obvious advantages to the party, he had to crack the problem that the party was hardly a party at all. Losing five out of six presidential elections had done more than just demoralize the Democrats. Without the unifying force of the presidency, the party had fractured into separate parts. Having bought into former House Majority Leader Thomas P. "Tip" O'Neill's famous dictum that "all politics is local," candidates, officeholders, state party officials, and contributors looked out for their own narrow parochial interests and were often as awry of each other as they were of Republican opponents.

"There were a lot of conversations in which we were told, 'You want me to coordinate with *him?*'" said a former DNC staffer. "'What's in it for me?'"

Brown hoped that the blunt answer to that would be money.

Thanks to a ruling by the Federal Elections Commission in the late 1970s that created what many reformers considered a loophole in election financing laws, national party committees could funnel unlimited amounts of contributions to state parties for so-called party-building operations—voter registration drives, get-out-the-vote campaigns, building voter lists, polling, even some types of advertising. As long as the funds—known as "soft money"—did not go directly into the campaign coffers of specific candidates, corporations and labor unions could donate as much as they wanted. In contrast, individuals and political action committees were limited by law to giving ($1,000). It was under this rubric that the Dukakis campaign and Bob Farmer were able to raise so much money during the 1988 campaign under what was called the Victory Fund—much of it from donors who gave in $100,000 chunks. That money was sent to state parties whose "party-building" activities all supported the Dukakis campaign.

Brown and Tully were, in essence, proposing to copy the Dukakis model and expand upon it. But instead of raising large sums of money and shoveling them out to state parties after the convention as Dukakis had, the idea was to raise the money and send it out to the states early and often—but only if campaigns in the states agreed to cooperate with each other. "The money was the carrot to get people to sign on to the coordinated campaign," said Steve Rosenthal.[15]

Whether they realized it at the time, Brown's and Tully's scheme would be another milepost on the road to transforming the American political process into one that was dominated by big money donors. What Dukakis—followed by Bush—had done in the presidential campaign was to use the soft money loophole to get around contribution limits. Brown and Tully were now proposing that the same thing be done on a massive scale in a congressional election—and that it be done two years before either party had named its presidential nominee.

Brown and Tully were also proposing another change. "One of the things we were saying to states is we don't want to send in, after the convention, some twenty-eight-year-old from Boston who arrives in your state and starts saying, 'Here's how to do things,' " said Steitz. "The way to avoid that was hire your own person now, who is not working for one or the other of the campaigns, but is working for this thing called the coordinated campaign and who is trying to knit all this together."[16] The person who was hired, of course, would be subject to Brown's and Tully's approval.

For Brown the coordinated campaign was the canvas on which he would paint his scenario for electing a president. It would create a campaign structure throughout the country that he could hand over to the eventual nominee. It would not only assist the Democratic presidential candidate but also aid party candidates up and down the ticket. It would prevent state party organizations from being ignored during the presidential campaign. It would give donors a reason to continue to contribute to the DNC while at the same time giving them a vehicle to donate to and therefore increase their influence with Democratic candidates for Senate, House, governorships, state legislatures, and further down the ticket. "Underneath the whole message was a unified party," said one former DNC staffer, "a coordinated effort that was going to win—from the courthouse to the White House. I mean, that was the mantra. We kept using that phrase."

Brown unveiled his plan at the Association of Democratic State Chairs meeting in Nashville in June 1989. It was a big moment for him, his first chance to articulate the action plan for his chairmanship. He and his staff revised his speech several times, making sure it hit the right tone. The night before he was to present his remarks, he and his senior staff gathered in a hotel room to go over it one more time. Toward the end of the meeting, Brown excused himself and walked out on the balcony of his room to practice the address a few more times alone.

"I'll never forget that image," said a former member of the DNC staff. "The reason why it's so indelibly etched is that for all the silkiness of Ron, there was a great deal of personal preparation that went into everything he did. He worked very hard. But it never showed; he never sweated. The way most politicians do it is they read their speech over once before and then they give it. He was literally standing there alone practicing it. From then on, every time I saw him as Mr. Smooth in a meeting I would think how much he had thought through how he would come across."

Standing behind the podium the next day, Brown emphasized that the 1989 races and the 1990 midterm contests would serve as "spring training" for the 1992 campaign using funds that the DNC raised as leverage to forge more cooperation up and down the ticket in New Jersey and Virginia. "Nineteen eighty-nine was like the Spanish Civil War to World War II," said Will Robinson.[17]

REALITY STRUCK in July. The *New York Times* reported that the DNC was having acute problems in raising funds. In a front-page story, one of the newspaper's political reporters, Richard L. Berke, said that one reason for the DNC's poor performance was that the chairman was not paying enough attention to fund-raising. Perhaps most critical, Berke wrote, Jewish donors remained reluctant to give because of Brown's close links to Jackson. "He's a very nice guy and a very articulate guy. But my feeling is he will not cast off the shackles of Jackson," one donor, William W. Batoff, a Philadelphia insurance executive, was quoted as saying.[18]

The story enraged Brown and members of his inner circle. "Believe me, it was a really bad day when that article came out," said one top DNC staffer. "We were all just mad about it. It was really unfair. He hadn't been in office as chairman for that long. Money hadn't been raised at all. And it was making a lot of assumptions that, I thought, were unfair to Ron and unfair to the institution and unfair to people in the Jewish community." Gary Barron, who is himself Jewish, felt that Berke had been talking to a group of disgruntled Jewish donors who were aligned with the Carter/Mondale wing of the party, where antipathy to Brown was the strongest. In Barron's view, the story did not reflect the efforts Brown had made with the Jewish community. "They were the wrong people to be the litmus test on where Ron stood," Barron said.[19]

Berke's story was not wrong in one important point. Through the first five months of the year, as Berke noted, contributions to the DNC were not only lagging behind donations to the RNC, but the committee had collected nearly $1 million less than it did in the same time period four years earlier under Kirk. What's more, Berke reported that the committee under Brown had spent $1.6 million more than it had taken in and was cutting into the surplus Kirk had left. Throughout his tenure, Brown had said the committee's performance should not be measured against the money-raising prowess of the RNC but against how well the DNC had done at a comparable period four years earlier. So even by his own standards, Brown was failing.

In the wake of the Berke article, Brown redoubled his efforts to woo traditional donors, including Jewish contributors. A group of Jewish Democrats led by Stu Eisenstat and Hyman Bookbinder approached Brown with the idea of setting up a new organization called the National Jewish Democratic Council. The group was formed amid fears that Jews were straying from their traditional Democratic roots and increasingly becoming Republican or Independent. The Jewish leaders also were concerned that Jewish Democrats were not playing a critical role at the grassroots organizing level and that, as a result, Republicans were making inroads in the Jewish vote. Brown threw his wholehearted support behind the new group. He spoke at their meetings and made it clear that he wanted them to play a major role in shaping the party's agenda.

Brown further broadened the party's fund-raising base by seeking more black, Hispanic, and Asian donors who were looking to play a larger role in politics. Like other groups with a large proportion of immigrants, Asians in particular wanted their success validated by being wooed by the country's political leaders. And they seemed to be asking for little in return. "Asian outreach was a good thing," said Mike McCurry. "The Asian crowd can produce money, and constituency-based fund-raising was a good thing. That was born during the Brown years as chairman."[20] Years later, in part because leaders in the Democratic Party paid too little attention to the sources of the money that came from some Asian American donors—even though Asian American activists told them that they should—the party's fund-raising activities would result in allegations that the Democrats illegally raised money from foreign donors. But at the time, Brown and his colleagues at the DNC were simply looking for a new source of money that was not already committed to other political committees.

From that summer on, in Brown's DNC there were only two sets of functions: those that led to the election of a Democratic president in 1992 and those that didn't. The former, like fund-raising, were nurtured and developed. The latter distracted from the goal of winning the White House and were to be kept down to the barest minimum or quietly stopped. They were what Tully derisively called "glue politics," internal political fights that once entered pasted you down and kept you from moving toward your objective.

"Ron distanced himself from the ideological fights early," said Jim Ruvolo, the chairman of the Ohio Democratic Party. "Over and over his speech was, 'If this helps us win, we're going to do it. But if it doesn't, we're not going to do it.' That sent a strong message to the ideological folks in the party. They thought that Ron was going to bring a big liberal ideological swing to the party or keep that liberal national party image that was anathema to many of the states. But Ron said, 'I'm not doing ideology. That's not what I'm here for.'"[21]

But if ideology was off the table, image was not. Brown and others perceived that the Democrats' difficulty went beyond money and mechanics. There was also the difficulty stemming from how the party was perceived, and it was more than a matter of being seen as too liberal. A major problem was that the party seemed not to have much of an image at all. Having been bludgeoned for eight years by Ronald Reagan, and facing George Bush's strong standing in the polls following the 1988 election, the party seemed to be retreating into what Edmund G. "Jerry" Brown, the then-chairman of California's state party, termed "me-tooism." The sense of frustration at the congressional Democrats' unwillingness to stand up to Bush, and in doing so define what the party stood for, pervaded the DNC. Privately, DNC staffers referred to the Hill Democrats as "the weenies."

Dan Carol, a young DNC staffer who became head of opposition research in the summer of 1989, recalled being in Tully's office one day in the early fall. Suddenly, Tully got up from his chair and started pacing the room. "He starts pointing over towards the Capitol and saying, "Just say *something*; say anything,'"[22] Carol recalled.

With the congressional Democrats reluctant to take on Bush, Brown stepped into the breach.

Not surprisingly, during a time when economic issues dominated the domestic agenda, the issue was taxes. In September, Bush attempted to rally the country to step up its enforcement of laws against illegal narcotics. Speaking from the Oval Office, holding up a plastic bag of crack cocaine that he said was purchased by undercover agents across the street from the White House, the president said he was declaring a "war on drugs."[23] The next day, Charles Rangel, the Democratic congressman from Harlem who had worked as a bellman in the Hotel Theresa when Brown was a child, agreed that special efforts were needed to combat drugs. Rangel, however, went on to propose a .5 to 1 percent surcharge on income taxes to pay for the drug war. Whatever the merits of Rangel's proposal—and given the fact that the federal deficit had ballooned to more than $200 billion, it had some—the idea of Democrats recommending new taxes struck Brown as harmful to the party's image. "You could hear America sigh," Brown stated very publicly. "'The tax-and-spend Democrats; there they go again.'"[24]

But Brown did not stop there in publicly chastising congressional Democrats and an old family friend. A week later, House Democratic leaders, including Speaker Tom Foley and Dan Rostenkowski, the gruff chairman of the Ways and Means Committee, suffered a stunning rebuke when a large number of Democrats joined with the Republicans to pass a reduction in the taxes paid on capital gains. The capital gains tax cut was one of Bush's favorite causes. Many Democrats, including Brown, had strenuously fought it, arguing that it would add to the deficit and that the main beneficiaries of the tax break would be the rich. But with Bush riding high on a 70 percent approval rating in the autumn of 1989, a large bloc of Democrats bolted to the Republican side on the issue, and the tax cut passed overwhelmingly in the House. Though the bill was defeated in the Senate, Brown felt that passage of a Republican tax cut in the House, where the Democrats held an eighty-one-seat majority, was a failure on the part of the House leaders. He specifically criticized Rostenkowski during a breakfast meeting with reporters, and, presiding over his first meeting of the Democratic National Committee, he denounced the tax break and, by extension, the Democrats for allowing it to be approved by the House.

"I'm proud to stand as chairman of the party that wants to help the middle class save for retirement, college, and homes instead of giving another massive, needless tax break to the wealthiest one percent—a giveaway that will cost working Americans billions," Brown said. He added, obliquely criticizing his own party, "When we state the choice clearly and consistently we win."[25]

The sight of the chairman of a political party publicly castigating some of its most powerful congressmen was startling for official Washington. It was even more so since Brown had strayed into the area of public policy, a territory that was the jealously guarded playpen of elected officials. In the past,

Democratic Party chairs had tentatively waded into the policy-making arena only to be reeled back in. Top congressional Democrats essentially told Brown to butt out, to confine himself to conducting voter registration drives and planning for the convention. "We don't need that kind of public criticism," snapped Senator Tom Daschle, co-chair of the Senate Democratic Policy Committee.[26] One angry Democratic Hill staffer angrily told the *New York Times,* "You don't see Lee Atwater criticizing Republicans."[27]

Brown did not back down, however, nor did he rein in other DNC staffers who voiced equally, if not more, caustic criticism of what they considered weak congressional leadership. That criticism had sparked huffy comments from congressional leaders that DNC staffers should essentially mind their own business. "We were all told that we don't need to have so much action by the overexcited DNC operation," McCurry recalled. "But Brown was defiant. He wanted good relationships with [Senate Majority Leader George] Mitchell and [House Speaker Tom] Foley. But he was determined to go forward, to continue to press the envelope on the political argument. And he did."[28]

A more critical test of Brown and the DNC loomed in November. Three major elections would be decided: the New Jersey and Virginia gubernatorial contests and the mayor's race in New York. All three Democratic candidates— James Florio in New Jersey, David Dinkins in New York, and Douglas Wilder in Virginia—led their Republican rivals in the polls by substantial margins. Brown had set his sights on winning all three races, hoping that victories would convince would-be donors and the Democratic political community to take the DNC and his coordinated campaign idea seriously. Even beyond that, each of the three races carried real and symbolic importance for Brown and the DNC. A New York City win for his friend since his family's days in Harlem would boost the turnout of the Democratic core voters in the key city come 1992. New Jersey was also a swing state in presidential politics. In Virginia, where his fellow Guardsman club member Wilder was trying to become the first black governor of a state since Reconstruction, a victory would go a long way toward quelling the constant refrain that the party was losing because it was too loosely identified with African Americans.

Partly because Democratic candidates in New Jersey were used to working together, Brown figured New Jersey would be a snap. It took little effort to get the candidates to buy into the DNC's coordinated campaign. "By the time '89 came around, we were pretty well versed in what worked and what didn't work," said Stephan DeMicco, who ran the coordinated campaign for the New Jersey Democratic Party.[29] The only thing the New Jersey Democrats needed was money, and Brown and Tully made sure they got it. They worked with DeMicco, helping him draw up a strategic plan for the state, and brought him around to a number of donors in Washington, including the AFL-CIO's Committee on Political Education. All told, the New Jersey party raised more than half of the $15 million in soft money it spent on the campaign in Washington, and Brown and Tully helped pull together a significant portion of that. "Basically, Brown and Tully guided us through where we had to touch all the bases down there and get as much Washington help as we could," said DeMicco. "It was tremendously successful. Lots of large checks were being written to the state party."[30]

New York City did not present the DNC with a monumental task, either. David Dinkins was the beneficiary of a solid Democratic organization in the city and had an overwhelming nine-to-one advantage in the number of Democratic voters. Still, Brown wanted to do all he could to help. It wasn't as if Dinkins did not need the help. His courtly, almost tepid style of campaigning and the fact that many white New Yorkers who were Democrats could not bring themselves to vote for a liberal black made the contest a nail-biter. Brown campaigned for his old friend and raised money for him. The Democrats could not afford to lose.

It appeared that Virginia would present the biggest challenge.

DOUG WILDER WAS poised to make history in 1989. Should he win the governor's race—and he held a solid lead in the polls at the end of the summer—he would be the first African American ever elected governor of a state. The other two major Democratic candidates, Mary Sue Terry, who was running for attorney general, and Don Beyer, who was campaigning for lieutenant governor, were also running strong campaigns. The state had a popular Democratic governor in Gerald Baliles, a strong statewide organization, and a U.S. senator, Charles Robb, with a national reputation and the ability to raise money both inside and outside of the state. Everything seemed primed for a Democratic sweep—except for one minor problem among the major Democratic players in the state. They hated each other—or more precisely, everyone seemed to strongly dislike and distrust Wilder. He felt the same way about them.

Winner of the Bronze Star in Korea, a lawyer, and a self-made millionaire, Wilder had a history of being a prickly, unpredictable politician. His was a personality forged from an uphill struggle. He had to claw his way up from humble beginnings to make it big as a black man in a state that was the capital of the Confederacy and whose politics was dominated by a Democratic machine cobbled together and defined by Harry Flood Byrd Sr., an archsegregationist. As a boy in Richmond's Church Hill section, Wilder had shined shoes and peddled copies of the *Richmond Planet,* the city's black newspaper, on the street. His values were shaped by his father, Robert J. Wilder Sr., a salesman for a black-owned insurance company. He was known as strict when it came to discipline and tight when it came to money.

As an undergraduate at Virginia Union University in Richmond, a historically black college less regarded than Virginia's Hampton Institute or Washington's Howard University, Wilder paid for his tuition, books, and upkeep by waiting on tables at all-white private clubs and the city's tony hotels. After graduating from Howard's law school, he entered the army and distinguished himself in combat during the Korean War.

Returning to Virginia at the height of the civil rights movement, Wilder eschewed participating in sit-ins or street protests and went about building a successful law practice. In 1970 he won his first political race, becoming the first black to serve in the state senate since Reconstruction, and later startling his white legislative colleagues by appearing on the floor wearing dashikis and styling his hair in an Afro. His first act as a lawmaker stunned conservatives and traditionalists—he introduced a bill to end the designation of James Bland's "Carry Me Back to Old Virginny," with lines like "that's where this ol' darkey's heart am long to go," as the state's official song. By 1989 Wilder had shucked his African garb, trimmed his Afro, and moderated his rhetoric. He moved toward the center and courted Virginia's political machine. He had run for lieutenant governor in 1985 and won, the first black person to win a statewide office in Virginia since Reconstruction. He was a self-made man, self-assured, with a copper-brown complexion, a mane of silver hair, a deep resonating voice, and a radiant smile. He was also a staunchly independent man whose life taught him to fear few and trust none. The way Wilder approached life, including relations with other politicians—according to his political adviser Paul Goldman—was to figuratively "put the gun on the table, fully loaded, and say, 'Normally you'd expect me to shoot myself. But I'm a different kind of person. If I'm going, then you're going with me. So either we both could die, or you stand a chance of living.' "[31] His independence and pit bull style had brought him to the near pinnacle of Virginia politics. He didn't get there because people loved him.

But as Wilder liked to say, "It takes two to argue," and in Virginia he had no shortage of sparring partners. Chief among them was Robb, the state's premier Democratic politician. Having aided Wilder in his winning race for lieutenant governor in 1985, Robb was stung when word leaked out that Wilder and Goldman resented his taking credit for the victory. Robb responded with a caustic letter to Wilder that said, in part, "Friends don't treat friends like you treated me recently. Unless you can find a way to repair the damage you and Paul Goldman did last week, there are some very large numbers of our mutual friends and supporters who just won't be there again for Doug Wilder."[32] During his tenure as lieutenant governor Wilder feuded with Baliles, the state's Democratic governor, over prison policies, a tax increase to pay for a mammoth highway program, and the governor's handling of a bitter coal strike in southwestern Virginia. Mary Sue Terry, a Robb protégé, was also displeased with Wilder. She had garnered more votes than he did in 1985, when he ran for lieutenant governor and she won the attorney general's job, and was considered the front-runner for the Democratic gubernatorial nomination four years later. But in 1989 Wilder hinted that if she did not step aside and let him get the nomination he would not support her and would urge blacks not to vote for her. Faced with the prospect of losing critical black support, Terry moved over for Wilder.

As much as Wilder and many of the other players in Virginia hated each other, they disliked outsiders, especially those from Washington, even more. In part it was an institutional distrust of the DNC; Virginia Democrats like to call themselves Virginia Democrats to distinguish themselves from the national party. Yet, Ron Brown wanted to use the state as one of his models to prove that Democrats could be successful if they worked closely together in a coordinated campaign. This clashed with Wilder's desire to be top dog and to not yield status or publicity to anyone else, especially anyone else who was black. Three decades after Middlebury College, Brown was again caught up in the F&O—first and only—syndrome. "Wilder was suspicious of Brown," said Will Robinson. "Doug Wilder saw himself as a national African American leader. And Ron was competition."[33]

The state seemed fraught with risks for Brown and the DNC. But Virginia was too important in Brown's grand scheme to let the state's internal political wars deter him. The DNC had to play.

Brown used the lure of money to bring the bickering parties in Virginia— and Wilder in particular—to the table. Wilder was being outraised by his Republican opponent, Marshall Coleman. Brown and other DNC staffers made it clear that he could expect financial help from the DNC only if he and the other statewide campaigns agreed to a written plan on how the funds were to be spent on voter registration drives, direct mailing operations, telephone banks, and get-out-the-vote efforts. Brown also insisted that the three candidates—Terry, Don Beyer, who was running for lieutenant governor, and particularly Wilder— show their commitment to the coordinated campaign by kicking in some of their own funds. At first Wilder balked. His strategist, Goldman, felt that some of the coordinated campaign activities, like the get-out-the vote effort focused on increasing black turnout in the Tidewater area of the state, were a waste of money. Blacks, Goldman reasoned, would come to the polls in droves anyway for the opportunity of electing the nation's first African American governor. Goldman preferred that the DNC simply help the Wilder campaign raise money for television advertising in northern Virginia. "We were getting assurances [from the Wilder campaign] that money would come, but nothing was happening," a strategist involved in the coordinated campaign said.[34]

Brown, however, would not back down. Symbolic or not, Wilder's race was not worth abandoning the broader vision of showing that joint efforts between Democratic candidates could work. In August, the DNC considered scaling back its efforts in Virginia.

Finally, Wilder relented. This change of heart was due mainly to Mark Warner's becoming Wilder's campaign chairman around that time. A lanky, carrot-topped, youthful-looking man who had made millions in the cellular telephone business, Warner was not beholden to the campaign for his next paycheck and therefore could stand up to Wilder and Goldman. "The good thing about Warner was that he could tell Wilder to fuck off," said Robinson. "He didn't need the money, so Wilder could fire him and he didn't care. It was Mark who basically brought Wilder to the table."[35] But it was also Brown's determination—or bluff, it was never clear which—that got to Wilder. Whatever his reluctance, the candidate needed the funds the DNC could raise. "There was a great deal of wariness," said Warner. "On the other hand, you had in the Wilder campaign great concern [about] whether we could raise money to match the Coleman effort, and the DNC offered funding."[36]

By the end of the race the budget of the coordinated campaign effort was $900,000. Unions kicked in at least another $600,000 in in-kind contributions, mainly through the manning of telephone banks. In addition, Brown helped Wilder raise money outside the state from labor by hosting fund-raisers for the candidate among Washington's black power elite, according to Frank Greer, who was Wilder's media consultant.

Even with Wilder's cooperation, Brown was not home free. Because of the possibility of Virginia's electing the first black governor in the country, the campaign was a magnet for numerous Democratic personalities, most notably Jesse Jackson. History was about to be made, and Jackson wanted to be a part of it. Wilder, however, did not want the famed civil rights leader anywhere near his state.

One again, the root cause of Wilder's feelings was a mixture of the political and the personal. The presence of the liberal Jackson campaigning for Wilder could have caused irreparable harm to Wilder, who was running as a moderate. Being identified with Jackson would have cost the candidate votes, especially in the conservative, though still highly Democratic, areas in the southwest corner of the state. But Wilder's arm's-length stance from Jackson was also personal. The candidate viewed Jackson as a potential rival, someone who would steal the spotlight and the publicity. Wilder was angling to become one of the country's premier black leaders—and possibly a candidate for president, which he became for a short time in 1992. Jackson's presence would only be a distraction. "You think I want him to be a part of this press story?" he once told a campaign strategist.

Yet Jackson wanted in and kept sending signals that he wanted an invitation from the campaign, to no avail. "I remember Jackson's emissaries calling Wilder and Wilder not responding," said one campaign strategist. "Jackson finally called him, himself, and Wilder said no." Jackson finally appealed to Brown to intervene so that he could travel to Virginia and campaign for Wilder. Brown, who controlled the money going to the coordinated campaign, clearly would have some leverage on Wilder. But after weighing the situation and the potential impact on Wilder's chances, Brown declined to try to twist arms to get Jackson into the state. "It would have been disastrous for Doug Wilder to have Jesse Jackson in the state, and Jesse Jackson sometimes likes to campaign on his own," said Frank Greer. "Brown was the one person who could say—in a very pragmatic way, but with the credibility of a long-term relationship—stay out."[37]

The prediction of Steve Cobble, one of Jackson's lieutenants who had helped Brown gain the DNC chairmanship, had come true sooner than anyone had expected. Cobble had said that the party would want Brown as chair because it was believed that only he, not some white party leader, would be able to say no to Jackson. That's exactly what had happened. But neither Cobble nor anyone else had realized that the first time Brown would have to block Jackson's desires would be on behalf of an African American candidate.

With Brown raising money and running interference against Jackson, the Wilder campaign could remain focused on its job. The campaign's strategy was essentially three-pronged. The candidate needed to hold on to traditionally Democratic areas in the southwest and boost its vote totals in the affluent northern Virginia suburbs across the Potomac River from Washington, D.C. It also needed to greatly increase voter turnout in black precincts that reliably voted Democratic. Wilder's chances in northern Virginia were greatly enhanced by Coleman's opposition to abortion. Because the campaign was taking place in the wake of a Supreme Court ruling in July in a case, *Webster v. Reproductive Services,* that gave states the right to limit the availability of abortions, the issue was center stage in the campaign. Wilder trumpeted his support for abortion in television advertisements targeted at female professionals, a group he would carry on election day.

The DNC offered more than just money. Robinson moved down to Richmond to oversee the coordinated campaign effort and to mediate between the still-distrustful Democrat candidates. "I tried to do as much as I could to move the discussion from who fucked whom to where do we need the votes," Robinson recalled.[38] Jill Alper, fresh from the Jill Long campaign, was also dispatched to the state to run field operations, especially the get-out-the-vote effort in heavily black precincts. That drive not only focused on predictable black neighborhoods in Richmond, Norfolk, and Alexandria, it also targeted small pockets of blacks living in white Republican areas. Paid campaign workers known as "flushers" earned forty dollars a day making morning runs through black precincts urging people to vote. Throughout the day on election day, campaign workers at various polling places in black neighborhoods would check totals to determine if the turnout was down from four years earlier, when Wilder ran for lieutenant governor. If it was, the telephone banks and flushers would concentrate their activity in those neighborhoods to get more people out to vote. It was, by some accounts, the most ambitious get-out-the-vote effort in Virginia's history.[39]

In the end, Wilder would need every vote he could get. Early polls had showed him well ahead of his opponent. But in the final days the race tightened—as it also did for Dinkins in New York.

On election night, Brown gathered at the DNC with Tully, Steitz, Alexis Herman, Carl Wagner, and others to monitor the returns. It was the first big test of whether the idea of the coordinated campaign would work. A lot was riding on the results. When early returns showed Dinkins and Wilder in neck-and-neck races, Brown could hardly contain his nervousness. He kept pacing back and forth.

"He was pumped," said Herman. "But pacing. Oh God, was he pacing. I remember thinking, 'God, this is really happening.' I wanted so badly to win. I wanted it for him. I wanted it for us. I knew this was a make-or-break election for so many things—resources, and money, and credibility. Ron had risked everything on this strategy."[40]

When the returns finally showed that both Dinkins and Wilder had made it—the latter winning by a razor-thin 5,533 votes, the closest gubernatorial win in modern Virginia history—Brown broke into one of his familiar smiles. "It was like, here we go!" said Herman.

In the aftermath of the victories in New York City, New Jersey, and Virginia, many in the DNC waxed enthusiastically about Brown's—and their—roles. As is often the case in politics, it is difficult to say conclusively that it was Brown, the DNC, and the coordinated campaign that made the difference. New York had its own political dynamic, and it is hard to see how Brown's contribution added greatly to Dinkins's win. The DNC and its chairman were much more of a factor in New Jersey, however. Though Florio's race was essentially a walk-over, Brown helped the state's Democrats raise significant funds for their coordinated campaign, which allowed the party to retake the state assembly.

And then there was Wilder.

It is true that the Virginia gubernatorial contest had its own political rhythms that were beyond Brown's or the DNC's ability to influence. But there was little question that the DNC's efforts were a key to Wilder's victory. The joint campaign allowed Wilder to shift more of his funds into television advertising, especially in the expensive Washington market, which covered the fast-growing northern Virginia suburbs. And the coordinated campaign's field operation help pump up black turnout, which ultimately carried Wilder across the finish line. Exit polls indicated that 73 percent of registered black voters went to the polls, compared to 65 percent of registered whites. The get-out-the-vote effort had achieved a stunning 19 percent increase in black turnout over 1985, when Wilder had run for lieutenant governor. The surge in black voting made up for the decrease in support for Wilder in suburban and rural districts compared to 1985.

"If it was not for Ron Brown and the national party, I seriously doubt that Doug Wilder would have been elected governor," said Will Robinson.[41] Some were not so sure, however. There would be those who argued that Brown's taking credit for Wilder's win was akin to the rooster claiming his crowing brought up the sun. But the argument over this issue isn't really relevant because of another unassailable fact: should Wilder have lost, Brown would have been crippled in his efforts to convince other Democrats to buy into the coordinated campaign or to heed the DNC's political advice. Hesitant Democrats would have had a ready answer for Brown's entreaties: your ideas didn't help Doug Wilder much. Brown's idea of playing a bigger role in the next round of elections and the 1992 presidential campaign would have been stillborn.

CHAPTER THIRTEEN

WE AIN'T RUNNING

B ASKING IN THE WINS of that golden November, Brown moved swiftly to expand his power. He had already persuaded the full DNC to officially extend his term in office to February 1993, assuring that he would remain on the job throughout the 1992 general election campaign. By spring 1990, he was ready to publicly declare his intention to assume an active role in the selection of the party's next presidential nominee and to work hand-in-glove with the eventual nominee during the general election. "This November will be the first test of the DNC as an effective campaign organization," Brown said in March. "The successes we enjoyed last year are prologue to this November and to the 1992 campaign."[1]

These were ambitious goals, unheard of for a DNC chairman. To have any clout in 1992, Brown would have to show that the coordinated campaign could make a difference in the 1990 midterm elections, when 36 governors' spots, 34 Senate seats, and all 435 seats in the House were up for grabs.

Brown and his DNC guerrillas could not just waltz into the fall campaigns and expect Democratic candidates—especially congressional Democrats—to welcome their help with open arms. Long before the first ad buys of the fall were made or the first telephone banks were turned on, Brown and his staff would have to prove their political smarts to the Democrats on the Hill. It was a tall order given the fragile state of the Democrats' psyche.

THE TIDE of public opinion had been running out on the Democrats for several months. In the fall of 1989, Democrats forlornly watched Bush's popularity soar as one stunning event after another occurred in foreign affairs, Bush's special area of expertise. The people of Poland, Czechoslovakia, Hungary, and the Baltic states threw off the shackles of communism. The Berlin Wall fell. Bush and Soviet president Mikhail Gorbachev met on the island of Malta in December to declare that the Cold War was over. It was obvious to all but the most obtuse that America had won. The breathless pace of foreign affairs continued unabated through December. American troops invaded Panama and captured its leader, General Manuel Noriega, who had turned his country into a way station for drugs flowing to the United States. Bush's approval rate hit 79 percent by the beginning of 1990, the highest of any president since World War II.

On the domestic front, the news for the Democrats was almost as bad. Throughout 1989 they were beset by scandal. In the spring, Jim Wright, the Speaker of the House, and Tony Coehlo, the House Whip, were forced to resign their seats amid allegations of financial improprieties. In the summer, Rep. Barney Frank of Massachusetts, an outspoken Democrat who also happened to be a homosexual, admitted that he had hired a personal assistant in 1985 and fired him two years later after discovering that he was running a prostitution ring out of Frank's home.

A survey of public attitudes toward the party conducted in June by Hickman-Maslin, a Washington polling firm, indicated that only 34 percent of the people trusted the Democrats to lead the country, compared to 43 percent who trusted the Republicans.[2] Press coverage of the party's views on economic matters portrayed the Democrats as out-of-date, too beholden to union bosses, and less dynamic than the Republicans.

"In 1989 the way the networks reported Capitol Hill was that the Republicans were pro-growth and pro-jobs and the Democrats were engaged in shopworn rhetoric," said David Dreyer, an aide to House Majority Leader Richard Gephardt. "They were the future. We were the past. They were strong. We were weak."[3] In the face of Bush's successes, the Democrats seemed to be imploding.

In what many Democrats considered a charred political landscape, Brown organized a campaign for the hearts and minds of congressional Democrats. One of his first moves was to hire Joan Baggett to be the DNC's congressional liaison, the first time the committee had ever had anyone working in that capacity. He and Baggett began attending the weekly meetings of Democratic whips, where the party's legislative strategy was devised. Some of the tradition-bound old bulls of the House began to grumble about permitting a non-legislator into their brainstorming sessions. Brown, however, disarmed the critics by never trying to take over any of the meetings, never making a formal presentation, even when asked, and speaking only when asked a specific question. Meanwhile, Tully and Steitz also made regular appearances at the daily "message" meetings instituted by Gephardt. In these sessions, the strategists hashed out the party's line on any given issue that day in order to have the Democrats at least appear unified and the party's philosophy clearly defined.

Brown and his associates searched the horizon for a way to break through the gloom. Then in July 1989 Alan Greenspan, chairman of the Federal Reserve Board, predicted that the U.S. economy would slow in the coming months.

Sure enough, on October 6, while much of the nation's attention was still focused on the crumbling Soviet empire, the Labor Department reported a jump in the jobless rate from 5.1 percent in August to 5.2 percent in September. The economy had begun to worsen.

There was a startling connection between the economic news and the polls commissioned by the DNC and by a group called Democrats for the '90s. Pamela Harriman, the wealthy Democratic dowager, had started the group, and it was about to prove its worth. The polls showed that despite the Republicans' efforts at refashioning themselves, the public still identified the GOP as the party of big business and the Democrats as the party of the average working family.

The combined polling research and economic outlook led Brown's and Gephardt's staffs to start taking a hard look at the issue of fairness. The theme had been trotted out during the embarrassing loss in the House on the capital gains tax cut, but those Democrats who voiced it had been hammered by the pundits as engaging in "class warfare." Now a realization began to set in: the class warfare rhetoric of the previous fall was not the liability many had thought.

Testing the theme, Brown began talking up a proposal by New York's Democratic senator, Daniel Patrick Moynihan, to cut Social Security taxes. Though Democratic leaders were aghast at the specifics, Brown jumped on the larger issue. "Let's cut taxes for those who need a tax cut most," Brown said in a television interview in April. "While this administration suggests a tax cut through a reduction in the capital gains tax for the wealthiest Americans, the Democratic party will always be on the side of the working men and women."[4] Moynihan's Social Security tax cut idea never got off the ground, but Brown's embrace of it helped get the DNC focused on a message of being on the side of middle-class and working-class families. "For the next three years it was working Americans, working Americans, working Americans," said Dan Carol. "We were just going to say it over and over again."[5]

The message was pumped out by McCurry's operation, which started "PartyLines," a computerized newsletter made available daily to Democratic officeholders and state party officials. In the days before the Internet and web pages, subscribers to "PartyLines" were given a special telephone number that would allow them to dial into the DNC's computer and receive the day's "talking points" via modem. It was technologically crude, but it was an attempt to have everyone in the party singing from the same hymnal. Brown stressed that, unlike a member of Congress, who had to fashion bipartisan compromises to get bills enacted, he could be more stingingly partisan to help define the public's view of the party. "We have a responsibility to help shape the political landscape of the country," Brown said on June 25, 1990.[6]

His timing was good. Polling done for the Democrats showed that while Bush remained personally popular, the percentage of people who expressed satisfaction with the direction in which the country was headed was plunging. Bush might still be well liked, but he was vulnerable. On June 26, as bad economic news kept pouring in, the president, showing signs of rising unease, announced that he was willing to enter into talks with Democratic congressional leaders over the federal budget for the next fiscal year. What's more, Bush said that everything—including his "Read my lips, no new taxes!" pledge at the 1988 Republican convention—was on the table in order to prevent a serious economic slowdown.

Bush's reneging on his no-new-taxes pledge was a godsend to the Democrats. In August, Iraq's invasion of Kuwait gave Bush's popularity a temporary uptick when he responded with a tough, unyielding position. But the budget negotiators finally reached an agreement that did raise some taxes. And the Democrats succeeded in moving the debate away from whether to raise taxes—a position that was a political loser for the party—to whose taxes should be raised. That was a position that allowed the party to play to its strength as defender of the middle class while the Republicans, who still resisted tax increases for the affluent, could be painted as favoring the rich.

Still, raising taxes is a risky political move at any time. As Democratic leaders struggled to maintain the party's support for their negotiating positions, Brown and the DNC played a critical behind-the-scenes role. Senior committee staff provided periodic briefings to Democratic lawmakers showing that the rhetoric of "tax fairness" was playing well in the country. "This gave them something to show that there's some value here," Baggett recalled. "There's some value in sticking together. We made the point that fairness is not a bad word when it comes to taxes."[7] Tully, Steitz, and others wowed the technologically backward lawmakers by making these presentations on laptop computers hooked to television monitors in House and Senate caucus rooms. The technology helped create the impression—and Brown always wanted to create impressions—of cutting-edge competence on the part of the DNC. The content helped stiffen Democratic lawmakers' spines. "The key to retaining the confidence of the [House] members was public opinion research and the demonstration of political acumen," said Dreyer. "That came from the DNC; that came from Ron Brown."[8]

As election day approached, the committee began training young operatives to work in the field. Robinson and others got state parties to sign agreements that they would implement joint campaigns. Brown secured an agreement from the AFL-CIO's Committee on Political Education—a traditional source of funding for many Democrats—that organized labor would not contribute to campaigns that did not come to an agreement on a campaign plan. By November the DNC had put together coordinated campaigns in thirty-three states and had directly contributed $4.5 million to state parties to run them. Using those contributions as seed money, the DNC was able to leverage an additional $30 million in soft money donations to state parties from unions and wealthy individuals.

On November 6, 1990, the Democrats won an additional eight seats in the House and one in the Senate. In addition, the party won governors' races in Florida and Texas, two of what Brown and others considered the top three gubernatorial races that year. True, they were mixed results. The party in the White House generally loses seats in an off-year election. The Democrats had failed to take the governor's mansion in the critical state of California. Brown and Tully laid much of the blame for the loss in California at the feet of Edmund G. "Jerry" Brown, the enigmatic former governor who had become state party chairman. During his tenure, Jerry Brown had done a poor job raising money and organizing the coordinated campaign in the state. Still, to Ron Brown, wins, no matter how modest, were good enough reasons to trumpet his effectiveness as DNC chair.

"Today there are more Democrats at every level of politics, except the White House, than there were in 1980," Brown said five months after the elections. "More governors, more senators, more congressmen, more mayors, more state legislators—more Democrats at every level."[9]

Brown could, and did, claim that under his leadership the Democrats had been transformed. When he took over, the party was a group of frightened copycats who couldn't defeat the capital gains tax cut in the House in 1989 and who prompted bold assertions from Bush's advisers that the GOP would pick up thirty seats in the 1990 elections.[10] By the end of 1990 the Democrats had been transformed to a party that had bloodied a sitting president for two election cycles in a row. And in 1990 it did so at a time when the United States had thousands of troops poised to go to war in the Persian Gulf, a time when the country normally rallies behind a president and his party.

As the Democrats—with Brown exhorting them—moved the debate from foreign affairs to the domestic economy, they moved it from the area of Bush's biggest strength to the field of his starkest weaknesses.

The lesson was not lost on two aides to Richard Gephardt—Paul Begala and George Stephanopoulos—who viewed the 1990 budget fight from close quarters. Both would become key advisers to the Democrats' 1992 nominee, Bill Clinton. "Clinton basically beat Bush on the economic argument, about who the party was willing to fight for and stand up for," said a key Gephardt aide. "The major issue in the '90 election was the whole tax fairness issue, and Clinton then built on that message." The fight sowed the seeds for the theme of Clinton's coming campaign. It was the economy, stupid.

As Brown took stock of the year, he reflected fleetingly on his own personal economic fortunes. In 1990 he and Nolanda Hill formed First International, Inc., an investment bank that tried to put together international deals, mostly in the newly emerging free nations of Eastern Europe. The company occupied the same office suite as Hill's own firm, Corridor Broadcasting and, according to Hill, was little more than a means to allow her to repatriate profits from the former communist countries. Worried about possible difficulties in bringing out profits, Hill said she set up First International as a subcontractor to Corridor. That way money could be brought out of places like Poland as business expense payments to First International rather than as profits. Brown invested no money in the company for his 50 percent stake. He paid scant attention to the details of how First International was run. As usual, he had other things on his mind. With the midterm elections behind him, Brown was itching to kick into a higher gear. He had forged closer links with Congress and won the confidence of many on Capitol Hill in 1990. He now trained his eyes and efforts on the big prize—the White House in 1992.

As Tully laid it out, the DNC would be engaging in a number of critical activities over the next eighteen months. It would help sharpen the party's message to convince the "persuadables" and energize reliable Democratic voters. It would try to figure out what to do about California. As the country's most populous state, California held a pivotal place in Brown's and Tully's road map to the White House. It was one of the three "C's"—along with cities and the coordinated campaign—that was at the basis of their strategy. But as important as California was, it was also currently a mess. After Jerry Brown's poor performance as state party chairman, Tully declared that it would be critical for the former governor to be removed from any important tactical job. "We desperately want our state chairman to run for the Senate or for anything else that requires his resignation," Tully wrote. "If he remains there, we could well be thinking about running 1992 out of an alternative structure to the party."[11]

Finally, Tully made clear that the DNC should move into a new posture, that of being the agent of the yet-to-be-named nominee. As he saw it, the committee would secure personal alliances with potential nominees. It would look out after all the possible candidates' interests, making sure the party did little or nothing during the nominating process that would harm the nominee's chances of winning. During the winter and spring of 1992, the potential nominees would be too busy focusing on the primaries to be concerned about the potential impact of DNC or party decisions. Tully suggested that the top DNC staff try to do that for them. It was, Tully reasoned, the only way to ensure that Brown and the DNC would play a role in the fall election. "If the political operatives of the nominees do not know what is happening at the DNC or do not trust us to make it happen, as soon as they are able, they will make sure that the only thing happening is that which is in their plans and within the control of their people," he wrote.[12]

ON JANUARY 16, 1991, an international crisis once again scrambled the political radar. As American, Saudi, and European aircraft initiated sorties over Kuwait and Iraq, the five-month "sitzkrieg" in the Persian Gulf came to an end. America was in a shooting war.

Brown's immediate response to the fighting was to convene the DNC staff—from his closest advisers to secretaries and receptionists. Surveying his troops on the fifth floor of the committee's headquarters building, near the Capitol, Brown was somber. "We have one message here," Brown told them. "We're going to support our troops. I'm a veteran myself. . . . We're going to be very supportive of our troops. We're not going to say anything that suggests otherwise."

As a former soldier who was once stationed near Warsaw Pact troops in Germany and North Korean troops on the Korean Peninsula, Brown could empathize with American troops in Saudi Arabia and Kuwait. As a politician, Brown, no doubt, had a clear enough recollection of how a few ill-considered words spoken about the Shah of Iran while American hostages were being held had helped kill Ted Kennedy's chances for the Democratic nomination in 1980. Brown was clear on one thing: the DNC would not hand the Republicans a cheap and easy issue. "If anyone learned from a mistake it was Ron," said Maria Cardona, a DNC media aide. "He wasn't going to repeat that one."[13]

The thirty-seven-day aerial bombardment of Iraq and Iraqi troops and the hundred-hour ground war ended with mixed results. Iraqi troops were chased from Kuwait with minuscule American casualties, but Iraq's president, Saddam Hussein, remained in power. Still, America erupted with an outpouring of patriotism and propelled Bush's approval ratings to 91 percent at one point, a stratospheric high that no other president had achieved since polling began. Suddenly all the plans and strategies of how to take on Bush seemed for naught. The president seemed a shoo-in. "My sense is George Bush is getting close to unbeatable," said Jim Ruvolo.[14] Republicans were anticipating a landslide victory the following year that would lead to big gains in both the House and the Senate as well. "I think it could be bigger than 1984; I think it could be 1980 all over again," said Sen. Phil Gramm, a Texas Republican.[15]

With the Iowa caucuses less than a year away, the Democrats looked in vain for a standard-bearer. Well into the summer, the only announced candidate was former senator Paul Tsongas of Massachusetts, a slight, unimposing figure. With a whiny lisp, he preached fiscal austerity that Tully liked to call "eat your peas." Neither Brown nor Tully was impressed. When they met with Tsongas in March 1991, they did their best to politely discourage his campaign.

But it looked like Tsongas was all the Democrats would get. Brown worked the telephones to potential candidates to make the case that, despite what seemed like long odds, a Democrat really could win in 1992. It was a tough selling job. At one staff meeting, Brown was startled to see his senior aides, including Baggett, Herman, and Steitz, sitting glumly around the table wringing their hands over what seemed to be the inevitable loss in '92.

"What's wrong?" he asked.

"Are you fucking kidding?" one answered.

Brown gave them all a tongue-lashing. They had a political plan. It was solid. It would work. Bush's poll numbers would come down. The Democrats would beat him in November. There was to be no defeatism. But the crisis of confidence within the DNC was compounded by a new round of financial woes. With Bush riding so high in the polls, donors became reluctant to fund Brown's and Tully's plans to build a campaign structure to beat him the next year. In December, Tully had spoken of the need to raise $60 million to put his and Brown's plans in place for the 1992 campaign. Now the DNC couldn't afford copier paper. "It was that bad," said Steitz. "We kept that out of the newspapers."[16]

Casting their nets for revenue from new sources who were not intimidated by Bush's daunting position in the polls, Brown and his staff were impressed by the potential of the burgeoning Asian American population. Immigration from East Asia in the 1970s and 1980s, especially from Korea, the Philippines, Taiwan, Vietnam, and the People's Republic of China, had swelled the Asian American community, particularly in the politically important state of California. As the Asian American population grew in both size and wealth, some urged it to become more active in the political process through voting or donating to candidates for office. It looked like a promising situation. No one foresaw the trouble ahead.

Among those pushing for a more robust role for Asian Americans were John Huang, a Taiwanese American banker who lived in Glendale, California; Maria Hsia, a Los Angeles woman, originally from Taiwan, who was an expert in immigration law; and Melinda Yee, the executive director of the Organization of Chinese Americans.

Hsia, who came to the United States as a student in 1973, began raising funds for state and local candidates in California in the 1980s. In 1988 she raised money for Lt. Gov. Leo McCarthy's unsuccessful race for the U.S. Senate, funneling soft money contributions through the Democratic Senatorial Campaign Committee. Two years later she put together a $250-a-plate fundraising dinner for the reelection campaign of Al Gore, the Tennessee Democrat. Huang also became politically active, believing that Asian Americans needed to be involved in politics, especially during the late 1980s when Congress was debating legislation to scale back legal immigration.

Hsia's political work, as well as that of Huang, was not solely the result of civic-minded altruism. Both also served as agents for James Riady and his father, Mochtar Riady, an Indonesian magnate whose company, the Lippo Group, included construction and banking operations in the Far East and, to a lesser extent, the United States. The Riadys saw political contributions as a way to further their business interest. They believed that the donations would produce close ties with American politicians, which, in turn, would boost their image in Asia. "Foreign businessmen who maintain political contacts in the U.S. are highly regarded in foreign countries," federal agents later reported that Huang told them. "For instance, a foreign businessman would be highly regarded in his country if seen greeting a U.S. Senator in a familiar way." The Riadys employed Hsia and Huang, the chief operating officer of the Lippo Bank of Los Angeles, owned by James Riady, to direct their political activity in the United States. Father and son helped Hsia and Huang set up the Pacific Leadership Council, a nonprofit organization that raised money, mainly for Democratic candidates for the Senate.

Riady's action differed little from activities of companies from Europe, Canada, and other foreign nations. But a combination of clumsy fund-raising that at times crossed the legal line, aggressive Republican congressional investigators, and the racism that saw attempts by Asians to influence American politics as more nefarious than similar attempts by Europeans were to cause the Democrats a host of difficulties in the ensuing years. Where others saw race, however, Brown's DNC saw only money.

In 1990, Yee left her job with the Organization of Chinese Americans to come to work for the DNC. Brown made her director of constituencies in the political division with the responsibility of doing outreach to Asian Americans. Though Yee's job was not supposed to directly involve fund-raising, in the summer of 1991 she put together a trip that put Brown face-to-face with political and business leaders in Taiwan, Hong Kong, and Hawaii to raise money for the DNC. The ten-day journey in December was paid for by a Taiwanese political party and the Lippo Group.

In an internal DNC memo, Yee spelled out her hopes for the trip's fruits. "Maria Hsia will play an important role in Taiwan. She sees this trip as the opportunity to finally fulfill her trusteeship to us," Yee wrote, referring to Hsia's commitment to raise $100,000 for the DNC.[17] Yee added, "John Huang is our key to Hong Kong. He is interested in renewing his trusteeship to us on this trip through his Asian banking connections. He has agreed to host a high-dollar event for us in Hong Kong with wealthy Asian bankers who are either U.S. permanent residents or with U.S. corporate ties."[18]

As stated by Yee, the fund-raising activities on the Asian trip would not violate American election laws. Candidates and parties are allowed to receive money from U.S. citizens or permanent residents who are living abroad and from the U.S. subsidiaries of foreign-owned companies. But the trip was one of the early signs of the Democrats' tapping donors in the Asian community, including ones who lived abroad. Such fund-raising would cause the party enormous woes in later years.

THE BASIC PROBLEM did not go away. It was Bush's commanding lead in the polls. Brown had to find a way to boost the lagging spirits of the Democratic fat cats, its principal fund-raisers. As a former DNC staffer put it, "We were trying to get people out of this notion that there was no hope; out of this wringing of hands syndrome; out of the feeling of, 'What are we gonna do? What are we gonna do?'"

Changing the attitudes of fund-raisers was crucial to luring high-quality candidates into the field. So Gary Barron set up a string of exclusive seminar-style meetings across the country for Brown, Steitz, and others to make the case for the Democrats to hang in there. In places such as Quincy Jones's base-ment, Pamela Harriman's Georgetown salon, and Larry and Shelia Lawrence's living room in their new house on Coronado Island, Brown attempted to change the emotional climate. It was a seeding of the clouds in the hope that those clouds would eventually bring a rain of cash.

Brown, Steitz, and sometimes Tully hammered away at Bush's vulnerabili-ties on the home front. "If you looked at the data, a Democrat could win," said Robinson. "Even at the height of the Gulf War, Bush's numbers on domestic stuff were in the toilet."[19] Indeed, polls showed solid majorities giving Bush failing grades on his handling of the economy, reducing the deficit, fighting the war on drugs, protecting the environment, and improving education. When asked in a Gallup Poll in March what was the most important issue facing the country, Iraq was listed by 4 percent.

The June seminar at Willow Oaks, Pamela Harriman's sixty-eight-acre coun-try estate near Middleburg, in the heart of the Virginia horse country, was piv-otal. Brown invited some of the richer and more reliable Democratic fund-raisers and a number of possible Democratic contenders. Although the session was closed to the public, the press was alerted in advance that the meeting was taking place. The DNC press operation figured reporters would find out about the gathering anyway. And besides, having coverage of top Democratic money men, party strategists, and potential candidates all plotting how to unseat George Bush sent the message that the Democrats were not going to roll over.

Brown and the DNC staff, led by Stein, spent a month and a half planning the event. Among the declared or potential candidates who attended were Tsongas and senators Lloyd Bentsen of Texas, Bill Bradley of New Jersey, Tom Harkin of Iowa, Bob Kerrey of Nebraska, George Mitchell of Maine, the Major-ity Leader, and John D. "Jay" Rockefeller IV of West Virginia. House Speaker Tom Foley, Gephardt, and Gov. Bill Clinton of Arkansas also showed up. Al Gore, Jesse Jackson, Doug Wilder, and Mario Cuomo decided not to attend.

In addition to Harriman, other big-time Democratic contributors included Ted Field, the heir to the Marshall Field fortune; Steve Grossman from Boston; Alida Rockefeller Messinger; and Monte Friedkin, a real estate developer from Boca Raton, Florida.

In the weeks leading up to the event, Brown, Steitz, and Stein worked with Tully on his presentation, which again showed how Bush could be taken down and was the centerpiece of the session. Tully hated being edited and would often rave or pout. But everyone knew the importance of his talk and wanted to make sure he did not lapse into his indecipherable "Tullyese" and lose everyone. "Steitz was pretty brilliant in dealing with Paul in terms of Paul's psychology, and we got it down to a pretty short but powerful pre-sentation," said Stein.[20] Mock sessions were run over and over for Brown. Each part of the seminar, from the chairman's opening remarks to possible approaches to donors, was thought through, practiced again and again, and presented to Brown over and over. Nothing was left to chance.

Rather than starting off with a presentation of the current political landscape, Brown walked around the room stopping by each of those in attendance to tell everyone who he or she was, explain why they were invited, relate a funny or poignant anecdote, describe his relationship with the person, and detail their importance in the Democratic Party. He then invited everyone to speak about why they came and what they expected to get out of the meeting. Subtly, Brown sucked everybody in, establishing a connection and making those who came feel like it was as much their meeting as the DNC's. "If we just started throwing information at everybody, there wasn't going to be an investment in the process and in us," said Stein. "But if people had a chance right at the beginning to say something, anything, we could maximize the degree of engagement."[21]

The plan worked to perfection. The politicians and fund-raisers became seriously engaged in the discussion. Tully's presentation not only laid out how Bush could be toppled, it also pointed to what the DNC would need to help do the job. Breakout sessions were held in which small groups would discuss various aspects of the DNC's plan and how it could be improved. Finally, just before lunch on the second day, the delicate subject of making financial commitments was raised.

"Well, what do you need from us?" Mark Mellman, who attended the session, recalled someone in the audience asking.

"I need your help; I need your assistance," Brown replied. "Let's have lunch and we'll talk about it."

"Wait a minute," piped up Monte Friedkin, the brash Floridian. Friedkin was a veteran of rough but highly effective fund-raisers held by the United Jewish Appeal. In those affairs there was none of this I'll-see-what-I-can-do. Cards were put on the table.

"We're not going to lunch," Friedkin said. "We gotta raise this money! I'm gonna give $100,000 and I want to know, right now, what everybody else is gonna give."[22]

As they went around the room, all but two of the Democratic donors pledged $100,000. In the end the event brought in more than $2 million for the DNC.

WHATEVER euphoria was generated at Middleburg soon dissipated in the heat of the summer. Though the economy continued to slacken, Bush's approval ratings remained high, and one by one big-name Democrats shied away from challenging him. In August, Gore opted out, saying he needed to attend to his family, especially his young son, Albert, who was recovering from a serious auto accident. The same month Jay Rockefeller also announced he would not run, declaring he was "not ready" to be president. "Rockefeller was this close to running," said one former DNC staffer, holding his thumb and forefinger a millimeter apart. "He had gone down South. He had done meetings with state chairs. He had gotten some tentative commitments. But his wife, Sharon Percy Rockefeller, was really skeptical. Tully went over to make the case to her. But basically she told him no Democrat can win now. We ain't running."

The withdrawal of Gore and Rockefeller to the sidelines, where they joined Gephardt, who had declined to run in April, hit the DNC hard. "August of '91 was definitely a low point in the building," said Dan Carol.[23] For want of a viable candidate, everything the DNC had achieved was going up in smoke. Opportunities outside the committee beckoned, and they looked more tantalizing than ever.

Will Robinson left.

Alexis Herman seriously considered quitting. She had told Brown when she took the chief of staff's job in the spring of 1989 that she would stay only six months. It had been two years, and she wanted to get back to running her own business. The possibility of her resignation hit Brown particularly hard. The two were exceedingly close, and because of that, he was concerned about the signal her departure would send. He asked her to reconsider.

The following evening, Herman went to Brown's office with a fifth of Wild Turkey for a chat. She told him she wasn't going anywhere so he need not give her any spin to convince her to stay. But, she asked after a few sips of the bourbon, did he really think they had a chance of winning in '92?

"Between you and me," she said. "No lights, no cameras. I know you have to say this stuff. But do you really believe this?"[24] Brown looked steadily at her and nodded his head. It was going to be hard, he said. But, yeah, he earnestly felt Bush could be beaten. Herman had already decided she would stay on, and now that she knew that Brown really did have the strength of his convictions, she had another concern.

"I remember thinking, 'What planet is this guy on?'" she said.[25]

CHAPTER FOURTEEN

VICTORY

A S 1991 WOUND DOWN, Democratic candidates slowly began to emerge.
Doug Wilder announced on September 13 that he would seek the nomination. He was followed two days later by Sen. Tom Harkin of Iowa. Sen. Bob
Kerrey of Nebraska and Jerry Brown followed in rapid succession. Over time,
Bill Clinton became a favorite of Tully. Virtually any other candidate would
have been sunk by the whiff of scandal that swirled around Clinton. But he
always bounced back from the dead, an attribute Brown and Tully in particular admired. "I know there were some in the political department who didn't
believe Clinton could be elected," said Steve Rosenthal. "There were others,
including the chairman and Paul, who flat out thought this guy had what it
takes to win the general election. I remember Tully saying one time that Clinton could take a punch better than anybody and just keeps coming back."[1]

In the beginning Brown was not especially enamored with Clinton. The
Arkansas governor had held back until the very last minute in 1989 before
endorsing Brown's bid to be DNC chairman. But as the Iowa caucuses drew
closer, Brown put aside the misgivings he had about Clinton.

One Sunday night, just before the caucuses, Gerald McEntee, head of
AFSCME, called Brown at home. McEntee wanted to talk about Clinton. The
union was about to endorse a candidate. Most other unions were leaning
toward Harkin, a liberal candidate with the best record on labor issues. Other
unions were holding back, hoping that Mario Cuomo would jump into the
race. But McEntee said AFSCME was strongly considering backing Clinton. "I
think that's the best choice," Brown told McEntee. "I think that he's going to
get the nomination, and I think he can win."[2]

Throughout the spring of 1992 Clinton began to pull away from the rest
of the Democratic contenders. But he seemed unable to catch fire with the
general public. He seemed stuck behind Bush in many polls; some had him
third, trailing Bush and H. Ross Perot, an eccentric Texan billionaire who, running as a third party candidate, tapped into the smoldering voter resentment
of both Republicans and Democrats. Worrying about a looming Clinton loss, a
number of Democratic notables and fund-raisers were desperately looking

around to draft another candidate, the ever-dithering Cuomo or Bill Bradley. Brown shut down that kind of talk as soon as he heard it.

By this time DNC insiders were not surprised to hear Brown cut off internal dissent. Early on as chair, Brown had quietly supported the blocking of Bella Abzug, a party icon but a left-wing ideologue, to be chairwoman of the DNC's Women's Caucus. He had also resisted pressure to reinstate the party's midterm convention, a meeting that had for a number of years taken place in the second year after the presidential election. The midterm convention generally was a place for the party's ideological differences to be played out in full flower in front of the assembled political reporters and once more paint the party as hopelessly split. Kirk had ended them during his reign, and Brown was in no mood to bring them back.

Brown went further to keep the party's internal bickering in the closet. At DNC meetings, which were open to the public and the press, he stationed staffers next to the microphones where members of the committee and the public could ask him and other party leaders questions. Before a person could pose his or her question, the staffer would quietly approach the questioner and ask what was on his or her mind. If the proposed query was deemed too incendiary, questioners were asked if they really wanted to bring up that subject now. What would be gained? Could they not contact the DNC staff in private and express their concerns? Among the true believers of an open DNC process, Brown's operation was mordantly called "Politburoesque."

In the late spring of 1992 as Clinton was wrapping up the nomination, Brown was not going to allow concerns over the candidate's character and electability to burst into public view. Ken Brody, a New York investment banker, recalled being with Brown on Manhattan's Upper East Side at a party held by a Bradley supporter. The mood was sour. Most of the crowd believed Clinton was going down to defeat and would drag other Democratic candidates with him. Wasn't there some way, they asked, to short-circuit Clinton's march toward the nomination? Brown, however, would hear none of it. The primaries had determined the party's nominee, he said. Clinton could win. They should back him and quit their carping.

"A crowd of angry New Yorkers is about as tough a crowd as you get to deal with," said Brody. "And Ron Brown, as the chair of the party, was brilliant in how he dealt with them. He was just fabulous."[3] Said Stein, "He could have really fucked Clinton big-time, but he stayed with him. His public statements were incredibly supportive. This was a period when everybody was saying, 'My God, we've got to get somebody else in the race because this guy is tanking.' Ron did everything he could, both out front and behind the scenes, to keep others from getting in."[4]

After the New York primary in April, Brown approached the Clinton campaign to say he believed that, barring some unforeseen circumstances, the

Arkansas governor would secure the nomination. He wanted to begin planning to integrate the DNC campaign operation with the candidate's. "He said, 'I can't say this publicly, but I can count, and I know who's going to be the nominee. It's time for us to start thinking about making the transition to the general election,'" said David Wilhelm, a top Clinton aide.[5]

Technically, Brown was breaking what had been a bedrock tradition. The party chairman was supposed to maintain a strict neutrality until the nomination was officially won. But such a quaint custom was made for tight, down-to-the-wire nomination battles and brokered conventions, when candidates were determined after several breath-holding ballots. Those times were gone forever. With a front-loaded primary calendar, the intense importance of having funds to mount television campaigns and the tendency of big-money donors scrambling quickly off a perceived loser's bandwagon, the nomination process was over relatively quickly. There would be no last-minute challenge to Bill Clinton. Why maintain the private fiction of neutrality, even if tradition called for its public pretense? Besides, Brown knew that if he was going to have a chance to have the DNC play a role in the general election campaign he had to move as soon as it was clear which candidate was going to emerge from the Democratic field. The longer he waited the less he would be negotiating from a position of strength.

Brown felt it was time to start talking about integrating staffs. He wanted to know who were the people in the Clinton campaign who were experts at field organizing, fund-raising, media strategy, message development, scheduling strategy, and other campaign activities. He wanted to put them together with their counterparts at the DNC. "He kept asking, 'Who is this Ram guy?'" Wilhelm recalled, referring to how Brown mangled the name of Rahm Emanuel, Clinton's chief fund-raiser.

By late spring, after the California primary, the Clinton campaign was flat broke. Discarding any pretense of neutrality, Brown arranged for the DNC to provide Clinton with a quick infusion of cash to buy a few television spots, according to Eli Sigel. Though he did not hold the title, Sigel served as the day-to-day manager of the Clinton campaign. "It was evidence of how Ron made the transition from being DNC chair to being cheerleader for the nominee earlier than it had been done before," said Sigel.[6]

Brown approached that summer's Democratic National Convention as if it were an integral part of the Clinton campaign. Partly as a favor to David Dinkins and partly because he considered New York his hometown, Brown had pushed the committee to designate New York City as the convention site. Others argued that it would be a mistake to hold the convention in the Big Apple, that it would reinforce the image of the Democrats as the party of northern liberalism and black people. But Brown held his ground. Holding the convention in New York would send a message that the party still cared about its urban base. "If the party couldn't show a commitment to New York and to urban centers, then it had real problems," said Mario Cooper, who worked on convention planning for the DNC.[7]

Remembering the debacle of the 1980 convention, Brown was determined that there would be little, if any, dissention at Madison Square Garden this time around. The Democrats would go into and come out of New York unified. There would be no rifts, even if they were repaired during the convention. The platform was worked out with a minimum of infighting. So instead of a long, drawn-out string of platform hearings, the DNC held one interminable day-long session. The overriding theme the political media came away with was not the clash of strident ideologies. It was tedium. "We had a day that ran from nine A.M. to midnight and bored people to tears," said Dan Carol.[8] No one was anticipating a fight over the platform at the New York convention.

Nor would there be battles over credentials. Hearing officers had been named months before to arbitrate credential challengers away from the media glare of the convention. No one would be allowed to speak at the convention unless that person had publicly endorsed the ticket of Bill Clinton and Al Gore.

Governor Robert Casey of Pennsylvania, perhaps the Democrats' most outspoken and highly visible foe of abortion, was not pleased. Casey, who had been one of the party's top vote-getters in the 1990 election, winning his race by more than 1 million votes, wanted to address the convention. But he would not, nor would he pledge to, endorse Clinton beforehand. Brown said no, even though in 1989 Casey had played a pivotal role in Brown's campaign for party chairman. It was worth using some political capital to avoid provoking boos, catcalls, and possibly even a floor demonstration by abortion rights opponents. The rules provided a convenient smoke screen. "If someone's not going to pledge their support to our candidate, Ron felt we needed to have some discipline and some consequences," said Cooper.[9]

Brown wanted more than just party unity. He wanted to make the public believe that Democrats were a patriotic party that could make government work for the average American. In the months leading up to the convention, he found just the backdrop he was looking for to make that statement. Garth Ancier, the young head of programming at Fox Broadcasting, had been brought in to provide some fresh ideas for staging the convention. He came up with the concept of constructing an eight-foot-by-seven-foot "video wall" made up of fifty-six television monitors whose pictures would be synchronized via a computer to produce one large, dynamic, and moving visual image.

At first, Ancier's idea was disparaged by many of the other convention planners. It was costly. The lighting in Madison Square Garden wouldn't allow it to work. There was a fear that the television networks, wary of being manipulated into presenting certain visual images, would decide not to show what was being broadcast on the wall. But Ancier's idea did have one important convert from the start: Brown. "He liked it immediately and he got it immediately," said Cooper. "His eyes lit up, and I think we all knew it was going to be a done deal, no matter what we said."[10]

"I remember sitting and negotiating with Ron and Alexis at Madison Square Garden," said Bill Lynch, who was Dinkins's chief aide. "It was hot and they had me in this room and I was trying to hold the line. But they convinced me that I should go convince Mayor Dinkins to spend $1 million that was not in our budget for this video wall."[11]

Brown was so convinced of the impact the wall's technical wizardry would achieve that he went to the mat for the idea when the Clinton campaign tried to shoot it down; the campaign even went so far as to try to cover the wall with a tarpaulin for Clinton's acceptance speech on the last night of the convention. Clinton's people feared that the audience would focus its attention on the video screens rather than the candidate. But Brown backed Ancier, and the wall, which was later to be praised as the most innovative part of the convention, remained uncloaked.

"The thing I liked about Ron Brown was that he was usually the person who would leap to your defense when you came up with something that was a fresh idea, as opposed to being the sort of older generation folks, people who had been around the Democratic Party forever, who had done things a long time and were just staunch defenders of the status quo," said Ancier.[12]

One more detail required Brown's personal attention. He would have to do some hustling to get Mario Cuomo to give Clinton's nominating speech at the convention. Traditionally, the host state's governor, if he or she is of the same party, gives a major speech at any convention, and Brown thought that Cuomo, the party's best orator next to Jesse Jackson, would be perfect to place Clinton's name in nomination during a prime-time speech. But the prickly New York governor was irked at Clinton for his remarks in a taped telephone conversation with his mistress, Gennifer Flowers, that compared Cuomo to a mafia hood. Clinton had survived salacious allegations of an extramarital affair with the Little Rock lounge singer, but Cuomo had neither forgiven nor forgotten the episode. The Clinton camp, on the other hand, was not enamored with the imperious Cuomo. They were not sure they wanted him in the first place. But Brown did, and he schemed to make it happen. He convinced Clinton that he should call Cuomo to at least make the pretense of asking him to give the nominating speech. Don't worry, Brown assured Clinton, he won't take your call. Brown then convinced Cuomo to accept the call. Don't worry, he told the New York governor, he won't ask you to give the speech. The reluctant suitors soon found themselves together on a telephone line. The offer was made and then accepted.

Just as the convention opened, Brown watched Ross Perot's emotional and, at times, incoherent press conference on television from his hotel suite. Perot, who had been stealing publicity if not votes from the Democrats, abruptly announced he was quitting the race. A huge smile split the party chairman's face. It was a long way from the time when he had seemed to be the only person in the country who believed the Democrats would win, when his close friend Alexis Herman had questioned his sanity. He could actually taste victory. "There was this palpable sense of, 'My God, we're going to win,' " said Dan Carol, who watched the Perot press conference with Brown. "I think it was the first time he knew it. There was no doubt. It was the first time he would be willing to go to Las Vegas and put lots of money on it."[13]

THE CONVENTION was a grand success. It held together. It presented a solid message for the ticket to run on. It presented Clinton and Gore as fresh young faces with new ideas. Yet as the Clinton/Gore campaign rolled out of New York on a bus caravan—another idea originated at the DNC—to start the general election campaign, Brown was growing uneasy. A casual observer might have wondered why, given Brown's accomplishments.

After all, he looked back on three years of putting meat on the idea of a coordinated campaign and selling it to the party. He had raised money, built the DNC into a savvy political operation, and proved its acumen. Modesty aside, he had expanded the party's base into new ethnic communities. There were clearly votes and revenue to be found among the country's growing Hispanic, Asian, and even Arab populations, as well as among African Americans. Brown knew these groups had not been properly attended to in recent years and sought to change that. Among his first acts as chairman was to invite Jim Zogby, executive director of the Arab-American Institute, a civil rights and lobbying organization, to meet with him in his office. During his tenure Brown also spoke a number of times at the group's convention, despite being warned by some Jewish activists that such an action might jeopardize Jewish support of the party. "I recognized that it wasn't about changing Ron Brown's politics," said Zogby, noting that Brown remained strongly pro-Israel. "It was about Ron Brown being fair. And he was, from that point on, an advocate for our inclusion."[14]

In 1990 the DNC had hired Maria Cardona, a young émigreé originally from Bogotá, Colombia, to beef up the outreach to ethnic media. Under her direction, the committee placed more stories in Spanish-language media, both print and broadcast, and in a number of Asian American publications. It was, Cardona recalled, relatively easy to do since many of these news outlets were so pleased to be taken seriously that they fell over themselves to give Brown and the DNC coverage. "They told us, 'This is great. Nobody had really ever gone out of their way to talk to us. We were sort of an afterthought or they would talk to us only if we initiated the phone call,' " said Cardona. "But here we were doing weekly radio feeds to Hispanic radio stations around the country."[15]

Brown had also made sure not to neglect the party's traditional ethnic support, either. The DNC press operation sent out a steady stream of press releases to black-owned newspapers. Often these publications had so little editorial staff that they ran press releases verbatim. So the DNC knew that tending to black newspapers meant getting the committee's message out in a completely unvarnished fashion to a segment of the black community. And Brown looked for every opportunity he could to mend fences with Jews.

All these actions were pointed toward assuring that when the fall presidential campaign began the DNC and its chairman would not be discarded like some well-worn but no-longer-needed old shoe. Now, despite all Brown's plans and work, that seemed to be happening anyway. He had not figured on how much the monumental egos, the distrust of outsiders among Clinton's inner circle, and the general chaos of the Clinton campaign operation would thwart his well-laid plans.

"He never complained. But he was treated like any other DNC chair; they're relegated to less importance," said Stein. "The campaign people did not take Ron real seriously. He did not like that one bit."[16]

There was not a wholesale disregard of the DNC, but neither was there the equal partnership that Brown had envisioned. Rahm Emanuel—that "Ram guy," as Brown called him—who was Clinton's chief fund-raiser, felt that the DNC had done a credible job of raising money through direct mail and courting large, $100,000 donors. But he felt the DNC had not paid attention to middle-level contributors, those who gave in $5,000, $10,000, or $15,000 amounts. Emanuel proceeded to virtually take over the money-raising function of the committee, easing out Melissa Moss, who had been doing the job since 1989. Moss complained to Brown, who could only tell her that she had to swallow her anger and go along with the program.

The takeover of the DNC fund-raising operation was made all the more galling because the Clinton campaign also placed a number of financial experts at the DNC to keep tabs on how the money was being spent. Much of the money being raised was passed along as soft money contributions to state parties. The Clintonites wanted to ensure that the money got to where it was supposed to go. This was hardly surprising; the campaign was raising enormous sums of money, and its officials naturally wanted to make sure it was being spent properly. But the Clinton campaign concern also stemmed from a distrust of Brown and other members of his inner circle like Alexis Herman and Bill Morton, Brown's personal aide. They were viewed within some parts of the Clinton campaign as profligate spenders who might divert funds to their own personal use. It was a suspicion that would surface later in the press.

"Ron Brown was respected, if not completely trusted," said one campaign official familiar with the situation. "He had a reputation for being slick, and the fact was this was his DNC. He brought it through some dark times and there was concern about whether or not he was going to give up control, whether or not they could really control the checkbook."

Brown refused to let the whispering get him down. It was the general disorganization of the Clinton campaign that really got on his nerves. Eventually, the rest of the country was to learn of Clinton's lack of discipline, his development of policies through late-night bull sessions with intimates over pizzas, his willingness to let things drift or to make a decision only to reverse himself after talking to a different set of advisers. But that was not well known during the 1992 campaign, at least not well known to Brown. It drove him nuts. It meant that his views as party chairman on campaign strategy could be overridden by any one of scores of other people just because he or she happened to be the person who talked to the candidate last. "I cannot fucking believe it," Brown told a former aide. "The only way I can get anything done on this goddamned campaign is to go sit on a bus for four days, talk to his wife, talk to him, talk to both of them, make sure nobody else talks to them, get a final decision, and then stay on the bus until it's implemented."

Brown was not the only one being sidestepped. Things were not going as expected for Tully, either. He had been reluctant to move from Washington to Little Rock and did so only after receiving assurances that he would play an important role in the campaign. Those promises had not panned out. Like Brown, he did not complain publicly. He continued to work away, preparing his famous spreadsheets to determine where and how the campaign should target its message. On September 24, forty days before the election, he was stricken with a massive heart attack in his room in a Little Rock hotel and died.

Tully's death shook Brown and the rest of the DNC staff to the core. In their grief, they looked to themselves, to their own mortality, and to their own culpability in allowing Tully to maintain a lifestyle that everyone knew would lead to an early demise. "Ron said at one point, 'I used to think we needed to force Tully to go to a spa,'" said Cooper. "He said that with kind of regret."[17] Cooper, openly homosexual, would have a particular reason to remember that comment. Soon after, he discovered that he had HIV, the precursor to AIDS. From the moment Brown heard the news, he would constantly call Cooper to inquire about his health and to remind him to make sure he took his medication.

But at the moment Brown's message to his shocked troops was not just to grieve but to keep working to elect Democrats, as Tully would have wanted. He went further, however. Brown stressed the importance of the staff's taking care of each other, of tactfully pointing out unhealthy habits, of making sure everyone got enough sleep and good food. Politics was important, and the best way to honor Tully's memory was to keep working for the Democratic ticket. But all that paled beside looking out for your friends and co-workers.

Press reports of Tully's death—virtually all of them painting sympathetic portraits of this committed and colorful Democratic warrior—emphasized the tragic irony of his leaving the scene so close to seeing his dream of finally electing a Democratic president fulfilled. But Tully knew what was going to happen. He had analyzed the race, voter attitudes, and other factors, and not only knew Clinton was going to win but which states he would carry. On one of his last spreadsheets he had used factors such as the increase in the selling price of single-family homes, the fall in unemployment, the growth in jobs, polling data, and traditional performance of Democratic voters to predict how the campaign would do in each state. He ranked Democratic chances in descending order of difficulty. On the day before he died, he showed Steve Rosenthal his predictions.

"This thing is over, Steve," he told his friend.

"Come on, Paul. It's not over yet," Rosenthal replied.

"No, it's over, Steve. Bush can't win."[18]

THROUGHOUT HIS ups and downs that summer and fall, Bill Clinton liked to call himself "the comeback kid." It was an apt metaphor highly descriptive of a candidate who, as Tully observed, "could take a punch" better than anyone he had ever seen. On election day, Clinton carried every state (except New Hampshire) that Tully had predicted the Democrats would either easily win or have a very good shot at winning. But if the language of the boxing ring applied to Clinton in 1992, it was equally descriptive of Brown and Tully, acting like the party's trainers, devising strategy, convincing their staggering pugilist it could work, yelling, exhorting, pleading, encouraging from the corner, refusing to throw in the towel. The final blow had been struck by Bill Clinton, but Ron Brown had been in the fight longer, willing his fighter along, refusing to let him give up. Despite the problems of the last days, Brown could legitimately claim a major stake in his party's victory. And he did.

"I remember the smile on Ron's face when he came downstairs with the first edition of the *Washington Post* that had the headline CLINTON WINS," said Steitz, recalling the Democrats' victory celebration at a Washington hotel on November 4. "The smile was just overwhelming. It could have lit up Yankee Stadium."[19]

From that day on, Brown traveled a different road than even he could have imagined. Accomplishments would exist alongside allegations; triumphs would be mixed with troubles. Brown and his advisers—more so his advisers than Brown himself—would ride an emotional roller coaster, trumpeting their boss's successes while waiting for the next shoe to drop. Clinton had raised Brown's profile, and in doing so increased Brown's sense of invincibility as well as his visibility. But in the post-Watergate, post-Abscam, post-Iran–Contra world of Washington that only meant that Ron Brown had become a bigger, more juicy target.

The chain of events that would cause Brown his greatest difficulties started innocuously enough. Shortly after the election, Lillian Madsen called and asked Brown if he would meet with an acquaintance of hers, Nguyen Van

Hao, a Vietnamese expatriate living in Coral Springs, Florida, to talk about easing U.S. economic sanctions against Vietnam. "I was asked that, since I knew
Ron Brown, that he was a friend, and a very powerful man, if he could arrange
to talk to him about the sanctions against his country," Madsen said.[20] Madsen
met Hao through her brother-in-law, Marc Ashton, a Florida businessman who
had once served as a financial adviser to Jean-Claude Duvalier. She said she
was moved by Hao's description of how much harm U.S. sanctions were causing among the poor in Vietnam. It reminded her of similar havoc that was
being visited on the poor in Haiti as a result of the economic squeeze the
United States was putting on the island in order to restore to power Jean-
Bertrand Aristide, the Haitian president who had been overthrown in a military
coup in 1991.

Brown, whose unwillingness to say no to friends was legendary, agreed.
In November 1992 he and Bill Morton met with Hao and Ashton in Fort Laud-
erdale, where Brown gave a perfunctory hearing to Hao's entreaties. "Bill's recollection was that [Ron] was more interested in the entrées—the food—than
in the discussion," one of his aides later said. The connection might have
ended there, but that was not to be.

ON A BLEAK DAY in Washington, Brown stood with Bill Clinton by the window of a suite in Washington's Hay Adams Hotel staring across Lafayette Park
at the White House. The presidential mansion stood out in stark relief against
the bleak, slate-gray sky on November 19, 1992. The weather, however, could
hardly dampen their moods. They had made history and they knew it. Fifteen
days earlier Clinton had become the first Democrat to be elected president in
twelve years and would soon occupy the stately mansion looming across
the park. Clinton gestured toward the White House and spoke the same words
he was to say on a more somber occasion: "I wouldn't have gotten it without you."

With his win, the president-elect was now doling out the spoils of victory.
Having acknowledged Brown's role, it would have been difficult for Clinton
not to offer him an important job in his administration. Politically, it would
have been suicidal to shun the party's most prominent African American.

Clinton and Brown, however, were on different wavelengths. Brown
longed to be secretary of State, the first of his race to be in charge of the
country's foreign policy. The job satisfied Brown's yearning to be a racial pioneer. There had never been a black secretary of State, and he was eager to
demonstrate that he could handle international diplomacy as well as run a
large bureaucracy. The position carried with it a wealth of prestige and patron-
age jobs to ladle out. But secretary of State was out of the question. From the
start, Clinton and his close advisers had it in their minds that the job should
go to Warren Christopher, a Los Angeles lawyer who had years of experience

in foreign affairs and who was heading up Clinton's transition team in Little Rock. Instead, Clinton wanted Brown to be ambassador to the United Nations.

The U.N. position, which Brown had heard about prior to the meeting, presented him with a difficult dilemma. It would allow him to indulge his interest in travel and other cultures, and it had wonderful perks. It would place him in New York, where he could solidify a base for a run for the Senate at some point, another one of Brown's ambitions. But it was not a cabinet-level position, and it was under the thumb of the secretary of State. Brown had seen how Andrew Young, the first black person to hold the position, had felt hemmed in by the secretaries of State in the Carter administration. Brown wanted to be what he considered a "serious" cabinet official, and wanted to show that he could run a large-scale department. Also, since Young and Donald McHenry, both of whom are black, had held the job during the Carter years, the U.N. job was becoming perilously close to being seen as another minority slot.

Still, Brown had seriously considered accepting it, much to the chagrin of several of his friends.

"That's a nigger job," Tommy Boggs joked to him when Brown said he was thinking of taking the U.N.

"Yeah," Brown replied with a smile in his voice. "But you ought to see the apartment and the car that come with it."[21]

By the time he arrived at the Hay Adams, Brown had made up his mind. No, he told Clinton, he did not want the U.N. ambassadorship. If the president-elect wanted him in his administration, he would have to come up with something else.

The importance of the moment was not just the offer of the U.N. job but the refusal. Brown no less than Clinton defined the new establishment. Black and white, born outsiders according to rules of the old order, deeply alike in their frank awareness of their mutual dependence and their shared vision of the future of American politics, they each had earned access to power the old-fashioned way—through hard work and outsized ambition.

Both Brown and Clinton were practical, pragmatic men. All that really mattered then—and it was enough—was this: it was payback time. A better deal for Ron Brown would just have to be worked out.

CHAPTER FIFTEEN

TRIUMPHS AND TROUBLES

T HE PHONE CALL came into the Democratic National Committee's office in the late morning of December 12, 1992, and was answered by Jim Desler, the DNC's deputy press secretary. Desler quickly recognized the voice of Ron Brown, who was calling from an airplane flying down to Little Rock. He was just the person Desler wanted to speak with. President-elect Clinton had been announcing the members of his cabinet during the past few weeks, and the previous day his aides had alerted reporters that another set of appointments would be made the next day. Speculation was rampant about who would be chosen, and a few enterprising network reporters, hearing that Brown was flying to Arkansas, had called Desler to see if they could pry out of him what job Brown was going to get.

"What is it, Jim?" each had asked. "The UN? Come on, you know. I know you know. You can tell me. It'll be on background. I won't say where I got it from. Come on, you know." In point of fact, Desler was as much in the dark as anyone. Now, with Brown on the other end of the line, the young DNC staffer could not resist asking his boss the same question.

"You don't need to tell me this," Desler said after a few moments of conversation, "and I will not tell any members of the press. You can trust me on that. But, what 'd'ya get?"

"It's Commerce, Jimmy," Brown replied.

"Commerce. That's great! Congratulations," Desler replied. "I think we need to start working on a statement for you for tomorrow. I can take the first crack at it. But first I kind of need to know one thing. What does the Commerce secretary do?"

Brown chuckled for a moment and then said, almost with a sigh, "To tell you the truth, Jimmy, I don't know myself. We're going to have to find out."[1]

Figuring out the functions of the department he was about to take over was a welcome relief to Brown, who for the past few weeks had been more concerned about whether he would be selected to any cabinet post at all. As the final round of cabinet appointees was being prepared, Brown wondered to friends whether he would be left out in the cold. Now the choice was whether he would take it. Suddenly, he wasn't sure.

The decision was not easy. Both Alma and Tommy Boggs counseled him against taking the offer. "He would have made a lot of money if he stayed out, which is what his wife and I were trying to convince him to do," said Boggs. "We suggested that he make some money, which he needed to do, and then go in. In a couple of years there is always turnover in the cabinet."[2]

Boggs had a point. Brown's lobbying and legal practice was finally bearing rich harvest. In 1992 Brown had earned $580,000 from his legal work. The election of a Democratic president and the Democratic majorities in both houses of Congress meant that his ability to attract new clients had just increased exponentially. He would be also relinquishing much of his outside income. In 1992 he had earned at least $90,000 from his work with PEBSCO and Capital/PEBSCO. His visibility after the convention, the campaign, and the election would only enhance his power to market to city, county, and state governments. He would be giving up all those potential earnings for a job that paid a mere $145,000 a year.

"Ron was at the top of his game," said his friend Jim Hackney. "He had just got the president elected. We thought he could go out and make a zillion dollars—and he could have."[3]

But Brown wanted in. He said yes to Clinton. "He wanted to be called Mr. Secretary—Mr. Secretary of something," said Hackney.[4] Many of his friends insist that a sense of duty and a desire to perform public service drove him. Perhaps he was taking a long view and felt that a stint in the cabinet would only further enhance his moneymaking potential. Whatever the reason, Brown was pulled in the direction of taking a cabinet position. He had achieved his goal of electing a Democratic president. He wanted the acknowledgment of that feat that a cabinet position would provide. "He said to me, 'If they take that first picture of the cabinet and I'm not in it, I'm going to be really pissed off,'" Hackney said.[5]

He need not have worried. There never was a time when President-elect Clinton did not consider appointing Brown to a cabinet-level position. The question was what. Brown had already made it clear he did not want the United Nations job. Warren Christopher, the head of the transition team, recalled a growing feeling among Clinton, Vice President–elect Gore, and other advisers that Commerce would be perfect. "This meets Ron's needs," he recalled being said at the discussions. "It's a very important post, and it also draws on the relationships he's already established. I recall . . . a gathering sense that this would be the right choice."[6] Ironically, the department was generally considered a refuse heap for political hacks and fund-raisers with mediocre talent.

That did not bother Brown. He had always taken underrated jobs and turned them into something else. No, it was the loss of income that weighed most heavily on his mind in the days after he got the offer. First, he had to sell his partnership in Patton Boggs. Because the law firm gave so much weight to the amount of business a partner brought in, the valuation of his percentage of the partnership was tricky. It had to include revenue from clients who had been billed but had not yet paid, plus earnings from legal work that Patton Boggs would do in the future for businesses Brown had recruited before he entered the cabinet. Patton Boggs wanted to continue to pay him a percentage of the earnings from those clients even after he became a government official. But the White House and the Senate, fearful of how it would look for a cabinet member to be receiving income from a politically connected lobbying firm, insisted that Patton Boggs estimate what those earnings would be and give Brown a one-time severance payment.

Patton Boggs called in outside accountants to estimate how much Brown's percentage of the partnership was worth, then and in the future. Looking at the billings to clients he had represented or brought in, Brown estimated his severance payment would be about $1 million. The firm estimate, however, turned out to be $700,000. Brown was disappointed and angry. "He really thought he was being hosed," said Timothy May, Patton Boggs's managing partner.[7]

May said that after he sat down and explained to Brown how the lower figure had been derived all parties went away satisfied. Still, the experience was a vivid reminder to Brown of how much of a financial loss government service would be.

Entering the cabinet also forced Brown to divest himself of his contractual relationship with PEBSCO. In negotiations with Brown to sever the relationship, Mark Koogler, PEBSCO's attorney, was shocked at how little Brown knew about the intricacies of the business and how much of the details of the financial transaction he had delegated to Nolanda Hill. "He did not appear to me to be a particularly organized person, to my surprise," Koogler recalled. "So when I say she was kind of his confidante or the person organizing it, she seemed to be comfortable in that role and he seemed to be comfortable in having her do [it]."[8]

Looking at Brown's financial picture as he approached his confirmation hearings, several of his friends, including Rob Stein and Hackney, advised giving up his partnership with Hill in First International Corporation, even if no laws were being broken. It just looked funny. It looked perilously close to something that would cause conflict-of-interest questions. If questions were raised, the issue of his personal relationship with Hill might surface. Even if it didn't, Hill's high-flying style of doing business might cause embarrassment.

"She was smart but she was never somebody who inspired any confidence—not someone your principal ought to be spending a lot of time with," said Stein. "As a serious staffer looking to put your principal's interest first and his best foot forward, it did not help to have her hanging around."[9]

At first Brown dug in his heels. When his advisers continued to raise the subject, he displayed rare flashes of anger. "You guys are trying to cost me money," he told a former aide. He did agree, however, to have the Commerce Department's ethics officer issue an opinion on whether he would be breaking government rules by holding on to his stake in First International. He also promised that any international business deals the company became involved in would be cleared by the department's ethics official to make sure they did not violate any conflict-of-interest prohibitions. With this agreement, Brown was able to deflect his advisers' concerns. But the agreement angered Hill, who did not want to have deals she was working on vetted through Commerce's leaky bureaucracy.

"You tell government people what you're doing and by the time it takes you to get back to your car it's on the street," Hill said. "You cannot be a private businessperson and put entrepreneurial kinds of information in government bureaucrats' hands 'cause they don't understand what you're talking about. Then they start asking questions, and then it's all over the street. And that blows deals."[10] To Hill, the idea also smacked of allowing the ethics officer, Barbara Fredericks, what was in essence veto power over the kinds of deals the company could enter into. "I said, 'I can't do this,'" Hill said. "So I told Ron he had to go away."[11]

Even with Hill's desire to end the partnership, the two couldn't split. Associates of Brown said that Hill could not come up with the money to buy him out. She insists that he was asking too much for his share and that they engaged in protracted and intense negotiations. It was difficult to determine the worth of his share of the business since he had put up no money for his share and had done no work on the partnership's behalf; he merely saw First International as a source of much-needed income. Throughout 1993 the two engaged in a financial tango as Hill slowly paid Brown money for his share of First International. Meanwhile, until the final, still-undetermined amount was paid, he maintained his partnership in the company.

TWO WEEKS AFTER Clinton took office, Brown had the opportunity to synthesize his vision for Commerce's mission during a retreat the president organized at Camp David for all his new cabinet secretaries. The retreat was pure Clinton: a mixture of policy shop talk and personal musings. On Saturday night, two weeks after the inauguration, all the cabinet members gathered together with the president and vice president in the living room of the president's residence at Camp David. A "facilitator" who was brought in to stimulate and direct discussion went around the room and asked each person to explain why he or she wanted his or her job, what life experiences each brought to the position, and what each saw as his or her prime mission. When it was Brown's turn, the new Commerce secretary had no difficulty in explaining his past, his future, and his presence there. He wanted the position to show that a black American did not have to be relegated to the traditional minority posts of HUD or Health and Human Services. He added that he wanted to show that the American economic system could work for all people at all rungs of the economic ladder.

Warming to his subject in front of a blazing fire in the hearth, Brown evoked his days at the Theresa Hotel, where he saw bright and talented black people whose abilities were limited by the segregation of the day. They were special people. They could have accomplished anything they set their minds to if only they had been given the chance. Now he had the chance. He would show the world what Theresa's son could do. "He said he grew up a proud African American at the Theresa Hotel in Harlem who knew that he was as good as anybody else and knew that he could do these things," recalled Henry Cisneros, the incoming HUD secretary.[12]

COMMERCE WAS A MISHMASH of programs and a warren of bruised egos and low morale. With a budget of slightly more than $3 billion, it was a pipsqueak of an agency, dwarfed by such giants as the Defense Department, with a budget of $281 billion, and Treasury, with a budget of $283 billion. Commerce was a midget in prestige as well. Treasury set economy policy, State conducted diplomacy between nations, and Defense fought wars. Commerce did trade fairs.

Commerce also lacked cohesion. Since its inception under Theodore Roosevelt, it had been patched together like a Rube Goldberg contraption with functions grafted onto it with no forethought and little concern for synergy. The jumble of functions had earned the department the nickname "the Hall Closet," the place to throw programs when no one could figure out where else to put them. Commerce housed programs that were directly related to American business, like the Patent and Trademark Office and the National Institute of Standards and Technology. It was also the home of the Census Bureau and the National Oceanographic and Atmospheric Administration (NOAA), which runs the country's weather service.

Where others saw cacophony, however, Brown saw connections. He looked at the seemingly disparate programs run by Commerce and saw a unifying theme. The Patent and Trademark Office handled the growing issue of intellectual property rights. The International Trade Administration promoted exports. NOAA conducted research on global warming. The Economic Statistics Administration produced economic and demographic data—including the census—that was needed by marketers and strategic planners. The Economic Development Administration tried to spur business development in economically depressed rural—and, at Brown's insistence, inner-city—areas. What they all had in common was trying to bring the benefits of the country's economic system to everyone.

Brown's predecessor, Robert Mosbacher, who had been George Bush's main fund-raiser, might have had a similar vision. He once tried to raise Commerce's profile, but the agency was never taken seriously. One joke that made the rounds of Commerce just as Brown was coming on was that the only thing Mosbacher did for the department was build an awning over the secretary's entrance on Fifteenth Street. And he did that so he would know which door to come in when he arrived in the morning.

Brown was different. He brought his formidable people skills to the position, displaying an uncanny ability to relate to people and a mastery of small talk with department employees whether they were secretaries or top management. He often ate lunch in the employees' cafeteria and engaged workers in chitchat on subjects ranging from their families to sports to their work.

Beyond a politician's deft touch with people, Brown brought clout. Like Mosbacher, Brown was seen as having a close personal relationship with the president and therefore was respected in the White House. Unlike Mosbacher, however, he brought results that moved the department off the policy periphery. Under Clinton and Al Gore, the techie and environmentally green vice president, Brown was in the enviable position of running programs that went directly to the interests of the administration's two top leaders. "What Gore was looking to do gave Ron an opportunity to emphasize the importance of the Commerce Department," said a former top aide to Brown. It also gave Brown an opening to work both the White House and Congress for a 12 percent increase in his department's overall budget.

But while Brown scored points with Gore, the programs were too small to gain the department headlines and acclaim. Brown soon realized that there was only one function of the Commerce Department that could provide that—international trade.

Promoting the exports of U.S. businesses had an immediate appeal to Brown. No one else in the cabinet was doing trade advocacy on a concrete level. Other agencies, like the office of the U.S. Trade Representative, negotiated treaties to help open foreign markets, but Brown felt that only Commerce could make the treaties real by helping American firms win contracts abroad. Making those deals could also help the administration politically, both through the jobs exports provided and by adding a new political constituency—American business—to the Democratic coalition. It was a perfect fit for his personality and his approach to life; it did not entail abstract theoretical concepts but down-to-earth, practical achievements.

"Ron was going to be assessed and his tenure graded on whether U.S. companies got deals, the volume of those deals, their effect on the balance of trade, how American business was perceived in the world, and, in turn, how American business perceived the administration," said Cisneros. "All of that is served by one end: more. More deals, more trade, more dollars, more exports. More."[13]

For the Commerce Department to aggressively pursue foreign contracts for American companies was a surprising new development, especially for a Democratic administration. The Reagan and Bush administration were presumably more business-friendly. But they both were in the thrall of the conservative Republican ideology that shunned government intervention in the marketplace. As such, beyond negotiating contracts to open up foreign markets, they did little to help American companies. "The United States, prior to this administration, had never aggressively advocated for the U.S. private sector," said Lauri Fitz-Pegado, who ran Commercial Service, a Commerce Department agency that had domestic and foreign offices to help American companies win foreign contracts. "Other countries had. France did it, the United Kingdom did it, Germany did it."[14]

Clinton administration officials, and especially Brown, realized that the Republicans' laissez-faire philosophy toward the economy had probably cost them the election. Clinton's victory had been based on the perceived poor performance of the American economy. "It's the economy, stupid," Clinton adviser James Carville kept reminding campaign workers during 1992. Once in office, administration officials knew that boosting international trade was another way to enhance the country's economic performance. The Clinton administration came into office feeling that America had lost its competitive edge to countries like Japan and Germany not because those countries produced better products but because their companies got help from their governments and U.S. firms did not. "Brown used to say we can't let a free market ideology get in the way," said Jeffrey E. Garten, a Wall Street banker Brown hired to run Commerce's International Trade Administration. "We have to do this in a very systematic way."[15]

EVEN AS BROWN was pulling Commerce together into a more cohesive unit and taking the lead in trade advocacy, however, a bank of dark clouds was rolling in from the past. First, there were Lillian Madsen and her Vietnamese associates. In December, Brown had met once again with Hao and Ashton, this time at the town house that Madsen had recently purchased in Washington. In February, Madsen had brought them along when he had invited her to visit the Commerce Department to show off his new office. According to aides and Clinton administration officials, nothing came of the meetings and Brown did not lobby for any change in U.S. policy toward Vietnam.

Hao's motives, however, were not completely altruistic. The previous July, he had formed an informal partnership with Binh Thanh Ly, another Vietnamese businessman in Florida, to explore investment possibilities in Vietnam once the U.S. embargo had been lifted. After the West Palm Beach meeting with Brown, Hao and Ly flew to Vietnam, where they met with government officials and the head of the country's Communist Party, according to Ly. Following that meeting, Ly later claimed that Hao asked him to draft a letter to Brown in

English spelling out the details on how to forge a closer relationship between the United States and Vietnam. Hao tried to give the document to Brown the second time he met with him, but Brown refused to accept it.

Then the unthinkable happened in the spring of 1993. Hao and Ly had a falling-out. Soon Ly was spreading a story among reporters, law enforcement agencies, and Republican congressmen that one subject of the discussions with Brown was the payment of a $700,000 bribe for his help in convincing the Clinton administration to ease restrictions on Vietnam. According to Ly, the money had been placed in a secret account that had been established for Brown in a Singapore bank. Ly, however, could offer no proof of his explosive allegations and, when questioned, acknowledged that his charges were based on secondhand and thirdhand hearsay.

The story might have died there except for a grievous error made by Brown and his aide, Jim Desler. In March, Desler began receiving telephone calls from reporters inquiring about Ly's charges. Desler, a relatively young press officer, did what he was supposed to do. He confronted his boss and asked him if Ly's allegations were true. "It's absolutely preposterous, Jimmy," Brown replied, "all of it."[16] Desler took Brown's emphatic denial to mean that nothing of what Ly had told reporters was true. He got back to reporters and told them that Brown denied everything, the bribe, the Singapore bank account, the meeting with Hao. On the last point, however, what Desler was telling reporters was, in fact, wrong. "With a little bit more experience, I probably would have handled it better," said Desler. "I pretty much presented Brown with the whole charge, instead of asking him point by point, going through it all and asking him his response."[17]

Desler might blame himself for the subsequent flap, but the real fault lay with Brown. On an allegation as serious as bribery, he had a responsibility to make sure that statements that went out in his name were accurate, and when going over the issue with Desler, it was his responsibility to make sure there was no misunderstanding. After all, it was his reputation that was on the line, not Desler's. More critically, even after Brown realized that a mistake had been made, according to aides, he made no move to correct the record, leaving what was in essence a lie to fester beneath the surface for months.

Meanwhile, there was more trouble coming from another quarter.

Brown and his advisers learned that Edward T. Pound, an investigative reporter with *U.S. News and World Report,* was researching an article claiming that Brown and some of his top aides at the Democratic National Committee had diverted DNC funds to their own personal use. Though Brown denied the charges, his successor at the DNC, David Wilhelm, was sufficiently worried about the pending story that he ordered a secret internal audit of committee spending during Brown's tenure. The audit did turn up lavish spending of DNC money by Brown and Alexis Herman and Bill Morton, another of Brown's close advisers, especially for hotels, meals, and limousine service. But with the exception of Morton, whom the auditors found to have used the committee's money to pay for limousines he used on dates with his girlfriend, all the spending could be directly tied to DNC functions. It turned out that Brown had used his DNC credit card to pay for some expenses related to his son's wedding. But a further check by the auditors revealed that Brown had reimbursed the committee for the expenses within the credit card's normal billing cycle.

Pound's story, which appeared in June 1993, did detail extravagant spending by Herman and other top DNC staff. Pound noted, for example, that "in 1991 and 1992 alone, the DNC spent $250,000 on limousine services," and that when she was in New York City planning the 1992 convention, Herman lived in a $4,000-a-month apartment on Central Park South, for which she contributed $500 monthly for the rent.[18] But Pound was unable to document any diversion of DNC funds to Brown's personal use. "It turned out to be a nonstory," said Desler. "But everyone was frightened—this is going to be an awful story, an awful story. It turned out to be nothing at all."[19]

BY FALL, in an operation called the Advocacy Center, Ron Brown's revitalized and refocused Commerce Department found its rhythm. Constructed to look like a trading room at a Wall Street brokerage, it was termed the "economic war room" by Garten. Deals were tracked like stocks or bonds; research was provided on various countries, on projects, and on competitors. How much did the projects involve? How many American jobs would be generated? Who were the real decision makers in the country? What was the competition doing? Was there any bribery involved? What government officials from the United States would be useful in helping an American company win a contract?

"If a guy came in and he had a $100,000 contract he was going for in Botswana, maybe that's something that ought to be handled by the commercial officer in the embassy in Botswana," said Ray Vickery, the assistant secretary for trade development who had set up the Advocacy Center. "But if this is a major transportation project, maybe we ought to get [Transportation Secretary Federico] Pena involved. Or if it's an energy project, maybe you get [Energy Secretary Hazel] O'Leary."[20]

Brown also beefed up Commercial Service, a division that had offices across the United States and around the world and was an entry point for companies wanting the department's help in securing business deals abroad. The approach to supporting U.S. business was not to be haphazard. It was to be done the same way Brown organized the Democratic Party for the presidential campaign—focused, well thought out, and using the full quiver of resources at his disposal. The Advocacy Center became headquarters.

Brown figured he could use the Advocacy Center to help solidify his position as lead dog when it came to trade promotion. Legislation passed by Congress in 1991 established something called the Trade Promotion Coordinating Committee (TPCC), a group of federal agencies that was to develop plans to boost U.S. exports and coordinate the execution of that plan. Brown, as head of Commerce, was supposed to be the chairman, but his general dislike of meetings kept his role to a minimum. Still, when the first meeting of the TPCC took place in November 1993, Brown used the Advocacy Center to impress the other cabinet officials who were members of the committee. About three weeks before the first meeting, the Advocacy Center did not even exist. But Brown wanted it up and running so that he could show it off to the other cabinet secretaries who were to assemble.

"We just kicked people out of spaces and started yelling and screaming and got it built," said Vickery. "By the time of the meeting we had computers in there and we had people working on projects. The other officials were somewhat in awe of Ron because he seemed to have taken the bull by the horns."[21] If Brown's awestruck contemporaries had looked closely, they would have discovered that the file cabinets were virtually empty and the computer drives held very little data. "It was kind of a Potemkin village," said Vickery. "It was pretty rudimentary. But they didn't know, either, exactly, what they were supposed to be doing. So their reaction was, Hey, this looks good."[22]

Early on, Brown focused his attention on winning contracts in the Third World, especially in the booming markets of Asia and Latin America. Garten recalled that when he was interviewing for his job as undersecretary of commerce for international trade, Brown made this clear. "I would ask him and say, 'This is what I want to do with ITA,' and he would wave his hand and say, 'You can do anything you want with ITA but, look, this is what I really want to do,'" Garten recalled. "Then he would go on to talk about something that was broader. We talked about the critical importance that emerging markets were going to play in America's future, and how there was too much emphasis being given to Europe and Japan and not enough to Latin America and the rest of Asia. We were both on the same wavelength."[23]

Garten and his principal deputy, David Rothkopf, put together a strategy focusing energies on ten "big emerging markets" (BEMs). They included Mexico, Brazil, Argentina, China (including Taiwan and Hong Kong), South Korea, Southeast Asia, India, Poland, Turkey, and South Africa; these were countries Commerce researchers estimated could have a $1 trillion increase in U.S. imports from 1990 to 2010. At first the idea of honing in on ten areas of the world did not appeal to Brown. Too exclusive. What would that mean for trade policy and trade advocacy in other countries? he wanted to know. But Brown agreed to the strategy as a way of achieving some focus, knowing full well that if an opportunity for trade deals came his way outside the framework of the BEMs, he would not let it pass. Brown also knew that selecting certain countries as BEMs served a public relations goal. It validated that country as an up-and-coming economic power worthy of U.S. attention. And it softened up the country's leaders for Brown's pitch when it came to contracts.

"When we announced India, the announcement of India as a BEM was on the front page of every newspaper in India," said Hackney. "Ron became a hero in India because this was an acknowledgement that it was among the top economies in the world. It was a big deal."[24]

The focus on the Third World was not just a matter of solidarity with people of color. Asia and Latin America were experiencing phenomenal economic growth rates, and many of their countries were in need of roads, bridges, power plants, dams, airplanes, and other big-ticket items to keep up with that growth and sustain it. Winning these contracts would produce huge, headline-grabbing deals for American companies and for Brown. And they also were the types of contracts where a government-to-government dialogue would make a difference. The department couldn't help companies increase exports to Germany or Britain. But it could intervene with governments in the Third World. "The commercial prizes in these markets were infrastructure projects," said Rothkopf, whom Garten hired as his principal deputy. "The decision makers on those were foreign governments. . . . So if we intervened with the foreign government we were dealing directly with the decision maker in a way that only a government could."[25]

ABROAD, BROWN was becoming a hero. But at home it was a different story. Washington is a fishbowl. The comings and goings of public officials are often better known than their policies. Their telephone calls are logged. Secretaries, aides, and security personnel monitor their movements. Keeping a secret, maintaining a lie, is tough. People talk. They talk to friends. Friends talk to reporters. Falsehoods in Washington are commonplace but they seldom have a long shelf life.

On September 26, the *Miami Herald* broke the story that, despite his denials, Brown had, in fact, met with Hao three times, including once after he had been confirmed as Commerce secretary. The newspaper's revelations were a bombshell. Suddenly it looked like Brown had tried to cover up something. Could it be that there was something to Ly's allegations? News organizations detailed more reporters to dig into the story. Republicans in Congress began demanding that Attorney General Janet Reno appoint an independent counsel to investigate the charges. Groups representing Vietnam veterans publicly called for Brown's resignation.

There was another factor that pumped more fuel into this story. When the story broke, the Clinton administration was, in fact, moving to normalize relations with Vietnam. The policy shift was being fiercely resisted by some unreconstructed hawks who never forgave Vietnam for defeating the United States in the war and by some who felt that Hanoi had never come clean on the fate of thousands of American servicemen and servicewomen who were officially listed as missing in action. The charges against Brown handed those opposed to an easing of relations with Vietnam a new argument—that the MIAs were being sold out by some black Judas Iscariot.

In the end the story amounted to nothing at all. A federal grand jury in Florida investigated the charges and by February had completely exonerated Brown. But before the panel completed its work Brown had to endure partisan attacks, continued questioning by reporters, and a spate of articles concerning the bribery allegations that many of his friends and family felt were unfair.

"Dad was enraged," Tracey Brown wrote in her memoir. "He couldn't believe that journalists with whom he had amicable relations would write stories about a lie. They should know better, he told us."[26] But Brown was ignoring his own part in the saga. The story had legs because of his lack of candor at the beginning. "When it hit, it hit with a little bit more force because of the original denial through me," Desler said.[27]

Why wasn't Brown candid? Friends and colleagues say that he was so dismissive of the bribery allegation because he knew it to be groundless. And in failing to set the record straight about the meetings he was engaging in what is a completely human activity. Once a bullet is dodged, why voluntarily present yourself as a target? Those who worked with Brown and knew him well knew that given an opportunity to walk through either a door labeled TRANQUILITY or one labeled TROUBLE, he would pick the former every time. "I think it was the compartmentalizing phenomenon more than anything else," said a former colleague. "Ron never believed any of this would go anywhere, so he thought it was over. I think that was it more than anything else."

There was another explanation. Brown did, in fact, have something to hide. It was not the receipt of dirty money. It was his relationship with Madsen. "That was a huge can of worms for him," said one intimate. "That was the bigger fear. He knew he hadn't taken any money, so he wasn't worried about that. What he was worried about was [the relationship with Lillian] coming out. Three meetings with a Vietnamese person. So who was there? He understood that once you go down that road, the setup of the meetings was going to be discussed. And that gets into who's Lillian?"

There were further complications. It turned out that in late 1992 Madsen was feeling restive in her small one-bedroom apartment across the street from Sidwell Friends, an exclusive private school in Washington where President Clinton would enroll his daughter, Chelsea. Madsen wanted a larger place and eventually found a town house she liked near American University. The problem was she was working part-time and couldn't afford the down payment or qualify for a mortgage. What's more, Haiti was in turmoil, with U.S. pressure building to return Aristide to power, and the wealthy, including Madsen's husband, said he could not provide her with the funds to buy a new house. So Brown asked another of his friends, Jose Amaro Pintos Ramos, a wealthy Brazilian businessman, to help out.

Brown's friendship with Ramos stemmed from the 1980s, when Ramos was a client of Brown's at Patton Boggs. At the time, Ramos was trying to close a business deal involving the construction of a telecommunications system in

Nigeria. The Nigerian government was giving him a difficult time, throwing up one bureaucratic obstacle after another to the project, on which millions, if not billions, of dollars of capital a group of investors led by Ramos had riding on it. As a result, Ramos retained Brown to help him negotiate his way out of the impasse. The two men flew to Nigeria, where Brown left Ramos in a hotel room and went off to talk to Nigerian officials. He returned a short time later to tell the surprised Ramos that everything had been taken care of and that Ramos would soon be getting the necessary clearances for the project to move forward. And he shocked Ramos even more. The clearances would be forthcoming without having to pay any huge bribe to the notoriously corrupt Nigerian officials. All Brown wanted was his fee of more than $30,000 for handling the legal work.

"He was absolutely stunned," a person familiar with the story said of Ramos. "Ron got the thing taken care of. He wanted absolutely nothing for himself, and he did it without paying any bribes. Or if any bribes were paid, Ron paid them out of his own pocket. The problem was solved, and the two men became friends."

Ramos would do almost anything to help his friend. So at Brown's behest, Ramos arranged a $108,000 loan from a French bank to Madsen for the down payment on the town house. The loan went to Madsen and not to Brown, one person knowledgeable about the transaction said, because the house was to be in Madsen's and not Brown's name. In addition, a loan from a wealthy Brazilian with international business connections to an incoming Commerce secretary who would have responsibility for international trade could raise some embarrassing questions. "It was going to be Lillian's property," said a friend. "Ron's point through all of this was that Lillian's relationship with her husband was faltering. He was a problem for her, the financial support. Haiti's in chaos. She needed a secure landing, and Ron was trying to accomplish it. And Ron was never a millionaire. Obviously, once he became a public official, his freedom of maneuverability on financial transactions was limited. So Ramos helped."

Even with the loan from Ramos, Madsen did not have enough income to qualify for the mortgage on the town house. To help, Brown and his son Michael, then thirty, were co-signers on a $250,000 mortgage on January 29, 1993. Madsen explained that the bank wanted two names on the mortgage. "Obviously, he couldn't ask his wife," she said.[28]

Ironically, Brown's attempt to keep his relationship with Madsen out of the news only served to ensure that it would become public. After the *Miami Herald* broke the story of Brown's lack of candor about his meetings with Hao, reporters began digging deeper into his affairs. It did not take them long to discover his connection to Madsen, though she was never described as anything more than a "close personal friend." Brown's worst nightmare concerning the Vietnam allegations had come true, even though the allegations themselves were not proven to be true.

"I think the Vietnam thing really hurt Ron," said one friend. "It really hurt him because of the Desler thing as well as it opened up the Lillian thing. Here he was, he had gotten through his confirmation. He had explained everything. And he was a kick-ass secretary of commerce in the first six, eight, ten months. He was on a roll. Here's the guy everybody had low expectations of and he takes on a new challenge and he's up to it. And then, bam!"

Brown was not one to sit around and wring his hands over his misfortune, however. Even as embarrassing disclosures poured forth out of the Vietnam affair, he worked to maintain a business-as-usual air, and he made sure that morale at the Commerce Department did not suffer. He knew it was critical for his effectiveness in his job that the White House maintain support for him both explicitly and implicitly.

In September, two days after the *Miami Herald* story broke, President Clinton voiced his support for Brown. Dee Dee Myers, the White House press secretary, told reporters, "The secretary told him the circumstances, said that he'd never done anything improper. The president accepts his explanation and stands by him."[29]

Even as Myers was speaking, members of the White House staff and Brown himself knew that reporters, legislators, lobbyists, and pundits would be watching closely to see if there were any signs that the president was backing away from his embattled Commerce secretary. In order to make sure such a perception did not develop, the White House took the offensive. It lobbied especially hard for the Commerce Department's budget in Congress and gave Brown extra visibility in the campaign to win congressional approval of the North American Free Trade Agreement (NAFTA), a proposal to create a free-trade zone that included the United States, Canada, and Mexico.

"We wanted to make sure that in the course of things he was perceived to still be a valuable member of the team," said John Podesta, then secretary to the cabinet. He was keeping track for the White House of the potential political fallout from the allegations against Brown. Podesta stressed that what Brown did to push NAFTA during this period was nothing that he would not have been asked to do anyway. The difference was, the White House went out of its way to publicize it. "It's the difference of whether he was speaking about NAFTA in the Rose Garden or in a motel in San Antonio," Podesta said.[30]

By the early part of 1994, Brown had emerged seemingly unscathed. He was about to embark on what would turn out to be his most successful year, one that would fix in place his claim that he was the most activist and, by all accounts, best Commerce secretary ever. In the early spring, he granted a series of interviews, all with the theme that he was back, happy to be relieved of the albatross of Vietnam, and ready to take on the challenges of his job. But the Vietnam bribery debacle would have a legacy that neither Brown, nor anyone else, could imagine at that moment.

CHAPTER SIXTEEN

TRANSITIONAL WORLD

P HIL LARSEN, a staffer for William Clinger, the ranking Republican member of the House Committee on Government Operations, was intrigued. As he read and listened to news accounts of the allegations and revelations flowing from Ron Brown's bribery charge, Larsen decided he would pull out Brown's official financial disclosure form and give it another look. What he found there surprised him. There was nothing in the document relating to Vietnam. But he did notice that many of the companies in which Brown had either held or still held a stake were involved in telecommunications, an area that falls under the purview of the Commerce secretary. Larsen took his findings to Clinger, and both of them thought Brown's holdings might raise conflict-of-interest issues.

"He did have responsibilities as secretary of commerce in the area of telecommunications, and First International ostensibly was in the telecommunications business," said Clinger. "That raised a red flag. We were looking at it for potential conflict of interest. It was only later that it became something else."[1] Brown's unwillingness to let go of First International in early 1993 had returned to haunt him.

On February 10, 1994, Clinger wrote to Brown expressing his concerns over Brown's stake in companies involved in information and telecommunications. "The mere holding of such interests may not, in fact, present a conflict of interest," Clinger wrote. "However, unless the public record is sufficiently documented to the contrary, the mere appearance of a conflict of interest could severely erode public confidence in [administration policy]."[2] Tacked on to Clinger's letter were two pages of questions regarding First International, Corridor, and other of Brown's businesses.

Three weeks later Barbara S. Fredericks, the Commerce Department's ethics officer, responded. "With regard to the specific questions you raise, we do not think it is appropriate to answer questions regarding the activities of financial interests of other persons or entities outside the Department," Fredericks wrote. "Therefore we are limiting our responses to matters concerning Secretary Brown's interests and activities"[3] It was a polite brush-off. Brown would answer some questions but he would not provide detailed information on his business activities, clients, or finances. He had, in essence, told Clinger to get lost.

The exchange of letters began a year-long quest in which Clinger continually asked for more and more details of Brown's outside business holdings—and felt that all he received in return was an acute case of stonewalling. "It was sort of arrogant," Clinger said. "He felt he didn't have to respond. We were in the minority, and at that point, we couldn't compel him to do anything. I wrote him very polite letters and got no answers."[4]

In this case Clinger was about half right. Brown and his staff did provide some of the answers he was seeking, but never enough to satisfy him. They also felt that Clinger was on a fishing expedition, and with a huge Democratic majority in the House ready to back them up, Brown and his aides felt confident in giving Clinger the cold shoulder. "Clinger was the minority person on the committee, and he was asking for tons of stuff," said one of Brown's lieutenants. "It felt so overreaching, so inappropriate, so invasive. He wasn't a chair. So . . . it felt legitimate to us not to create an avalanche of materials for him." So while his staff held Larsen and Clinger at bay, Brown hurdled ahead to put Commerce on the map and make his best case for the secretary of State job he still coveted.

A SERIES OF TRIPS to the Middle East in January 1994 bore fruit almost immediately. Under Brown's prodding, the Arab League pledged to reconsider its forty-three-year-old economic boycott of Israel. Brown urged Israeli officials to be more flexible in their dealings with the Palestinians. He met with Yasir Arafat, head of the Palestine Liberation Organization, on ways to spur economic development on the West Bank and Gaza, and became the first Commerce secretary to visit that forlorn strip of land jutting into Israel's southwest corner.

He was appalled at the conditions he found in Gaza. Unlike the West Bank, the area had been completely ignored by Israeli and Western businesses. He later termed its conditions worse than those of Soweto, the teeming black township southwest of Johannesburg, South Africa. It was in Gaza, he later said, where the importance of private investment from the West and from the United States was most critical. Peace, he believed, would not come to the Middle East through treaties and resolutions passed by the United Nations Security Council. It would come by providing the residents of Gaza with jobs.

Brown was trying out the themes that his staff would later come to call "commercial diplomacy." He was saying that relations between nations would depend more on economic development and economic interdependence than on guns, soldiers, or treaties. "One thing that concerned me was that too often the business leaders were way ahead of the political leaders," he said in January 1994. "The business leaders seemed to understand what this was all about: this is about changing lives. The political leaders were saying, 'No, we have to dot every *i* and cross every *t* before we can get on with economic development. I think that's nonsense. I think there is no time to waste."[5]

When Brown arrived in Riyadh, Saudi Arabia, to close the $7 billion contract for Boeing and McDonnell Douglas to supply jets to Saudi Arabia, the goals were clearer but the prospects for success were not. The American firms were in close competition with Airbus, the European aerospace consortium. Brown was there with only his close aides—and he wanted to speak directly with King Faud.

That was impossible, Brown was told by Saudi officials. The king was in his summer palace and would not be able to see Brown. Fine, Brown replied, I'm going home. According to Hackney, who accompanied Brown on the trip, the Saudis were unused to such brashness and said they would see what could be done. Brown stayed in Riyadh for two days, making a round of speeches, meeting with Saudi officials, and expressing optimism that they would eventually get to see the monarch—a view that Hackney doubted would come true. Kings see heads of state, not trade ministers.

But two days later, as Brown was leaving one of his speeches, the American ambassador to Saudi Arabia cornered him. "The king would like to see you," Brown was told. The visit took place at one of Faud's gilded summer palaces outside of Riyadh. Brown had been briefed on what to expect. The king might possibly talk nonstop for two hours, and it was both unwise and impolite to interrupt him. That was exactly what happened, but within the first five minutes of his soliloquy he told Brown and the other Commerce officials that he was agreeing to buy the commercial aircraft from Boeing and McDonnell Douglas. All that was left for the Americans to do was try to stay awake during the rest of the speech.

Out of these personal forays, a grand strategy emerged. The rest of the business trips that year were not just trade missions. They were also shows. They were meticulously planned and reflected Brown's concern about details in his public life. Advance teams both in the United States and abroad carefully gathered data to help Commerce officials select companies that were near consummation of their contracts and might just need a little extra push from the U.S. government to put them over the hump. Certain rules had to be followed. If more than one American firm was bidding on a foreign project, for example, Commerce could not advocate for one business over another. Companies had to be vetted to make sure that none had significant contracts with the Commerce Department, that none of the top officials had been in the news for some nefarious act, and that the FBI or the CIA background checks had come back clean. Brown left nothing to chance.

He wanted CEOs on these trips. He did not want the vice president in charge of Asia, or the sales rep for Chile. He wanted the top. And he wanted all the executives to arrive together with him on an air force jet. "His view was—and this goes back to the point about creating image and impressions— if you all sort of sneak into town on commercial aircraft and got together later at some hotel, that did not make the same impression as when you come in on a U.S. Air Force plane with the American flag on the tail, endorsed by the president of the United States," said Vickery.[6] The image was clear: this was not a mere covey of American businessmen. They represented the United States. They had the imprimatur of the president and the support of his Commerce secretary.

Before leaving the country, the CEOs were given a pep talk at the White House, sometimes by President Clinton or Vice President Gore. Amid the hand-shakes and speeches a subtle message was conveyed: you are not going on a crass commercial venture. You are carrying the prestige and promise of the United States. On the plane, Brown made sure that he was briefed by each one of the CEOs on the project that was being sought, its costs, the sales pitch, the potential obstacles, and the people who needed to be stroked. He displayed his remarkable ability to soak up vast quantities of information and regurgitate it back in cogent—sometimes better crafted—ways.

Maria Cardona, who followed Brown to Commerce from the DNC, recalled a trip when Brown seemed so fatigued that his eyes drooped and his head nearly fell onto his chest as he listened to the CEOs brief him about their potential deals. "I think all these CEOs were thinking, 'What good is this doing me if he's falling asleep?'" Cardona said. "The next day he got into the meeting and he spit out every single thing these CEOs had told him. I was taking notes, and I said, 'Oh my God, he's got all of it.'"[7]

The trips were to generate their share of controversy. At one point in 1995, the *Chicago Sun Times* printed the contents of a DNC memo that spoke about the possibility of donors being able to get a place on a "DNC trade mission" for a contribution of $100,000. And documents obtained by Judicial Watch, a conservative public interest law firm that focused heavily on what it considered the misdeeds of Brown, clearly indicated that companies used lobbyists and friends within the administration to try to secure seats on these trips. But investigations by two committees of Congress and news organizations were not able to turn up a smoking gun to prove the charge that Brown or Commerce officials were actually selling spots on trade missions. With the lack of solid proof of the charge, it was constantly mocked by Brown's allies.

"I can't say unequivocally that everybody on that plane did not get there by some political connection," said Desler. "We're in Washington. It's a political town. If people want to get on the plane, how do they do it? They have their lobbyist contact people they know. That's how Washington works. You can't completely divorce it from the political process.

"But Brown's motives were what deals can we make. He didn't give a shit if somebody who was on the plane is donating a lot of money to the Republican Party or the Democratic Party. If we could get somebody from a foreign government to sign on the dotted line, and he's standing there . . . hell, we're going to do it."[8]

His supporters said Brown would never be so crude. He was unashamedly a liberal, a believer that government existed to provide services to people, especially poor people and people like minorities who had been or were still being denied opportunities. By showing companies that government worked for them as well, he hoped to convince corporate leaders not to swallow the Republicans' antigovernment line. "His feeling was, 'Look, I can show by being an activist champion for business that there is a role for government, that we all benefit from government,' " said a former aide. " 'If I do that, then how can they legitimately object to government's providing services to those who are less fortunate?' "

In the early days of the trade missions, Commerce officials had a difficult time filling planes. Coordinating the schedules of twenty to twenty-five CEOs was turning into a nightmare of logistical planning. "It's not the case that people were lining up and saying, " 'Oh my God, Ron Brown's going to India. Where can I make my contribution so I can get on that plane?' " said Vickery. "It was more like, you'd be on the phone with the subordinates, saying, 'Don't you think we could get your CEO? I know he's got a board meeting next week, but, wait a minute, this is the president and the secretary of commerce asking. It's important. Think what you'd be doing for your country.'"[9]

To be able to lure more CEOs, Brown needed a high-profile commercial transaction that would grab the spotlight and make the case that if you wanted to do foreign business deals, Commerce was the place to go. He got his deal in a place many Americans did not—and probably still do not—think of as a major U.S. trading partner.

In June, the Brazilian government was poised to award a mammoth $1.5 billion contract. Brazil needed a country-wide surveillance and air traffic control system. Known by the acronym SIVAM, the system would monitor the health of the Amazonian rain forest, combat illegal mining and drug trafficking, and monitor the country's borders. SIVAM was the classic case Brown had been hoping to find. It involved computers, technology, and environmental protection issues that Clinton and Gore sought to promote. And it was being built by one of the countries that Commerce had targeted as a "big emerging market."

One of the finalists in the intense global competition for the contract was the Raytheon Company, based in Lexington, Massachusetts. It was Raytheon, an electronics and defense company, that manufactured the Patriot missile. The public would remember the Patriot missile because it had been used to intercept Scud missiles during the Persian Gulf War. Raytheon's chief competitor was Thomson CSF, a giant French electronics company.

At the beginning, Raytheon was said to have the inside track on winning the contract, but as the decision drew close the Central Intelligence Agency detected evidence that the French were bribing Brazilian officials.[10] Commerce let out all the stops. Members of the TPCC met daily to plot out strategy to support Raytheon's efforts. The committee directed the head of the Federal Aviation Administration to tell his counterpart in Brazil that future cooperation on aviation issues would depend on whether Raytheon had gotten fair consideration on the contract. Similar messages to their Brazilian counterparts were conveyed by Carole Browner, head of the Environmental Protection Agency, and Jim Baker of NOAA. The Export-Import Bank put together a financing package that provided low-interest loans to Raytheon. Garten, Commerce's undersecretary for international trade, made an advance trip to Brazil to make Raytheon's case and gently twist arms. The State Department was requested to ask President Clinton to write a letter to the president of Brazil in support of Raytheon.

When the State Department dragged its feet, Brown contacted Clinton directly and asked for the letter. "This blew away the French," one American official was quoted as saying at the time.[11] Arriving in Brazil on June 26, Brown himself met with top Brazilian officials to again make Raytheon's case. The American full-court press made the difference. In the end Raytheon won the contract.

Brown had gotten his trophy. The business community suddenly began to take notice. A heretofore sleepy little agency that had existed on the margins of Washington's power institutions now was leading the way to help American companies compete internationally. And it was doing so in a Democratic administration. Who would have thought it?

By August, Brown was off again. This time the political stakes were even higher than they had been in Brazil. He was leading a delegation of twenty-four CEOs on a trade mission to the People's Republic of China. With the world's largest population, and having made a decision to spend more than $600 billion to modernize itself, China presented an enormous potential market for American businesses.

In May, the Clinton administration had taken the controversial step of announcing that the United States would no longer consider Beijing's human rights record during the administration's annual review of China's "most favored nation" (MFN) trade status—an official declaration that granted reduced tariffs on Chinese exports to America. Clinton, in the wake of lobbying from U.S. business interests, argued that commercial engagement with China was the best way to prod Beijing to improve its human rights record. Among those in the cabinet who argued strongly for this position was Brown.

With his finely honed sense of timing, Brown knew he would be the first cabinet official to travel to China since the delinkage of MFN from the human rights issue. This trip had to be about more than just signing business deals.

Garten traveled twice to China, holding talks with virtually all the Chinese leaders Brown was to meet. Projects that American companies were bidding on were analyzed and vetted by lawyers to make sure there was no violation of American law. About $5 billion in contracts was already nailed down, and in most cases required only signing and press announcements.

"That's not enough," Brown told Garten a few days before the trip.

"Could you tell me, in your view, what would make the trip a smashing success?" Garten asked. Two major deals, an agreement for Chrysler to construct a plant to build minivans and a contract for McDonnell Douglas to supply jet aircraft to the state airline, were still pending. But Commerce officials felt that even if these did not materialize Brown's trip was still poised to be a commercial success.

"I want to make some progress on human rights."

"That would be terrific," Garten replied. "But if you mix the two, there's the chance you won't get anything."

"I think I can," Brown said. "I'd like you to go to the State Department and find out what I could do that would be significant."[12]

State Department officials told Garten that the Chinese had months ago stopped participating in a forum known as the Human Right Dialogue—bilateral talks over specific human rights issues. Since the Clinton administration had renewed China's MFN status, Beijing's leaders seemed not to be inclined to restart these talks. When told about the issue, Brown decided that the resumption of the Human Rights Dialogue would be his trophy. It would demonstrate that commercial engagement could yield political benefits. And, parenthetically, it would demonstrate his skill at diplomacy. In typical fashion, Brown raised the stakes by stating even before he left that he felt he could make some progress with the Chinese on the human rights front. "My own background, having been with a civil rights organization for a good part of my professional career and being very sensitive to these issues and being perceived by the Chinese as someone who has political gravitas in the United States . . . gives me an opportunity," he said.[13]

Brown decided to raise the issue of the Human Rights Dialogue for the first time during his meeting on August 29 with Li Ping, the Chinese prime minister, best known in the West for ordering the brutal crackdown by Chinese troops on pro-democracy demonstrators in Tiananmen Square in 1989.

Li was surprised. He had not expected Brown to interject the subject into the talks on the Chrysler and McDonnell Douglas deals. But Li was not dismissive. The Chinese, it seemed, wanted something, too. Chinese leaders, especially Wu Yi, the trade minister, pressed for U.S. support of China's entry in the General Agreement on Tariffs and Trade (GATT), a treaty among the world's industrialized countries to maintain low tariffs for each other's goods. Looking for U.S. help to be included in GATT, which would later be renamed the World Trade Organization, the Chinese were in somewhat of a dealing mood.

Brown continued to raise the issue of the Human Rights Dialogue in private sessions. But he declined to publicly hector the Chinese on the general subject of its treatment of its people. Instead, he insisted publicly that his trip—like the administration's new approach to China—was primarily about forging trade and commercial links. "By moving beyond the specific linkage between MFN and human rights, we can pursue all the broad interests of the United States in a more effective manner," he said in a breakfast speech to the American Chamber of Commerce. "The United States government is now playing an activist role on your behalf, and we plan to turn up the heat. We are not ideological or philosophical about this. We are relentlessly pragmatic, bottom-line oriented."[14]

The crucial meeting came the following day, when Brown sat down to make his pitch for the Chrysler and McDonnell Douglas projects with President Jiang Zemin. In his talks with Jiang, Brown displayed impressive knowledge of the details of both projects, something that cabinet secretaries seldom show. After speaking at length, and seemingly reaching the end of his presentation, Brown paused and said he would like to change the subject and talk about human rights. Garten, who witnessed the exchange, recalled that Jiang visibly tensed.

"I used to be a civil rights lawyer," Brown said. "That's how I got my start. And you know, I can tell you right now that our society, the United States, has some of the worst human rights problems. We've got people living on the streets, we've got children living in poverty, we've got people shooting and killing each other. So I come here not to tell you that we've got a perfect society, but that everybody can do better. I think all of these things have been miscommunicated to you. This is something you could do for your own sake. You'll never be a great respected power as long as other countries think you treat your own people in a way that is degrading."[15]

Jiang was taken aback, and then apparently pleased. "You're the first American who has come here and admitted that your own situation is nothing to brag about," he said. "You're someone I can deal with."[16]

Jiang spoke for a time on how he felt the human rights situation in China was improving and how no one ever seemed to acknowledge it. Brown did not argue the point. He let Jiang have his say. But he did say there was one specific measure the Chinese could take, and he brought up the subject of resuming the Human Rights Dialogue forums with the United States. Jiang told him that Li Peng had mentioned this. He said he would think about it, as if signaling that this round of discussions was finished.

Brown did not miss a beat. The minute Jiang was done, Brown went right back to the Chrysler and the McDonnell Douglas deals, saying that he would be in the country for another day. Further, his idea of a successful trip was that there would be announcements on both deals and that the human rights talks would be restarted.

"You should have seen the president," Garten said. "He couldn't believe it. He couldn't believe this guy at the other end of the table just wouldn't let go.

. . . I remember the president chuckling like he couldn't believe the chutzpah of this guy."[17] Sitting there watching his boss, Garten's mind brought forth an image of a person pushing a poker chip across a table, moving it closer and closer to the edge. Garten was convinced the chip would fall off and everything would collapse. But Brown seemed to know exactly where to stop. What stayed in Garten's memory was not so much Brown's nerves but his coolness. "There wasn't one ounce of tension displayed," he said. "There was no evidence that he thought he was taking a risk."[18]

A few hours after the session with Jiang, while Brown was meeting with other Chinese officials, a message arrived from the foreign ministry. The Chinese had agreed to restart the human rights talks. Again, without missing a beat, Brown immediately asked, "Can I announce it?"[19]

A day later, after saying he was "exhilarated" by his trip, Brown left China having secured the resumption of the talks but without commitments on the Chrysler and McDonnell Douglas deals. Those took a while longer. In the end China did agree to finalize its purchase of the jets, but in an apparent attempt to not seem to be granting too much, it set so many stringent conditions on the minivan project that Chrysler eventually backed out of the deal.

Critics have asserted that the resumption of the human rights talks was a rather small concession for the Chinese to make. But diplomacy is generally nothing more than a series of small moves forward that help build confidence between antagonists. And that Brown had won this concession in the midst of a trade mission was evidence of the possibility of commercial diplomacy, of how starting from the point of commercial engagement, policy could be moved in a direction that the Untied States desired. Brown also displayed his ability to make personal connections with people.

Wu Yi, Beijing's notoriously tough trade minister, invited Brown on a personal tour of the Forbidden City. For a while, the two strolled amiably, sometimes hand in hand, chatting about sports and children. "There probably has not been anybody in this country who had a good chemistry with as great a diversity of world leaders as Ron did," said Rob Stein. "It's an intangible. I can't put precise words on the quality of the relationships that I observed him establish with foreign dignitaries. There was a warmth; there was a connection; there was a nonverbal level of comfort."[20] Brown's ability to relate to world leaders—especially, though not exclusively, Third World leaders— was a direct outgrowth of his interest in people and other cultures. It allowed him to develop a personal diplomacy that was at times startling to those around him. He, like other powerful people, had a well-developed ego. But throughout his years in the spotlight, he did not always flaunt it. Instead, he worked hard to establish connections. In a world that seemed always to be defined as "us against them," he tried his best to convince whoever he was with that they were both part of "us."

"Most big-time cabinet-level people like to talk," said David Rothkopf, a white aide at Commerce. "Their thing is to get their message across. Ron always began by listening, and in doing so he established rapport with more people than one had any reason to expect he could."[21]

In his last years, his position—whether real or perceived—as one of Clinton's trusted political advisers gave him clout with foreign leaders. When he traveled abroad, he wasn't relegated to meeting with just foreign trade ministers. Heads of state wanted to talk. Foreign ministers sought him out. They knew they were not dealing with a mere commerce secretary but with someone of substance in the American government. It was an image he cultivated with his large entourages and with statements like the one he made on the eve of his trip to China when he spoke of having "political gravitas."

All this was true. But it would not have mattered as much if Ron Brown had not been driven to play a central role as a man of his times. As such, he came to embody that nexus of America's political and commercial strength that was so critical in a world that had radically changed since the fall of the Berlin Wall and the toppling of Lenin's statue in Red Square. No longer could Third World countries play the United States and the Soviet Union off against each other. There was only one top dog that could bring peace and prosperity.

"When he went to the Middle East, Arafat didn't seek him out because he thought Brown knew the intricacies of the territories," said Jeffrey Garten, the top Commerce official for international trade. "When Ron went to Russia or to Ireland, they wanted to talk to him because they also knew he was sitting on top of what they wanted: investments, capital, entry into the U.S. market. They didn't want to hear jawing about theory or America's long-term foreign policy interests. They needed something very immediate, and that's what Brown would talk to them about."[22]

Into this global sea change Brown brought his own personal diplomatic style. He liked to be accompanied by huge entourages, but he was by no means imperious. His trips did not entail dashes from the airport to the Presidential palace in a long, tinted-window Mercedes, a quick meeting with the head of state, and then a sprint out of the country. Brown spent time making connections. He met with mayors and provincial leaders. He played soccer with poor children in Brazil. He walked the streets of Gaza. Despite the expressed concern of the State Department, he appeared on a televised town hall meeting at a university outside Bangalor, India. You have no idea what these students are going to ask, the State Department warned him. They are notoriously left-wing and will be relentless in their criticism of American commercial imperialism. That's all right, Brown told them, as long as we can have a dialogue.

"Perhaps it was the politician in him," said Garten.[23] Perhaps it was. But it was those political instincts that made him an uncanny fit in the New World Order. Brown seemed to know instinctively that the world was different. To see it no longer as a bipolar world with Soviet Union vanquished was to see only half of the change. The victory of Western democratic capitalism meant that the Third World was changing as well. Its economies and its politics were becoming decentralized. There were more power centers. No more were all decisions going to be made in Brasilia or New Delhi. Municipal officials, provincial governors, and student leaders had to be won over as well. If they could not be fully convinced, Brown worked to get them to the point where they would give him—and therefore America, and therefore American companies—the benefit of the doubt. As a politician whose skills with people were finely honed, Brown was in the perfect place at the perfect time. After his death he was often depicted as a transitional figure in America's changing racial environment. That is an accurate but pinched analysis. In reality, his destiny was to be a transitional man in a world in transition.

As an African American, Brown often succeeded in relating to world leaders on the basis of race and ethnicity. He looked for those images that connected him to them as descendants of people who had been victimized by racism and colonial exploitation. In nearly all of his speeches abroad, Brown reminded his audience that he grew up in Harlem at a time of racial segregation. His life—and theirs, he seemed implicitly to be saying—was one of struggle and achievement in a world dominated by white Americans and white Europeans. "This was someone they could trust," said Fitz-Pegado, head of the Commerce Department's Commercial Section and herself black. "They could have confidence that this wasn't America, the big guy, coming in, trying to impose its will, the traditional Ugly American that often haunts us. He never suffered from that imagery. They did not see him that way. They saw him as, perhaps, one of them."[24]

Brown did not take that connection for granted. He worked hard to nurture it. In India, he celebrated the birthday of Martin Luther King Jr. by visiting the Gandhi *raj got*—the site where the ashes of Mahatma Gandhi were laid—and spoke of two spiritual and ideological streams of nonviolence that connected the two men. His talk the next day was less about nonviolence. Instead, Brown folded Gandhi's pragmatism into an appeal for the importance of commercial development. "Gandhi wrote, 'I am not a visionary. I claim to be a practical idealist,'" Brown said in New Delhi. "This is the spirit in which we come to your great nation. We believe that commerce between our nations has the potential to help millions of people. That we can speed growth and the spread of prosperity in both India and the U.S. And that in doing these things we can create not just [a] more affluent society, but a better society: more just, more tolerant, more inclusive."[25]

That he used the imagery of racial solidarity and justice to enhance the profits of American businesses, both large and small, and even his own reputation and ambition, seemed not to bother Brown at all. It was all part of The Deal. To Brown, life was not a zero-sum game. Everybody benefited. Corporate profits rose. American jobs were created. The standard of living in developing countries rose, and with it, hopefully, more freedom. He gained acclaim. Do what you can for your client. Do what you can for your people. Do what you can for yourself. It was a philosophy of The Deal that he lived by. It had worked when he worked for Ted Kennedy in 1980. He had tried to make it work when he was a lobbyist for Haiti. It worked to elect Bill Clinton. The Deal never changed; the dealmaker just kept moving to larger stages.

As Brown cruised through 1994 wowing world leaders and corporate chieftains, however, a parallel series of events began unfolding in the shadows.

WHAT WAS A solid strategy for dealing with Congressman Clinger in early 1994 turned horribly sour after November of that year, when the Republicans won majorities in the Senate and the House, giving them control of Congress for the first time since 1954. Suddenly, Clinger no longer was the easily ignored ranking minority member of a key congressional committee. He was the chairman and could ask for any documents he pleased. If Commerce refused, Clinger could issue a subpoena that would carry the full weight of the committee or, if necessary, that of the House. "Suddenly, he said he wished he had answered our questions earlier," Clinger said. "We really had their attention. People would come up from the Commerce Department and sit down with us. We got a greater sense of urgency."[26]

Even as Clinger turned up the heat, reports began appearing in the press concerning Brown's ties to Nolanda Hill and financial transactions that raised eyebrows, if not questions.

Newspapers had already reported that First International, the company Brown owned in partnership with Hill, was closely linked with Corridor, Nolanda Hill's company. In addition to the fact that Hill ran both firms, the two companies shared office space and telephone numbers.

In January 1995, the *Washington Post* reported that Hill had paid more than $190,000 of Brown's personal debts (the figure would later turn out to be much higher, $300,000) the year before. The payments were part of a December 15, 1993, agreement between Brown and Hill to buy out his share of First International. The two had finally settled on how much Brown would be paid for his portion of the company. In addition to the $300,000 payment of Brown's debt, Hill paid him $135,000 in three installments of $45,000 during 1993. She also agreed to forgive $72,000 in debts Brown owed to the company. On his financial disclosure form, filed in May, Brown reported that the buyout was worth between $250,000 and $500,000. Hill gave a more accurate figure, placing the value closer to the half-million-dollar figure.[27] Other than the fact that Brown was getting a return of $500,000 from a business that he had not invested a dime in, nothing particularly suspicious had been disclosed—yet.

Ten days later, Clinger revealed that First International's "primary source of income" was interest that accrued on a $875,000 promissory note that was held by Corridor and funneled to First International. The arrangement raised questions since at the same time Corridor was paying First International $12,000 a month it was failing to repay a $23 million debt to the Federal Deposit Insurance Corporation (FDIC). Corridor had borrowed the money from a savings and loan to purchase television stations in Washington and Needham, Massachusetts. When the savings and loan went bankrupt, the FDIC assumed the debt. Clinger's disclosure was embarrassing to Brown since it meant that he was receiving money that should have been going to the taxpayers. But though embarrassing, there was nothing illegal in Brown's being paid the money.

Hill was making enemies. Employees at her television stations were beginning to suspect she was looting them. Even after she lost the stations, she was hired to run them, and some employees suspected she was diverting their assets for personal use. In early 1995, however, employees from the stations began leaking documents to Clinger. "As we began to develop the Hill connections, we had some stuff coming over the transom from some of her employees," Clinger said.[28]

One crucial piece of evidence fell into the committee's hands: copies of three checks, each totaling $45,000, that were paid to Brown from First International in April, July, and October 1993. The checks indicated that he had received income from First International before he sold his stock in the company. He had not reported this income—as income—on his financial disclosure form as was required by federal law. Clinger used this piece of evidence as a major part of his request to Attorney General Janet Reno that an independent counsel be appointed to investigate Brown's finances. On May 16, 1994, Reno complied. In doing so, she authorized the prosecutor to investigate whether Brown deliberately misled the bank when he took out a mortgage on the town house he helped Lillian Madsen secure. Reno asked the special prosecutor to look into Brown's failure to state the source of the down payment for the property and the fact that he listed the house as rental property.

Whether Brown would have been indicted on the key charges of failing to disclose income and providing misleading information to his bank on his mortgage application is an open question. Friends and advisers insist that although he might have been hooked up with a business partner who played fast and loose, Brown himself did nothing illegal. They might have a point. In fact, Hill was charged in March 1998 of illegally siphoning off assets from her other companies in order to funnel money to Brown. But if it could be shown that Brown was unaware of what she was doing, then he had not committed any crime. Brown was notorious for not paying attention to the details of his business dealings. Mark Koogler, the lawyer for PEBSCO, was surprised when he found out how little Brown knew about the details of his business arrangement with that company. And Hill and others have said that Brown left much of the running of First International to her. "The truth is he liked doing deals but he didn't know business," said Stein. "He didn't care much for the details of business."[29] This personality trait was not confined to business. As much as Brown liked smooth running operations and things going off like clock-work, he generally left the details of getting those operations organized to other people.

"As an administrator, oh, Lord, he was horrendous," said his old friend Carl Wagner. "I wouldn't trust him to pick up my laundry . . . he wasn't into the details."[30] Brown had placed his trust in many people along the way, confident that in the end they would come through for him. Why should his business dealings with Hill have been any different?

Moreover, Brown had disclosed that he had received payments from First International. He had listed them as revenue from the sale of his stock in the company to Hill rather than as income. Technically, this might have been incor-rect since he received $135,000 before he actually dissolved his stake in First International in December 1993. The Internal Revenue Service could have cited Brown for incorrectly listing the revenue as a capital gain, rather than as income, and therefore paying a lower tax rate on the earnings than he was allowed. But such a citation probably would have led to Brown's having to pay interest and penalties on the difference, not an indictment.

The allegations related to the town house were another problem. Brown clearly did not list the loan from Ramos to Madsen as the source of the down payment for the property, nor did he list the town house as a rental property until December 1993, after its existence and the fact that Madsen was living there had been disclosed in the press. But it is difficult to discern who was the victim of any crime here. Brown was meeting his obligations on the mortgage, and, indeed, when Reno appointed the special prosecutor the payments on the mortgage were being made on schedule. Presumably, the bank could have charged Brown a higher rate on his mortgage had it known the town house was being rented. But when Brown changed the mortgage to reflect the prop-erty's real status, the rate remained the same. It is true that making false state-ments on a mortgage application is against the law, but the question is whether prosecutors would have sought an indictment on such a trivial charge. Prose-cutors make judgment calls on whether a transgression is sufficient to warrant a formal indictment. They often base such a decision on the possibility of gain-ing a conviction and how embarrassing it would be to lose in court. Given that, the possibility that they would have brought a politically well-connected, wildly popular black man to trial in Washington, D.C.—a city so annoyed at the con-duct of federal prosecutors that it reelected its mayor, Marion Barry, even after he had been caught on videotape smoking crack cocaine—strains credibility.

Still, as picayune as the allegations were, they did reflect an appalling lack of judgment on Brown's part, especially in his dealings with women.

In public, Brown appeared to be unmoved. But in his private life, he seemed to be courting danger with almost rebellious recklessness. He was having another affair, this one with an employee directly under his supervision. Her name was Kathryn Hoffman, a statuesque, brown-skinned woman who worked as one of his senior advisers. Hoffman, originally from Atlanta, had gotten her first taste of politics working for Julian Bond's unsuccessful bid for Congress in 1986.

"She was just a strikingly beautiful young woman, and a hard worker," Bond recalled. "She was really good at all the kinds of little stuff you need to do in a campaign."[31] She had worked for a time for Time-Life Co. in New York and later for Sony Entertainment Corp. in California. Things apparently did not work out well at Sony, and in 1992 she left and took a job with the Clinton campaign in California, where, according to one source, she got to know Brown. After the election she came to Washington, where Brown placed her at the Commerce Department. Their romance was an open secret at Commerce; some officials say that neither made much of an attempt to hide it. Indeed, Brown reportedly bought her a large ring that she often boasted about. "She really dug him," one acquaintance said.

That Brown would be carrying on an affair with a close subordinate in the post–Clarence Thomas and Anita Hill world and during a time when he was under intense press scrutiny could not have been coincidental. He seemed intent on proving his supreme confidence in his ability to live on the edge and survive. With Jean Chisholm at Middlebury, he had bowed to contemporary mores. With other women later in life, he had at least taken pains to cover his tracks, but now he refused to change his behavior. Here was the same bravado and willingness to take risks that had gotten him to the chairmanship of the Democratic National Committee and to the top job in a cabinet department in an area he knew little about.

But his willingness to take chances had gotten him in serious trouble this time. Whether, as Reid Weingarten, Brown's lawyer, insists, Brown felt confident about the ultimate outcome of the independent counsel's investigation, he had never faced the weight and power of such an investigation. Though seemingly limited in what allegations they could explore, investigators checked into his businesses, including PEBSCO, to make sure that he had properly disclosed his income. They interviewed friends, business associates, bankers, accountants. The scope and intrusiveness of the probe for once pierced Brown's normally sunny and optimistic disposition. He worried that Clinton and the White House would not stick by him. In October 1994, Mike Espy, the black secretary of agriculture, who was the subject of an investigation by an independent counsel for allegedly accepting gifts from businesses that did business with his department, abruptly resigned. There was widespread belief, including by Brown, that the White House essentially pushed Espy out the door. Though Clinton publicly expressed support for his Commerce secretary, Brown at times wondered aloud if he would suffer the same fate.

"The media was taking potshots at him. The people in the White House saw him as a liability," said Jesse Jackson. "People wanted to remove him. He felt a strong kinship with the president and felt the president would support him. But the way things work in Washington is that the president can love you to death, but forces around him are awesome in their power."[32]

There were, in fact, discussions in the White House about moving away from Brown, or even asking him to step down. "I don't think the president would have done it," said George Stephanopoulos. "But sure. You . . . didn't know; you didn't have all the answers and you didn't know how it was going to work out. There was always the question of is it right for someone to stay in a job if they are creating any kind of problem for the president."[33] Leon Panetta, the former White House chief of staff, said discussions about asking Brown to step aside were nothing more than "back room talk" among Clinton's political advisers. "I think there were moments when, as the thing heated up and you began to get more headlines as to where the investigation was going, that there were some who were concerned about whether Ron could survive the allegations and whether it would be better to move on."[34]

But Stephanopoulos recalled that the discussions about asking Brown to leave were "pretty high level," and there were those in the White House whom he declined to identify who were pushing for Brown's ouster. However, Clinton, himself the object of continued allegations of wrongdoing, said he would not abandon his beleaguered Commerce secretary. "The president put his foot down," Stephanopoulos said.[35]

The probe made Brown uncharacteristically despondent. For once, he began to second-guess decisions he had made and actions he had taken or not taken in his business if not his private life. "He didn't have the experience of running anything from a business perspective," said Nolanda Hill. "He was really ill-equipped. He mentioned this to me a week before he died: how much of his problems stemmed from his inexperience in business."[36]

In early 1996, as the independent counsel's probe was intensifying, Rob Stein visited Brown at the Commerce Department. The two men sat in Brown's office talking about the investigation. Stein had not seen his friend in six months and was shocked at both Brown's anger and his sadness. "He said to me, 'Rob, you wouldn't believe it,'" Stein recalled. "'They are even going to my golf club and getting all of my receipts at the golf club and calling every person who has ever known me. People must regret having known me.'"[37]

Stein had never heard Brown talk like this. This worldly man, so self-assured, so comfortable with himself and others, who reveled in his vast network of friends and acquaintances, enjoying their company and making connections between them, was, for the first time in Stein's experience, speaking of himself as a burden. It wasn't so much the anger or hurt in Brown's voice that shocked Stein. It was the doubt. Stein had never heard Brown question his own worth to others before. It shook Stein. "It was a moment," he said.

"Whether or not the day before or the day after he was to show doubts, who knows? But at that moment he did. At that moment he was vulnerable."[38]

ANOTHER PROBLEM added to Brown's woes. From the moment the GOP swept into control of Congress, leaders in the Senate and House wanted to make good on their promise of cutting federal spending and reducing the size and scope of the federal government. Everyone, it seemed, wanted to get rid of the Commerce Department. Plans put forward by the Republican-controlled budget-writing committees in both the House and the Senate called for abolishing the department.

It turned out, though, that the battle over the dismantling of Commerce displayed him at his best. His problems with Vietnam and First International highlighted his lack of attention to detail, his willingness to trust people who might not have been deserving of that trust, and a sense of arrogance and disdain toward his political adversaries. The dismantling battle showed his political astuteness, his unwillingness to give any quarter, his ability to rally troops and keep allies on his side. It showed that, even as he was under investigation for his role in First International, once the issue moved into the political arena there were few better than Ron Brown.

"The complicating factor with regard to Commerce was, obviously, the investigation of Ron and whether or not that would impact on what would happen to Commerce itself," said Leon Panetta. "But if there was anything that all of us, and certainly myself, appreciated about Ron it was his tremendous capacity to work the issues on Capitol Hill. He brought the same kind of operation that he used in Commerce, in the trade area, and in politics, and brought all of those skills to bear during the budget battles involving Commerce."[39]

Brown held things together by the force of his personality. From the start, his view was give no ground, make no compromises, everyone hangs together, and we'll face 'em down. By contrast, Henry Cisneros, with HUD on the chopping block, decided that the way to save his department was to agree with the Republicans that it needed reforming. He came forward with a plan to radically change the way HUD did its business. Brown decided early on not to go that route.

"Ron liked Henry and respected him a lot," said one senior Commerce Department official. "But he really thought Henry was wrong on how to deal in the dismantlement battle. I remember him . . . disparaging that strategy and saying Henry had ceded the battle before it had started."

"There were people in the department who thought if you cut off one of your arms and fed it to the sharks, the sharks would swim away," said another former top Commerce official. "Ron understood from day one that wasn't how you made the sharks go away, that if you put something on the table they'll say, 'Thank you very much, what else d'ya got?' "

In the summer of 1995, Brown convened a meeting of his top aides in his office. They hashed out the pros and cons of the proposal to slim down the department, and Brown let both sides have their say before weighing in. His view was, simply, united we stand, divided we fall. "I think many people disagreed with him or were skeptical of the strategy," said Desler. "But Brown didn't move from it at all. Given their personal respect for him and given the fact that the guy showed no doubt, the feeling was, 'He's playing our hand. We'll just let him play it. We don't have a better card player than this guy. Let's see if he can bluff our way into survival.' "[40]

The strategy seemed risky since Brown and many of his aides were not sure how much support they would get from the White House. After the election, Clinton moved to the center, bringing on board as a key adviser Dick Morris, an operative who had worked as much for Republicans as he had for Democrats and was personally close to Trent Lott, the Senate Majority Whip. Morris was constantly counseling Clinton to figure out ways to accommodate the Republicans, even if that meant throwing Brown and Commerce out of the lifeboat. "His constant theme was to always throw Congress some kind of bone," said Panetta. "And he would kind of indicate that with his backdoor discussions with Trent Lott that if the administration could throw this bone or that bone at Congress, somehow that would pacify them and they could resolve budget issues. So I think Ron had a real concern that he would be sold out in that process."[41]

In private, Brown argued his case with the White House. In public, he insisted that Clinton was standing squarely behind the department, even if the words emanating from 1600 Pennsylvania Avenue were not always that strong. If a presidential spokesperson said that Clinton would consider a veto of any appropriations bill that eliminated Commerce or his aides would recommend a veto, Brown would take that a step further and declare that Clinton would definitely reject any measure that scrapped the department. "I've had a number of direct and specific conversations with the president, as recently as two days ago," Brown told a gathering of Commerce Department employees. "He is unalterably supportive of this department, unalterably supportive of its continuation and, in fact, its preeminence."[42]

Brown believed in his department and honestly felt that Commerce was doing important work. But it was also against his nature to back down or to exhibit any doubt about the rightness of his cause. To do so, he believed, would mean defeat. His speech to Commerce employees was classic Brown, pounding home the message of maintaining a positive attitude. "If we are projecting a kind of hangdog, isn't this terrible, isn't this awful what they're doing to us, oh my goodness, what's going to happen to me, what's going to happen to our department—all of the bad things will happen," Brown told the employees. "If we're out there, projecting a sense of confidence, a sense of belief in ourselves—not arrogance, not arrogance but confidence—that will have a major impact on the outcome of this battle."[43]

But Brown also felt it was not just Commerce the Republicans were after. It was him. "They needed a scalp," said one top Commerce official. "I never heard him say it was personal. But I suspect he thought it was personal. . . . Everybody else thought it was personal. The message that was being conveyed by those partisan Republicans who weren't reluctant to be nasty was that Ron Brown had a significant role in making sure that George Bush lost and Bill Clinton won. There were a lot of Republicans in the Congress that blamed Brown for the '92 election—probably still do. And I think there was a determination that said, 'This was the guy who wiped us out and we're going to get even.'" Brown's acceptance of this view meant that seeking a compromise with Congress by agreeing to slim down Commerce would be fruitless. If, as he believed, they were out to personally humiliate him, they would not be deterred by any kind of plan to reorganize the agency.

Throughout the fight, Brown was quick to point out the lack of cost saving in getting rid of the department and how the Republican plan was merely shifting parts of Commerce to other agencies. "This talk of wholesale dismantlement has become a joke," he once said. "We're headed toward creating even more agencies—each with its own inspector general, each with its own public affairs office, each with its own personnel office. Where's the savings in that?"[44]

Realizing that the more partisan House was a lost cause, Brown focused his attention on the Senate, personally lobbying Senators not to eliminate his department. He found allies in his fight to keep NOAA as part of Commerce in senators from coastal states who sat on committees that oversaw the Commerce Department's programs and controlled its budget. These senators from places like Alaska, Oregon, and Maine were concerned that if NOAA was transferred to another agency they would lose their ability to direct funds to the fishing industries in their states. He hammered away with his message that the breakup of Commerce would not save money, and won a critical procedural victory in the Senate that required that passage of any budget measure to eliminate the department in that chamber would require sixty votes rather than a simple majority of fifty-one. Finally, Senator Robert Dole, the Senate Majority Leader, met with Brown in October and essentially threw in the towel. "Ron, we don't have the votes," Dole said to him, according to Will Ginsberg, Brown's chief of staff during Brown's last year at Commerce.[45] The Republicans were not going to go after the department during this round in the budget wars. They might do so in the future. But, for now, the department was saved.

Technically, the fight wasn't over. Brown and Commerce had prevailed in the fashioning of the budget where Congress sets broad outlines of how the federal government will spend its money. But he still had to contend with the appropriations process, when the lawmakers pass bills that actually allocate the funds. The Republicans could still use those spending bills to strip agencies or programs away from Commerce. But as autumn turned into what was to be one of the harshest winters in several years in Washington, the fight over dismantling Commerce was subsumed into the more titanic struggle between the White House and the Congress over enacting a balanced budget, restructuring Medicare, and other spending proposals. The tussle led to shutdowns of the federal government in November and December after Clinton vetoed spending bills that he found distasteful.

The brinkmanship that characterized the budget wars of late 1995 would set off rounds of debate within the administration over how tough or accommodating it should be with congressional Republicans. Clinton's natural bent toward compromise, the entreaties of Morris, and the political disaster of the 1994 elections pulled in the direction of coming to terms with the Republicans. Brown, however, was one of those inside the administration who argued forcefully for the president to hang tough. He asserted at cabinet sessions and other meetings with the president and White House officials that the Democrats were pursuing the proper policies for the country and that if you faced down the Republicans they would eventually fold or shoot themselves in the foot. Look what had happened in the dismantling fight over this department, he would say. Finally, he would tell Clinton in no uncertain terms that compromise would be a political disaster. The Republicans were portraying Clinton as a weak, vacillating leader—a second Jimmy Carter—whom they could steamroll and get their way. For Brown, who was hypersensitive to the importance of perception in creating a new reality, this was not the portrayal the president would want to project going into the 1996 elections. "He had a pragmatic sense to say to the president, 'Your political ass is on the line in terms of these decisions,' " said Panetta.[46]

The advice was not unique to Brown. But it carried weight because Clinton respected Brown's political judgment. Helped by others voicing the same views, and by the stridency of the Republicans, Clinton was persuaded. He did not yield to Republicans. The government shutdowns were a political disaster for the GOP. The public did—contrary to some Republicans' belief—miss some governmental services, and they blamed the Republican Party for taking them away. The White House was able to paint the Republicans as ideologues and the president as fighting to maintain a sensible course against their extremism. That definition—along with a still superbly performing economy—allowed Clinton to coast to victory in 1996. It was a victory that Brown would not live to see.

ON JANUARY 31, 1996, Richard Holbrooke, the American diplomat who had negotiated the Dayton peace treaty, stopped by Brown's office to ask him a favor. "I asked him to undertake an important mission to Bosnia," Holbrooke would later write. "Brown had been exceptionally effective in strengthening American exports and supporting business, and I thought his imagination and drive could give a huge boost to the economic reconstruction effort, one of the key long-term tests of our policy."[47]

In November 1995, leaders from the remnants of Yugoslavia, Bosnia-Herzegovina, and Croatia had met at an American air force base in Dayton, Ohio. They reached an agreement that would halt the fighting in the Balkans, where war had been raging for years. The agreement called for the deployment of twenty thousand NATO troops, including American forces, as peacekeepers, as well as American efforts to rebuild the region's shattered economy.

Holbrooke's idea intrigued Brown, and it especially appealed to Bill Morton, one of his top personal advisers. Morton had been with Brown since the Jesse Jackson campaign. "Bill was a low-key guy, but Ron really valued him," said Ray Vickery. "One of the reasons he did was that Bill could think outside the box. . . . Bill was a very good strategic thinker when it came to advance ways of how this guy was going to be perceived."[48] Morton was also one of the advisers to Brown who was constantly pushing the idea of his boss's becoming secretary of state.

Brown was beginning to reexamine his goals. With the Independent Counsel investigation making confirmation by the Senate more and more difficult, he was beginning to think more seriously about entering the private sector. Morton was one of those who kept the State Department dream alive, and the Balkans trip could help in that effort. "Bill wanted to do that trip for a long time because he thought that it really made the point very plainly about the relationship between commercial and business activity and national security," said Vickery.[49]

There was, however, opposition within the department. David Rothkopf lobbied hard against the mission, arguing that given the controversy over selling seats on trade missions to contributors to the Democratic Party, Brown ought to be very careful what trade missions he led. "There was a lot of scrutiny about these trips," said Rothkopf. "It seemed only prudent to be very careful to make sure the trips were a useful exercise and had a high return on investment."[50] This one did not look like it was going to bring about any immediate results and might not be worth the effort. "It looked like it was going to be a purely symbolic trip," Rothkopf said. "There were not going to be a great deal of deliverables, deals that would happen." There was another reason Rothkopf argued against the Balkan trip. Sure, a peace treaty had been signed, but the cease-fire that had been achieved was a fragile one. There were reports of sporadic fighting, roads might still be mined, and foes of the peace treaty might want to conduct a headline-grabbing act like assassinating a top U.S. official. "I thought it was still a dangerous place," Rothkopf said.[51]

For a time Rothkopf's arguments prevailed. Brown wanted to keep his schedule focused and was willing to cut down on the number of trips over all. So he listened to Rothkopf's objections and for a time was not willing to give the Balkan trip his go-ahead. But in early 1996 Rothkopf left the department. With Rothkopf gone there was no effective counterweight to those in favor of the Balkans mission. At the insistence of Morton and others, Brown began to see the trip as a means to once again be in the headlines and further his case for the secretary of State job. He felt that by the end of the year his legal problems would have cleared up, and with Clinton's reelection, he still had a shot at heading the State Department. A few more successful trips to show his diplomatic bona fides would help make a stronger argument for the job. Just a few more.

LENADRA GLUHAN WAS SEATED in her kitchen having a cup of coffee on April 3, 1996, when she heard the airplane roar overhead. The sound was not unusual. Gluhan, an assistant air traffic controller at the airport in nearby Dubrovnik, was used to the sounds of aircraft. And her house was located on the beach just north of the airport, smack in the middle of the airport's landing approach pattern. So hearing jets scream over her dwelling was a normal feature of her life. It wasn't the sound that caught Gluhan's attention. It was the direction. It was coming from the north. There was no mistake about it. It had been raining for some time in and around Dubrovnik.

The rain had momentarily halted—though clouds still hung low on the nearby mountains—and Gluhan had flung open the kitchen windows to get some fresh air. It was through those windows, located in the rear of her home, that the sound of jet engines could be clearly heard. What that meant was that whoever was flying the plane was dangerously off course. In front of her house was the Adriatic Sea, a safe, unobstructed approach to the airport, the way pilots were supposed to bring their aircraft in. Behind her home lay the mountains, which rise abruptly from the coast and create a hazard to anyone who has strayed too far north. "That captain is an idiot because he is flying that way," Gluhan thought to herself.[52]

Tragedies have many parts and many causes. And, of course, there are mysteries that will never be solved, though probably far fewer than conspiracy theorists would have us believe. With a little prodding from aides like Morton, Brown had decided to go to the Balkans. He had not necessarily wanted to go to Dubrovnik, however. The original schedule drawn up for the trip called for stops in Zagreb, the capital of Croatia; Tuzla, in Bosnia-Herzegovina, where he would visit American troops; and the Bosnian capital of Sarajevo. That was about all he could do and still get his party back to the United States for Easter Sunday. But Croat officials prevailed upon Brown and his staff to see if they could add Dubrovnik to the itinerary. The twelve-hundred-year-old walled city, an ancient port on the Adriatic, had been one of the region's prime tourist spots before it was chewed up by Serbian artillery during the war between Serbia and Croatia. Croat officials, seconded by Peter Galbraith, the U.S. ambassador in Zagreb, hoped Brown's visit would help boost the tourist trade to its former glory. "Tourism is Croatia's most important industry," Galbraith later said. "So, for reasons both relating to American business and as a symbol of our good relations with Croatia, I recommended this strongly."[53]

The trip was essentially a photo op. Brown would have his picture taken against the backdrop of the quaint old city and mouth a few well-chosen words about the beauty of the Dalmatian Coast and the good investment opportunities in the tourist industry.

The weather was atrocious on the day of the flight to Dubrovnik, with intermittent driving rain and broken clouds down as low as four hundred feet. But five planes landed at the airport without any major problems just before Brown's aircraft was due to arrive. Each had a difficult approach. First of all, the airport had sustained more than $30 million worth of damage during the war with Serbia from shelling and equipment was missing. Dubrovnik lacked an instrument landing system, an electronic navigational aid that guides pilots, telling them when they are off course or are too high or too low. The system is critically important when rain or fog makes it impossible for pilots to see the runway. But when Serbian troops overran the airport in 1991 they had taken it. Croatia, its treasury depleted as a result of the war with Serbia, had not had the funds to replace the system. "Croatia does not have any money to repair all the infrastructure very fast," Tonci Peovic, the airport manager, later told air force investigators. "Probably this was also the reason why Secretary Brown was here, to find a way how to rebuild the infrastructure."[54] David Rothkopf was turning out to have been right. The war had made this a dangerous place, and this landing was more difficult and harrowing than it would have been in more peaceful times.

No one can say what Brown's thoughts were during the final seconds of his life. It had been another good trip. In his element as an American politician abroad, he could almost forget his legal problems at home. He was an optimist. He felt he had done no wrong in his public trust. Things were going well for his family despite the controversy. Things always had a way of working out for him if he didn't let them get him down. Even on this improbable trip he had gotten out the image he wanted—bringing McDonald's hamburgers to American troops in Tuzla. His trade mission was successful and nearly over.

Knowing how well Brown liked to prepare for his appearances, it is easy to imagine that he was trying to go over his notes for the next stop as the plane careened through the wretched weather. No one will ever know. Suddenly, the pilots, probably seeing the craggy mountain emerge out of the fog, powered up the left engine in a panicky attempt to swerve right.[55] It was too late. Traveling at 138 knots, the 737 slammed into the mountain. The sound of the jet crashing and the screams of lives ending were all lost amid the desolate terrain and the thunderclaps of the dreary Dalmatian storm. The fatal plane crash snuffed out his life along with the lives of the thirty-four other passengers and crew.

DEATH OFTEN deifies people. In *Black Enterprise* magazine in June 1996, reflecting on Brown's memorial service, publisher Earl G. Graves Sr. captured the mood of a stunned nation in the week after the crash. "About four hours into the service, around midnight, the standing-room-only crowd rose to its feet applauding the achievements of this great American hero. . . . The clapping of hundreds of hands filled the room with a thunderous roar that went on and on and on." As Graves wryly noted, "At Brown's memorial, Rev. Jesse Jackson joked about the occasional need for eulogists to 'hallucinate a life' for the survivors' benefit. No such false effort was needed in the case of Ron Brown."

But even in death Ron Brown was unable to escape controversy. Questions exploded on December 3, 1997, exactly twenty months after the plane went down, when the *Pittsburgh Tribune Review* suggested that, rather than being a victim of a tragic accident, Brown might have been murdered. The front-page story by Christopher Ruddy noted that a circular hole slightly left of the top of the former Commerce secretary's head bore a striking resemblance to a gunshot wound. "Essentially . . . Brown had a .45-inch inwardly beveling circular hole in the top of his head, which is essentially the description of a .45-caliber gunshot wound," Lt. Col. Steve Cogswell, a pathologist who handled some of the forensic investigation of the plane crash, told the *Tribune Review.*[56]

Cogswell did not stop with that provocative assertion. He did more than merely suggest foul play. He accused his superiors of a cover-up for not conducting a more thorough examination of the cause of Brown's death. "Even if you safely assumed accidental plane crash, when you got something that appears to be a homicide, that should bring everything to a screeching halt," he said.[57] Cogswell said that at the time he learned of the hole, he had implored his superiors to conduct a full autopsy on Brown's body to determine a precise cause of death. "Open him up. This man needs an autopsy," Cogswell said he told Col. William Gormley, who conducted the postmortem on Brown. "This whole thing stinks."[58]

The mystery deepened even more when the air force admitted that it had lost the original X rays taken of Brown during the postmortem examination. Air force officials said, however, that they had copies. One set of those copies showed curious-looking tiny fragments inside Brown's skull. Such fragments could be evidence of a "lead snowstorm," minute particles from a disintegrating bullet.

Armed with Cogswell's charges, which were spread far and wide over the Internet, Ruddy, several civil rights activists like Dick Gregory, and black radio talk show hosts began clamoring for an investigation and called for Brown's body to be exhumed so that a complete autopsy could be conducted. The seeds of doubt sown by the Ruddy story found fertile ground among a number of black people whose suspicion of the federal government had been primed by past events like the FBI attempts to discredit Martin Luther King Jr. and the long cover-up of the notorious Tuskegee experiments, in which government doctors injected unwitting black patients with the virus that causes syphilis.

Yet from the beginning there was more than adequate reason to doubt the doubters.

First of all there was the newspaper that broke the story. The *Pittsburgh Tribune Review* was published by Richard Mellon Scaiffe, the scion of the steel-producing Mellon family and a noted bankroller of right-wing causes. Though his politics should not automatically discredit Scaiffe—and by extension his newspaper—he had funded far-right groups who consistently charged the Clinton administration with covering up all manner of wrongdoing, including the alleged murder of Vincent Foster, a deputy White House counsel who, according to a number of investigations, had committed suicide. The undercurrent of the Brown "murder" story that was being spread on the Internet—and suspected by some in the black community—was that someone in the Clinton administration had arranged for Brown to be killed to prevent him from telling what he knew about fund-raising improprieties during the 1996 campaign.

Col. Gormley probably had no such conspiratorial thoughts in his mind when he discovered the strange hole in Brown's skull during his postmortem examination, but he was intrigued by his find. Having worked in military pathology since 1983, and as the air force's chief medical examiner and its leading forensic expert on aircraft accident investigations, he had traveled to Dover, Delaware, on April 6 to head the team that would examine the bodies of those killed in the crash near Dubrovnik. He immediately noticed the hole, which in the argot of pathology was termed a "depressed skull fracture," and wanted to know its origin. He did not immediately jump to the conclusion that the .41-inch hole—actually smaller than one that would be produced by a .45-caliber bullet—was caused by a gunshot. But he was suspicious and wanted to know how it did happen.

Gormley ordered that a second full set of X rays be taken of Brown's head and body. Like the first set, and another third set that was taken later, these X rays gave both a frontal and a side view of Brown's head. The following day, Gormley also telephoned Col. Cogswell in Germany. Cogswell, who never actually saw any of the bodies from the plane crash, was on his way to Croatia to conduct an examination of the crash site. Gormley told him of the hole in Brown's skull and asked him to examine the wreckage to determine what could possibly have caused it. It was during this conversation that Cogswell vehemently demanded that an autopsy be conducted. For his part, Gormley said he does not recall the details of the conversation, but acknowledged that Cogswell may have mentioned the need to conduct an autopsy.

Cogswell was never able to find anything at the site that would have explained the existence of the hole, a fact that only served to deepen the mystery about its origin. But a close examination of the X rays has laid the matter to rest, at least to the satisfaction of Brown's family who, after being briefed by the air force, declined to give the consent authorities needed to exhume the body so that a full autopsy could be conducted.

A closer examination of the first set of X rays showed that at the site of the hole, a small bone fragment had been pushed down on Brown's skull but had not separated from it. The second set of X rays showed that the same fragment, oddly resembling an inverted mushroom cap, had broken away from the skull. Such a difference in the location of the fragment could have been caused only by the movement of Brown's body as the pathologists went about their grisly tasks during their examination. Because bullets travel at such high velocities, if the hole had been caused by a slug, the fragment would not have been still attached to the skull.

The frontal shots taken as part of the second set of X rays once again show the tiny particles that were later to be described as the "lead snowstorm." But while they showed up on the left side of Brown's brain cavity in the first set of X rays, they now were on the right. Also, the second set of X rays taken from the side show no particles at all. The snowstorm had suddenly disappeared. Such an occurrence led air force pathologists to believe that rather than a disintegrating bullet, the specks on the X ray pictures were probably caused by dust on the X ray film. Indeed, the X rays taken of at least one other victim of the crash whose body was examined that day also showed a shower of particles inside the skull, and the pattern of the speckles were also exactly the same as Brown's.

Perhaps the most conclusive piece of evidence was not what the X rays showed, but what they didn't show. All sets of the X rays showed the hole in the top of Brown's skull, which, if it was caused by a bullet, would clearly be an entry wound. None of the X rays showed the presence of a bullet inside Brown's cranium, nor did they show an exit wound.

Of course, the mystery remains: what did cause the hole in the top of Ron Brown's head? No one is quite sure. But what is less mysterious is what killed him—a plane crash.

LIKE MALCOLM X, John and Robert Kennedy, and Martin Luther King Jr.— men who were cut down in the prime of their careers—Brown will probably always be the object of conspiracy theories. Perhaps this is the fate of men whose legacy is as much about what they might have done as it is about their accomplishments. Brown was, it has been said, a transitional man, a person in the vanguard of change for black people, the Democratic Party, and America itself. He showed the country how well an African American could play at the top. He helped nudge the Democrats toward the political center and away from the ideological wars that had consumed the party since Vietnam. He helped push American trade policy out of a hidebound laissez-faire and toward the dynamism that could be found in emerging Third World markets. But his death meant he was not around to finish the job or see what was wrought by the forces he either helped put in motion or recognized and tried to harness.

"I've been to the mountaintop," King had said the night before he was killed. "I've seen the promised land." Brown could make no such claim. He and the rest of the country did not have any idea of the contours of the domestic and international landscape he was working toward. But he knew that the country and the world were changing.

That his public journey was filled with such peril and influenced millions outside his race was a sign that those spheres were themselves changing in unpredictable ways. Diverse waves of voters seeking justice and America's bounty ushered in a new era of ethnic politics. A relentless and expanding news media started keeping politicians and government officials under its never-ending gaze. Soft money contributors played a larger and larger role in elections. American business interests stretched out overseas. Eventually, Brown would both epitomize and influence trends as familiar as any evening's news broadcast or morning's newspaper headlines.

But through it all, Brown was about building bridges, making connections, brokering deals. There could be links between blacks and whites, centrists and liberals, labor and business, corporations and government. He believed less in choices than in combinations. In the new global landscape, that made him a master of the deal.

NOTES

PART ONE   Four Generations (1894–1958)

Chapter One   Out of the South

1. Yetter, John B., and Kerns, Harold L., *Steelton, Pennsylvania: Stop, Look, Listen,* Triangle Press, p.1.
2. Bodner, John E., "Peter C. Blackwell and the Negro Community of Steelton, 1880–1920," *Pennsylvania Magazine of History and Biography,* April 1973, p.200.
3. Bodner, Ibid. p.199.
4. Wright, Richard R., *The Negro in Pennsylvania,* Arno Press, pp. 218, 229.
5. Stewart, Charlotte Brown; interview, January 20, 1999.
6. Warner, Mary, "Sisters Recall Their Family's Years," *Harrisburg Patriot,* February 29, 1996, p. C-1.
7. Ibid.
8. Ibid.
9. *Hilltop,* November 1, 1936, p. 1.
10. Washington, Walter; interview, August 27, 1997.
11. Brooke, Edward; interview, August 5, 1997.
12. Washington, op. cit.
13. Ibid.
14. Brooke, op. cit.
15. Brown, Tracey L., *The Life and Times of Ron Brown,* William Morrow and Company, Inc., 1998, p. 31.
16. Brooke, op. cit.
17. Brown, Tracey L., op. cit., p. 38.
18. Bill Brown obituary, *Amsterdam News,* October 1, 1988.
19. Stewart, op. cit.
20. Wilkinson, Frederick D., Jr., "Reflections: An Essay on Ron Brown," *Opportunity Journal,* August 1996, p.46.
21. Interview, George Lopez, December 10, 1997.
22. Interview, Frank Morris, December 7, 1997.
23. "The Waldorf of Harlem," *Ebony Magazine,* April, 1946, p. 8.
24. Jones, Nicholas Brown; interview, January 6, 2000.

Chapter Two   Theresa's Child

1. Middlebury College Personal Record Form.
2. "Bias Charged to Restaurants," *New York Times,* March 3, 1951, p. 18.
3. " 'Bias' at Stork Club Brings Bomb Threat," *New York Times,* October 21, 1951, p. 72.
4. Cunningham, Evelyn; interview, January 13, 1997.

5. Ibid.
6. Cunningham; interview, February 3, 1999.
7. Cunningham; interview, February 1, 1999.
8. *Ebony,* op. cit.
9. Ibid.
10. "Negro Vote Gains Expected by G.O.P.," *New York Times,* April 11, 1954, p. 56.
11. Brown, Tracey, *The Life and Times of Ron Brown,* William Morrow, 1998, p. 43.
12. Lewis, Martha; interview, March 6, 1997.
13. Howard, Dr. Juanita; interview, February 18, 1999.
14. Wilder, L. Douglas; interview, January 17, 1997.
15. Hubert, James; interview, March 25, 1997.
16. Brown, Ronald H., speech to International Tourism Conference, February 10, 1993.
17. Lewis, op. cit.
18. Brown, Peggy (Bill Brown's second wife); interview, January 29, 1999.
19. Lopez, op. cit.
20. Brown, Tracey, op. cit., pp. 46–47.
21. Lopez, op. cit.
22. Brown, Tracey, op. cit., p. 46.
23. Parks, Gordon, interview, February 6, 1999.
24. Ibid.
25. Cunningham; interview, January 13, 1997.
26. Harper, Dessie; interview, March 25, 1997.
27. Clarke, Kenneth; interview, August 6, 1997.
28. Brown, Tracey, op. cit., p. 34.
29. Walker, Sally; interview, November 14, 1998.
30. Nailor, John; interview, March 6, 1997.
31. Hinton, Lois; interview, February 15, 1997.
32. Ibid.
33. Ibid.
34. Ibid.
35. Ibid.

PART TWO   On His Own (1958–1979)

Chapter Three   Twilight's School

1. *First Annual Report of the Vermont Anti Slavery Society,* February 18, 1835, p. 9.
2. Buckeye, Robert, Middlebury archivist; interview, January 29, 1999.
3. Brown, Ronald; interviewed by *Middlebury Campus,* October 13, 1989.
4. Nailor, John; interview, March 6, 1997.
5. Reynolds, Thomas H.; interview, December 30, 1998.
6. Meehan, Thomas; interviewed in *Middlebury Magazine,* Summer 1996, p. 50.
7. Dulles, Juliet, "Jackson Advisor Brown Is Newest Trustee," *Middlebury Campus,* August 16, 1988, p. 5.
8. Cobb, Ralph; interview, January 23, 1997.
9. Ferguson, Joseph Fielding; interview, February 6, 1997.
10. Lucas, Wallace; interview, February 1, 1997.
11. Ibid.
12. Sullivan, Jean; interview, February 3, 1997.
13. Ibid.
14. Hinton, Lois; interview, February 15, 1997.
15. Ibid.

16. Ibid.

17. Hall, Carla, "Ron Brown & the Party's Acid Test," *Washington Post,* March 14, 1989, p. E2.

18. Walsh, Sharon, "Ron Brown, as Complex as His Finances; Commerce Secretary Described as Driven by Money, Public Service," *Washington Post,* February 26, 1995, p. A-1.

19. BettyJean Murphy; interview, March 14, 1997.

20. Owren Gilbert; interview, January 31, 1997.

21. Halpin, John; interview, January 22, 1997.

22. Orth, Sam, "Sigma Phi Epsilon Abolishes 'White Christian' Clause at Washington Conclave," *Campus,* October 1, 1959, p. 1.

23. Lardner, Breck; interview, January 22, 1997.

24. Farrell, Al, "Sig Ep Tries to Get Back into National," *The Campus,* December 8, 1960.

25. Middlebury College, Person Record Card.

26. Walsh, op. cit.

27. Poole, Isaiah J., "Brown Set to Lead Democrats after Final Foe Drops Out," *Washington Times,* January 31, 1989, p. 4.

28. Steitz, Mark; interview, September 25, 1996.

29. Middlebury College, Person Record Card.

30. Reynolds, op. cit.

31. Dulles, Juliet, op. cit.

32. Middlebury College, Person Record Card.

33. Ronald Brown writing in a Middlebury publication, n.d.

Chapter Four   The Army

1. LeTowt, Jon; interview, February 7, 1997.

2. Ronald Brown writing in a Middlebury publication, n.d.

3. Hill, Nolanda; interview, July 21, 1997.

4. Jaffe, Harry, "Mr. In-Between," *Washingtonian,* November 1992, p. 65.

5. Performance evaluation, December 11, 1963.

6. Performance evaluation, April 30, 1964.

7. Armed Forces of the United States Report of Transfer or Discharge for Ronald Brown.

8. Performance evaluation, January 5, 1965.

9. Carol, Dan; interview, April 9, 1998.

10. Moskos, Charles C., and Butler, John Sibley, *All That We Can Be: Black Leadership and Racial Integration the Army Way,* Twentieth Century Fund Books, 1996, p. 103.

11. Moskos and Butler, op. cit., p. 104.

12. "The Negro in the Armed Forces: A Statistical Fact Book," prepared by the Office of the Deputy Assistant Secretary of Defense (Equal Opportunity), September 15, 1971.

13. Powell, Colin L., *My American Journey,* Random House, 1995, p. 52.

14. Brown, Tracey L., *The Life and Times of Ron Brown,* William Morrow and Company, 1998, p. 94.

15. Jaffe, Harry, "Mr. In-Between," *Washingtonian,* November 1992, p. 65.

16. Hall, Carla, "Ron Brown & the Party's Acid Test," *Washington Post,* March 14, 1989.

17. Armed Forces of the United States Report of Transfer or Discharge for Ronald Brown.

18. Brown, Tracey, op. cit., p. 99.

19. Skaggs, David Curtis, "The KATUSA Experiment: The Integration of Korean Nationals into the U.S. Army, 1950–1965," *Military Affairs,* April 1974, p. 53.

20. Ibid.

21. Performance evaluation, April 30, 1967.

22. Ibid.

23. Frankel, Max, "Million in Seoul Cheer President at Last Asian Stop," *New York Times,* November 1, 1966, p. 1.

24. United Press International, November 2, 1966.

25. Performance evaluation, April 30, 1967.

26. Ibid.

Chapter Five   The League

1. Puryear, Mahlon; interview, June 15, 1997.

2. Bond, Julian; interview, March 19, 1997.

3. Weiss, Nancy J., *Whitney M. Young, Jr., and the Struggle for Civil Rights,* Princeton University Press, p. 73.

4. Mack, John; interview, February 26, 1997.

5. Johnson, Napoleon B. II, former director of Urban League Labor Programs; interview, April 29, 1997.

6. Gegan, Bernard; interview, February 16, 1999.

7. Ibid.

8. Cuomo, Mario; interview, January 17, 1997.

9. Ibid.

10. Brown, Ronald; unpublished interview with Richard L. Berke of the *New York Times,* February 10, 1989.

11. Hamilton, Charles; interview, April 2, 1997.

12. Valentine, Paul W., "Program for Urban Poor," *Washington Post,* July 29, 1969.

13. Mack, op. cit.

14. Jaffe, op. cit.

15. Kaufman, Vi; interview, April 21, 1997.

16. Weiss, op. cit., p. 200.

17. Garment, Leonard, memo to President Nixon, December 21, 1970, National Archives.

18. Garment; interview, February 17, 1997.

19. Patterson, Bradley; interview, February 17, 1997.

20. Patterson, *Ring of Power,* Basic Books, p. 204.

21. Safire, William; memo to Alexander Butterfield, December 22, 1970, National Archives.

22. Mart & Lundy, Inc., "Fund-Raising Study Prepared for National Urban League, Inc., September 1972, Urban League papers, Library of Congress.

23. Carpenter, May; interview, April 4, 1997.

24. Reich, Herb; interview, March 25, 1997.

25. McCarthy, Marie; interview, April 26, 1997.

26. Reich, Herb, op. cit.

27. Reich, Geri; interview, March 25, 1997.

28. Reich, Herb, op. cit.

29. Ford, David Sr.; interview, April 3, 1997.

30. Ibid.

31. McCarthy, op. cit.

32. Davis, Daniel S.; interview, March 23, 1997.

33. Payne, Les, "In the Footsteps of Whitney Young," *Ebony,* July 1972, p. 98.

34. Ibid.

35. Johnson, Robert E., "Interview with Vernon Jordan," *Ebony,* December 1980, p. 31.

36. Hunter-Gault, Charlayne, *In My Place,* Vintage Books, p. 158.

37. Hunter-Gault, op. cit., p. 157.

38. Ward, Horace; interview, April 23, 1997.

39. Gibson, James O.; interview, May 2, 1997.

40. Polly, Frances; interview, May 2, 1997.

41. Cleghorn, Reese; interview, October 7, 1997.

42. Jordan, Vernon; interview, December 22, 1997.

43. Cleghorn, Reese, op. cit.

44. Branch, Taylor; interview, October 5, 1997.

45. Cleghorn, op. cit.

46. Jordan, op. cit.

47. Davis, op. cit.

48. Hackney, James; interview, April 29, 1997.

49. Jordan, op. cit.

50. Mack, op. cit.

51. Williams, Faith; April 2, 1997.

52. Adair, Andrew; interview, May 4, 1997.

53. Hill, Robert; interview, October 18, 1996.

54. Adair, op. cit.

55. Jordan, op. cit.

56. Gibson, Carol; interview, May 1, 1997.

57. Gibson, James O., op. cit.

58. Jordan, op. cit.

59. Adair, op. cit.

60. Davis, op. cit.

61. Papers of National Urban League, Library of Congress.

62. Ibid.

63. Gibson, Carol, op. cit.

64. Alpern, David A., "Vernon Jordan: Keeping Contact," *Newsweek,* February 19, 1973, p. 30.

65. Jordan, op. cit.

Chapter Six   Homecoming

1. Shuster, Alvin, "Integration Gain in Capital Hailed," *New York Times,* October 7, 1955, p. 19.

2. Baker, Russell, "Behind Washington's Postcard Façade: Change, Trouble and Danger Afflict Capital," *New York Times,* June 10, 1963, p. 25.

3. Parker, Marjory H.; interview, December 1, 1997.

4. Adams, Betty; interview, April 8, 1997.

5. Haskins, Bill; interview, April 30, 1997.

6. Ibid.

7. Ibid.

8. Yergin, Daniel, *The Prize: The Epic Quest for Oil, Money & Power,* Simon & Schuster, 1991, p. 608.

9. Jordan, Vernon, memorandum to Ronald Brown, December 19, 1973, Papers of the National Urban League, Library of Congress.

10. Ibid.

11. Brown, Ronald, memorandum to Vernon Jordan, January 3, 1974, Papers of the National Urban League, Library of Congress.

12. Ibid.

13. Ibid.

14. Hernandez, Antonia; interview, February 27, 1997.

15. Ibid.

16. Gibson, Carol; interview, May 2, 1997.

17. Norton, Eleanor Holmes; interview, September 19, 1997.

18. Butler, Landon; interview, December 22, 1997.

19. Adair, Andrew; interview, May 4, 1997.

20. Norton, op. cit.

21. Gibson, Carol, op. cit.

22. Mack, John; interview, February 26, 1997.

23. Jordan, Vernon; interview, December 22, 1997.

24. Jordan, Hamilton, memorandum to Jimmy Carter, undated, Carter Library.

25. Jaffe, Harry S., and Sherwood, Tom, *Dream City: Race, Power, and the Decline of Washington, D.C.,* Simon & Schuster, p. 28.

26. Gibson, James O.; interview, May 2, 1997.

27. Coleman, Milton, "A New Face for Next Year's Mayor's Race?" *Washington Post,* November 17, 1997, p. C-1.

28. Ibid.

29. Hechinger, John; interview, April 28, 1997.

30. Coleman, Milton, "Mayor 'Candidate' Isn't One," *Washington Post,* February 14, 1978, p. C-2.

31. Johnson, Thomas, "Black Leaders Air Grievances on Jews," *New York Times,* August 23, 1979, p. A-12.

32. Jordan, Vernon; text of speech to National Conference of Catholic Charities, papers of National Urban League, Library of Congress.

33. "U.S. Blacks Visit Israeli Unionist and Stress Dislike of Terrorism," *New York Times,* October 16, 1979, n.p.

34. Mack, op. cit.

35. Ibid.

36. Johnson, Thomas, "2 Black Leaders Seeking to Avert Rift on Mideast," *New York Times,* October 15, 1979, p. A-1.

37. Smith, John T.; interview, January 7, 1998.

38. Statement of Black American Leaders at Press Conference, October 15, 1979.

39. Ibid.

40. Ibid.

41. Shipler, David K., "Rustin Delegation Confers with Begin," *New York Times,* October 18, 1979, p. 1.

42. Smith, op. cit.

43. Haskins, op. cit.

44. Barney, Clarence; interview, April 21, 1997.

45. Jordan, op. cit.

46. Edsall, Thomas, "Brown Takes Reins as Democratic Chief," *Washington Post,* February 11, 1989, p. 1.

47. Edelman, Peter; interview, December 24, 1997.

48. Jordan, op. cit.

49. Ibid.

50. Ibid.

51. Ibid.

52. Hill, Robert; interview, October 18, 1996.

53. Ibid.

54. Mack, op. cit.

PART THREE   The View (1980–1988)

Chapter Seven   Kennedy

1. Jackson, Jesse; interview, January 2, 1998.

2. Kraft, Tim, speaking at a 1980 conference on presidential campaign decision making, Institute of Politics, John F. Kennedy School of Government, Harvard University, December 5, 1980.

3. Jaffe, Harry, "Mr. In-Between," *Washingtonian,* November 1992, p. 65.

4. Chavez, Fernando; interview, August 5, 1997.

5. Ibid.

6. Hernandez, Antonia; interview, February 27, 1997.

7. Ibid.

8. Quinn, Tom, speaking at John F. Kennedy School of Government conference on 1980 presidential campaign decision making, December 5, 1980.

9. Kirk, Paul G. Jr., speaking at John F. Kennedy School of Government conference on 1980 presidential campaign decision making, December 5, 1980.

10. Buchanan, Christopher, "Kennedy: The Long Delayed Quest Begins," *Congressional Quarterly,* October 27, 1979, p. 2397.

11. Brown, Ronald H., speaking at the John F. Kennedy School of Government conference on 1980 presidential campaign decision making, December 6, 1980.

12. Ibid.

13. Herman, Alexis; interview, April 7, 1997.

14. Podesta, Tony; interview, May 23, 1997.

15. Brown, op. cit.

16. Ibid.

17. Shrum, Robert; interview, April 3, 1997.

18. Kirk, op. cit.

19. Lynch, Bill; interview, November 23, 1998.

20. Ibid.

21. Wagner, Carl; interview, September 26, 1996.

22. Wagner, op. cit.

23. Ibid.

24. Ibid.

25. Podesta, op. cit.

26. Tunney, John; interview, February 17, 1997.

27. Ibid.

28. Teicher, Orin; interview, October 16, 1996.

29. Ibid.

30. Ibid.

31. Wagner, op. cit.

32. Meyer, Richard E., "Kennedy TV Campaign for State Put at $195,000, Carter's at $150,000," *Los Angeles Times,* May 29, 1980, p. 20.

33. Kirk; interview, op. cit.

34. Sasso, John; interview, January 27, 1997.

35. Shrum, op. cit.

36. Ibid.

37. Garmenzy, Kathy; interview, February 25, 1997.

38. Shrum, op. cit.

39. Wagner; interview, op. cit.

40. Shrum, op. cit.

41. Ibid.

42. Reid, T. R., and Walsh, Edward, "Kennedy: 'Planning to Be Nominee,'" *Washington Post,* June 6, 1980, p. A-1.

43. Stearns, Kennedy School seminar, op. cit.

44. Ibid.

45. Brown, Kennedy School seminar, op. cit.

46. Podesta, op. cit.

47. Hernandez, op. cit.

48. Herman, op. cit.

Chapter Eight   The Player

1. Breyer, Justice Stephen; interview, April 20, 1997.

2. Ibid.

3. Eidenberg, Gene; interview, August 21, 1997.

4. Manatt, Charles; interview, February 7, 1997.

5. Kuznik, Frank, "Unify and Conquer," *Dossier Magazine,* September 1989, p. 41.

6. Bernstein, Carl, "King of the Hill," *Vanity Fair,* March 1998, p. 174.

7. Ibid.

8. Ibid.

9. May, Timothy; interview, May 20, 1998.

10. Greider, William, *Who Will Tell the People: The Betrayal of American Democracy,* Simon and Schuster, 1992, p. 484.

11. Ibid., p. 45.

12. Ibid., p. 47.

13. Bernstein, op. cit.

14. Greider, op. cit.

15. Ibid., p. 256.

16. Boggs, Thomas; interview, April 20, 1998.

17. Kuznik, op. cit.

18. Boggs, op. cit.

19. Ibid.

20. May, Timothy; interview, March 10, 1999.

21. Boggs, op. cit.

22. Buc, Nancy; interview, June 25, 1998.

23. Eidenberg, op. cit.

24. Stein, Rob; interview, March 14, 1997.

25. Boggs, Thomas; remarks at memorial service for Ron Brown, telecast by Black Entertainment Television, April 9, 1996.

26. Stein, op. cit.

27. Hill, Nolanda; interview, July 22, 1997.

28. Ibid.

29. Boyer, Peter, J., "Ron Brown's Secrets," *New Yorker,* June 9, 1997, p. 64.

30. Hill, Nolanda; interview, November 21, 1998.

31. Fisher, Bart; interview, February 16, 1999.

32. Hill, op. cit.

33. Ibid.

34. Brown, Tracey L., *The Life and Times of Ron Brown: A Memoir,* William Morrow and Company, Inc., 1998, p. 16.

35. Reports of lobbying activity filed by Patton Boggs and Blow with the Justice Department.

36. Howill, Richard; interview, February 5, 1997.

37. Horblitt, Steven; interview, June 9, 1998.

38. *Counterpunch,* December 1983, quoted in *Harper's Magazine,* February 1984, p. 18.

39. Ibid.

40. Schwartz, Bob; interview, June 16, 1998.

41. Ibid.

42. Howill, op. cit..

43. Bernstein, "King of the Hill."

44. May, op. cit.

45. Masden, Lillian; interview, June 7, 1998.

46. Stein, op. cit..

47. Koogler, Mark; interview, June 15, 1998.

48. Ibid.

49. Leland, Mickey; unpublished interview with Richard L. Berke of the *New York Times,* February 10, 1989.

50. Jackson, Jesse; interview; January 2, 1998.

51. Barney, Clarence; interview, April 27, 1997.

Chapter Nine   Jesse

1. Frady, Marshall, *Jesse: The Life and Pilgrimage of Jesse Jackson,* Random House, 1996, p. 75.

2. Ibid., p. 78.

3. Godwin, Lamond; interview, March 2, 1998.

4. Jackson, Jesse; interview, January 2, 1998.

5. Godwin, op. cit.

6. Jackson, op. cit.

7. Berke, Richard L., "Jackson Trails Other Democrats in Fund-Raising," *New York Times,* October 22, 1987, p. B-6.

8. Borosage, Robert; interview, September 12, 1996.

9. Cobble, Steve; interview, September 16, 1996.

10. Brown, Willie; interview, June 10, 1997.

11. Ibid.

12. Ibid.

13. Godwin, op. cit.

14. Herman, Alexis; interview, April 7, 1997.

15. Jaffe, Harry, "Mr. In-Between," *Washingtonian,* November 1992, p. 65.

16. Jackson, op. cit.

17. Austin, Gerald; interview, March 8, 1997.

18. Ibid.

19. Godwin, op. cit.

20. Kuttner, Robert, "Ron Brown's Party Line," *New York Times Magazine,* December 4, 1989, p. 44.

21. Ibid.

22. Herman, op. cit.

23. Brown, Tracey L., *The Life and Times of Ron Brown: A Memoir,* William Morrow and Company, Inc., 1998, p. 153.

24. Edley, Christopher, Jr.; interview, January 29, 1997.

25. Ibid.

26. Godwin, op. cit.

27. Brown, Tracey, op. cit., p. 153.

28. Brown, Willie, op. cit.

29. Kuznik, Frank, "Unify and Conquer," *Dossier Magazine,* 1989, p. 41.

30. Cobble, op. cit.

31. Ibid.

32. Weinraub, Bernard, "Jackson Says He Deserves Thought as Running Mate," *New York Times,* June 1, 1989, p. A-22.

33. Brown, Willie, op. cit.

34. Jaffe, op. cit.

35. Oreskes, Michael, "Jackson Caravan Heads for Georgia," *New York Times,* July 14, 1988, p. B-6.

36. Estrich, Susan; interview, February 26, 1997.

37. Ibid.

38. Brountas, Paul; interview, January 27, 1997.

39. Borosage, op. cit.

40. Ibid.

41. Ibid.

42. Brountas, op. cit.

43. Ibid.

44. Ibid.

45. Ibid.

46. Dionne, E. J., "Dukakis and Jackson Agree to Unite for Fall Campaign as Party Opens Convention," *New York Times,* July 19, 1988, p. A-1.

47. Cooper, Mario; interview, April 17, 1997.

48. Lewis, Martha; interview, March 6, 1997.

49. Devine, Tad; interview, February 18, 1997.

50. Zogby, Jim; interview, March 3, 1998.

51. Herman, op. cit.

52. Kirk, Paul; interview, March 17, 1997.

53. Corrigan, Jack; interview, January 29, 1997.

54. Cobble, op. cit.

55. Sasso, John; interview, January 27, 1997.
56. Ibid.
57. Cobble, op. cit.
58. Jackson, Jesse; interview, January 2, 1998.

PART FOUR   The Deal (1988–1996)

Chapter Ten   The Races We Win

1. Robinson, Will; interview, December 13, 1996.
2. Travis-Germond, Alice; interview, January 23, 1997.
3. Lunde, Brian; interview, January 4, 1997.
4. Herman, Alexis; interview, April 7, 1997.
5. From, Al; interview, April 10, 1997.
6. Ibid.
7. Cobble, Steve; interview, September 16, 1996.
8. Brown, Ron; press conference, December 6, 1988.
9. Ibid.
10. Ibid.
11. Wagner, Carl; interview, September 26, 1996.
12. Ibid.
13. Travis-Germond, op. cit.
14. Steitz, Mark; interview, September 25, 1996.
15. Cobble, op. cit.
16. Cuomo, Mario; interview, January 17, 1997.
17. Jackson, Jesse; speech, Democratic National Convention, July 20, 1988.
18. Bradley, Bill; interview, April 7, 1997.
19. Wagner, op. cit.
20. Cuomo, op. cit.
21. Mercer, David; interview, April 14, 1997.
22. Steitz, op. cit.
23. Travis-Germond, op. cit.
24. Ibid.
25. Brady, James; interview, April 12, 1997.
26. Lunde, op. cit.
27. Ibid.
28. Lunde, Brian; confidential memorandum to Jim Brady, January 17, 1989.
29. Lunde, interview, op. cit.
30. Lunde, memorandum, op. cit.
31. Slagle, Bob; interview, April 9, 1997.
32. Wiener, Richard; interview, January 27, 1997.
33. Casey, Robert; interview, May 8, 1997.
34. Ibid.
35. Lunde, interview, op. cit.
36. Richter, Allan, "DNC Race Raises New Fears of Black-Jewish Split," *Jewish World,* January 13, 1989, p. 3.
37. Stein, Rob; interview, November 18, 1996.
38. Ibid.
39. Ibid.
40. Grossman, Steven; interview, March 12, 1997.
41. Hirsh, Stanley; interview, March 24, 1997.
42. Baggett, Joan; interview, November 4, 1996.
43. Horowitz, Rochelle; interview, October 5, 1996.

44. Ibid.

45. Gould, George; interview, April 17, 1997.

46. Horowitz, op. cit.

47. Ibid.

48. Ibid.

49. McEntee, Gerald; interview, January 9, 1999.

50. Horowitz, op. cit.

51. Ibid.

52. Wagner, op. cit.

53. Jones campaign material.

54. Statement issued by Ron Brown's campaign for DNC chairman, n.d.

55. Herman, Alexis, April 7, 1997.

56. Horowitz, op. cit.

57. Slagle, op. cit.

58. Wiener, op. cit.

59. Ibid.

60. West, Paul, "Jones Quits Race to Lead Democrats; Backs Brown," *The Sun,* January 31, 1989, p. 5A.

61. Brown, Ron; speech, February 9, 1989.

62. Ibid.

63. Herman, op. cit.

Chapter Eleven   Such a Bloody Mess

1. Hall, Carla, "Ron Brown & the Party's Acid Test: The New Democratic Chairman, Reaching Out," *Washington Post,* March 14, 1989, Style Section, p. 1.

2. Leifer, Neil; interview, July 17, 1998.

3. Ibid.

4. Brown, Ron; interview on *Meet the Press,* NBC News, February 12, 1989.

5. Steitz, Mark; interview, September 26, 1996.

6. Cooper, Mario; interview, April 17, 1997.

7. Kirk, Paul; interview, March 17, 1997.

8. Steitz, op. cit.

9. Price, David E., *Bringing Back the Parties,* CQ Press, 1984, p. 40.

10. Reichley, A. James, *The Life of the Parties: A History of American Political Parties,* Free Press, 1992, p. 355.

11. Ruvolo, Jim; interview, August 6, 1997.

12. Blumenthal, Mark; interview, April 22, 1997.

13. Alterman, Eric, "G.O.P. Chairman Lee Atwater: Playing hardball," *New York Times Magazine,* April 30, 1989, p. 30.

14. Steitz, op. cit.

15. Manatt, Charles; interview, February 7, 1997.

16. Brown, Ron; speech to the Democratic Leadership Council, March 11, 1989.

17. Rosenthal, Steve; interview, May 20, 1997.

18. Barnes, James A., "A Democrat Who Never Said Never," *National Journal,* October 3, 1992, p. 2281.

19. Gersh, Mark; interview, June 27, 1997.

20. Hickman, Harrison; interview, April 18, 1997.

21. Herman, Alexis; interview, April 7, 1997.

22. Gersh, op. cit.

23. Ibid.

24. Steitz, Mark; interview, November 22, 1996.

25. Stein, Rob; interview, December 5, 1996.

26. McCurry, Mike; interview, June 11, 1997.

27. Stein, Rob; interview, December 5, 1996.

28. Herman, op. cit.

29. Ibid.

30. Steitz, Mark; interview, November 22, 1996.

31. Stein, op. cit.

32. Ibid.

33. Ibid.

34. Barron, Gary; interview, April 29, 1998.

35. Stein, Rob; interview, April 19, 1998.

36. Brown, Tracey L., *The Life and Times of Ron Brown,* William Morrow and Company, 1998, p. 177.

37. Barron, op. cit.

38. Stein, op. cit.

39. Ibid.

40. Ibid.

41. Ibid.

42. Steitz, op. cit.

43. Robinson, op. cit.

44. Godwin, Lamond; interview, March 2, 1998.

45. Jackson, Jesse; interview, January 2, 1998.

46. Hill, Nolanda; interview, March 2, 1998. The circumstances by which Brown shared the letter with Hill, his business partner and mistress, are a matter of some dispute. She insists it was over a candlelight dinner on Valentine's Day 1989. The Brown family say emphatically that could not have happened since February 14 is Alma Brown's birthday and her husband always took her out to dinner on that date. Whatever the circumstances, Hill was the first to disclose the existence of Jackson's letter, which was later confirmed by Jackson and by other DNC staffers. While Jackson declined to discuss many of the letter's specifics, he did, through a spokeswoman, say he did not dispute Hill's characterization of it.

47. Wilhelm, David; interview, July 21, 1997.

48. Dold, Bruce R.; and Reardon, Patrick, "New Party Chief Would Back Daley," *Chicago Tribune,* January 31, 1989, Section 2, p. 1.

49. Mianowany, Joseph, "The New Race Problems in Politics," *U.P.I.,* March 20, 1989.

50. Jackson, op. cit.

51. Herman, op. cit.

52. Axelrod, David; interview, July 20, 1997.

53. Steitz, op. cit.

54. Brown, Ron; speech at National Press Club, February 15, 1989.

55. Estrich, Susan; interview, February 26, 1997.

Chapter Twelve   The Plan

1. Eller, Jeff; interview, April 21, 1998.

2. Ibid.

3. Alper, Jill; interview, May 18, 1997.

4. Robinson, Will; interview, May 14, 1998.

5. Smulkstys, Inga; interview, May 19, 1997.

6. Steitz, Mark; interview, May 12, 1998.

7. Barnes, James A., "Ron Brown's Fast Start," *The National Journal,* May 6, 1989, p. 1103.

8. Gorman, Steven J., "West Offers 'Land of Opportunity' for Democrats," *United Press International,* December 15, 1989.

9. Steitz, op. cit.

10. Steitz, Mark; interview, May 12, 1998.

11. Mayhew, David, and Russett, Bruce, "How the Democrats Can Win in '92," *New Leader,* January 9, 1989, p. 13.

12. Lewis, Ann; interview, July 21, 1997.

13. Steitz; interview, op. cit.

14. Brown, Ron; interviewed by reporters, June 25, 1990.

15. Rosenthal, Stephen; interview, May 20, 1997.

16. Steitz, op. cit.

17. Robinson, Will; interview, December 13, 1996.

18. Berke, Richard L., "Democrats Trail in Fund-Raising, and Many Blame New Chairman," *New York Times,* July 17, 1989, p. A-1.

19. Barron, Gary; interview, April 29, 1998.

20. McCurry, Mike; interview, April 29, 1998.

21. Ruvolo, Jim; interview, August 6, 1997.

22. Carol, Dan; interview, April 30, 1997.

23. It was later determined that agents from the Drug Enforcement Agency lured a young drug dealer to Lafayette Park, across Pennsylvania Avenue from the White House, in order to make the drug buy there so that Mr. Bush could use it as a prop to highlight that drugs were being sold adjacent to the presidential mansion. The young drug dealer did not even know where Lafayette Park was and had to be given direction by DEA agents.

24. Oreskes, Michael, "Party Chief Faults Democrats for Asking Drug War Taxes," *New York Times,* September 12, 1989, p. A-1.

25. Brown, Ron; speech to the Democratic National Committee, September 28, 1989.

26. Toner, Robin, "Democratic Party Chief Faces Uphill Battle in Effort to Rouse a Troubled Party," *New York Times,* September 29, 1989, p. A-12.

27. Ibid.

28. McCurry, Mike; interview, February 14, 1997.

29. DeMicco, Steve; interview, May 23, 1997.

30. Ibid.

31. Goldman, Paul; interview, February 4, 1997.

32. Edds, Margaret, *Claiming the Dream: The Victorious Campaign of Douglas Wilder of Virginia,* Algonquin Books, 1990, p. 47.

33. Robinson, op. cit.

34. Edds, op. cit., p. 171.

35. Robinson, op. cit.

36. Warner, Mark; interview, February 3, 1997.

37. Greer, Frank; interview, April 25, 1997.

38. Robinson, op. cit.

39. Edds, op. cit., pp. 229–230.

40. Herman, op. cit.

41. Robinson, op. cit.

Chapter Thirteen   We Ain't Running

1. Brown, Ron, "The Chairman's Report to the [DNC] Executive Committee," March 23, 1990.

2. Edsall, Thomas B., "DNC Chairman Criticizes 'Dirty' Republican Politics," *Washington Post,* June 17, 1989, p. A-11.

3. Dreyer, David; interview, January 10, 1997.

4. Brown, Ron; interview on *Face the Nation,* April 8, 1990.

5. Carol, Dan; interview, May 23, 1997.

6. Brown, Ron; Sperling breakfast, June 25, 1990.

7. Baggett, Joan; interview, November 6, 1996.

8. Dreyer, op. cit.

9. Brown, Ron; speech to Democratic Leadership Council, May 7, 1991, Cleveland, Ohio.

10. Rollins, Ed, *Bare Knuckles and Back Rooms: My Life in American Politics,* Broadway Books, 1996, p. 197.

11. Tully, Paul; "Memorandum Re: 1991–92 DNC Mission and Operational Considerations," December 17, 1990.

12. Ibid.

13. Cardona, Maria; interview, April 14, 1998.

14. Toner, Robin, "Bush's War Success Confers an Aura of Invincibility in '92," *New York Times,* February 27, 1991, p. A-1.

15. Ibid.

16. Stetz, Mark; interview, November 22, 1996.

17. Yee, Melinda; memo to Ron Brown titled "Asia Trip," October 15, 1991.

18. Ibid.

19. Robinson, op. cit.

20. Stein, Rob; interview, December 5, 1996.

21. Ibid.

22. Mellman, Mark; interview, February 8, 1997.

23. Carol, op. cit.

24. Frisby, Michael K., "Kingmaker, Rainmaker: The Irreplaceable Ron Brown," *Emerge,* June 1996, p. 30.

25. Herman, op. cit.

Chapter Fourteen   Victory

1. Rosenthal, Stephen; interview, May 20, 1997.

2. McEntee, Gerald; interview, January 9, 1999.

3. Brody, Ken; interview, May 12, 1997.

4. Stein, Rob; interview, November 18, 1996.

5. Wilhelm, David; interview, July 21, 1997.

6. Sigel, Eli; interview, July 22, 1997.

7. Cooper, Mario; interview, April 17, 1997.

8. Carol, Dan; interview, May 23, 1997.

9. Cooper, op. cit.

10. Ibid.

11. Lynch, William; interview, November 23, 1998.

12. Ancier, Garth; interview, May 4, 1997.

13. Carol, op. cit.

14. Zogby, Jim; interview, March 3, 1998.

15. Cardona, Maria; interview, April 14, 1998.

16. Stein, Rob; interview, November 18, 1996.

17. Cooper, op. cit.

18. Rosenthal, op. cit.

19. Steitz, Mark; interview, May 12, 1998.

20. Madsen, Lillian; interview, June 7, 1998.

21. Boggs, Thomas; interview, April 20, 1998.

Chapter Fifteen   Triumphs and Troubles

1. Desler, Jim; interview, May 8, 1998.

2. Boggs, Tommy; interview, April 20, 1998.

3. Hackney, James; interview, April 29, 1997.

4. Ibid.

5. Ibid.

6. Christopher, Warren; interview, June 18, 1998.

7. May, Timothy; interview, March 10, 1998.

8. Koogler, Mark; interview, June 18, 1998.

9. Stein, Rob; interview, March 14, 1997.

10. Hill, Nolanda; interview, January 16, 1999.

11. Ibid.

12. Cisneros, Henry; interview, February 26, 1997.

13. Ibid.

14. Fitz-Pegado, Lauri; interview, January 10, 1997.

15. Garten, Jeffrey; interview, July 6, 1998.

16. Desler, op. cit.

17. Ibid.

18. Pound, Edward T., and Cohen, Gary, "Living Well Is the Best Revenge," *U.S. News & World Report,* June 7, 1993, p. 30.

19. Desler, op. cit.

20. Vickery, Ray; interview, April 30, 1998.

21. Ibid.

22. Ibid.

23. Garten, op. cit.

24. Hackney, op. cit.

25. Rothkopf, David; interview, February 20, 1997.

26. Brown, Tracey L., *The Life and Times of Ron Brown,* William Morrow and Company, Inc., 1998, p. 257.

27. Desler, op. cit.

28. Madsen, Lillian; interview, June 7, 1998.

29. Behr, Peter, "Clinton States His Support for Brown," *Washington Post,* September 29, 1993, p. F-1.

30. Podesta, John; interview, February 16, 1998.

Chapter Sixteen   Transitional World

1. Clinger, William; interview, May 27, 1998.

2. Clinger, William; letter to Ron Brown, February 10, 1994.

3. Fredericks, Barbara S.; letter to William Clinger, March 2, 1994.

4. Clinger; interview, op. cit.

5. Brown, Ron; speech to the Arab American Institute's Challenge '94 Leadership Conference, January 22, 1994.

6. Vickery, Ray; interview, April 30, 1998.

7. Cardona, Maria; interview, April 14, 1998.

8. Desler, Jim; interview, May 8, 1998.

9. Vickery, op. cit.

10. Sanger, David E., "How Washington Inc. Makes a Sale," *New York Times,* February 19, 1995, Sec. 3, p. 1.

11. Ibid.

12. Garten, Jeffrey; interview, March 19, 1997.

13. Behr, Peter, "Brown Has Two Tough Sales Challenges on China Trip," *Washington Post,* August 24, 1994, p. B-10.

14. Mufson, Steve, "U.S., China Act to Boost Trade Ties," *Washington Post,* August 30, 1994, p. A-1.

15. Garten, op. cit.

16. Ibid.

17. Ibid.

18. Garten; interview, July 6, 1998.

19. Ibid.

20. Stein, Rob; interview, December 5, 1996.

21. Rothkopf, op. cit.

22. Garten, Jeffrey; interview, March 20, 1998.

23. Ibid.

24. Fitz-Pegado, Lauri; interview, January 10, 1997.

25. Brown, Ron; speech, Indian Institute of Technology, Town Hall Meeting, January 17, 1995.

26. Clinger; interview, op. cit.

27. Hill, Nolanda; interview, March 2, 1998.

28. Clinger, op. cit.

29. Stein; interview, March 14, 1997.

30. Wagner, Carl; interview, September 26, 1996.

31. Bond, Julian; interview, February 11, 1999.

32. Jackson, Jesse; interview, January 2, 1998.

33. Stephanopoulos, George; interview, May 2, 1997.

34. Panetta, Leon; interview, June 16, 1998.

35. Stephanopoulos, op. cit.

36. Hill, op. cit.

37. Stein, Rob; interview, May 31, 1998.

38. Ibid.

39. Panetta, op. cit.

40. Desler, op. cit.

41. Panetta, op. cit.

42. Brown, Ron; speech to Commerce employees, n.d.

43. Ibid.

44. Ibid.

45. Ginsberg, Will; interview, May 21, 1998.

46. Panetta, op. cit.

47. Holbrooke, Richard, *To End a War,* Random House, 1998, p. 329.

48. Vickery, Ray; interview, May 12, 1998.

49. Ibid.

50. Rothkopf, David; interview, June 1, 1998.

51. Ibid.

52. Gluhan, Lenadra, quoted in U.S. Air Force CT-43A Accident Investigation Board Report, interviewed, April 10, 1996, p. 1656.

53. Galbraith, Peter, quoted in U.S. Air Force CT-43A Accident Investigation Board Report, interviewed, April 12, 1996, p. 1836.

54. Peovic, Tonci, quoted in U.S. Air Force CT-43A Accident Investigation Board Report, interviewed, April 17, 1996, p. 2426.

55. All Dubrovnik Airport had by way of navigational aids were two nondirectional beacons. These sent out Morse code beeps—dots and dashes—to help the pilots line up on approach. The first beacon was located 11.8 miles west of the runway. Pilots were supposed to pick up its signal as they passed over it, telling them they were on the right course for landing. The approach then called for pilots to maintain a heading of 119 degrees, which would guide them over the second beacon, located about 1.9 miles from the runway. If they did not spot the runway by the time they passed over the second beacon, they were to abort their landing, climbing to 4,000 feet and executing a right turn out over the sea.

This tricky approach was made even more daunting by the fact that the plane carrying Brown and members of his party was a modified twenty-two-year-old 737 using outmoded equipment. The nondirectional beacons sent out their signals on different frequencies. More modern aircraft carried two automatic directional finders, essentially radio receivers, each set to the frequency of the directional beacons. Flight crews could therefore hear the first beacon's signal on one receiver and then listen for the second beacon on the craft's second receiver. Brown's plane carried only one directional finder. Its pilots would have to hear the signal from the first beacon and then find a new radio frequency on the same receiver. What was worse, the one directional finder the air force plane did carry was not a digital one that would have allowed them to move from one preset frequency to the second merely by flipping a switch. Instead, they had to dial their radio until they found the new frequency. This had to be done while watching airspeed and course and talking to the control tower.

The air force made things difficult in other ways. The Croat civilian airline had a rule that no plane is allowed to land at Dubrovnik Airport if neither the pilot nor the co-pilot had ever landed there before. In the case of the 737 that carried Brown, neither the pilot, Capt. Ashley Davis, nor his co-pilot, Capt. Tim Shafer, had ever seen the Dubrovnik Airport. Moreover, the air force had a standing order that pilots based in the United States could land at Dubrovnik only in clear weather. But air force squadrons in Europe did not follow that order.

Considering the bad weather, their lack of knowledge of the area, and their outdated equipment, one wonders why the pilots even attempted to land. They could have—and arguably should have—either circled the airport for some time to see if the weather would break or turned around and headed west to Split, another picturesque seacoast town west of Dubrovnik.

Davis and Shafer were members of the 76th Airlift Squadron of the air force's 86th Air Wing, based at Ramstein Air Base in Germany. The squadron's prime function is to fly military and civilian VIPs on official trips in Europe and the Middle East. Davis and Shafer were veteran pilots, though Davis had not had much experience flying 737s. Yet the 86th was a troubled outfit. Pilots grumbled that its commander, Brig. Gen. William E. Stevens, was too willing to sacrifice safety concerns to get civilian and military bigwigs where they needed to go—and on time. Pilots told of feeling pressure coming from above to maintain schedules. One pilot told investigators of being told that delays could mean their jobs. "The word was out," said one pilot. "You better make on-time takeoffs," according to the testimony of Lt. Col. Donald M. Cochick on April 15, 1996, in the Accident Prevention Board Report.

Davis and Shafer actually left Tuzla about five minutes early on the final flight, flying in an approved corridor through the so-called no-fly zone over Bosnia, an area where only approved NATO combat aircraft were allowed. But the flight plan Davis and Shafer had filed called for them to fly along a section of the corridor that was closed at that time. As they entered that section the pilots were warned by air traffic controllers that they were entering a forbidden zone and had to divert to the west for several miles before turning back toward Dubrovnik. The diversion cost the crew fifteen to twenty minutes. Now, instead of being early, they were running behind schedule.

Rainstorms, spotty visibility, no instrument landing system at the airport, antiquated equipment aboard the aircraft, a tricky approach, a crew totally inexperienced in local conditions, and, perhaps, feeling pressured not to cause any more delays. The sun, the moon, and the earth were lining up.

At 2:50 the crew received a radio call from Sehic, the pilot of the Croat plane that delivered Galbraith, Prime Minister Matesa, and other government officials. The Croat pilot told the crew of Brown's 737 that he had landed about an hour before and that weather conditions were at the minimal level for a safe landing. If the American plane had to execute a missed approach procedure, the crew should divert to Split, another town farther along the coast. The other officials would meet Brown there. Sehic was trying to be helpful. But all he did was create another diversion for the crew of the 737. Now, in addition to trying to make sure their airspeed, course, and altitude were correct; finding the new radio frequency for the second directional beacon; communicating with the control tower; and trying to see the airport runway, the crew was engaging in a conversation with another pilot.

The crew was by now probably on task overload. Too many things were being required of it. None of them was particularly difficult on its own. But given their lack of familiarity with their surroundings and their aircraft, having to do all of them at once meant that something could easily be forgotten. As the plane passed over the first beacon, the crew apparently forgot to begin searching for the signal from the second directional beacon, and the pilots failed to notice that their course heading was a full 9 degrees off course. Instead of heading toward the runway, they were barreling directly toward St. John the Baptist Mountain, 1.8 miles north of the airport.

At 2:56 P.M. the pilots received clearance to land from the Dubrovnik tower. It was the last communication they would have with the ground. Three minutes later they, and nearly all their passengers, would be dead (one passenger, a flight attendant, died several hours after the crash).

56. Ruddy, Christopher, "Experts Differ on Ron Brown Head Wound," *Pittsburgh Tribune Review,* December 3, 1997.

57. Ibid.

58. Ibid.

INDEX